P9-EDD-501

THE PAPACY

Endpapers St Peter's Square in 1668
taken from a book of engravings
of the buildings of Rome
by Giovanni Battista Falda

THE PAPACY

AN ILLUSTRATED HISTORY FROM ST PETER to PAUL VI

Edited by Christopher Hollis

The Macmillan Company, New York

Designed by Jane Mackay *for George Weidenfeld and Nicolson*

Library of Congress Catalog Card No. 64 – 12539

Nihil obstat Joannes M. T. Barton S.T.D., L.S.S. *Censor deputatus*
Imprimatur ✠ Georgius L. Craven. *Episcopus Sebastopolis. Vic. Gen.*
Westmonasterii, die 26a Feb. 1964

The *Nihil obstat* and *Imprimatur* are a declaration that a book
or pamphlet is considered to be free from doctrinal or moral error.
It is not implied that those who have granted the *Nihil obstat* and *Imprimatur*
agree with the contents, opinions or statements expressed.

Printed in Switzerland by Conzett & Huber, Zürich

CONTENTS

Introduction 9

1 *THE TOMB OF ST PETER* 10

Engelbert Kirschbaum SJ *Professor of Christian Archaeology and Art History, The Gregorian University, Rome*

2 *THE FIRST POPES* 22

ST PETER to SIXTUS III 33-440

Vincenzo Monachino *Dean of the Faculty of Ecclesiastical History, The Gregorian University, Rome*

3 *ROME AND BYZANTIUM* 32

LEO I to ZACHARY 440-752

Francis Xavier Murphy C.SS.R. *Professor of Patristic Moral Theology, Academia Alfonsiana, Rome*

4 *THE REBIRTH OF THE EMPIRE* 44

STEPHEN II to ALEXANDER II 752-1073

Douglas Woodruff *Editor of* The Tablet, *London*

5 *GREGORY VII AND THE STRUGGLE FOR INDEPENDENCE* 54

GREGORY VII to CELESTINE III 1073-1198

Gervais Dumeige SJ *Professor of the History of Patristic and Medieval Theology, The Gregorian University, Rome*

6 *THE ZENITH OF THE MEDIEVAL PAPACY* 66

INNOCENT III 1198-1216

John A. Watt *Lecturer in Medieval History, University of Hull*

7 *THE PAPACY AND THE HOHENSTAUFEN* 74

HONORIUS III to INNOCENT IV 1216-54

Brian Tierney *Professor of Medieval History, Cornell University*

8 *THE FRENCH PREDOMINANCE AND THE AVIGNON POPES* 84

ALEXANDER IV to GREGORY XI 1254-1378

Bernard Guillemain *Professor of Medieval History, University of Bordeaux*

9 *SCHISMS AND COUNCILS* 96

URBAN VI to EUGENIUS IV 1378-1447

Joseph Gill SJ *Rector of the Pontifical Oriental Institute, Rome*

10 *THE RENAISSANCE POPES* 106

NICHOLAS V to LEO X 1447-1521

Gerard Culkin *Professor of Church History, Ushaw College, Durham*

11 *THE BASILICA OF ST PETER AND THE VATICAN PALACES* 120

Paolo Brezzi *Professor of Ecclesiastical History, University of Naples*

12 *THE CHALLENGE OF THE REFORMATION* 136

ADRIAN VI to JULIUS III 1522-55

Hubert Jedin *Professor of Ecclesiastical History, University of Bonn*

13 *THE TRIUMPH OF THE COUNTER-REFORMATION* 148

MARCELLUS II to LEO XI 1555-1605

Eusebio Rey SJ *Professor of History, College of San Jose, Valladolid*

14 *THE POPES AND THE CITY OF ROME* 160

Paolo Brezzi *Professor of Ecclesiastical History, University of Naples*

15 *THE GROWTH OF THE ETERNAL CITY* 172

Paolo Brezzi *Professor of Ecclesiastical History, University of Naples*

16 *THE POPES AND THE THIRTY YEARS WAR* 184

PAUL V to URBAN VIII 1605-44

Quintin Aldea SJ *Professor of Ecclesiastical History, The Gregorian University Rome*

17 *THE POPES AND THE ABSOLUTE MONARCHS* 194

INNOCENT X to INNOCENT XII 1644-1700

Michel Dierickx SJ *Professor of Ecclesiastical History in the Faculty of Jesuit Theology, University of Louvain*

18 *THE AGE OF REASON* 204

CLEMENT XI to CLEMENT XIV 1700-74

Ferdinand Maass SJ *Professor of Ecclesiastical History, University of Innsbruck*

19 *THE YEARS OF REVOLUTION* 214

PIUS VI and PIUS VII 1775-1823

Burkhart Schneider SJ *Professor of Modern Ecclesiastical History, The Gregorian University, Rome*

20 *REACTION AND REVOLUTION* 226

LEO XII to GREGORY XVI 1823-46

Kenneth Scott Latourette *Sterling Professor of Missions and Oriental History Emeritus, Yale University*

21 *PIUS IX: THE END OF TEMPORAL POWER 1846-78* 234

E. E. Y. Hales

22 *THE PAPACY AND SOCIAL REFORM: THE GREAT ENCYCLICALS* 244

Anne Fremantle

23 *THE POPES IN THE MODERN WORLD* 250

LEO XIII to PIUS XII 1878-1958

E. E. Y. Hales

24 *CARDINALS AND THE CONCLAVE* 260

Christopher Hollis

25 *THE CENTRAL GOVERNMENT OF THE CHURCH* 270

Peter Canisius Van Lierde *Vicar General of the Vatican City and Prefect of the Pontifical Sacristy*

26 *JOHN XXIII AND THE SECOND VATICAN COUNCIL 1958-63* 278

Christopher Hollis

Maps 292

Chronological List of Popes 296

The General Councils of the Church 299

Acknowledgements 301

Index 303

INTRODUCTION

Christopher Hollis

TO THE STUDENT OF HISTORY, WHETHER CATHOLIC or Protestant, believer or unbeliever, there can hardly be a more remarkable institution than the Papacy. The Catholic believes that a divine promise has protected it over two thousand years and will continue to protect it through the rest of time. There were Popes who were great saints, who inspired the world to high spiritual achievement, and before whom even the most hardened sceptic must be tempted to say that 'the finger of God is here'. Other Popes were great statesmen, whose achievements were memorable on the secular plane. And still others were great patrons of the arts and of architecture. The non-Catholic historian is equally ready to recognize the remarkable nature of the institution and its achievements, and even though he is not able to admit its uniquely divine foundation, he recognizes that there is no other institution at all remotely comparable to this.

Today the world seems to be growing happily weary of the *odium theologicum* with which so much of the past history of Christendom has been filled. Scholars discuss their differences in kindlier and more charitable terms than used to be the fashion. To this new climate many of all religions, and of no religion, have made their contribution, and among them Popes, most notably the late Pope John XXIII. Many people quite outside the Catholic Church – more by far than in past generations – are today prepared to admit that the voice of the Pope has, and must necessarily have, an important word to say in the settlement of all the world's problems. That being so, this is a good time to lay before the public a volume which, by text and illustration, tells the whole story of the Papacy from St Peter's time to our own. The contributors are all of them distinguished scholars, each a specialist in his own period or subject. The illustrations take us from affairs to art and tell us of the contribution which papal patronage has made to the world's art and architecture.

Perhaps – who knows? – we stand at the threshold of a new age. Today, when one looks for examples of papal artistic achievements, one finds them predominantly in Rome and exclusively in Europe. By an accident the Catholic Church has been in its government a predominantly European body until this century. Recently we have seen an extraordinary broadening of the base of that government. There are Cardinals now of every race and from every corner of the world. It looks as if we are soon destined to see a real internationalization of the Curia. Probably before many years – as the Church counts years – we shall see a non-Italian, and even perhaps a non-European, Pope, and it may be that one consequence will be that in coming centuries the main monuments of Christian architecture and art will be found outside Europe and in other than European styles. However that may be, nothing will obliterate the memory and love of those origins from which we sprang, and the three great creative cultures to which Pontius Pilate paid his immortal and unwitting tribute when he bade them write up over the Cross 'in letters of Greek and Latin and Hebrew'.

NERO
ROMA
ROM

1 THE TOMB OF ST PETER

ENGELBERT KIRSCHBAUM

The site of the present St Peter's and of Constantine's first basilica has been venerated by Christians from the earliest times as the site of St Peter's tomb. The first Memoria *over his grave was built in about 160 and subsequent generations have vied with one another to honour the apostle's tomb. The evidence produced by the full scale scientific investigation of the shrine ordered by Pius XII has provided a wealth of information about the early Christian Church.*

DURING THE FIRST HALF OF THE FOURTH CENTURY A large five-aisled basilica was built by Constantine the Great on the Vatican hill, above the grave of St Peter. It is beyond dispute that from that time onward this site, in the centre of the apse, has been venerated as the tomb of the apostle. Countless pilgrims have come, and still come, to honour the first Pope in his last resting place. Constantine's basilica has long since been replaced by the present massive structure, which took a century and a half to build (it was begun in the early sixteenth century and not completed until halfway through the seventeenth) and whose dome is the finest in the world. The one thing that has not changed is the veneration of St Peter's tomb, which continues at the very spot marked out by the tradition received and perpetuated by Constantine.

It was Pius XII who took the courageous decision to break with centuries of tradition by ordering a full-scale scientific examination of the shrine. To date there have been two series of excavations, from 1940 to 1951 and from 1953 to 1957. Their purpose was not so much to discover whether this was in fact the tomb of the apostle, since there was no reason to doubt the authenticity of the ancient tradition, but rather to establish what, if anything, has survived of the original grave and what evidence exists of its primitive form and later evolution.

In the space allotted here it is impossible to follow the excavation through all its various phases or to single out individual pieces of evidence for a discussion of their significance for the picture as a whole. All this has been very thoroughly discussed elsewhere by a number of eminent scholars. In this article I can mention only the most important of those finds, which help us to trace the history of the tomb of St Peter from the beginning down to the Pontificate of Gregory the Great (590–604). The later history is so well known that I shall allude to it only briefly in conclusion.

Unfortunately, we cannot be sure of the exact date of St Peter's martyrdom under Nero. The choice of year is usually held to lie between 64 and 67. However that may be, the apostle's body was buried on the Vatican hill, at a spot close to the gardens of Nero and their famous circus, which was actually more like a sports stadium. The grave was a plain earth trench and must have been covered with large tiles. We cannot say with certainty that there were already other graves nearby, but it seems likely since in time the whole area came to be occupied by one of the largest pagan burial grounds in Rome. The apostle's grave became hemmed in by others, some of them dating from the seventies and eighties of the first century and thus more or less contemporary with his. The tomb of a child on the south side, however, dates only from *c* AD 120. The number of tombs in the immediate neighbourhood gradually increased, as is consistent with the early Christian custom of seeking burial close to a martyr's grave. Sometimes, in an effort to come as close as possible, tombs were allowed to overlap. Soon it became necessary to build a little protective wall round the apostle's grave, a fragment of which has been found.

From *c* 130 onwards there was a substantial increase in the number of mausolea erected near the apostle's tomb.

St Peter was crucified upside down according to an ancient, but unsupported, tradition which is depicted on the fifteenth-century bronze doors of St Peter's by the Renaissance artist Filarete. On the right is the Emperor Nero, whose persecution of the Christians *c* AD 65, was confined to Rome

The Tomb of St Peter

Access to the older burial ground was secured, as was required under Roman law, by leaving an alleyway clear. At the same time a fundamental alteration was made to the lay-out of the area occupied by the older Christian graves. It seems likely that the responsibility for this lay not with a private individual but with the entire Christian community at Rome.

What happened was that the Christian burial ground, now no doubt the exclusive property of the Christian community, was divided into two open graveyards of unequal size, surrounded by walls. The two were separated by a common wall some eight metres long, the so-called 'Red Wall'. The larger of the two graveyards, which lay east of the Red Wall, had a mausoleum to the south. The smaller western graveyard was eventually overshadowed by a large double mausoleum. Since the graveyards and the surrounding mausolea lay on a slight incline, the alleyway giving access ran uphill, passing between the pagan mausolea and ending in a steep flight of steps (south–north) leading into the western graveyard. The larger eastern graveyard was now accessible only from the north and east. The creation of these two open graveyards must have entailed some levelling off of the hilly ground and the filling up of the hollow southern sector east of the wall. The apostle's grave lay more or less exactly in the centre of the Red Wall, and to mark the place a simple but dignified Memoria was erected at the time when the wall itself was being built.

This structure consisted of two superimposed semi-circular niches, recessed into the Red Wall itself and separated by a projecting travertine slab supported on two marble colonnettes. The digging for the foundations of the Red Wall and the Memoria must have exposed the graves in the vicinity, including that of the apostle. It would be seen that the alignment of the older graves deviated considerably from the axis of the more recent mausolea (in fact by as much as eleven degrees). This difference was faithfully preserved in the alignment of the seating provided for the movable slab which sealed off the Memoria from the grave below, although the resulting asymmetry must have been obvious. This fact is itself striking testimony to the sincerity of contemporary belief that under the Memoria lay the authentic grave of the apostle. This belief also accounts for the presence of yet a third niche, in the portion of the Red Wall below ground and an exact vertical continuation of the two niches visible above. Stamps on tiles used to cover

A view of the *clivus*, the sloping pathway which gave access to the early Christian graveyards. This path runs across the church above it and is almost immediately beneath the High Altar. The back of the Red Wall, built *c* 160 and dividing the two Christian cemeteries, is on the right, with the site of the apostolic tomb behind it

Above In the course of time a buttress was built to support the Red Wall. A number of early Christian *graffiti* were scratched on it. At the top can be seen the Christian monogram consisting of the two first Greek letters (Chi and Rho) in the name of Christ. This is preceded by the words *Vivite in* (May you live in Christ)

Left Early Christians sought burial as close as possible to St Peter's grave. These tombs are the nearest and adjoin it. The Red Wall is on the left

Right The nearest approach possible to a photograph of the apostolic tomb – 'a tangle of fragmentary remains'. The inscribed marble slab is that of a neighbouring grave

The Tomb of St Peter

The second-century mausoleum of the Caetennii was found not far from the grave of St Peter, but the formal tomb belonging to a rich, cultured family is very different from the poorer part of the cemetery where the apostle was buried

A reconstruction of the *aedicula*, or 'little house', built as a memorial above the grave of St Peter, at the same time as the Red Wall (*c* 160) and half-way along it. The actual alignment of the grave beneath is shown on the floor. About 200 this Memoria was said by the priest Gaius to be an object familiar to all Roman Christians

the drain running behind the Red Wall help to establish the date of the Red Wall and the Memoria as *c* 160.

Early Christians used to scratch inscriptions or graffiti on the venerated graves of martyrs. These inscriptions usually invoked the powerful protection of the martyr on behalf of the author or his deceased friends; pious hopes for the dead are also found, for example VIVAS IN CHRISTO, 'Live in Christ'. A late second or early third century graffito written in Greek has been found cut into the Red Wall itself. Unfortunately some letters are missing, which has given rise to considerable dispute over the correct restoration and reading. There can be no doubt, however, that the graffito refers to the apostle Peter. It runs as follows: *ΠΕΤΡ*[*ΟΣ*] *ΕΝΙ*[...?]

In course of time the Red Wall developed a vertical crack and had to be supported by a quite substantial buttressing wall. To make room for it the travertine slab had to be shortened on its northern edge and the northern colonnette shifted an equivalent distance southward. A light wall was also built projecting from the Red Wall on the southern side of the Memoria, no doubt in an effort to remedy the asymmetry produced by the buttress. The inner surfaces of these flanking walls were faced with marble, as were the niches and the adjoining parts of the Red Wall. It was about this time too that the ground round the Memoria was given a tessellated paving of white and green mosaic.

Around the year 258 a cult-centre in honour of the apostles Peter and Paul was inaugurated on the Appian Way. Our knowledge of this is based on an entry in the so-called *Depositio Martyrum*, a Christian calendar compiled in the mid-fourth century. Of the many theories advanced to account for this cult-centre, the most likely is that the

apostles' bodies had been removed out of the city to safety during the persecution under Valerian, when a watch was set on Christian cemeteries, and that when the persecution was over the place became a shrine. The translation of St Peter's body must have entailed considerable disturbance both of his grave and of the foundations of the buttressing wall. At all events the grave's original covering of slab tiles is now missing.

A recess under the lowest niche of the Memoria in the Red Wall was found to contain the bones of a man of advanced years and powerful build. The skull was missing. Who, we may well ask, is this old man in St Peter's grave? In view of the fact that the head of the apostle has for centuries been preserved and venerated in the Lateran church, the conclusion that these are the bones of the apostle himself is well-nigh irresistible. Complete certainty, however, is out of the question, because of the condition of the grave.

A number of graffiti were scratched on the outer face of the buttressing wall in the years between the end of the third century and the time of Constantine. Some of these scribblings overlap. At this period certain letter combinations were given a meaning of their own; the best-known examples are probably the Christ monogram formed from the Greek letters *X* and *P* (Chi and Rho) and the association of the two apocalyptic letters, Alpha and Omega. A new combination appears to have been made by the addition of *E* to the *P* of the Christ monogram. Thus when we find the combination PE, if we read them as Latin letters and can associate them with the Christ monogram, they must surely if they are to yield any meaning at all be regarded as shorthand for Peter. Several other letter combinations have been found cut into this wall, but scholars have so far failed to agree over their interpretation. What is definite is that the graffiti are important evidence for the veneration of the apostle's grave in the pre-Constantine era.

Before going on to discuss the great transformation of St Peter's tomb under Constantine, we must return briefly to the smaller Christian burial ground west of the Red Wall. Square in shape, its north, east and west sides were furnished with two carefully constructed burial places, each surmounted by a wide niched arch cut into the wall rising behind it. The Christian character of this burial ground, like that of its eastern neighbour, is established by the absence of cremations, still very frequent in other parts of the necropolis at this time. The two Christian burial grounds seem to have been laid out at the same time and as part of the same plan, which suggests the guidance of a single mind. The date of the whole complex can with some confidence be fixed as *c* 160. The Bishop of Rome at this time

This pillar was discovered during the excavations in the wall south of the site of the Memoria. It is one of the original pillars of the *aedicula*

The Tomb of St Peter

One of the columns used in the Constantinian Church to support the canopy over the Memoria. Some of these columns were used by Bernini in the dome of the new St Peter's

was Pope Anicetus (155–65). The *Liber Pontificalis*, written in the sixth century, ascribes the building operations undertaken by this Pope at the apostle's grave to Anacletus, St Peter's successor. The similarity of the two names probably led to their being confused, and with the passage of time the confusion became permanent. The *Liber Pontificalis* also says that 'Anacletus' arranged a burial place for the Bishops of Rome adjoining the Memoria over St Peter's grave. In view of this, it seems reasonable to identify the western burial ground with its six tombs as the first papal cemetery: Anicetus and his successors would naturally have wished to be buried as close as possible to the martyr's grave. The famous papal vault in the catacomb of Calixtus came into use only in the third century.

Although the Memoria built under Anicetus was already a substantial departure from the simplicity of the original grave, it was insignificant when compared with the elaborate reconstruction of the site under Constantine. Nothing of the great necropolis was allowed to remain. Only the Memoria was left standing, isolated among the surrounding debris. Everything else was razed to the ground – pagan

A reconstruction of the apse and decorations built around the Memoria in the Constantinian Church. Pilgrims were able to approach and pray at the tomb

mausolea, Christian graveyards – and where necessary the empty hollows were filled with earth. In order to create a level platform large enough to accommodate a five-aisled basilica over the apostle's grave, an escarpment had to be cut into the flank of the Vatican hill on the north side of the site and huge foundation walls built up from the valley bottom, in places to a height of ten metres, on the southern side. The tomb was contained within a wide apse, connected with the nave by an impressive transept. The Memoria, set in the centre of the apse, was buttressed with side walls and encased in a covering of white marble interspersed with panels of dark red porphyry. A canopy, carried on four fantastically spiralled columns of white marble, was set over the shrine. Two further identical columns were placed in line with those supporting the canopy at the rear, to provide a formal screen separating the apse from the transept. The spaces between the four columns of the canopy were spanned by a low marble balustrade, delimiting the precincts of the shrine.

All the essential features of this structure have been recovered. The columns were actually used by Bernini to decorate the pillars supporting the dome of the new St Peter's. The remaining details can be reconstructed from a relief on an early fifth-century ivory casket.

Within the rectangular enclosure quite a large area in front of the shrine was left free. Over the middle of it hung a golden lamp, marking the spot where an altar was set up for the solemn masses celebrated on the apostle's feast days. During the rest of the year the space was left clear, to allow pilgrims access to the shrine, where they were allowed to pray; pieces of linen which had been in contact with the grave itself were taken home as treasured relics. Having come so close, the pilgrims would be able to admire the gold cross placed within the shrine by Constantine and his mother St Helena, as an imperial votive offering.

With the passage of time the number of pilgrims increased. They came from all over the known world; many of them threw a coin or two down the shaft which opened into the grave. Over a thousand such coins, doubtless intended as votive offerings, have been recovered; they range in date from the early Christian period to the seventeenth century.

A reconstruction of the changes made under Gregory the Great. The pavement around the Memoria was raised leaving only the top of the shrine exposed, which was then used as an altar, so that mass could be said immediately above the martyr's tomb. Four of the columns were moved forward to make a screen

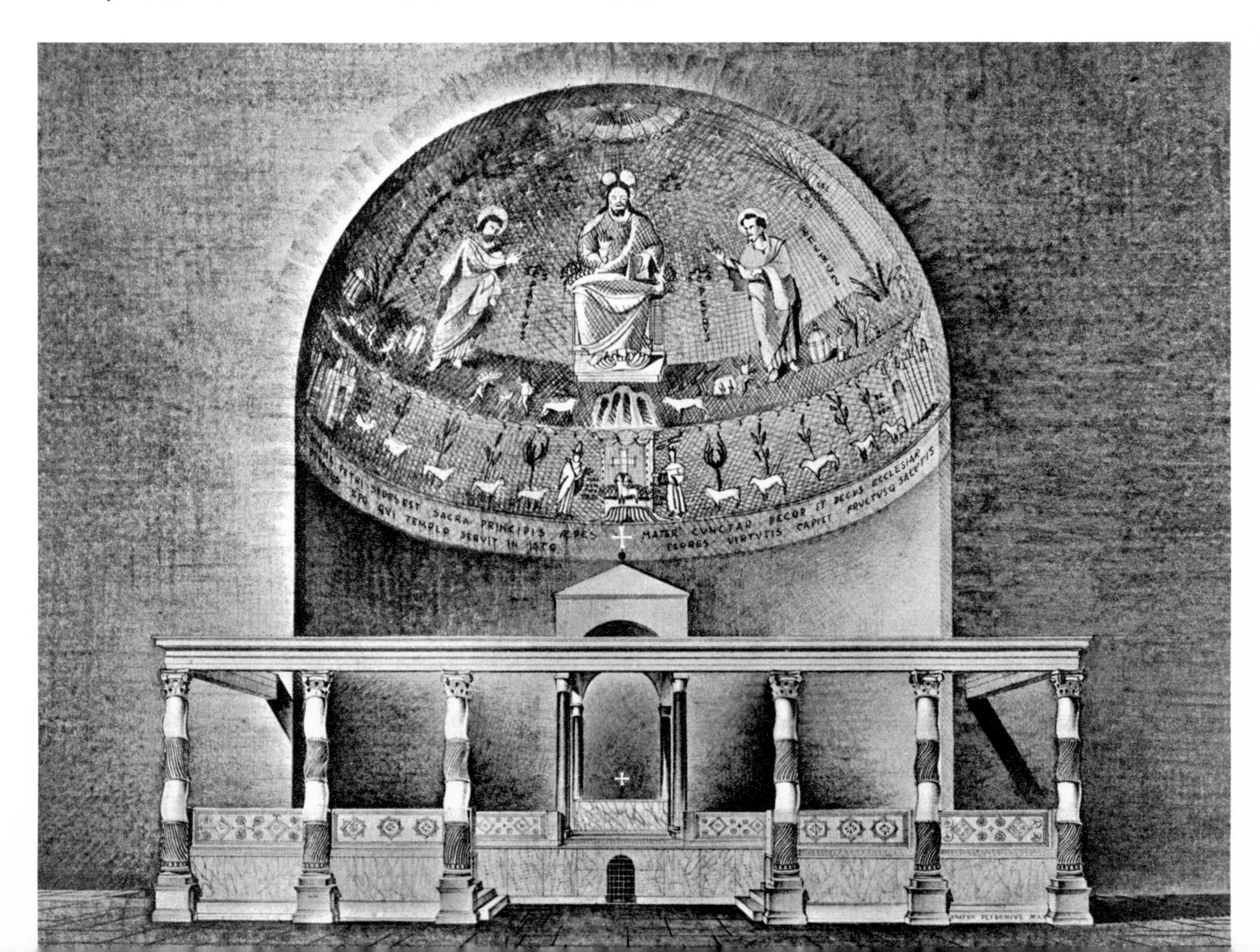

The Tomb of St Peter

Right Arnolfo di Cambio's famous statue of St Peter in the nave of his church.
The toe is worn by the kisses of the thousands of pilgrims who have flocked to St Peter's.
The statue is robed in these magnificent pontifical vestments and the triple crown on 29 June, the festival of St Peter and St Paul, and on certain ceremonial occasions when the Pope is present in the Vatican Basilica

Left A sixth or seventh-century gold Christian votive offering, *ex voto*, found in the Confessio of St Peter's.
Such valuable offerings are often made to the Saints in thanksgiving for an act of healing or a similar event

This ever-growing stream of pilgrims, coupled with the desire to associate the apostle's grave more directly with the altar, prompted Gregory the Great (590–604) to make further alterations in the area round the shrine. The first step was to bring forward the four spiral columns which had formed the apse-screen and to place them beside the pair which supported the front of the canopy. The pavement round the Memoria, apart from the portion immediately in front, was then raised to such a height that only the top of the shrine was left exposed; this portion, 'altar high', now in fact became the altar. The Pope was putting into practice the current theological theory linking altar and martyr's tomb; mass should be celebrated as nearly as possible over the apostle's body. In front of the altar a flight of steps on either side led up from what had been ground level to the raised presbytery. From this side, therefore, pilgrims could continue to visit the shrine on the same level as before. To secure access from the other side, Gregory provided an underground passage running along the inner face of the apse wall. A short gallery branching off in the centre of the apse formed an approach to the back of the shrine. This ingenious and simple device of a circular crypt, first adopted for St Peter's tomb, was to become an established feature of European architecture. Under Gregory III (731–741) a second row of almost identical spiral columns was added to the first, so that the shrine was now protected by a double screen.

Such was the basilica as Charlemagne saw it, when Pope Leo III crowned him as the first Emperor of the new Roman Empire on Christmas Day 800. This was neither the first nor the last great historical drama to be played out at the shrine of the prince of the apostles. It might be difficult to forgive the Renaissance Popes for destroying an edifice so hallowed by centuries of history and devotion, had they not had a valid excuse for their building mania in the serious deterioration of the fabric. It would in any case be ungenerous not to admit that their century-long labours, in which vast resources were deployed and the best artists of the day enlisted, resulted in a structure which has yet to find its equal.

Anyone who stands before the Confessio of St Peter as it is today in the knowledge of what lies beneath must be impressed by the ascent from the dark and humble beginnings to the splendid lustre shed by Michelangelo's great dome. This '*Tu es Petrus*', in honour of the poor fisherman raised by the Lord to be first Pope of his Church, strikes the ear with a swelling crescendo as it rises over the centuries from the low mutter of the grave to this final grandeur.

2 THE FIRST POPES

ST PETER to SIXTUS III 33-440

VINCENZO MONACHINO

There is strong evidence that St Peter was from the first recognized as the head of the Church, and that his authority was transferred to his successors because they were his successors, rather than because they were resident in the capital city of the Empire. There are numerous examples of the acceptance of the authority of the bishops of Rome in the controversies and heresies which beset the early Church. Under Constantine the Papacy was treated with comparative neglect, but its power was reasserted under later Emperors.

THE PARABLE OF THE GRAIN OF MUSTARD SEED applies both to the Church and to the history of the Papacy, which, although it had humble and almost invisible origins, developed with time into the visible and unquestioned centre of the Church.

The origin of the Papacy and the primacy of the Bishop of Rome derive from the promise made by Jesus to Peter to establish him as the cornerstone of His church, as the custodian of the keys of heaven, with the power to bind and to loose. This promise was subsequently confirmed when Jesus, after his resurrection, entrusted Peter with the task of feeding his lambs and his sheep.

Peter quickly took his place as head of the rising church. It was Peter who organized the election which appointed Matthias in place of the traitor Judas. At the first Pentecost Peter bore witness boldly to the risen Christ, explained the action of the Holy Ghost and called on those present to be baptized. He again spoke to the people of Jerusalem after healing the cripple near the door of the Temple, and he represented the new Christian community before the Sanhedrin. He was the first to speak at the Apostolic Council and established the conditions for admitting the Gentiles. It was he who greeted Paul on his visit to Jerusalem and formally acknowledged Paul's mission to the Gentiles.

It may be that even before the Council of Jerusalem Peter had transferred the seat of his apostolate to Rome, from which however he often absented himself to visit other Christian communities and to preach the good tidings elsewhere. When he reached Rome, there was already a small group of Christians, but there is no evidence that any kind of hierarchy had been set up: hence he may be regarded as the founder of the Roman Church, because with him begins the Roman hierarchy. A mass of literary and archaeological evidence makes it clear that Peter went to Rome, where he and Paul suffered martyrdom between 64 and 68, and was buried at the foot of the Vatican hill.

No valid literary and archaeological evidence can be produced to support the traditions concerning the places where Peter is said to have lived in Rome – the *domus Petri* at St Sebastian and the house of Pudens which is said to be on the site of the later basilica of St Pudentiana, or the places where he is reputed to have administered baptism near the catacombs of Priscilla or in the *Coemeterium maius*. The same must be said of other localities in Rome traditionally associated with St Peter: the *Quo Vadis*, the spot in the Roman Forum where Simon Magus is said to have fallen, the chains of St Peter in Fetters, the place on the Janiculum where Peter is said to have been crucified.

Does the episcopal see of Rome owe the pre-eminence, which it enjoyed from the very beginning, to the fact that it lay in the capital of the Roman Empire? This fact must certainly have influenced Peter in his choice of headquarters. Nevertheless the early Christian church clearly regarded the bishops of Rome not primarily as the bishops of the Empire's political capital, but as the inheritors of the *locus Petri*, possessing by right of succession the place and throne of Peter, called on to continue its functions and therefore entitled to special prerogatives.

The Emperor Constantine bestowing the primacy of the Church and rule over the West on his contemporary Pope Sylvester (314–35). This legend, known as the Donation of Constantine, was used to support papal claims to temporal power in the Middle Ages. A thirteenth-century fresco

Some twenty years after the death of the Apostle Peter, the intervention of his third successor in the dissensions of the Church of Corinth may be regarded as evidence of the Bishop of Rome's authority. This intervention has been defined as 'the Epiphany of the Primacy'. When news of the serious quarrels in Corinth, which had resulted in some of the community's younger members expelling a number of the elders, reached Rome, the Church there considered it its duty to intervene. This took the form of a long letter written by Bishop Clement (*c* 90–100), which while confining itself to exhortation and counselling harmony and submission to the leaders of the Church, does not hesitate at times to adopt a commanding, almost threatening, tone, revealing a determination to be obeyed:

It is to you, the authors of this sedition, that I now turn: submit to the priests and accept punishment as a penance. Learn to live in submission and cast off vain words and haughty speech dictated by idle presumption ... If one of you should not obey what Jesus has spoken through us, let him know he commits a grave sin and lays himself open to dire peril. We are not to blame for their false works ... You will give us great joy if, by obeying what we have written in the Holy Ghost, you cast off the unrighteous vehemence of your anger, according to the admonitions we have expressed in this letter in favour of peace and concord ... All has been done to persuade you that our every concern was bent and is still bent on quickly re-establishing peace among you.

If one bears in mind that this intervention was spontaneous and had not been requested by Corinth, that at the time Clement wrote the letter the Apostle John was still alive in Ephesus, from where communications with Corinth were easier, and that the letter expresses more than the normal solidarity between churches, such as that shown, for instance, in the epistles of Ignatius of Antioch and Polycarp, it seems legitimate to conclude that at the end of the first century, the Church of Rome, represented by its bishop, was already aware of possessing a higher authority, which was to emerge even more clearly later. Moreover the way the letter was greeted in Corinth, where it was almost accepted as an inspired writing and was still being read seventy years later at dominical liturgical assemblies, shows this authority was also acknowledged by other churches.

Ignatius of Antioch's letter to the Romans, written round about 110, exalts the Roman Church more directly. One is struck by the elaborate laudatory epithets which Ignatius pours out and which are more numerous and significant than those he uses in other letters.

Ignatius, known also as Theophorus, to the Church which received mercy from the magnificence of the Father in the highest and of Jesus Christ, to the Church loved above all and enlightened by the will of Him who has willed all that exists, which presides over the region of the Romans, worthy of God, worthy of honour, worthy to be called blessed, worthy of success, which presides over charity, which bears the law of Christ, which bears the name of the Father.

An early Christian lamp in the shape of a ship, with St Peter and St Paul, the apostles of the Roman Church, guiding the vessel. In Christian art and imagery the ship is a recurrent symbol of the Church

It is not difficult to discern in this assemblage of titles Ignatius's faith in the pre-eminence of the Roman Church. It is particularly significant evidence when it is remembered that Ignatius himself was the successor of Peter in Antioch and upholder of the authority of each bishop within his own church.

Ignatius's acknowledgement of the Roman Church's pre-eminence is echoed some decades later by Irenaeus of Lyons (*c* 202). In combating the deviations of the Gnostics, he demonstrates that orthodox faith is the one preached by the apostles and preserved unaltered among those communities which, through the uninterrupted succession of bishops, can trace their origins back to the apostles. Since it would take too long to demonstrate the apostolic

The First Popes

Above The Christian monogram formed from the initial Greek letters χ and ρ of the name of Christ. This early fourth-century bronze also incorporates the mystic letters Alpha and Omega – Christ the beginning and the end

Left The Good Shepherd, the most common representation of Christ in the early Church, carved on the side of a third-century sarcophagus

succession in all the churches, he considers the Roman one, founded by the apostles Peter and Paul, which has maintained its apostolic character through an uninterrupted succession. Having laid down this premise, he establishes the maxim that every church must agree with that of Rome, because it is there, above all, that the apostolic tradition has been preserved unaltered. The difficulty presented by the text, which has survived only in an imperfect Latin translation and lacks a consistent terminology, means that we cannot claim that it clearly asserts Roman primacy of jurisdiction. It does however assert the special importance of the Roman Church as the most reliable witness and most assured interpreter of the apostolic tradition and, consequently, its primacy amongst all churches.

In the testimonies of Ignatius and Irenaeus it is to the Church of Rome that special pre-eminence is attributed. But according to the principles held by these same men, the Church is the bishop; it is to the bishop, then, that this pre-eminence belongs.

This is the context in which we must consider the attraction of Rome between the second and third centuries both for heretics – for example, Cerdo, Valentinus, Marcion, the Montanists, the Monarchians – who came to Rome seeking approval for their theories, but returned carrying with them the condemnation of the Popes, who defined the main articles of faith and the canon of inspired writings; and for the orthodox, who journeyed there to draw on the unfailing source of the genuine apostolic tradition.

More clearly than in the doctrinal field, the superior jurisdiction of the Papacy emerges in matters of discipline and practice. Two questions particularly involved the authority of the Popes: in the second century the date for celebrating Easter and in the third the validity of baptism administered by heretics.

The First Popes

The epitaph on the tomb of Pope Cornelius, who died in exile in 253. He ruled at a troubled time, but was able to enlist the help of Cyprian of Carthage

As to the first, Pope Anicetus (154/55–66) had already called on the Asians to adopt the Roman date of Easter, as being in conformity with the apostolic tradition. St Polycarp went to Rome to discuss the matter with the Pope, who, though no agreement was reached, did not exclude the Asians from his communion. But the question was energetically taken up again around 190, by Victor (189–98). The majority of the Asians adopted the Roman usage, but Polycrates of Ephesus maintained that their customs were also apostolic in character, turning for support to the great figures of the Asiatic churches, probably because Pope Victor had based his command on the authority of the apostles Peter and Paul. Victor then excommunicated the recalcitrant Ephesians; but we do not know if this sanction was maintained after the mediation of Irenaeus of Lyons. In any case these churches were also conforming to the Roman usage before the Council of Nicaea.

The second controversy, involving Pope Stephen and Cyprian of Carthage, is equally important. Before the controversy came to a head a number of episodes and statements by Cyprian had made it clear that he acknowledged the pre-eminence of the Bishop of Rome: for example the case of the Spanish Bishops Basilides and Martial, and of Bishop Marcion of Arles, whom Cyprian called on the Pope to condemn. Writing about his opponents Cyprian said: 'they dare to sail towards the see of Peter and the principal church from which priestly unity is derived.' In the recension A of chapter 4 of *De catholicae Ecclesiae unitate*, he wrote 'Does he who abandons the see of Peter, on which the church is founded, still think he is in the church?': and 'certainly the others too were as Peter was, *sed Petro primatus datur*, and thus is demonstrated a church and a see'. Cyprian saw in the *cathedra Petri* the prime source of ecclesiastical unity, but he did not altogether maintain this attitude in his relations with Pope Stephen. Cyprian held that only baptism received in the Catholic Church was valid and that the Roman usage of not rebaptizing those christened by heretics was mistaken, although he allowed each bishop to act as he thought fit. Stephen threatened the Africans with excommunication if they did not accede to the Roman custom, basing this requirement on his authority as Peter's successor, whereupon Cyprian had his own judgment confirmed by the Council of September 256 and sent several bishops to Rome to report the result of these deliberations. The bishops were, however, not received by Stephen. It should be noted that although Cyprian criticized the Pope's harshness, he did not dare break his communion with Rome or ultimately question the Pope's authority. Stephen, on the other hand, was prepared for a break, convinced of possessing the authority of the see of Peter. It has rightly been pointed out that this episode constitutes the most significant demonstration of the pre-eminence of Rome up to this date.

About the year 260 certain improprieties of language used by Bishop Dionysius of Alexandria (*c*264) in formulating the Catholic doctrine of the Trinity provided an opportunity to denounce Dionysius before the Pope of the same name. Pope Dionysius intervened authoritatively, judging and condemning the doctrine upheld by the bishop, who in fact enjoyed the greatest prestige in the East. The latter accepted the Pope's ruling, admitting the impropriety of certain similes he had used to define the relationship of the Son to the Father and providing explanations on other points in order to demonstrate the coincidence of his doctrine of the Trinity with that of the Pope.

After Dionysius (259–68) there are almost no records of the Papacy for well over forty years. It is not until the Pontificates of Miltiades (311–14), Sylvester (314–35) and Julius (337–52) that reliable information exists about the activities of the Roman bishops, or any significant affirmation of authority can be found. In fact, contrary to what one might expect, during the vital period of the reign of Constantine, the Popes played a very modest role. There was, it is true, a promising start when Constantine, at the suggestion of Hosius and his ecclesiastical counsellors, referred to Pope Miltiades rather than to the bishops of Gaul as he had been requested to do, the first appeal addressed

The fourth-century church at the entrance to the catacomb of St Calixtus, Pope from 217 to 223. These underground cemeteries had to be outside the walls of the city. Being sacrosanct as burial grounds, they became good hiding places for the early Christians during persecution. Later they were the scenes of great ceremonies on the feast days of the martyrs

The crypt of the Popes in the catacomb of St Calixtus, where some of the early Bishops of Rome were buried. A typical gallery, with the niches in which the bodies were placed arranged in tiers. The inscription refers to Pope Damasus who died in 384

Above The catacombs contain some of the earliest examples of Christian art. The crypt of St Cornelius in the catacombs of St Calixtus, with wall frescoes
Below Popes Sixtus II (badly effaced) and Liberius, on either side of an allegorical representation of Susanna and the Elders

A fourth-century wall fresco of Adam and Eve from the catacombs of SS Peter and Marcellinus

The First Popes

Many early Christian symbols have been found in archaeological excavations. A third-century representation of a praying man with a dove and the Christ symbol

to him by Christian bishops. Nevertheless when the bishops maintained their position, as is shown by the decisions of the Council of Arles (314), by the synodal letter to Pope Sylvester, and by the judgment of Bishops Eunomius and Olympius, Constantine seemed to forget the Bishop of Rome.

When the Arian controversy, which asserted that the Son was begotten of the Father in time, arose, Sylvester learned of it from Alexander of Alexandria and the Council of Antioch (324), and gave his judgment. At the Council of Nicaea (325) his legates were not given precedence because they were only priests; nor did the elders make a solemn act of homage to Sylvester as the elders of Chalcedon did to St Leo. Yet Sylvester was not ignored – the inclusion of the definition of the term *homoiousios*, proposed as much as sixty years earlier by Pope Dionysius, the honourable place assigned to his legates and the adoption of a number of canons, where the Roman inspiration is discernible, bear witness to this. On the other hand after the Council of Nicaea the Papacy withdrew within itself, due to the indifference of Constantine and of the bishops, led by Eusebius of Nicomedia, who, by flattering the Emperor and making him the arbiter of the peace of the church, won his favour and ruled the church, ignoring the Pope completely.

Later, under the sons of Constantine, on the occasions when the imperial power did not attempt to deal on its own authority with ecclesiastical affairs – disputes or questions of doctrine, jurisdiction and discipline arising from the Arian controversy – church matters proceeded normally and were referred for solution to Rome. However, when the imperial power came under the domination of the Eusebian faction, the Pope's right to decide on questions affecting the Eastern church or to review judgments pronounced by the councils of the East was contested. There were several significant episodes in the history of the Papacy at this time: the Council of Rome in 340 and Pope Julius' letter to the Eastern church, in which his consciousness of his authority over the entire church and his determination to exercise it are clearly expressed, and the Council of Sardica, which codified the right of appeal to the Pope. But when Constantius II remained the sole Emperor, he not only ignored the authority of Rome, but went so far as to humiliate Pope Liberius (352–66), banishing him and bringing pressure on him to denounce Athanasius and accept the Eastern communion and new formulas of faith. This is sometimes referred to as the defeat of Pope Liberius; but the description is inaccurate because he only consented to condemn Athanasius and to subscribe to a formula of faith which did not contain the term *homoiousios* but which, with the declaration he added to it, was none the less orthodox. The culminating point in the humiliation of the Papacy at the hands of Constantius came at the Council of Rimini-Seleucia (359), in which Liberius took no part at all.

When Constantius died the Papacy quickly reasserted its authority. Liberius declared the Council of Rimini invalid, the rebels from the Eastern church came to Rome and accepted the conditions for return to the Roman communion.

A Christian sarcophagus of the fourth century, elaborately carved with scenes from biblical history. On the left Jonah and the whale and on the right the baptism of Christ

The First Popes

A giant fourth-century bronze head of Constantius II, who brought the political power of the Empire to bear on the Church to reverse the decision of the Council of Nicaea. In 358–9 he forced the exiled Pope Liberius to condemn Athanasius, the 'orthodox' champion, and to side with the detractors of the Nicene Creed

Right The papal basilica of S Maria Maggiore was founded by Pope Liberius in 352. According to legend, the Virgin Mary appeared to him and commanded him to build a church on the spot where he found snow on August 5th.
A representation by the fifteenth-century painter Masolino

Far right above Sixtus I (*c* 117–*c* 127) and St Timothy with Christ holding wreaths or haloes over their heads.
The bottom of a glass bowl decorated in gold

Far right below Innocent I (402–17) from an early fresco.
Innocent made more substantial claims for the Papacy than any of his predecessors

In other words the Papacy, under Liberius and later under Damasus (366–84), resumed its role as leader of the church in both West and East. In fact the East sent repeated appeals to Damasus for help in re-establishing orthodoxy and peace in the Church, while the Council of Antioch in 379 accepted the formularies sent by Damasus. In the West, in spite of Palladius of Ratiaria's invectives, Ambrose and the Council of Aquileia in 381 proclaimed the Roman Church the head of the Roman Empire and the fount and centre of the Catholic communion. Damasus's documents proclaim the see of Rome as the 'Apostolic See': in the solemn proclamation made at the Council of Rome in 382, refuting the third canon of the Council of Constantinople in 381, he states that the primacy of Rome is not derived from synodal constitutions, but is founded on Peter through the words of Christ himself.

Popes Siricius (384–99) and Anastasius (399–402) were succeeded in 402 by Innocent I (402–17) whose many activities were inspired not only by the aim of establishing the primacy of the Apostolic See, but also by pastoral care and a realization of the duty incumbent on him as 'head and apex of the episcopate' to foster the observance of the canons, to safeguard the unity of the Church, threatened in the West by the break-up of the Empire, and to preserve the faith in all its purity. This is borne out by his decretal letters to the Bishops of the West and Illyricum, his actions in defence of St John Chrysostom and his intervention in the Pelagian controversy. Such intervention had been requested by the African bishops who, while jealous of their autonomy in matters of discipline, were however convinced that in matters of faith, they needed the sanction of a higher, more universal and effective authority, in other words that of the Apostolic See. Innocent condemned Pelagius and Celestius, *apostolici vigoris auctoritate*, and Augustine exclaimed: 'The case is finished: may Heaven will that once and for all the error ceases.'

An attitude similar to that of the Africans was shown by the Eastern church, which, whilst accustomed to acting independently and only turning to Rome in extreme cases, invoked the intervention of Pope Celestine (422–32) in the Nestorian heresy. The Council of Ephesus (431) did no more than carry out Celestine's sentence: 'Urged on by the canons and according to the letter of our most Holy Father and co-servant Celestine, we have proceeded with the sentence against Nestorius.' Later during the reign of Sixtus III (432–40), the metropolitans Eutherius of Thiana and Helladius of Tarsus made a moving appeal for the Pope's help in re-establishing discipline: 'We pray that he may stretch out his salutary hand and calm the tempest of the world, that he may command all cases to be examined, so as to bring heavenly correction to injustices and set up once more the holy shepherds unjustly removed from their sheep, so that the order and concord of the past may be restored to the flocks.'

SVSTVS
TIMOTEVS

3 ROME AND BYZANTIUM

LEO I *to* ZACHARY 440-752

FRANCIS XAVIER MURPHY

When the centre of imperial power shifted to Constantinople, conflict between Popes and Emperors became inevitable. The barbarian invasions and continual doctrinal conflicts caused confusion throughout the Empire; and while Rome and the West looked to the Papacy for spiritual and political leadership, the Emperors felt themselves impelled to intervene in ecclesiastical matters. Two great Popes emerged, Leo the Great, who made sweeping reforms in church organization and liturgy and championed the Roman people against the invading Huns, and Gregory the Great, during whose reign the Papacy reached a new height of authority and missionary enterprises flourished all over the Western world.

TO UNDERSTAND THE DEVELOPMENT OF THE PAPACY and its relations with the Romano-Byzantine Empire during the three hundred years that run from St Leo the Great (440–61) to Zachary (741–52) it is necessary to keep in mind two facts. The Popes considered themselves the direct successors of St Peter, governing the Church which was the *civitas dei* in the place of Christ. It was at once a mystical ideal and a practical idea. The terms in which it was expressed, as well as the political situation in which it was exercised, were inevitably those supplied by the later Roman Empire, and the Roman concept of law and order. This is abundantly evident from the actions and decisions of Leo and Gelasius in the fifth century, of Gregory the Great at the close of the sixth, of Martin, the Johns and Sergius in the seventh and the eighth.

At the same time, the Eastern Emperors, who inherited an absolute tradition of universal law from the Caesars and the Constantines, could not but assert their overall supremacy in the oriental context of the ruler as the immediate representative of Almighty God, the *pantocrator* or governor of the universe.

These two concepts were bound to clash in dealing with the Christian polity, for Christianity demands the loyalty of the whole man. It was to avoid duality of allegiance that, once the Roman Emperor became a Christian, Eusebius of Caesarea referred to Constantine as the *Isapostolus* – the equal of an apostle; and speaks of the imperial *Christomimesis* – the Emperor as imitator of Christ the divine ruler.

In the practical sphere of the Church's life, both sets of concepts were applied respectively by Pope and Emperor to the enunciation of the Catholic faith, and the government of clergy and laity. But the social, political and economic factors also played a part in determining policy and supplied the occasion for conflict between the two powers.

The election of the Roman deacon Leo in September 440 as Bishop of Rome marks a new era in the history of the Papacy. Leo brought to the papal office a mystical sense of the destiny of the Roman pontiff as custodian of traditional doctrine, and then, a clarification of the power – the authority of Christ – exercised by himself and his predecessors as the direct representatives of St Peter, 'in whose place we function'. Trained in the law, experienced in the care of Rome's indigent, accustomed to the ideological and political movements of the age as deacon to Celestine and Sixtus III, Leo as Pope immediately proclaimed his 'solicitude for all the churches'.

In Italy and the provinces of the west, he set out pastoral prescriptions intended to ensure the election of worthy priests and competent bishops. He insisted on the holding of frequent regional synods to preserve orthodoxy and order. Determined to achieve unity through the liturgy, he laid down rules regarding the mass, baptism and marriage, penance, the repression of heresy and the rehabilitation of schismatics. Finally he set a precedent as protector of the city of Rome by negotiating the withdrawal of Attila and his Huns from the Mincio, and mitigating the depredations of the Vandals in the Eternal City itself. Turning to the East, he entered headlong into the political and doctrinal

Leo the Great brought a new sense of power and responsibility to the Papacy. He reformed and unified Church organization and in 452 protected Rome from Attila and the Huns. A miniature from St Basil's Calendar of Saints

difficulties sapping the strength of the later Roman Empire. Accused of a certain superficiality in his theological thinking, Leo justified his stand by indicating that profundity in theology was a luxury in ecclesiastical affairs. He extracted from the scriptures and patristic tradition a clear statement of the truth involved in the incarnation and was ready with his *Tome to Flavian* when in 448 the anti-Nestorian fanaticism of the archimandrite Eutyches became an international issue. His doctrinal statement triumphed at the Council of Chalcedon in 451, but his intransigence in refusing to accept the '28th canon' which recognized Constantinople, the 'new Rome', as the second see in Christendom, hampered the Emperor Marcian in dealing with the rebellion of the Egyptian monks that spread through the Orient as the heresy of Monophysitism.

Leo's successor, Hilary (461–68), had a comparatively peaceful reign, challenged only by the anti-Chalcedonian activity of the Egyptian and Syrian monks. Pope Simplicius (468–83) followed Leo's lead in advising the Emperor Zeno to remove heretical bishops such as Timothy the Cat and Peter Mongos in Alexandria, and Peter the Fuller in Antioch. He established a vicariate in Seville for Spain and strengthened the authority of the Bishop of Arles in Gaul. It was during his reign that the barbarian regent Odoacer deposed the last of the Western Emperors, Augustulus (476), and returned the imperial insignia to Constantinople. This decisive act rendered the Papacy the final source of authority in the West, and awakened the Roman nobility to the value of the papal office as a family possession. To circumvent local intrigue, however, Odoacer informed the Romans that thereafter confirmation for the newly elected Pope would have to come from Constantinople; and that the new Pope would have to pledge not to alienate any of the vast property holdings of the Roman see. Felix III (483–92), of ancient Roman stock, accepted these conditions. Nevertheless, in 484 he condemned the Archbishop of Constantinople, Acacius, who had assisted the Emperor Zeno in issuing his *Henoticon* or doctrinal decree intended as a compromise statement of the Chalcedonian doctrine on the incarnation. The result was schism between Rome and Constantinople.

Pope Gelasius (492–96) inherited this situation. Writing to the Emperor he formulated his famous thesis concerning the relationship between Church and Empire, and speaks of the 'world being governed by two sovereignties, the papal authority and the royal power, which come from

The election of Pope Symmachus (498–514) was disputed between pro- and anti-Byzantine factions. Once established, he was an energetic Pope. A mosaic portrait from S Agnese fuori le Mura, Rome

The triumph of the Christian Empire represented in the fifth-century wooden doors of S Sabina, Rome. The carving gives a vivid picture of the clothes and architecture of the time

In the fifth and sixth centuries the Church was deeply divided by the Monophysite heresy, which originated in Egypt. It concerned the definition of the relation of the divine and human natures of Christ. This sixth-century fresco from a Monophysite church shows St Cosmas and St Damian and in the background the burning in the fiery furnace

God, the supreme Sovereign'. While separate and independent, the imperial power is intended by divine providence as a complement to the spiritual authority, which then has a right to judge the Emperor's use of his power. This theory fell on the deaf ears of the Emperor Anastasius II, a Monophysite by conviction. When the new Pope, Anastasius II (496–98) wrote to his namesake the Emperor in a conciliatory fashion, two factions formed in Rome. Upon that pontiff's death, the followers of Anastasius elected Symmachus (498–514), while the anti-Byzantines put forward the deacon Laurentius. The dispute was referred to the Ostrogoth king, Theodoric, who supported Symmachus. After a campaign of calumny by the Laurentian party, the Pope was called before the Ostrogothic king in Ravenna. The matter was finally dealt with by three synods in Rome; and there in 502, after declaring the Roman See 'beyond man's judgment', Symmachus cleared himself of the charges.

Hormisdas (514–23) ended this local Roman schism; then turned his attention to the troubles between Rome and Constantinople. In the East, the man who was to fuse the Monophysite movement into a church, Severus of Antioch, had emerged; while in 518 the new Emperor Justin I proved to be both a Catholic and a Latin. He turned at once to Pope Hormisdas for a settlement of the doctrinal problems, and the Pope sent a legation to Constantinople with a new formula to be signed by the bishops of the Empire. It asserted the indefectibility of the faith of the Roman Church, condemned Nestorius, Eutyches and Dioscoros, made explicit recognition of the decisions of Ephesus and Chalcedon, accepted Leo's *Tome*, and condemned the Monophysite bishops including Acacius and his supporters. It likewise forbade receiving in communion anyone not in agreement with the Apostolic See. The imperial soldiery were employed to gather signatures from the bishops and leading monks, in what amounted to a direct persecution of the Monophysites. Pope John I (523–526) was sent to Constaninople by the Ostrogothic king, Theodoric, to persuade the Emperor Justin to restore the churches taken from the Arians. While his mission was partially successful, he was imprisoned and died soon after his return to the Eternal City in an outburst of anti-Byzantine fury that resulted likewise in the death of the Christian philosopher Boethius.

During the reign of Pope Vigilius (537–55) the Empress' favourite Monophysite, the Cappadocian Bishop Theodore Ascidas, demanded as a reprisal for the condemnation of the ancient Alexandrian theologian Origen by Pelagius, that Pelagius condemn three theologians who had supported the decision of the Council of Chalcedon. Summoned to Constantinople, Vigilius published three contradictory documents: the *Judicatum* (or verdict) of 548, condemning the writings, though not the persons of the three writers. This caused a furore of protest among the Western

A jewelled reliquary cross belonging to Justin II, Emperor of Byzantium 565–78. Called the *Crux Vaticana*, it is the oldest surviving relic in the Treasury of St Peter's

bishops, and the Pope withdrew the document. Abused and bullied by the Emperor's men, Vigilius refused to take part in the second Council of Constantinople, called by the Emperor in May 553. Instead he published his *Constitutum* or Resolution, defending the deceased theologians, while pointing out the errors in some of their works. In having the Council repudiate the Pope, Justinian made it clear that he remained loyal to the Apostolic See by appealing from the *sedentem* to the *sedem*. Six months later, he forced the Pope, now a broken old man, to accept the Council's decisions in a new *Constitutum*. Historians have been harsh in judging Vigilius, making little of his bravery under great pressure and his humble attempt to arrive at a solution for the terrible religious difficulties of his age.

Apparently to ease the situation in the West where political anarchy reigned, Justinian granted Vigilius a *Pragmatic Sanction*, which his successor, Pelagius I (555–561), utilized to organize the temporal government in the territory occupied by the Ostrogoths, over which he was practically sovereign. The Pope thus became the protector

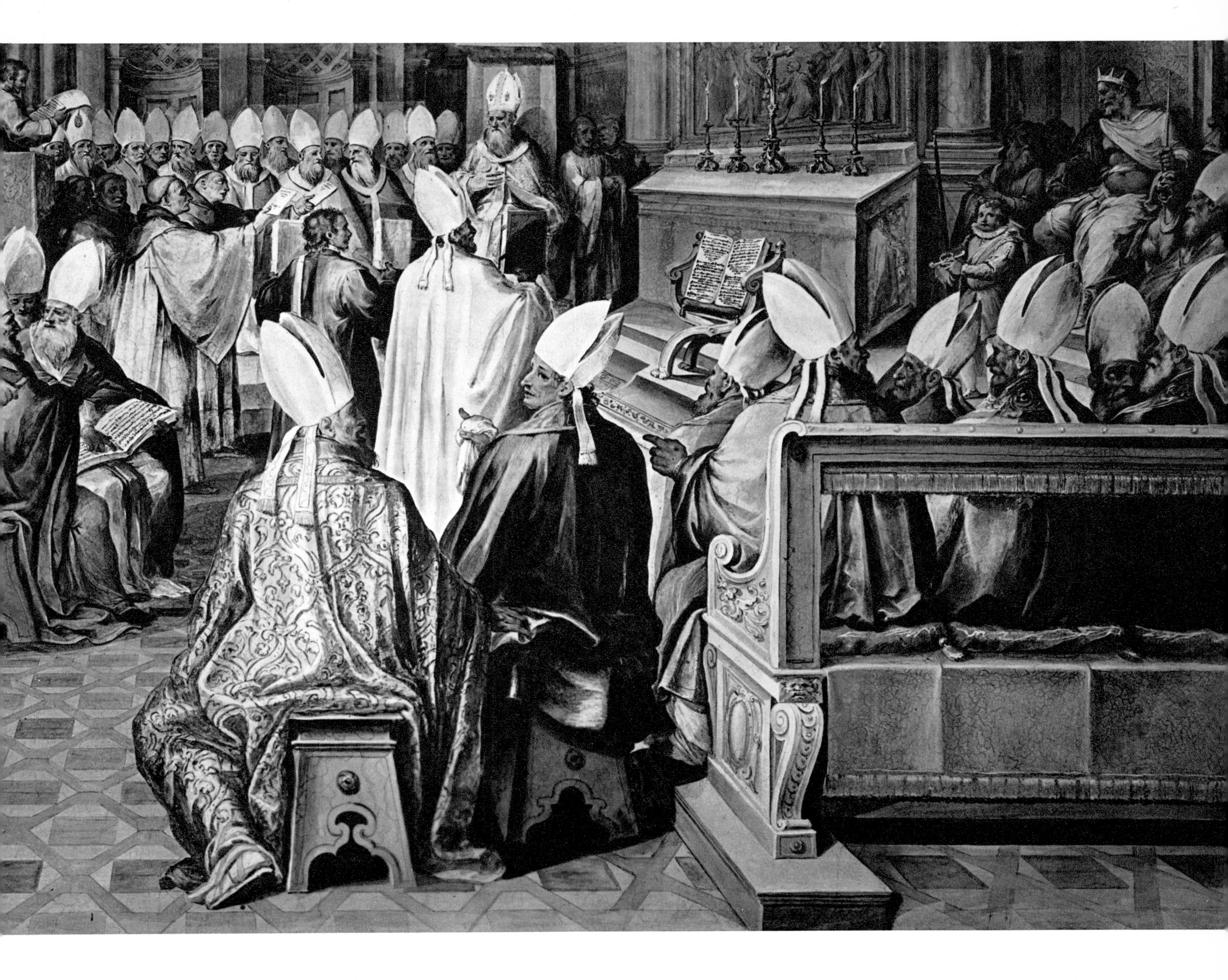

of the civil population against tax gatherers and the depredations of the soldiery. John III (561–74) had to deal with the Lombard invasions that overran Ravenna and threatened both Rome and Naples. Benedict I (574–79) waited a whole year for imperial confirmation; hence his successor, Pelagius II (579–90), turned to the Franks, converted a century earlier, for protection against the 'deadly race of Lombards', and had the satisfaction of learning that the Arian Visigoths of Spain had turned Catholic under King Reccared and St Leander of Seville.

The Second Council of Constantinople, summoned by the Emperor Justinian in 553, marked a crisis in relations between the Papacy and the Empire, typical of the intricacies of the doctrinal disputes of the time and the struggle for power between East and West. Pope Vigilius refused to join Justinian in the condemnation of three fifth-century heretics, but was later forced to submit. This Renaissance fresco in the Vatican is one of a series covering the Councils of the Church

Rome and Byzantium

By tradition the Byzantine Emperors were raised on a shield for their coronation. This tenth-century miniature illustrates the ceremony, while depicting the biblical story of David

Below The silver cover of a contemporary copy of Justinian's *Digest* or *Pandects*. Justinian made a great contribution to the codification and simplification of Roman law, which was in a state of chaos. His *Codex* (529) and *Digest* (533) are among his most important achievements

Right The reign of Justinian (527–65), statesman, soldier and lawgiver, was the most brilliant period of the Byzantine Empire. A mosaic portrait in San Vitale, Ravenna

MAXIMIANVS

SANC THEODORVS

Opposite St Theodore (642–9), a near contemporary mosaic in the apse of SS Cosmas and Damian, Rome. Theodore's reign was disturbed by the Monothelite heresy, concerning the relation of divine and human will in Christ

Left St Benedict (*c* 480–547) was the virtual founder of Western monasticism. His famous *Rule* (*c* 540), with its simple yet flexible ordering of monastic life, is the basis not only of the Benedictine, but of many other Orders. A tenth or eleventh-century fresco from the catacomb of St Ermete

Rome and Byzantium

Left Gregory the Great (590–604) is known as the father of the medieval Papacy. He laboured to restore peace to Italy, virtually taking over the political power, and did much for the mission of the Church, especially in sending St Augustine to England. This portrait shows the gentleness which was allied to his outstanding ability.

Right above Gregory's throne in S Gregorio Magno, Rome

Right below A manuscript illustration of Gregory the Great's funeral, showing the old basilica of St Peter's in the background

Gregory the Great (590–604), great-grandson of Pope Felix III, governed Rome as civil administrator, then became a monk in Rome, before being sent as papal ambassador to the Byzantine court. As Pope, he represented Roman law and order in a century of chaos. He reorganized the patrimony of the Church in Sicily, Gaul and Italy; spread Benedictine monasticism, and by intensifying the conversion and romanization of the barbarian nations, set the stage for a later break with the Byzantine domination of the Papacy. Considering himself 'God's consul', he despatched St Augustine of Canterbury to England, and sent some 848 letters, still preserved in the Papal Register, to bishops all over Christendom. As the *Servus servorum Dei*, with his *Commentary on Job* for monks, his *Moralia*, his *Homilies* and his *Pastoral Rule for Bishops* – translated into Anglo-Saxon by King Alfred – which are all of deep though simple piety, he created the moral, doctrinal and pastoral atmosphere that prevailed in the early Middle Ages.

His immediate successors, Silverian, Deusdedit and three Bonifaces, continued his missionary efforts, cut off as they were from the East by the Persian invasions under Chosroes II until the military genius of the Byzantine Emperor Heraclius (610–41) rescued the Empire from extinction.

Pope Honorius I (625–38) was brought into the Monothelite controversy by the eighty-year-old archbishop of Jerusalem, Sophronius, to combat the teaching of Sergius of Constantinople that there was only one source of action or 'energy' in Christ. This teaching was eventually enunciated in an imperial *ecthesis* or doctrinal decision. Unfortunately, as his immediate successors in the Papacy – John IV (640–42) and Theodore (642–49) – maintained, Honorius missed the point behind the argument, and spoke of 'only one will in Christ', intending to clarify the harmony or moral union of natures with which Christ acted, after having correctly asserted that while the divine and human natures of Christ are united in one person, 'each nature operated in its own sphere'. Martin I (649–55) summoned a Roman Synod to condemn a new Monothelite definition, call a *Typos*, or outline of the faith, by defining the fact that there are in Christ 'two wills, the divine and the human,

Right Martin I (649–55) was another victim of the struggle between Rome and the Byzantine Emperors. He was banished and died in exile, being the last of the Popes who is venerated as a martyr.
Fresco from S Maria Antiqua, Rome

hence two operations, the divine and the human'. Kidnapped and brought to Constantinople he was tried for treason, degraded, and exiled by the Emperor, Leo III. For a further three-quarters of a century controversy raged between Rome and Constantinople, particularly about the question of whether the veneration of images was legitimate. In a council at Rome (731) Gregory III (731–41) excommunicated whoever condemned the veneration of images or destroyed sacred pictures. When the fleet sent by the Emperor to capture the Pope foundered in the Adriatic, vengeance was taken by depriving the Pope of the patrimony of Sicily and Calabria. But by now, the tremendous missionary zeal of the Englishman, St Boniface, in the Germanies was supported by the Frankish Mayors of the Palace, Pepin of Héristal and Charles Martel. This brought about an alliance between the Papacy and the new dynasty emerging in Gaul. Thus the Church was in a position to profit from the coalition between the next Pope, Zachary (740–52), and Pepin the Short in preparing for the rise of Charlemagne and the Carolingian renaissance.

SCS PE TR VS
DN LE O PP
CARVLO REGI
BEATE·PETRE·DONAS
VITA·LEON·PP·E·BICTO
RIA·CARVLO·REGI·DONAS
BONE VOLVN
TATIS

4 THE REBIRTH OF THE EMPIRE

STEPHEN II to ALEXANDER II 752-1073

DOUGLAS WOODRUFF

On Christmas Day 800 Leo III crowned Charlemagne, King of the Franks, as Emperor and the Holy Roman Empire founded on that day endured in different forms until the time of Napoleon. Under Charlemagne's successors the Carolingian Empire lost its vigour and coherence, and the period saw the growth of new kingdoms and the establishment of papal temporal power in the West. In the East the quarrel between the Patriarch Photius and the Pope, Nicholas the Great, began the rift between Rome and Constantinople.

THIS NEXT PERIOD IS DOMINATED BY THE EXISTENCE of the Carolingian Empire of the Franks whom the Popes had called to their aid. Pepin's son, Charlemagne, when he came to Rome in 774, extended his father's gift of lands; Corsica, Venetia, Istria, all north of Ravenna, were included in his Donation to create the States of the Church. He was building up an ecclesiastical state to contain the Lombards to the north-west of it. The Papacy was not able to make its authority real in so great a territory, and was never effectively in control of Venice or Istria or Corsica. But the lands it could control brought new wealth, so that Adrian I (771–95) in one of the longest Pontificates, of twenty-four years, was able to endow, to restore, to decorate the churches of Rome in a way his predecessors had been quite unable to do; and this continues to be the mark of successive Pontificates for a hundred years. It showed an unconquerable optimism to spend so much money on buildings and their adornment when there was all the time such imminent risk of invasion and pillage by the Saracens. The Mohammedans had taken all Spain. They reached half across France, until the Franks drove them back at the Battle of Tours. They could easily land on any part of the long Italian coast-line. From this enemy the Franks could not effectively defend them.

When Pepin first gave the lands taken from the Lombards to the Church, the Emperor in Constantinople wrote and demanded them as part of the Empire and the Popes then looked to the Franks as their defenders not only against the Saracens and Lombards, but against Constantinople. The Popes had other enemies to contend with, now that to be Pope was also to be a king of a fine kingdom, and it was these acquisitive Roman families who assaulted and tried to mutilate, in the form favoured at the time – blinding and cutting out the tongue – St Leo III (795–816), who reigned after Adrian. Though attacked in this fashion, he must have escaped to make his way to Charlemagne, who returned with him to Rome. It was on this occasion, on Christmas Day in the year 800, that the historic event took place, when the Pope suddenly produced a crown and an imperial robe and crowned the King of the Franks as Emperor, with the congregation shouting 'To Charles Augustus, crowned by God; to the great and peace-bringing Emperor'. According to Einhard, Charlemagne's secretary and biographer, the king was both taken by surprise and displeased, probably because he did not wish to seem to receive his authority, already sufficiently great, from the Pope. It may have weighed with Leo that a little earlier the Empress Irene, of Constantinople, had proposed a marriage between her House and the Franks, a proposal which had filled Rome with alarm, and was effectively prevented when the Franks assumed the imperial title, which had hitherto been the prerogative of the direct successors of Augustus now residing in Constantinople. Leo's letters to Charlemagne have disappeared, and we are left to conjecture about the Pope's motives, but what he did was of momentous significance. He was founding a European Christian Empire which was to pass from the Franks to the Germans, to remain one of the great institutions of European life and

St Peter conferring the pallium, or stole, symbolizing spiritual authority on Pope Leo III, and the imperial banner, symbol of temporal power, on Charlemagne. A restored eighth-century mosaic from S Giovanni in Laterano

The rebirth of the Empire

Pépin III, King of the Franks, the father of Charlemagne, came to the help of Pope Stephen II against the marauding Lombards, so that the Popes came to look upon the Franks as their allies and defenders. This manuscript illumination shows him with two priestly attendants, while a divine hand places a diadem on his head

An equestrian statue of Charlemagne in the Musée Carnavalet, which some scholars believe to be of almost contemporary workmanship

not finally to disappear until 1806. The successful attempt of the Emperor of Austria to veto the election of a particular cardinal to the Papacy in 1903 goes back all the way to that Christmas Day in 800. Unfortunately, the Carolingian Empire fell a victim to the quarrels of Charlemagne's grandchildren and proved unequal to defending Italy. In the middle of the ninth century, Leo IV (847–55) built the walls enclosing an area still known as the Leonine City, roughly corresponding to the Vatican City State, to make an inner keep against the Saracens.

These Carolingian emperors were by agreement to enjoy the temporal rights which the Emperors of Constantinople had enjoyed, and their sanction had to be sought before the choice of the Roman clergy and people could be consecrated as Bishop of Rome. While the Bishop was to have jurisdiction in temporal matters, there was to be an ultimate appeal to the Emperor.

But the position of Pope had become something to be coveted for its material possessions and power, and from now onwards the noble families seek to play, and often succeed in playing, a successful hand in placing one of their members in the papal chair. As the power of the Carolingian emperors begins to wane, so does that of the local nobles become more important. If we look at the Pontificate of Pope Gregory IV (827–44) we can see the whole process at work. Nearly all the authorities for his Pontificate are the Carolingian chronicles, and it is from Franks who have left literary records like Nithard, Charlemagne's priestly grandson, or Agobard of Lyons, that we can get the clearest picture of the difficulties with which the Popes now had to contend. It was far better to deal with the Franks than with the Greeks. The Frankish emperors were far less sure of themselves, far more impressed with the authority and majesty of Rome, and when they usurped, as they occasionally did, part of the Pope's spiritual jurisdiction, as when Charlemagne inserted the *filioque* clause in the creed, the Popes reacted vigorously. Gregory IV did not hesitate to reaffirm the supremacy of his office over that of the Emperor, since a spiritual jurisdiction must take precedence of a temporal one, and in this the Carolingian emperors acquiesced.

The real trouble was the virtual disappearance for a hundred years of the office of emperor, through the feeble character of Charlemagne's son, who is rather lucky to live in history under the alternative titles of 'the Pious' or 'the Debonair'. From the quarrels of his sons, their actions

Right The coronation of Charlemagne by Leo III on Christmas Day 800 marked the foundation of a Western Christian Empire, which was to succeed to the rights and status previously enjoyed by the Byzantine Emperors. An illustration from the fourteenth-century *Grandes Chroniques de France*

The rebirth of the Empire

Left Nicholas I (858–67) was the outstanding Pope of this period. He fearlessly asserted the authority of the Church in dealing with Charlemagne's successors and in the theological controversies of the Eastern church. An eleventh or twelfth-century fresco of Nicholas officiating at the transfer of the bones of St Cirillus to the church of S Clemente

Right Charlemagne's son was a weak character, who divided the Empire between his sons, of whom Lothair, seen here, was the senior. Lothair claimed the whole Empire and fought with his father and brothers, but finally received Italy and the lands between the Rhine, the Rhône and the Meuse

against him and against each other, there came the division of Europe. Lorraine still preserves the name of Lothair, who received Italy and the territories between the Rhine, the Rhône and the Meuse, while one of his brothers, the Emperor Charles the Bald, had what was soon to be France, and another brother lives in history as Louis the German, because his portion of his grandfather's empire was the land between the Rhine and the Danube; and it was in his territories that the Empire was to be restored early in the next century. But in the ninth century, the Carolingian Empire was going downhill, and the inability of the successive descendants of Charlemagne who held the title of Emperor, to intervene much more effectively in Italy than their Byzantine predecessors had been able to do, prepared great evils for the Papacy. In the first half of the ninth century this was not yet apparent. The Pontificate of Gregory IV was full of pastoral work, extending as far north as Denmark and Sweden where he made St Anscar his Apostolic Delegate. Pope Gregory it is to whom we owe All Saints' Day on November the First, for he extended this Roman feast to Western Europe. It was in his day, too, that bishops were taught that though the Bishop of Rome would call them Brother, they were not to call him Brother in return. Soon, neither the Eastern nor the Western Emperor could any longer exact his claim that his sanction was necessary for a papal election, and the ceremony of crowning the Pope appears in this century and takes on more and more a character of its own. It was in Europe generally a great century for the growth of territorial kingship, still a weak institution because of the invasions on every frontier, but an institution that the lawlessness of the times made ever more necessary, and it saw also a monarchical character being more and more underlined in the bishopric of Rome. Pepin had not intended this, nor had Charlemagne, but it came about as his successors proved unable to live up to the proud title of Defender of the Holy Roman Church, while that Church learnt to maintain itself in possession of the inner portions only of its wide territories.

Historically, the Roman noble families like the Crescenti, with their materialist ambitions, justify their existence only by their co-operation in the defence of the city.

But before they came on the scene, there appears a Pope, one of only three with St Leo and St Gregory to whom history has allowed, in addition to sainthood, the appellation 'the Great'; this was Pope Nicholas I (858–67). The election of his predecessor, Benedict III (855–58), had been immediately succeeded by a plot to supplant him by a Cardinal Anastasius, who had been condemned for his intrigues in the time of Leo IV. Anastasius had advanced on Rome, invaded the Lateran Palace, had seized and ill-treated the Pope. But although Cardinal Anastasius had by misrepresentation secured the backing of imperial Carolingian envoys, public feeling in Rome was too strong, and the imperial envoys abandoned their protégé. (It was this Pope Benedict to whom King Ethelwulf of England presented his young son, the future Alfred the Great.) When Pope Benedict died suddenly in 858, the Emperor Louis II happened to be in Rome, and his recommendation secured the election of Nicholas, a well-born Roman, but no more than a deacon. It might have seemed that this showed the Frankish Emperors still in the ascendant, but Louis II had a very strong sense of the Pope's exalted office, and himself led the Pope's horse by the bridle, in a way that was to prove a constant embarrassment to later Emperors when they were told that this act of homage and deference was expected of them, as the precedent had been set. In fact, Nicholas is called 'the Great' because both towards the Franks and the Greeks he was able to assert the independence and the pre-eminence of the papal office.

His strength lay in his fearlessness. One illustration must suffice. He did not hesitate to pass judgment on the private morals of the Frankish rulers. The second son of the Emperor Lothair, King Lothair II of Lorraine, divorced his wife and married a concubine, to find himself immediately threatened with excommunication if he did not return to his lawful wife. He obeyed, but treated her so badly that to secure a judicial separation, she pleaded guilty to various charges. The Archbishops of Cologne and Trèves seized on this confession to proclaim the marriage null and to tell Lothair he could go back to his concubine. But Pope Nicholas promptly excommunicated both archbishops. They then persuaded the Emperor Louis, their King's brother, to march with an army on Rome to compel the Pope to change his judgment. Nicholas stood firm, and Louis gave in and promised to accept the Pope's judgment. But, as may be imagined, King Lothair did not treat his first wife any more kindly when the Pope had compelled him to return to her for the second time, and soon she was begging to be allowed to become a nun. Nicholas summoned Lothair to come and submit to judgment in Rome, and the King was preparing to set out in obedience to the summons, when, to his great relief, he learned that the Pope had died.

Nicholas's successor, a gentle character called Adrian II, was at once told by Lothair that Nicholas had misunderstood him, and Lothair tried to get the question reopened. But Lothair himself died shortly after, and the two wives

The apse mosaic in S Marco, Rome, shows Christ flanked by Popes and saints. Gregory IV (827–44) is on the left with a square nimbus, showing he was alive at the time. He was unsuccessful in bringing peace to the imperial family, but gave active support to the evangelization of Denmark and Sweden by St Anscar

The rebirth of the Empire

Above Leo IV (847–55), on the left, depicted in a ninth-century fresco as a contemporary observer with the apostles at the Ascension. He built the walls of the Leonine city, roughly corresponding with the present Vatican State, as an inner citadel against the attacks of the Saracens

Below The nomination of Michael Cerularius as Patriarch of Constantinople, illustrated in a fourteenth-century Greek manuscript. He was the Patriarch under whom the breach between the Greek East and the Latin West finally took place in 1054, although the Churches had been drawing apart for centuries

ended their days in convents. Perhaps it was in these centuries that the Holy See learned how often difficulties resolve themselves by the intervention of human mortality. Not only violent and unreasonable temporal rulers tended to be cut off in their prime, but even the bishops succeeded one another the more rapidly, the more tempestuous and quarrelsome they were.

The greatest event of the Pontificate of Nicholas took place at Constantinople. It is known as the Schism of Photius. Ignatius, the Patriarch of Constantinople, refused Communion to a certain evil-living member of the Imperial family. As a result Ignatius was driven into exile and Photius declared Patriarch in his place. Pope Nicholas refused to consent to the consecration of Photius, but the Emperor and Photius stood their ground, and the Pope agreed that a Synod should be held to establish the rights and wrongs of the matter. He sent legates from Rome who allowed themselves to be tempted by bribes into siding with Photius and the Emperor against Ignatius. It was some little time before the Pope learned of this, when he not only degraded but excommunicated his unworthy legates, and wrote strong letters both to the Emperor Michael and to Photius. The reply of Photius was to attack and reject the authority of the Pope.

The authority of Rome had always been accepted previously, on the principle that the See of Rome, being the Apostolic See *par excellence*, had a primacy not only of honour but of jurisdiction. But Constantinople was intended to be in scarcely an inferior position; it was the seat of the Empire, and often styled 'the new Rome'. Indeed when Constantine made it his capital, he intended to make it the Christian Rome, thinking the Rome which he was leaving was incurably and profoundly pagan, full of senatorial families deeply attached to the old Roman religion. If Rome was the city of St Peter, the most was made of the tradition that his brother St Andrew, who had been called by Our Lord first and had introduced St Peter to the Lord, was the founder of the Christian community in what was then the small city of Byzantium. The Emperors and their Bishops took advantage of the remoteness of Rome and they claimed for the See of Constantinople not only patriarchal standing but authority over the patriarchates of Jerusalem and Antioch, older Sees than Rome itself, and Alexandria. They disliked it very much when these patriarchs and other bishops in the Levant looked to Rome as a final court of appeal. The Emperor Michael was particularly incensed when the newly converted Bulgarians, though adjoining the Metropolitan area and plainly in the Patriarchate of Constantinople, sent to Pope Nicholas in Rome for spiritual guides and guidance.

Photius was the first to take the step of severing the tie with Rome, and though it was to be two hundred years before the breach was made final, what he began was to endure for eleven hundred years until this present day.

Above The heads of Benedictine monks from a fragment of a tenth-century fresco. During the ninth and tenth centuries the Benedictines spread from Monte Cassino throughout Europe and were responsible for some of the great missionary work of the time

Below The sarcophagus of Gregory V incorporating fourth-century carvings of the lives of St Peter and St Paul. Gregory was the first German Pope and a cousin of the Emperor, but his election was disputed and much of his reign spent in strife

During the late tenth and early eleventh centuries the Papacy was the victim of disreputable rivalries between Italian noble families. An inscription of John XVIII – Dom(i)n(u)s Ioh(anne)s XVIII Papa – (1003–9), who was one of three successive Popes nominated by the Crescenti family

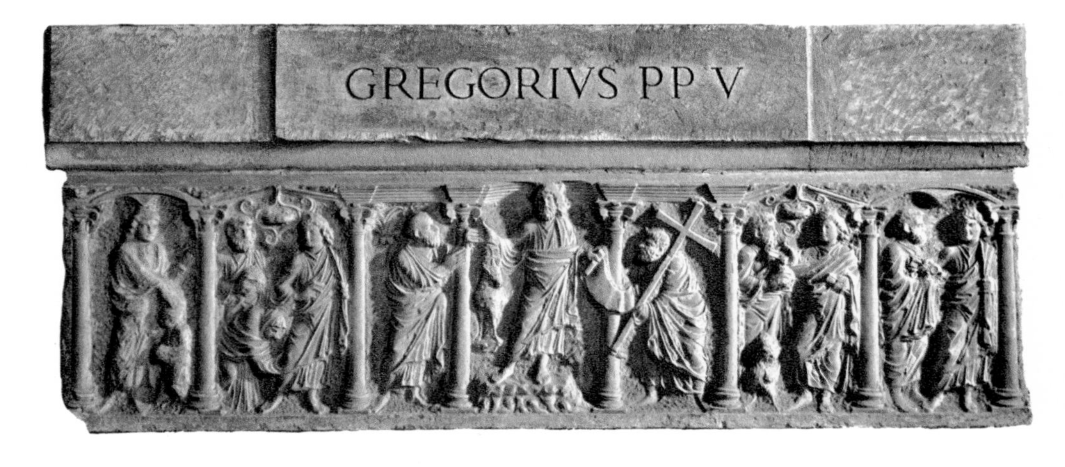

The rebirth of the Empire

The authority of the Holy Roman Emperors was effectively restored by the reign of Otto the Great, who was crowned by John XII in St Peter's in 962. A French manuscript illustration showing Otto receiving the homage of the nations

Among the charges he brought against the See of Rome was the insertion of the word *filioque* in the creed, making the Holy Spirit proceed from the Son as well as from the Father, but this was put in because he was plainly looking for every sort of grievance to justify his repudiation of papal authority.

By the end of the ninth century, the Carolingian Empire had had its day, so that the Pope, Adrian III (884–85), decreed in 884 that in future the Emperor must be a prince from the Italian peninsula, where there were many powerful nobles, of whom one or two, like the Duke of Spoleto, were ambitious enough to try to be emperors. But they had not sufficient strength; the Empire went to the Germans early in the tenth century, and they were strong enough to keep it. The Saxons succeeded the Franks.

What the Italian and Roman nobles were strong enough to do was to degrade the Papacy by intimidating the Roman clergy and inflicting on the Church for half a century the humiliation of a number of unsuitable and often quite unworthy scions of their own families, whose only saving grace was that they seldom lived long. The average life of a Pope was under three years. Sometimes this was because they were very old compromise candidates, and worthy men in themselves; but sometimes the reasons were more violent and sinister than old age. In the first half of the tenth century, the chief argument for doubting the assertion of the chronicler about one of them, Benedict IX (1033–47), that he was twelve years old was that his debaucheries show he must have been nearer twenty.

In the middle of the tenth, and again in the middle of the eleventh century, there is a humiliating reversal of roles and the Saxon Emperor has to come to Rome to secure the election of a worthy priest.

So Otto the Great came, in whose person the Empire was fully restored when the Pope, John XII (955–64), crowned him in St Peter's in 962. But nearly a hundred years later we find another German Emperor, Henry III, again playing an essential role, to make a change from the nominations of the Roman nobles. He secured the election of the Pope who became St Leo IX, who came from near Strasburg, and with him a new era opens for the Papacy, as other Popes, like Urban II, come from Northern Europe.

Above Gregory VII (1073–85) was the originator of a movement for church reform, which continued after his death, and in which the first necessity was to free the Church from domination by the temporal powers. This led to the controversy over the appointment and investiture of bishops. A manuscript illustration showing Gregory with the Abbot of S Sophia

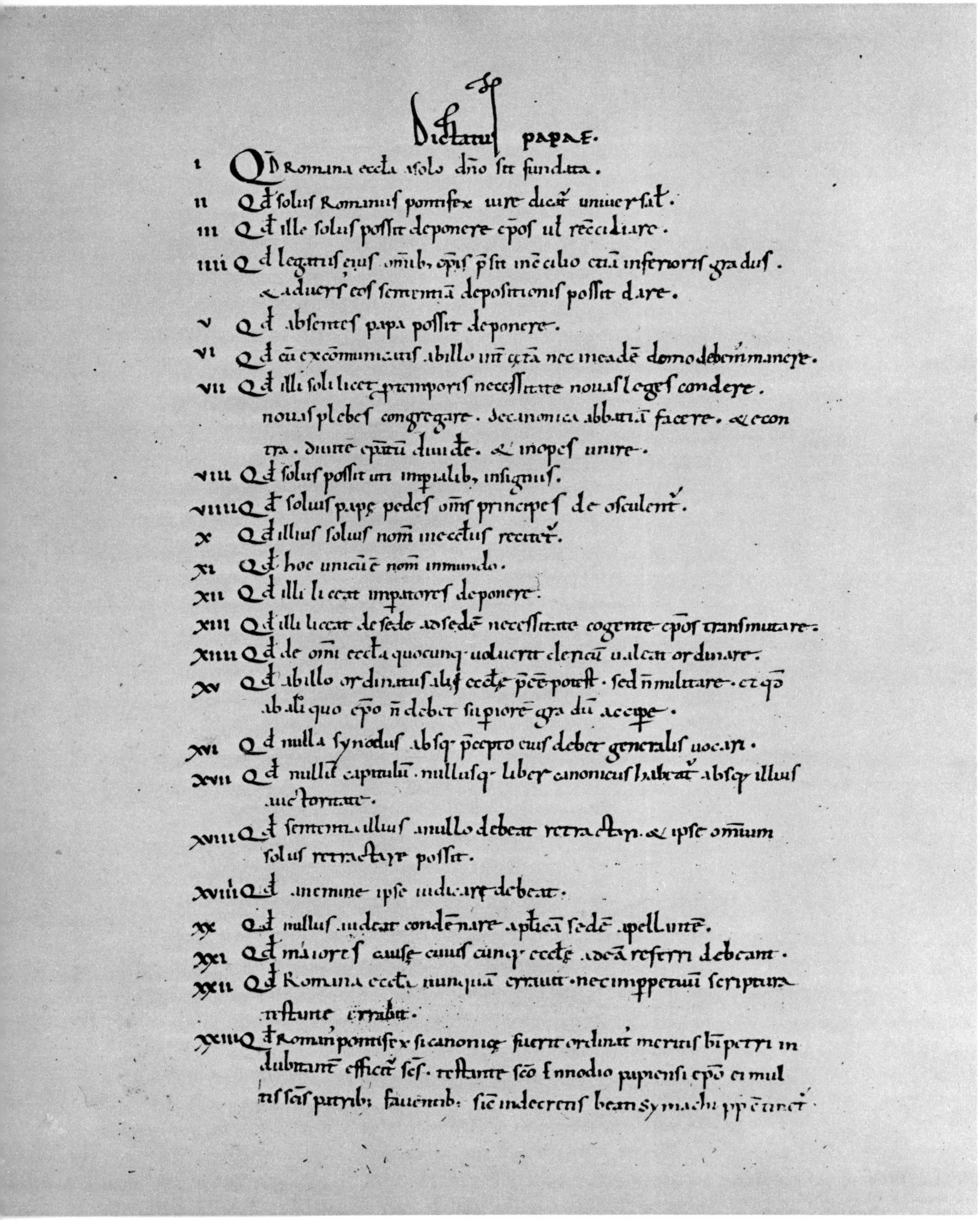

Left The opening page of the *Dictatus Papae*, twenty-seven propositions drawn up by Gregory VII in 1075 at the time of the investiture controversy. These propositions set out in categorical form the supreme power of the Pope in Church and State. For example XII states, 'The Pope can depose Emperors'

5 *GREGORY VII AND THE STRUGGLE FOR INDEPENDENCE*

GREGORY VII to CELESTINE III 1073-1198

GERVAIS DUMEIGE

In the reign of Gregory VII the struggle between the Papacy and the Empire reached its height. Gregory's policy of reform and his firm assertion of papal authority led to an immediate clash with the Emperor Henry IV, who was excommunicated in 1076 and forced to do penance at Canossa. Later fortune turned against the Pope, who died miserably in exile. After Gregory relations between the secular and religious authorities turned mainly on the question of the investiture of prelates. A compromise solution was finally achieved by the Concordat of Worms in 1122. It was a confused period of disputed successions, dominated by the personality of St Bernard.

THE PONTIFICATE OF GREGORY VII (1073–85) IS marked by attempts to reform the Church and free it from dangerous subjection to the temporal powers, in particular the German Emperors, who had succeeded in gaining control of the episcopal elections.

Gregory VII, who was elected by popular acclamation in a strange but nevertheless legal manner on the very day of his predecessor's funeral, at first refused the pontificate. When he finally accepted it, he carried out his duties resolutely. This Tuscan mystic had already had considerable experience as a reformer and had served Alexander II as papal legate in France and Germany. He was a deeply religious man, with an inflexible will, and his first concern was with the salvation of souls. His policy can be summed up in his own words: 'I have done everything possible to ensure that the Holy Church, the Bride of Christ, our mistress and our mother, should take her rightful place and remain free, inviolate and Catholic.' A whole organization was established: letters were sent to the bishops, councils called to legislate against the Simoniacs, who sold benefices for money, legates despatched to make known the Pope's wishes and see that they were carried out, all in order that the Church could achieve the freedom which was necessary for her to accomplish her mission. At the beginning of his reign Gregory VII tried to reach an agreement with the Emperor. He was also influenced by the principles of the Italian reformers. At the Council of Rome in 1074 war was declared on abuses, and clergy guilty of simony, or of having contracted matrimony, were to be banished from the Church. But these measures were either ignored or met with fierce opposition. However, the Council held in Rome in the following year censured several prelates and the attitude changed. Simony was declared a heresy.

Gregory's ideas and the principles on which he based his policy are contained in the *Dictatus papae*. These revive earlier canonical statutes and set out with relentless logic the precise scope of papal authority, Roman primacy and the subordination of the temporal to the ecclesiastical power. The papal monarchy and theocracy are clearly defined. As soon as lay investiture 'by the ring and crozier' was forbidden, a bitter struggle began; the supporters of Pope and Emperor hurled insults at one another and Gregory's interdicts were met with armed force from Henry IV. A synod of the German clergy declared that the Pope had forfeited his right to rule. Henry IV was deposed and excommunicated on 22 February 1076. He had to fight internal political enemies and Germany was invited to choose a new ruler if the Emperor did not mend his ways. The troubled state of the Empire induced Henry IV to yield and do penance and he was finally received back into the Church at Canossa. Gregory was more concerned with Christian charity than political advantage, whereas the Emperor broke his word, and as soon as he had settled the internal disturbances in the Empire he stirred up an anti-Gregorian movement, which was responsible for appointing the anti-Pope Clement III, who crowned the Emperor in Rome at Easter 1083. The only support that Gregory VII could rely on was from the Normans. But they were not satisfied simply to release the Pope but laid Rome waste, and the Pope was forced by popular indignation to flee the city in the wake of his embarrassing allies. He died at Salerno on 25 May 1085. Was his pontificate then a failure? From his own standpoint, perhaps, but from the Church's point of view it was not. Certain reforms had been achieved; there had been a period of strict government, and already the distinction between temporal and spiritual authority was becoming clear.

The Holy See remained vacant for a year. It was doubtful whether Victor III (1086–87) would be able to continue the work of his predecessor with the same vigour. He had been chosen in the hope that he would pursue a policy of moderation and make agreement with the Empire possible. He was elected according to canon law on 21 March 1087. He called a council at Benevento which excommunicated the anti-Pope and forbade lay investiture, but did not expressly mention Henry IV. Victor died soon afterwards on 16th September. He had been an excellent reforming abbot at Monte Cassino but as a Pope he was somewhat irresolute. But at least relations between the Papacy and the Empire had not deteriorated further.

The next Pope, the French Cardinal Eudes de Chatillon, who took the name of Urban II (1088–99), was also a confirmed Gregorian, but he preferred the subtleties of diplomacy to the direct approach. He was elected and consecrated at Terracina and made sure that the German bishops were fully informed of his election. He won over the kings of England and France and granted dispensations, which further underlined his authority. As soon as he had established his position more firmly, he reverted to Gregorianism in its purest form and at the council of Piacenza (1095) condemned the ordinations made by Clement III and issued a number of reforming decrees. In 1095 the situation in France, under the adulterous King Philip I, called for the Pope's presence in his own country. While

Gregory's determined policy, particularly his condemnation of lay investiture of bishops, inevitably led to a clash with the Emperor Henry IV, whom Gregory excommunicated in 1076. The struggle was temporarily resolved when Henry did penance at Canossa and was received back into the Church. He is seen here in St Nicholas' Chapel at Canossa asking Matilda of Tuscany and the Abbot of Cluny to intercede for him

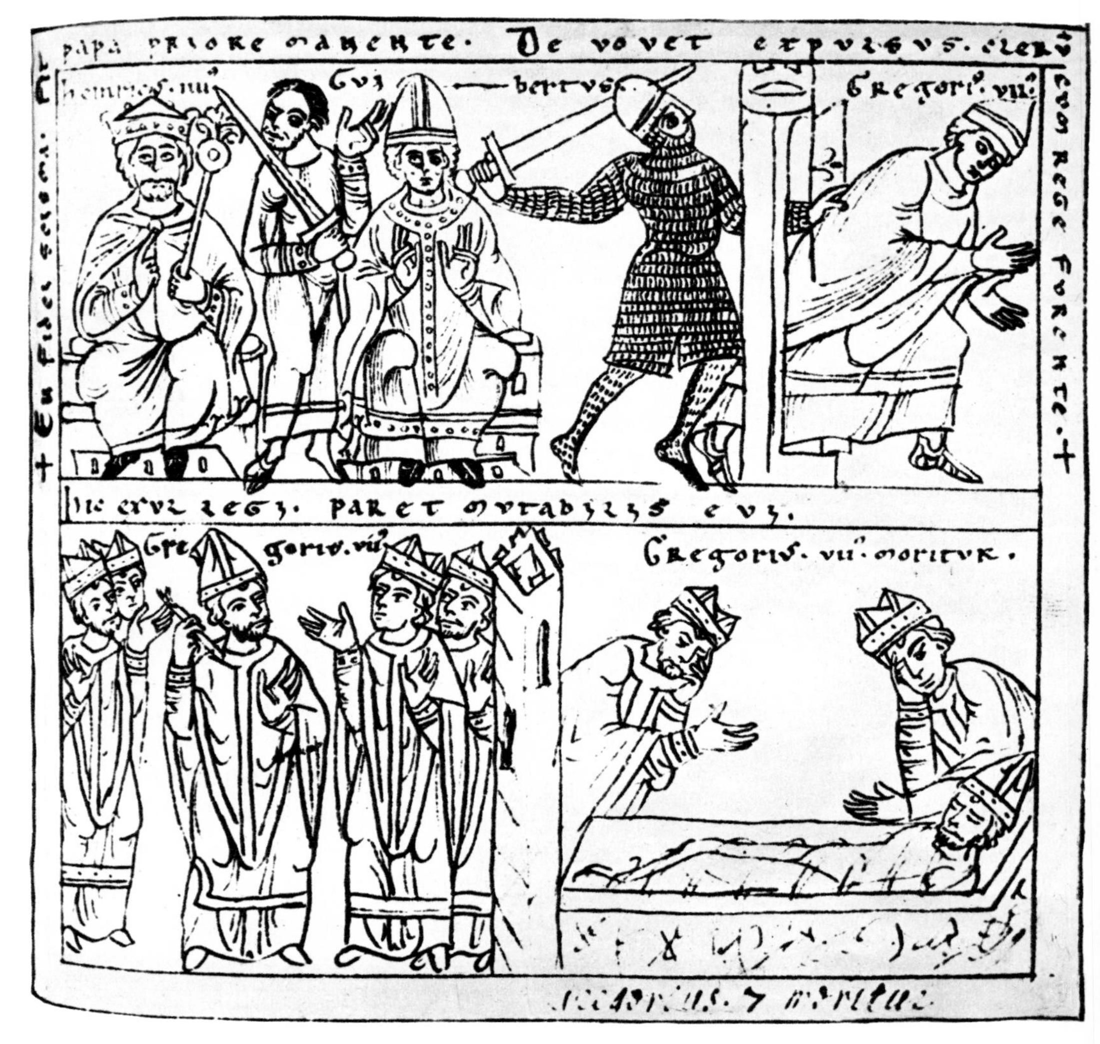

The concord was short-lived and Henry IV soon appointed an anti-Pope, Clement III. The twelfth-century chronicle of Otto of Freising shows, in the upper picture, Henry and Clement expelling Gregory from Rome by force of arms and, in the lower, the death of Gregory at Salerno in 1085

he was there he held the Council of Clermont (18 November 1095), which helped to restore the Church's discipline and also inspired the preaching of the First Crusade. The schismatics were expelled from Rome and the Pope held two councils there. He died on 29 July 1099, too soon to hear the news of the capture of Jerusalem by the Christian armies a fortnight previously.

As the danger of schism had been averted for the moment, Paschal II was elected without much difficulty. He was a former monk of Vallombrosa and papal legate in Spain and he was to pursue the task of liberation in troubled times. Some rulers already appeared more willing to cooperate. Louis VI le Gros seemed to have abandoned lay investiture by the ring and crozier in France. In England the agreement signed in London in 1107 made a more precise distinction between spiritual and temporal jurisdiction, but only after many vicissitudes, during which Henry I had driven St Anselm of Canterbury into exile. The king would no longer invest bishops, but they would swear fealty to him as vassals and pay homage to him before their consecration. In Spain the legate Archbishop of Toledo succeeded in negotiating an acceptable solution to the problems of jurisdiction raised by the *Reconquista*. But the problem of Germany remained unsolved and the obstinacy of Henry IV unchanged, although he did declare himself willing to go on a crusade. However, he was forced to abdicate during a rebellion led by his son. He escaped the country and died in 1106. Would Henry V prove more conciliatory than his father? After re-affirming the condemnation of lay investiture, the Pope made an unexpected proposal to the Emperor who was in Italy for his coronation: in return for freedom from interference by the temporal power, the Church was willing to give up ecclesiastical claims to temporal sovereignity and public privileges to which financial reward was attached. Paschal II's idealism would indeed have restored to the bishops their pastoral function, but at the same time it deprived them of both their income and their political power. This agreement, signed at Sutri on 4 February 1111, had been kept secret. When it was read out in St Peter's the German bishops protested. The Pope refused to crown the Emperor, who retaliated by taking him prisoner. After sixty days of threats and coercion, Paschal II agreed to crown the Emperor, to whom he had conceded the right of lay investiture. This *privilegium* was condemned outright by the Pope in 1116. In the spring of the following year the Emperor came to Rome and the Pope was forced to take refuge at Benevento. His stormy Pontificate came to an end on 21 January 1118.

When Paschal II died the Emperor's supporters were the strongest party in Rome. In the space of three days Gelasius II was elected, then imprisoned by Cencio Frangipani and finally released by the nobility and populace of Rome. But his stay there was brief. The Emperor arrived, proclaimed an anti-Pope, Gregory VIII, and then returned across the

The struggle for Independence

Henry IV was deposed by his son Henry V, who continued the struggle with the Papacy over lay investiture. In 1111 he forced Paschal II to concede the point and to crown him in St Peter's, a concession the Pope later withdrew. The coronation ceremony is shown in a German manuscript illumination

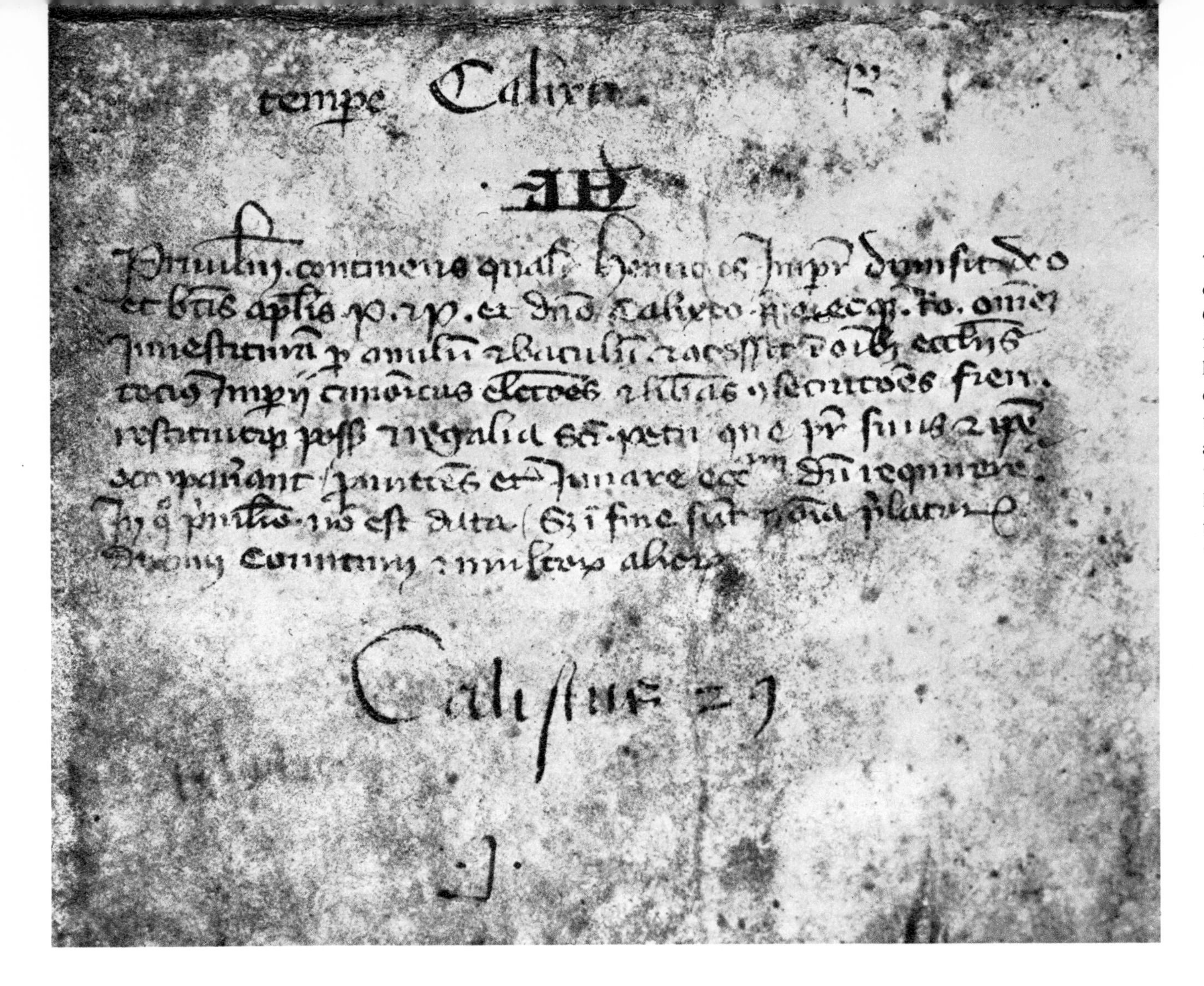

The signature of Calixtus II on the last page of the Concordat of Worms, 1122, which finally solved the dispute over lay investiture. By this compromise the Emperor renounced the appointment of bishops and their investiture with 'ring and crozier', but retained his right of investiture with the symbols of temporal authority, 'regalia and sceptre'

Alps. Gelasius II travelled to France and hoped to negotiate some kind of an agreement with the Emperor. He died at Cluny, recommending as possible successors either the Abbot of Cluny or Guy, Archbishop of Vienne. His Pontificate was too short to allow much scope for expansion.

Calixtus II was elected by two cardinal archbishops, according to the decree of 1059, and was later acclaimed by the Romans. This Burgundian cardinal was an uncompromising man, who had criticized Paschal II for his weakness. Now that he was Pope he felt everything must be done to reach an understanding with the Emperor. He was in fact related to the reigning houses of Europe and his prestige and his own capabilities enabled him to conclude the peace which both the Church and the Empire desperately needed. But the way was not easy. Finally, after delicate negotiations, the document incorporating Henry V's renunciation to the right of lay investiture was signed. But the opposition was not over. The Pope, who was holding a council at Rheims, was to have met the Emperor at Mouzon, but at the last minute complications arose – the agreement had not been adequately prepared. Calixtus returned to Rheims, excommunicated the Emperor, the Simoniacs and the anti-Pope Burdin, who was later besieged at Sutri and then set free by the inhabitants. After terrible humiliations he ended his days in the monastery of Cava. The Emperor urged on by his vassals decided to make peace once and for all. 'Henry, the Church does not seek to claim that which is yours by right', the Pope had once written to him. At the Diet of Worms a Concordat was drawn up in which the Emperor renounced investiture with 'ring and crozier', at the same time retaining, and later exercising, his right of investiture with 'regalia' and with 'sceptre', preceded by homage and the oath of fealty. The Emperor also promised to grant the Church its freedom. Calixtus agreed to episcopal elections being held in the presence of the Emperor, who was granted absolution on 23 September 1122. It was an honourable enough compromise in which the loosely defined terms allowed for different interpretations by the two parties. One result at least was achieved: a bishop's duties were many and varied, therefore his investiture could be by more than one authority. Church and Empire were never again to cross swords on this issue.

The real work, that is to say the task of reform which was the chief aim of the Papacy, could begin. The 1st Lateran Council (IXth Oecumenical Council) in 1123, which was attended by a large number of bishops, once again condemned simony and lay investiture, strengthened discipline and made fiscal reforms, granted indulgences to

The struggle for Independence

A stone altar of 1123, in S Maria in Cosmedin, Rome, with a dedicatory inscription to Calixtus II, 'the father of peace'

The tomb of Adrian IV (1154–59), Nicholas Breakspear, the only English Pope. The tomb is a third-century pagan sarcophagus, with two heads of Medusa

the crusaders and ratified the Concordat of Worms. Calixtus II, the 'Father of peace', died on 11 December 1124 and Henry V five months later.

After a great deal of intrigue by aristocratic Roman families, who each tried to forward their own interests, Lambert, Cardinal of Ostia, author of the Concordat of Worms, was elected. He took the name of Honorius II (1124–30). He established good relations with Lothair of Supplinburg, Louis VI of France, and Henry I of England, but not with the Normans. Even before he died, Rome was once again in a turmoil. There was disagreement among the cardinals about the best methods of promoting reform and fierce rivalry between the Frangipani and the Pierleoni families. Cardinal Papareschi, Innocent II (1130–43) was elected hastily and without conforming to the rules laid down by Nicholas II. The Pierleoni faction were dissatisfied with the results of the election and, according to an old Roman practice, elected a cardinal of their own family, Anacletus II, without, however, invalidating the preceding election. Anacletus was consecrated at the Vatican and occupied Rome, but he faced the hostility of the whole of Europe, which, led by St Bernard, regarded him only as the anti-Pope. His generosity towards the people of Rome, and his Hebrew ancestry, did him more harm than good. Germany and France, influenced by St Bernard and St Norbert, declared themselves for Innocent II. Anacletus then sought the help of the Normans in Sicily. The Emperor brought Innocent back to Rome, where Innocent crowned Lothair, while his rival was immured in the Castel Sant' Angelo. The sudden death of Anacletus on 28 January 1138 put an end to the schism and St Bernard ensured the immediate abdication of his successor, Victor IV. The following year, Innocent II was able to hold the 2nd Lateran Council (xth Oecumenical Council) in which he combined genuine and drastic reform of the clergy with a violent attack on his opponents' former supporters who were forced to submit to his authority. Roger of Sicily was excommunicated, but when war delivered the Pope into his hands he was granted absolution and the title of King of Sicily. If the Pope's authority was acknowledged fairly generally in Europe, it was contested in Rome which did not accept his temporal power and dreamed of re-establishing the Senate. The Pope died on 24 September 1143.

The city maintained its rebellious attitude towards his successor, Celestine II (1143–44). This cultured Tuscan was, however, reserved in his dealings with the Normans. He reigned for six months, and three days after his death,

The struggle for Independence

St Bernard of Clairvaux (1090–1153) Cistercian abbot, reformer and mystic, was the greatest religious leader in Europe in his time. He threw the weight of his spiritual authority behind the Papacy and the crusading movement. *Below* a detail from the embroidery of his cope and *right* a mosaic portrait attributed to the fifteenth-century artist Melozzo da Forli

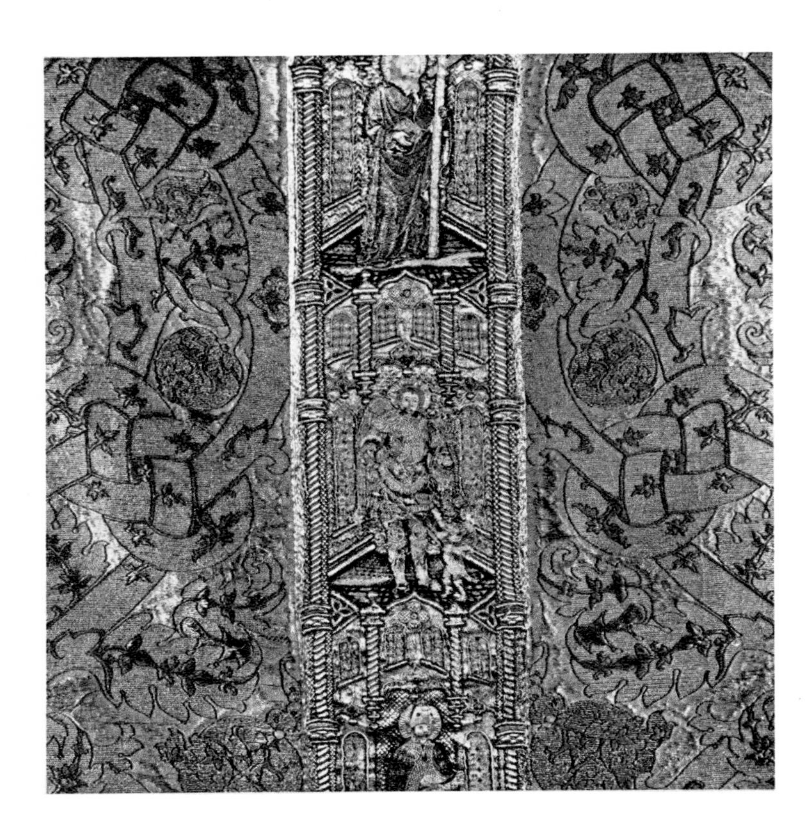

on 12 March 1144, Gerardo Caccianemici was elected, and took the name of Lucius II (1144–45). In an attempt finally to crush the opposition in Rome Lucius made an alliance with the Normans and died after storming the Capitol, seat of the Roman Senate. The fact that the burial place of these last two Popes is unknown tells us a good deal about the troubled times in which they lived.

There were many, including St Bernard, who doubted whether the self-effacing Cistercian, Abbot of Tre Fontane, Eugenius III (1145–53) was the right choice for the next Pope. And yet, this monk, who was thrown into the maelstrom of world affairs, proved able and resolute. When the Romans demanded a Republican constitution he refused, and in the fighting that ensued he starved the city and the Senate into subjection. He then had to leave for Viterbo because Arnold of Brescia, an austere reformer and pupil of Abelard, had put himself at the head of the Republicans and subjugated the town, demanding the total separation of spiritual and temporal affairs. Eugenius III went on to France, where he renewed the crusade. Back in Rome, his position became untenable, to such an extent had Arnold's ideas stirred up the people. To add to

A memorial inscription from S Maria in Trastevere to Innocent II, who owed his election largely to the support of St Bernard and as a result showered privileges on the Cistercian order

Right Innocent II (1130–43), whose election led to a fierce struggle between rival factions in Rome. A portrait from an apse mosaic in S Maria in Trastevere, the church which he rebuilt, and of which, according to custom, he is holding a model

Above The ruthless ambition of the Emperor Frederick Barbarossa harried the Papacy for a period of thirty-eight years.
This carving at the entrance to Freising Cathedral shows him with Otto, Bishop of Freising

Left In England the attempts of Archbishop Thomas à Becket to free the Church from the domination of the crown led to his murder in 1170 at the instigation of Henry II.
Becket was canonized by Alexander III four years later and his shrine at Canterbury became the great pilgrimage centre of England. A fresco from SS Giovanni e Paolo, Spoleto

the difficulties the Emperor Conrad III was succeeded, on 15 February 1152, by Frederick Barbarossa, who during his reign of thirty-eight years relentlessly pursued the realization of his imperial ambitions. Just as he was about to wrest from the Roman Senators the authority they had usurped, Eugenius died at Tivoli on 8 July 1153.

After the comparatively peaceful reign of Anastasius IV, which lasted only seventeen months, Nicholas Breakspear, the only Englishman in the long line of Popes, succeeded as Adrian IV. Adrian was tactless and stubborn. In the course of an unfortunate quarrel with one of the cardinals he employed a spiritual weapon which the Romans – a people still excited by memories of the days of Republican greatness – had never seen turned against themselves. An interdict was hurled upon the city. Holy Week was approaching. Rome was like a city of the dead. Then the Senators asked for pardon. Arnold of Brescia was exiled and then delivered by the Emperor to the Prefect of the city, who had him executed. Frederick scornfully reminded the Senate that the glory of Rome belonged to the past. '*Olim fuit*.'

The agreement between the Pope and the Emperor was short-lived. Frederick was determined not to repeat the traditional gestures of homage to the Pope, considering them a humiliation. The new Chancellor, Reinhard von Dassel, was hostile to the Curia, and Roman law which was upheld by the jurists of Bologna would endorse the attempts of the most powerful of the Germanic Emperors to achieve a united Empire. A letter of protest from the Pope was mistranslated by Chancellor von Dassel, who changed the phrase 'accord favours' into 'confer benefices'. This incident was much exploited and provoked the indignation of the German Princes and of Frederick, who arrived in Italy and held a Diet at Roncaglia where his sovereign rights were proclaimed. '*Tua voluntas jus est*', declared the Archbishop of Milan. Adrian IV died in September 1159 when he was on the point of excommunicating the Emperor.

The election of his successor was complicated by the rivalries of the pro-German and pro-Norman factions. Roland Bandinelli, the Sienese jurist and theologian from Bologna, was to have a turbulent but fruitful pontificate as Alexander III (1159–81), but a minority group elected Victor IV. Who was the legitimate Pope? The Emperor, following the example of Constantine and Theodosius, declared that the Church should decide and summoned a council at Pavia which was attended by about fifty Lombard and German bishops. A further series of councils resulted in Alexander III being accepted as Pope by France, England, Castile, Aragon and the Holy Land. In 1160 the Emperor and the anti-Pope were excommunicated. Victor IV's death solved nothing, as a successor had already been

The struggle for Independence

Left The reign of Alexander III (1159–81) was disturbed by the rival claims of an anti-Pope Victor IV, which even a Council could not settle. Alexander's stormy relations with Frederick Barbarossa ended with reconciliation at the Peace of Venice in 1178, depicted in a fresco by Francesco Salviati

Right Celestine III (1191–98) was eighty-five on his election and was too old effectively to resist the depredations of the Emperor Henry VI. This fresco by Domenico di Bartolo shows Celestine granting autonomy to the Ospedale di S Maria di Scala in Siena

elected. During Frederick's fourth expedition to Italy, in a St Peter's still marked by the violence committed within its walls, Paschal III was enthroned and Barbarossa crowned (30 July 1167). The Emperor was master of Rome, but his army was being decimated by malaria, a judgment of heaven according to many of his contemporaries. Lombardy then went over to Alexander III. After the Battle of Legnano, Frederick was ready to negotiate and on 1 August 1178 the Peace of Venice ratified agreements that had already been worked out at Anagni. Alexander III was recognized as Pope. The Emperor was given absolution and agreed to lead the Pope's mount by the bridle and ever afterwards regarded the Pope with great veneration. On his return to Rome the Pope called the 3rd Lateran Council (XIth Oecumenical Council). He laid down the regulations which required that the Pope should be elected by a majority of two-thirds. The twenty-seven canons of the Council with their lengthy preambles, in which the practised hand of the Bolognese jurist can be recognized, reaffirmed previous decrees. Alexander III died on 30 August 1181. He had succeeded in winning greater spiritual freedom for the Church and his triumph had not degenerated into ecclesiastical dictatorship.

The struggle continued under the reigns of the next five Popes which lasted a total of seventeen years. In 1190 Frederick Barbarossa was drowned on his way to the Holy Land to take part in the Third Crusade, and was succeeded by Henry VI. In 1191 Celestine III was elected Pope at the age of eighty-five and embarked on a reign which was to last seven years and see the crimes of Henry VI, the violation of the Concordat of Worms and the invasion of Southern Italy. Henry VI died before him in 1197 at the age of thirty-two. Time and time again innumerable obstacles prevented the Church from achieving the independence which she needed in order to fulfil her mission. But under Innocent III, a young, energetic scholar and politician, the Church was to make rapid strides forward and the prestige of the Papacy was greatly increased.

PP III
+ INNOCENTIUS EPS SERVUS SERVORV DI. DILECTIS FILIIS
PRIORI ET FRIB IUXTA
SPECV BEATI BENEDICTI REGLARE VITA SERVANTIBUS IN. INTER HOLOCAUSTA
VIRTUTV NULLV MAGIS EST MEDULLATV. QUA QD OFFERTUR ALTISSIMO DE PINGUEDINE
CARITATIS. HOC IGIT ATTENDENTES. CV OLI CAUSA DEVOTIONIS ACCESSISSEM AD LOCV
VRE QUE BEATUS BENEDICT SUE CONVERSIONIS PRIMORDIO CONSECRAVIT. ET IVENISSEM VOS
INSTITUTIONE IPIUS LAUDABILITER DNO FAMULANTES. NE PROTEMPORALIS SUBSTENTATIONIS
SPIRITUALIS OBSERVANTIE DISCIPLINA TORPERET. APOSTOLICV VOBIS SUBSIDIV
IMPENDENDV. SPERANTES QD IDE BEATISSIM BENEDICT NRE DEVOTIONIS
ET PRECIB APUD PIISSIMV PATRE ET IUSTISSIMV IUDICE COMMDABIT.
NECESSITATIB PUIDERE. SEX LIBRAS USUALIS MONETE VOBIS ET SUCCESSORIB VRIS
CAMERA BEATI PETRI SINGULIS ANNIS PCIPIENDAS CONCESSIM. DONEC INALIQUO CERTO LO
VOBIS ESSENT UTILITER ASSIGNATE. STATUENTES UT EA QUE ADSUSTENTATIONE VRAM CO
SUEVISTIS PCIPERE DE MONASTERIO SUBLACEN: VOBIS ETSUCCESSORIB VRIS PPTER
MINIME NEGARENTUR. POSTMODV AUTE CV REVERSI FUISSEM ADURBE QUOSDA DE
VRIS AD NRAM PRESENTIA DESTINASTIS HUMILITER IMPLORANTES UT CONCESSIO
IPSA INALIQUO CERTO LOCO DIGNAREMUR PPETUO STABILIRE. DE QUO PREFATAS
SEX LIBRAS PCIPERE VALERETIS. NOS IGITUR HABITO FRATRV NRORV CONSILIO
ASSENSV. IA DICTAS SEX LIBRAS VOBIS ET SUCCESSORIB VRIS PCIPIENDAS SINGULIS
ANNIS DE ANNUO CENSU CASTRI PORTIANI CONCEDIM. ET CONCESSIONE
PRIVILEGIO CONFIRMAM. NULLI ERGO OMNINO HOMINV LICEAT HANC PAGINA NRE
CONCESSIONIS ET CONSTITUTIONIS INFRINGERE VEL EI AUSU TEMERARIO CONT
IRE. SIQUIS AUTE HOC ATTEPTARE PRESUPSERIT: INDIGNATIONE OMNIPOTENTIS
ET BEATORV PETRI ET PAULI APOSTOLORV EIUS SE NOVERIT INCURSURV. AMEN

6 THE ZENITH OF THE MEDIEVAL PAPACY

INNOCENT III 1198-1216

JOHN A. WATT

Under Innocent III the Papacy attempted to play a larger part in world affairs than ever before or since. The problem of heresy and the spiritual renewal of the Church occupied the early part of his reign. He organized the crusade of the Northern French against the Albigensians and encouraged the missionary work of St Dominic and St Francis. Under his inspiration the Fourth Crusade set out for the Holy Land, but in one of the most shameful episodes in Christian history the fleet was diverted and the Sack of Constantinople took place in 1204. The Pope's temporal jurisdiction was greatly extended and in 1215 King John was forced to acknowledge England as a papal fief. Innocent also attempted to ensure that the Holy Roman Empire should not absorb Sicily into part of its kingdoms. His conception of the Papacy as the feudal overlord above all the rulers of the world represents the climax of papal influence in international affairs.

SHORTLY AFTER THE DEATH OF INNOCENT III A distinguished academic observed that 'his like had not been found occupying the Fisherman's chair for a very long time back'. Later opinion has generally endorsed this first judgment and has frequently added that though many aspired to follow in his footsteps, his like was not to be found again. This earliest critic was a eulogist to whom Innocent was a Pope 'of most sharp-sighted genius and consummate understanding ... who ennobled the Church'. If many later assessments have been less enthusiastic both about his ability and his achievement, few of them have denied their central importance for the understanding of the medieval Papacy as a whole. For in his Pontificate are to be seen writ large the characteristic aims, the typical outlook, most of the strengths and many of the weaknesses of the Papacy in the medieval phase of its history.

The election of Lothair dei Conti de Segni caused surprise and some criticism. He was only thirty-seven (there has been no younger Pope since) and a German poet summed up the reaction of many in the prayer he put into the mouth of a hermit: He cried to God, 'Thy kingdom come!'
Alas, the Pope is far too young;
In mercy help thy Christendom.

But the electors knew what they were about. Celestine III had been ninety-two at his death and had been virtually incapable of personal government during most of his Pontificate. The times demanded papal vigour, energy and courage. These Lothair possessed in abundance, with other qualifications. He was unusually well educated, having studied theology in Paris and law at Bologna. This blend of the speculative and the practical in his formation was reflected in his work as a cardinal. The fruits of the one were shown in his religious writings – in the *De miseria humanae conditionis* (one of the most popular of all medieval books), the *De sacro altaris mysterio*, and other treatises; and of the other, in an established reputation as a jurist. He was known as a zealous reformer. Moreover, his family was powerful in the Campagna, no mean consideration, given the weakness of the papal position in Rome and Italy. Lothair's personal character – *fortis*, *stabilis*, *magnanimus et astutus* said his first biographer – his spirituality, scholarship and outstanding legal ability and his important family connection overcame the electors' early hesitation about his youth. Their decision was endorsed by thirteenth-century opinion. The *navicula Petri* ran into heavy weather in this period. For better and for worse it was held to a course set by Innocent III.

What this course should be Innocent often proclaimed. For him reformation of the Church and the recovery of the Holy Land were the objectives 'closest to our heart'. Such a view of what constituted the main aims to be pursued was conditioned by a century and more of papal thought and action. It aligns Innocent's Pontificate with the tradition of Gregory VII and Urban II in the search to establish a Church reinvigorated by means of a tighter organization round the Papacy, and a Christian world, its 'civil wars' composed, united and regenerated through the penance of the holy war. What was new was neither the policy itself

Innocent III with St Benedict from a thirteenth-century fresco in the Lower Church of Sacro Speco, Subiaco, where Benedict founded the first of his monasteries. The text stresses Innocent's many favours to the Benedictine Order

nor the underlying conception of the Pope as leader of Christendom, but the vehemence of the directing personality. In one sweeping vision of the role of the Papacy, Innocent synthesized the aspirations of a papal epoch. It was his attempt to translate this vision into practice which in turn defined the evolution of papal action in the thirteenth century.

When Innocent spoke of the reformation of the Church the problem of heresy was uppermost in his mind. Of the diverse errors then current, the heresy of the Cathars predominated. This claimed that spirit alone was of God's creation, matter was of the principle of evil. On this basic premise and its necessary denial that God had become man to redeem His creature, the Cathars developed a way of life which seemed to the orthodox as destructive of the fabric of society, as it was of the sacramental order. The heresy had spread from the Balkans and Constantinople along the trade routes into Italy, whence it had become endemic in the area between the Rhône and the Garonne. Protected by the nobility, unchallenged by the local clergy, it affected all classes and had in the twelfth century defied all attempts at eradication. Innocent III, with a drastic wielding of the axe to the root, applied a remedy which was to become fully effective during the remainder of the century.

The campaign against the heretics of Languedoc began along lines suggested by earlier effort. Clerical reformation, particularly the restaffing of the episcopate, was the first aim. Special preaching missions to convert by word and

Above A contemporary mosaic portrait of Innocent III from the old basilica of St Peter. Innocent was responsible for considerable restoration work on the basilica and other churches in Rome

Left The repression of the Albigensian heresy was one of the most important preoccupations of Innocent's reign. This painting by Fra Angelico, himself a Dominican, shows St Dominic handing a book containing an account of the true faith to an envoy of the Albigensians and, on the right, the book miraculously leaping out of the flames to which the heretics had consigned it

Right The early attempts to convert the Albigensian heretics in Languedoc took the form of special preaching missions. St Dominic and his Order of Preachers were leaders in this work. A portrait of St Dominic by his contemporary Guido da Siena

example, and to adjure nobles and town governments to police action, were to supplement a regenerated local clergy. But clerical renovation proved slow and difficult. Nor were the missions conspicuously successful, led though they were to be by the abbot of Cîteaux himself, later reinforced by St Dominic and his earliest followers. As early as 1204 Innocent's mind turned to more forceful methods and he appealed to the French king to intervene. Philip Augustus, however, had good reasons of his own for not complying. In January 1208 matters came to a head when the papal legate was murdered in circumstances implicating Raymond VI, Count of Toulouse and the leading noble of Languedoc. Raymond had long been suspected of heresy, and had been excommunicated in 1207.

Once again Philip Augustus held back. But the voracious nobility of northern France needed little prompting. In March 1208 Innocent called for a crusade against Raymond, declared afresh a heretic and murderer of the legate. Thus began the Albigensian Crusade, notorious for the savagery of its course, complex in its military and political detail, but decisive in the long run for the suppression of heresy in Languedoc.

The crusade was only fitfully under the control of Innocent III. The sudden submission of Count Raymond in June 1209 and his acceptance of the crusading cross proved in the end but a temporary respite for the house of St Gilles. For Simon de Montfort and his crusaders, during five years of hard fighting, advanced the interests of the French crown against the nobles of Languedoc. When the King finally intervened, Languedoc lost its political independence (and, some think, its culture). It was the co-operation of the crown with the Inquisition that finally eliminated the Cathars.

Repression of heresy, however, was only the negative aspect of reform. It was to be complementary to positive renewal of the life of the spirit throughout the Church. Innocent's great contribution was to identify the Papacy with the twin forces which were to mould the religious and intellectual climate of the century: the friars and the university of Paris. Innocent it was who first gave official approval to the apostolic efforts of St Dominic and St Francis, and who lent the weight of papal support to the masters of Paris in the critical period when the schools were maturing into a definite and independent university organization.

His most characteristic contribution to reform was as a legislator. This work was epitomized in the Fourth Lateran Council. Much of the legislation of this most ambitious of medieval General Councils proved of great consequence in the years to come. Particularly significant were the codification of the law of episcopal elections and the penal law for heretics; the introduction of a constitutional system for the very numerous autonomous houses of monks and canons, hitherto prone to laxity through the absence of corrective organization; the imposing of the obligation of annual Confession and the reception of the Holy Eucharist on all the laity. But this Council was far from representing the sum of his legislative work. When, in 1234, Gregory IX promulgated a revised version of canon law, nearly one third of its canons were Innocent III's: his permanent imprint on the structure of the medieval Church.

From the very beginning of his reign Innocent sought fervently to stir the conscience of Christendom to a sense of shame at the loss of the Holy Sepulchre and a determination to avenge what he presented as an injury done to the Crucified. The call to fight the 'battle of Christ' was propagated in a steady stream of personal letters, by specially appointed crusading preachers and by cardinal legates who also busied themselves with the details of practical organization. By the end of 1200 a considerable force had been assembled. Officered by the flower of the younger nobility of northern France, the army numbered nearly ten thousand. An Italian noble of military repute, Boniface of Montferrat, was appointed commander-in-chief, a covenant was signed with Venice for transport and approved by Innocent. All seemed ready for a major assault on the Moslem.

That it became instead a major assault on the Greeks was the biggest single disaster of Innocent's Pontificate. In April 1204 Constantinople was captured by the crusaders, sacked and the establishment of a feudal Latin kingdom set in train. Did Innocent III plot with Boniface and the Venetians to divert the crusade? The very limited evidence that exists suggests that he had no precise foreknowledge of any plan, that he would have been opposed to it but that in any case, since it was the Venetians who were calling the tune, there was little enough he could have done about it.

The zenith of the Medieval Papacy

Innocent wrote many spiritual and theological works and many of his letters and records have survived. This detail from a page of his *Registro* deals with the power of the Church to punish sins and sinners. The vivid illustration shows two wolves, one in Friar's clothing, probably assisting in an heretical or black mass

Throughout his Pontificate Innocent strove to mount an effective crusade to win back the Holy Sepulchre. But the great force of European chivalry which he assembled and which set out for the Holy Land in 1203, was diverted in 1204 to the capture and sack of Constantinople. Innocent welcomed the establishment of a Latin kingdom there as a means of Church unity, though in fact the breach between East and West was widened. The capture of Constantinople by Giovane Palma in the Doge's Palace, Venice

No ambiguity, however, attaches to his attitude to the *fait accompli*: 'by the just judgment of God is the kingdom of the Greeks translated from the proud to the humble, from the disobedient to the faithful, from schismatics to catholics'. The Latin Empire was welcomed as being at once the means of healing the breach between the Greek and Latin churches and the base for future operations in the Holy Land. The judgment – which was observed as a policy directive by future Popes – could hardly have been more fallacious. The contribution of the Latin Empire to the crusade was wholly on the debit side, a drain on the limited manpower and wealth available for crusading purposes. More significantly, the Fourth Crusade and the hatred engendered by Latin rule contributed more than any other historical episode to making the rift between the Churches an unbridgeable gulf.

The repression of heresy and the mounting of a crusade concerned, directly or indirectly, all rulers of any consequence. Other ecclesiastical issues, too, involved Innocent deeply in politics, and the national histories of most European countries record at least one significant example of his intervention. That concerning England was, perhaps, more striking than many, but it was nevertheless typical of Innocent's cast of mind.

Canonical freedom of episcopal election, always a major issue for reformers, was at stake. After England had lain under interdict for over six years, Innocent and King John reached agreement about the respective roles of the ecclesiastical and royal powers in the making of bishops and their concordat marked the definitive solution of the 'investiture' problem for medieval England. Furthermore, John acknowledged that he held England and Ireland as papal fiefs. Innocent in turn was to discharge his suzerain's duty in condemning *Magna Carta*.

Innocent's political *cause célèbre*, however, concerned Italy and the Empire. His objective was to prevent the union of the Empire and the kingdom of Sicily under one ruler, the career of Henry VI having revealed how dangerous this was for papal independence. Further, the Papal State was to be enlarged and welded into a coherent entity both to ensure this separation and to build up the material bases of papal power. It was to be the guarantor of a sure foothold in the shifting sands of Italian politics.

The achievement of these aims became possible after the sudden death of Henry VI. The power vacuum thereby created in Italy left the way open for a vigorous assertion of papal rights to various territories in central Italy. It presented also an opportunity of influencing, even of deciding, the destination of the imperial and Sicilian crowns.

Basing his claims on Carolingian and later imperial grants, freshly re-edited in the *Liber Censuum* as recently as 1192, Innocent gave the Papal State the form it was to retain down to early modern times. He also did much to demonstrate the techniques by which independent-minded

Innocent's reign saw a great renewal of the Church centred on the foundation of the Dominican and Franciscan Orders. Innocent granting St Francis and his 'little band' the right to preach, and confirming the first Franciscan Rule in 1209. A predella by Giotto from the Louvre

The zenith of the Medieval Papacy

The Fourth Lateran Council of 1215 was one of the great events of Innocent's reign and an essential instrument of his reforming policy. A page from Mathew Paris's *Chronica Maiora*, written in about 1255, showing the Fathers of the Council and stating the number of Archbishops, Bishops and Abbots present

authorities might be brought to obedience. Despite some personal success, Innocent bequeathed to his successors the Sisyphean task of making papal rulership a reality within the State.

Sicily was a papal fief. Henry VI had left a three-year-old son. It was good law that Frederick, on the death of his mother, should be recognized as the ward of the Roman Church and good tactics to ensure that when he assumed his inheritance he should have cause to be grateful to its guardian during the troubled years of his minority.

The imperial crown, however, was a more complicated matter. The emergence of two candidates for the honour was Innocent's opportunity. To the Curia, papal right to choose between candidates in the event of a double election was not in doubt. The view had been gaining ground in twelfth-century papal circles that the Roman Empire of the West owed its origin to the Papacy. The particular function of a Roman emperor, it was argued, was to give protection to the Roman Church. When the emperors in Constantinople had failed in this duty, the Empire had been 'translated' from East to West. In the very purpose of its existence, then, and in the manner of its coming to the Germans, the Holy Roman Empire was of papal origin. Hence, in a conflict as to who should be emperor, it was for the Pope to decide.

It was one thing to formalize a theory, and another to make it politically effectual. Innocent had to establish himself as arbitrator before choosing the more suitable man; the candidate's disposition to further papal policies being his criterion. In concrete terms this meant willingness to co-operate with the Pope – in leading a crusade, suppressing heresy in Italy, respecting ecclesiastical liberties generally and, in particular, the integrity of the Papal State as the Curia now defined it.

The problem dragged on. First Otto of Brunswick showed himself apparently the more tractable, while Philip of Swabia as the brother of Henry VI was suspect. But Otto's position in Germany weakened beyond repair and Philip must have been the Pope's choice had not his assassination forestalled a decision. Otto was crowned Emperor in October 1209, with a coronation rite specially revised to emphasize the imperial position as the Pope's strong right arm and with renewed oaths to uphold the Roman Church in all its undertakings and to respect its liberties, not least its possessions in Italy.

Whatever Innocent's hopes of Otto as a crusader, he was speedily disillusioned because of his Italian ambitions. Relations between the two deteriorated rapidly when Otto invaded papal territories and schemed to wrest Sicily from the young Frederick. Excommunicated by Innocent in 1210, rejected by a substantial section of the German electoral princes in 1211, destroyed militarily by Philip Augustus in 1214, Otto faded from the imperial scene.

In his place Innocent raised up Frederick of Sicily. After long years of tortuous papal diplomacy, the danger of the union of the imperial and Sicilian thrones was more real than ever – avoided only by one man's word. Frederick promised he would renounce Sicily in favour of his son, once crowned emperor. A second commitment bound him to observe the guarantees Otto had failed to keep in relation to the Papal State. A third had signed him with the crusading cross. If Innocent had any qualms about the fulfilment of these obligations he kept them to himself. It was left for his successors to attend to their implementation: Innocent had but set the stage for the most destructive of all the clashes of Empire and Papacy.

The problems of Italy, the crusade and heresy put the Curia in the forefront of international politics. Action once initiated, however, Innocent as often as not was following the course of events rather than controlling it. His achievement as a reformer was more impressive. The Papacy was once again in the van of the reforming movement.

The dream of Innocent III, in which the Pope sees St Francis supporting the falling church of S Giovanni in Laterano, a dream symbolic of the spiritual work of St Francis and his followers in the thirteenth century. A predella by Giotto from the Louvre

7 THE PAPACY AND THE HOHENSTAUFEN

HONORIUS III *to* INNOCENT IV 1216-54

BRIAN TIERNEY

The quarrel between the Papacy and the Empire became more embittered during the reign of Frederick II, the last great Emperor of the Hohenstaufen dynasty. Frederick broke the promise he had given to Innocent III and attempted to unite under his rule the Empire and Sicily. Honorius III acquiesced in the Emperor's ambitions, but Gregory IX and Innocent IV both stood firm. Gregory twice excommunicated Frederick and died while imperial troops surrounded Rome. Innocent IV retired from Italy to Lyons and at a General Council held there in 1245 pronounced the Emperor's deposition, while Frederick retaliated with a total denunciation of the rights of the Church. Innocent also attempted to bring about a reconciliation with the Greek Church, but negotiations were cut short by his death in 1254.

THE YEARS BETWEEN 1216 AND 1254 WERE YEARS OF great achievement for medieval civilization. Gothic art, scholastic philosophy, the literature of chivalry were all coming to their finest flowerings, and from Scandinavia to Spain the Pope was acknowledged as head of a single Church, united in a common faith and ruled by a common law. Yet this was also an age of grievous new perils for the Church. Toward the middle of the thirteenth century there were unforeseen disasters on the borders of Christendom – in 1241 a horde of Tartars from Central Asia raided deep into the Christian lands of Eastern Europe and in 1244 the holy city of Jerusalem was captured by the Khwarazmanian Turks. During this same period there was also going on a bitter and prolonged struggle in the heartland of Italy itself where, for decade after decade, the Papacy had to fight – it seemed for its very survival – against the last great emperor of the Hohenstaufen dynasty, Frederick II.

This ruler has fascinated and baffled modern historians as much as he did his own contemporaries. Brilliantly intelligent, ruthlessly amoral, dedicated only to a cult of his own omnipotence, he was the most dangerous enemy that the medieval Popes ever had to face, and the history of the Roman See during his lifetime is inextricably entangled with the story of his ambitions and achievements. The outbreak of open conflict between Frederick and the Papacy was delayed for several years after the death of Innocent III only through the extreme forbearance of the next Pope, Honorius III (1216–27). Honorius was an elderly, pacific man who gave the Church eleven years of quietly efficient administration, a necessary period of consolidation, perhaps, after all the stress and change of Innocent's Pontificate, though his acquiescence in Frederick's Italian policies laid up grievous problems for his successors in the Papacy.

Frederick was by hereditary right King of Sicily (including South Italy), which he held as a fief from the Papacy and also, in his capacity as Emperor-elect, overlord of North Italy and Germany. Innocent III, fearing the extension of imperial power, insisted that Frederick should relinquish his Kingdom of Sicily upon becoming Emperor. Frederick accepted this condition and gave the most solemn assurances that he would never seek to unite the Sicilian and imperial crowns. The arrangement agreed upon was that Frederick would have his infant son Henry crowned co-king of Sicily and then, immediately after his own coronation as Emperor, would relinquish the direction of government there to a regent who was to be approved by the Pope. The child Henry was duly crowned as co-king but Frederick never gave up his personal control of the Sicilian government. Moreover, in 1220, he had his son elected as king by the German princes also, which, in effect, designated Henry as the next successor to the imperial throne. By this manoeuvre Frederick abandoned his whole undertaking to avoid a future union of the Sicilian and imperial territories. All his subsequent conflicts with the Papacy, and the 'persecution' that he complained of, sprang from this initial, carefully calculated act of treachery.

At the time Frederick assured Pope Honorius that the German princes had acted without his knowledge, an

Gregory IX (1227–41) made a great contribution to the codification of ecclesiastical law in the *Decretals*, which remain the foundation of canon law in modern times. Raphael's fresco shows him handing a copy of the *Decretals* to a consistorial lawyer

The Papacy and the Hohenstaufen

Above A seal of Frederick II. The inscription in the centre refers to his campaign of 1228 when he won back the Holy Places and crowned himself King of Jerusalem

Right Honorius III (1216–27) succeeded in averting open conflict with Frederick II, but only by acquiescing in the Emperor's reversal of his undertaking not to unite his Sicilian and imperial territories. Honorius approved by a papal bull the Rule of the Franciscan Order and this detail from Giotto's fresco at Assisi shows him listening to the preaching of St Francis

excuse almost insulting in its effrontery. He also renewed an earlier pledge to go on crusade and proffered numerous concessions on various points concerning clerical privileges and disputed territorial boundaries. Honorius allowed himself to be persuaded of the Hohenstaufen's good will and, shortly after this episode, crowned him as Emperor.

Frederick spent the next few years consolidating his power in Sicily. All possible sources of opposition to his despotic rule – the nobility, the towns, the clergy – were in turn subjected to his absolute will. Honorius repeatedly reminded the emperor of his vow to lead a crusade. Frederick prevaricated with endless excuses. Then, in 1226, he turned his attention to Lombardy, summoning a Diet at Cremona where, he announced, the restoration of imperial rights in Italy would be considered. The example of Sicily had taught the Lombard cities what a 'restoration of rights' meant to Frederick and they came together in a league to defend their traditional autonomy. Moreover, at this latest turn of imperial policy even the patient Honorius became exasperated, the more so since Frederick in his progress northwards had marched his armies through the Papal States without seeking permission, just as though he were rightful lord of those territories as well as of Sicily and Lombardy. There was an exchange of bitter letters and a breach between Pope and Emperor seemed imminent when, in 1227, Honorius died.

Right Honorius III approving the Carmelite Rule. A detail from a painting by the fourteenth-century Sienese artist Pietro Lorenzetti

The Papacy and the Hohenstaufen

The next Pope, Gregory IX (1227–41) was a man of different mettle. Like Honorius he was already an old man at the time of his election, but there was combined in this Pontiff an unusual mixture of hard-headed legal craft and fiery-hearted zeal for religion. It was Gregory who first organized the papal inquisition; his great work of legal codification, the *Decretals*, remained a living part of the law of the Church down to modern times; but this shrewd canon lawyer had also been a friend to Francis of Assisi from the earliest days of the saint's mission and was chosen by Francis to be the first Cardinal-protector of his new order of friars. Such a man was not likely to accept further prevarication, still less provocation, from the Emperor, and Frederick did in fact set off on the long-deferred crusade a few months after Gregory's election. He returned almost at once, however, pleading ill-health. The Pope promptly excommunicated him for breach of his crusader's vow and, in a subsequent letter, denounced him for a long series of crimes against the Church.

Left Gregory IX (1227–41) took a firm stand against the ambitions and prevarications of Frederick II. He died while the imperial armies were besieging Rome.
A mosaic head from the old basilica of St Peter

Below Frederick II was twice excommunicated by Gregory IX, in 1228 and 1239, but the Emperor claimed that he was being persecuted by the Church and continued the struggle undeterred. A dramatic representation of the excommunication by Vasari

In 1241 Frederick's fleet captured two cardinals and a hundred bishops who were on their way to a Council summoned by Gregory IX to depose the Emperor. A manuscript illustration showing Frederick in the ship on the left, while his soldiers assault the prelates in the ship bearing the papal ensign

The Emperor's next move was bold and clever. While still under the papal ban he actually did travel to the Holy Land and, without waging a military campaign, he was able to exploit the existing dissensions in the Mohammedan world so adroitly as to persuade the Sultan to hand over to him the holy places of Jerusalem, Nazareth and Bethlehem – a considerable triumph. During Frederick's absence papal armies invaded the Kingdom of Sicily, but on his return he easily routed them and carried the war into the Papal States. Gregory was for the time being at the end of his resources and accepted a negotiated peace in 1230.

The hostility between Pope and Emperor smouldered through the 1230s and flared into open war again over a dispute concerning the papal fief of Sardinia in 1239. Gregory now denounced the Emperor as a blasphemer and a heretic and summoned a General Council to meet in Rome, presumably to enact a formal sentence of deposition against him. There ensued the greatest disaster of Gregory's Pontificate. A Genoese convoy bringing bishops from the North to the Council was intercepted by the Emperor's fleet and defeated in a sea battle. Two cardinals and some hundred prelates were captured and held prisoner by the Emperor. Frederick then marched on Rome itself, anticipating a triumphal entry into the city 'amid the acclaim of the whole Roman people' (as he wrote); but for once the fickle Roman mob, moved by an impassioned appeal from the aged Pontiff, stood loyally by their Pope in the face of an imperial threat. In the midst of this crisis, with the Emperor's armies encamped ten miles from the city, Gregory's life came to its close. He died in August 1241. Frederick openly exulted when the news was brought to him at Grottaferata.

On Gregory's death the ten cardinals who were in Rome were imprisoned by the governor of the city and ordered to make an immediate election. Some of them favoured a compromise with the Emperor. Others bitterly opposed such a policy. It seemed impossible to find the necessary two-thirds majority for any candidate. Several cardinals became sick because of the harsh circumstances of their confinement in the fetid heat of the Roman summer and

Stone head of Frederick II, a brilliant and unscrupulous statesman, who made no secret of his attack on the Church and his repudiation of its claims to political power

Frederick's armies marched and counter-marched in Italy, where his territories in the north and south bordered the Papal States. Among the many fortified castles built by him is the Castel del Monte, Bari

one of them, the English cardinal, Robert Somercote, died during the conclave. After two months the exhausted electors agreed on a Milanese cardinal, Godfrey Castiglione, who took the name Celestine IV; but he was already sick at the time of his election and died seventeen days later, before he had even been consecrated as Pope.

There ensued a long vacancy. One group of cardinals had fled to Anagni on being released from the conclave, others remained in Rome, and two of the Sacred College were still held prisoner by Frederick. It required the intervention of King Louis of France to bring about their release so that at last all the cardinals could come together in a new conclave in 1243. This time they quickly agreed on a candidate, Cardinal Sinibaldo Fieschi, who became Pope Innocent IV (1243–54).

Innocent IV is famed as a great lawyer and administrator, pre-eminent as a jurist in an age when many outstanding churchmen were distinguished as canonists. But historians have usually judged this Pope harshly when assessing his Pontificate as a whole. It has commonly been maintained that, throughout his reign, he concerned himself exclusively with worldly politics in a fashion unbecoming to a spiritual pastor; and it is true that, in Innocent IV, we find little trace of Gregory IX's mystical fervour or of the real passion for moral reform that underlay all the political preoccupations of Innocent III. His whole Pontificate was one long war in which all the spiritual and temporal resources of the Church were mobilized to serve the overriding purpose of defeating Frederick II. But it is also true that Innocent IV did not create the political problems with which he had to cope. They arose from ambitions of the Emperor that would have been intolerable to any Pope, and it may be that, in such a time of desperate crisis, the Roman See needed above all else the qualities that Innocent brought to his task, an adamantine will and a courage that never faltered.

At the very beginning of the Pontificate there were negotiations between Innocent and Frederick, each ruler probing the other for any possible weakness, but soon it became evident that there could be no settlement between them. The Emperor next invited the Pope to a personal conference. Innocent knew that to let himself fall into Frederick's hands would jeopardize his whole cause, that the Emperor would treat a visiting Pope with no more courtesy than he had shown to the captive cardinals. He resolved therefore on a radically new tactic to meet the situation. By night, in disguise, the Pope fled to Civitavecchia where a fleet was waiting to carry him safely to his native city of Genoa. Innocent became ill at Genoa and stayed there several months, then pressed on over the Alps to the city of Lyons on the border of France where he could rely on the protection of King Louis against any imperial attack.

As long as Frederick lived Innocent ruled the universal church from Lyons. His first major act was to summon a General Council to meet there in 1245. According to the letters of convocation the Council was to consider the succour of the East European lands devastated by the Tartars, the launching of a new crusade to recapture Jerusalem from the Turks, the schism between Greeks and Latins in the Eastern Empire, and the persecution of the Church by the Emperor Frederick. All of these matters received some attention at the Council and afterwards. In 1245 Innocent did send an embassy to the khan of the Tartars and then missionaries to preach to them; in 1248 King Louis launched a Crusade against the Saracens; and one of the main preoccupations of Innocent's last years was the conduct of negotiations to bring about a reconciliation with the Greek Church. (The negotiations seemed on the point of success in 1254 but foundered after the Pope's death.)

However, in spite of the Pope's real concern over all these matters, everyone understood that the essential purpose of the Council was the condemnation of Frederick II. At the opening session Innocent rebuked the Emperor for his treacheries to the Church and for maintaining unseemly relations with the Saracens. This latter accusation was well calculated to arouse the anger of all the members of the Council and it was not without substance. (Frederick maintained an army of Saracen mercenaries whom he had settled at the town of Lucera in South Italy and he was popularly supposed to maintain also a harem of Saracen wives.) The Emperor was represented in the proceedings before the Council by Thadeus of Suessa, one of the most distinguished jurists of his realm. Thadeus pleaded his master's case with eloquence but the task was a hopeless one and, at the third session of the Council, Innocent proceeded to the expected act of deposition. The prelates assembled in the nave of the cathedral bearing lighted tapers. The Pope, seated on a raised throne in the choir, read a long

On Gregory IX's death Rome was without an effective Pope for two years.
Innocent IV (1243–54) fled to Lyons after preliminary negotiations with the Emperor had failed.
He summoned a General Council there in 1245 to excommunicate and depose the Emperor.
This manuscript illustration shows Frederick's representative, Thadeus of Suessa,
leaving the Council as the sentence is pronounced

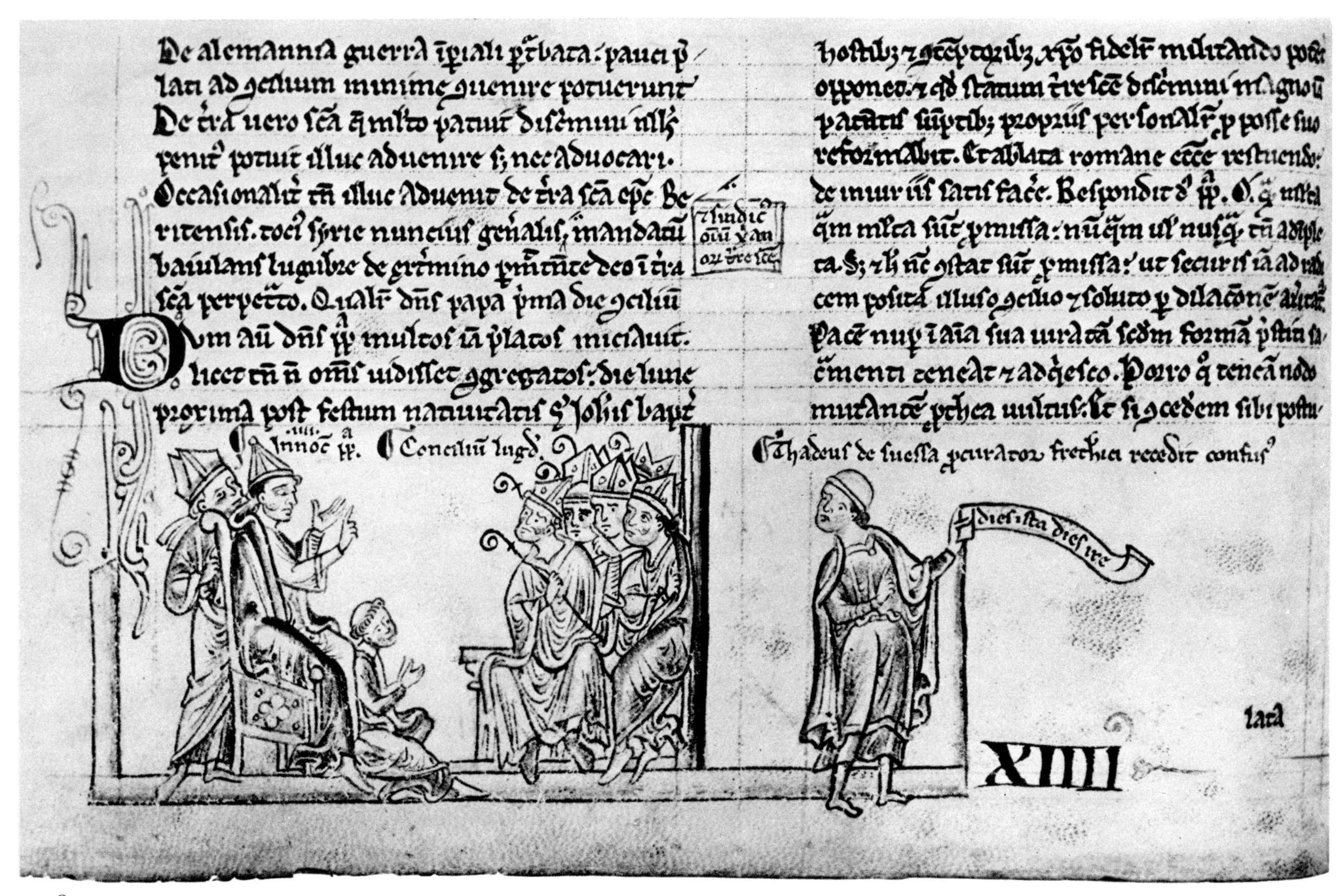

recital of Frederick's offences – heresy, sacrilege and perjury prominent among them – and then came to his appointed conclusion. 'After careful consultation with our brothers and the holy Council we declare that the aforesaid Prince ... is rejected and deprived of all honour and dignity by God, to which we add our sentence of deprivation also.' As the words of condemnation rolled forth the prelates extinguished their tapers, Thadeus of Suessa swept out of the Cathedral crying that a day of wrath had come upon the world, and, as he left, the fathers of the Council began to intone a solemn *Te Deum*.

Frederick received the news of his deposition with fury. Up until this point he had generally claimed to be a loyal son of the Church who was being persecuted through the individual malice of misguided Popes. Now he denounced the whole structure of existing ecclesiastical society in letters addressed to the kings of Europe. The priests and prelates of his time who concerned themselves with war, politics and the pursuit of worldly possessions were no true followers of Christ, he declared, and he made it clear that he would henceforth treat it as a royal duty to strip the Church of its wealth under pretext of reforming it. The letters provide a first foreshadowing of a distinctively laical, anti-sacerdotal theory of the state.

Meanwhile, in the period immediately after the papal condemnation, the continuing war in Italy went badly for Frederick. He suffered a major set-back in 1247 when the imperial city of Parma went over to the papal cause and was defeated again in 1248 when an attempt to recapture the city ended in the virtual destruction of the besieging army. During the next year Frederick's most gifted and best loved son, Enzio, was taken prisoner in a skirmish near Modena. But, after all these reverses, Frederick still controlled all of South Italy and many cities in the north, and during 1250 he again won a series of victories. The outcome of the struggle still hung in the balance when the whole scene was transformed by the death of Frederick in December 1250. Innocent greeted the news with the same open joy that Frederick himself had shown at the death of Gregory IX.

With the disappearance of his great antagonist Innocent was able to return to Italy, first to Perugia, then in 1253 to Rome. Throughout 1254 he was concerned principally with the settlement of the papal fief of Sicily. For the time being he recognized Frederick's son, Manfred, as regent, leaving the ultimate disposal of the fief to be determined in future negotiations, but at the end of the year Manfred led the Saracens of Lucera in a rebellion against his papal overlord. When the news came to Innocent at Naples he was already sick to death. His life ended before he could plan any counter-stroke, on 7 December 1254. The best summary of his reign was written by a contemporary chronicler. 'He sat as Pope for eleven and a half years or, rather, he did not sit. He stood on his feet fighting.'

Louis IX (1214–70), king of France, gave protection to Innocent IV during his stay at Lyons. Louis embodied the highest ideals of medieval kingship and died on his second crusade. He was canonized by Boniface VIII in 1297. A portrait by El Greco from the Louvre

8 THE FRENCH PREDOMINANCE AND THE AVIGNON POPES

ALEXANDER IV to GREGORY XI 1254–1378

BERNARD GUILLEMAIN

During the second half of the thirteenth century the Papacy was dominated by the influence of Charles of Anjou, brother of St Louis IX. But in 1294 the election of Boniface VIII brought about a disastrous struggle with Philip IV of France and Boniface's extravagant claims to papal supremacy culminated in his humiliation at Anagni in 1303. After his death the Holy See was occupied by a succession of Popes who were dominated by the French crown. For seventy years the Popes were resident at Avignon, where they built up a complicated bureaucratic administration. The extravagance, the national composition and the fiscal system of the papal court were severely criticized. In 1377 Gregory XI finally returned to Rome and the 'Avignon Captivity' came to an end.

BY THE MIDDLE OF THE THIRTEENTH CENTURY THE claims of the Papacy were clearly defined. The Vicar of Christ, Peter's successor, exercised an absolute authority over the religious life of the whole community. This spiritual power was superior to any temporal authority. Secular princes, of course, had the authority to rule over their subjects, but they could only exercise this authority if they conformed to the rules laid down by the Pope. The most important of these was that the Empire could only be conferred on a candidate approved by the Holy See.

For this system to work effectively, it was essential for the Papacy to be politically independent. The death of the Emperor Frederick II in 1250 lessened the danger of encirclement, but did not remove it. His successors wanted to remain in control of both the Empire and the Kingdom of Sicily. Pope Innocent IV, who died in 1254, and Alexander IV (1254–61) struggled hard against Conrad IV and Manfred, sons of the Emperor. In 1261 the conclave elected a Frenchman, Urban IV, an energetic man who, according to a Sienese ambassador, 'does what he wants'. An agreement was concluded in 1264 with Charles of Anjou, brother of St Louis, King of France. The prince undertook to conquer the Kingdom of Sicily and hold it in fief for the Roman Church.

But Charles was consumed with ambition. He forced Rome, the Papal States and Tuscany to submit to his will; he dreamed of establishing himself in Byzantium and dominating the Mediterranean. The Papacy had thought to gain a servant but found themselves with a master.

A French, or rather an Angevin party was formed in the Sacred College, but it did not have the two-thirds majority necessary for the election of a Pope. And so the Holy See remained vacant for three years between 1268 and 1271, until the accession of an Italian, Teobaldo Visconti as Gregory X (1271–76). He was succeeded by three Popes, nominees of Charles of Anjou, who followed one another in rapid succession between 1276 and 1277. As 'Keeper' of the conclave the King of Sicily used to feed his supporters lavishly and virtually starve his opponents! Nicholas III, a member of the powerful Roman Orsini family, attempted to resist him (1277–80). But his successor, Martin IV, who had studied in Paris and had been in the service of the King of France, was convinced that the interests of the Papacy coincided with those of the Capetian dynasty and as a result appointed his countrymen to high offices.

In 1282 Charles of Anjou's reign came to an abrupt end. He lost the island of Sicily in the revolt of the 'Sicilian Vespers' and the rebels called in the Aragonese. Martin IV undertook a Holy War, but the crusade he launched against Aragon with troops under the command of Philip III of France was short-lived. By the beginning of the fourteenth century the Papacy had been forced to recognize a junior branch of the House of Aragon as rulers of Sicily and to promise Corsica and Sardinia to the senior branch, stipulating that these lands were held as papal fiefs.

The setback to the Angevin family could ultimately have proved advantageous to the Holy See, especially as German power at this time also seemed to be on the decline. In

The Palace of the Popes at Avignon, built during the reigns of Benedict XII and Clement VI. Half fortress and half royal palace, it housed the papal court and administrative centre until 1377

Charles of Anjou, brother of St Louis of France, whose territorial ambitions were centred on the Kingdom of Sicily. For some years he dominated the conclave and secured the election of Angevin nominees to the Papacy

Nicholas III (1277–80), a member of the great Roman Orsini family, resisted the influence of Charles of Anjou and attempted to free Rome from foreign interference. The standing bear (*orso*) is the emblem of the Orsini family

these circumstances, there was a good opportunity for the Papacy to press its temporal ambitions.

In an attempt to put an end to the bitter rivalry between the Orsini and Colonna families, which had divided the College of Cardinals since the death of Nicholas IV in 1292, Charles II, King of Sicily, son of Charles of Anjou, had suggested calling on a pious hermit from Abruzzi. This man had attracted a large number of followers and his influence had resulted in the reform of several abbeys. Pietro di Murrone became Pope Celestine V in July 1294. But his inadequacy was soon very obvious. He settled in Naples and became a tool of the Angevin government. Moreover, his devotional and penitential practices made him quite unfit to carry out the duties of his high office. He soon began to think of resigning his office and Benedetto Caetani convinced him that such an act would be legitimate. On 13 December 1294 Celestine V abdicated. On Christmas Eve the conclave elected as Pope Cardinal Benedetto Caetani, Boniface VIII (1294–1303). His enemies did not hesitate to cast doubts on his integrity and encouraged stories such as one that he had engineered a vision in order to help Celestine V overcome his doubts about abdicating.

Boniface VIII is one of the outstanding figures of the medieval Papacy. He came from an aristocratic family who had settled in Anagni and his pride and ambition were matched by his imposing appearance. His logical mind developed the principles instilled by his legal training to their ultimate conclusion, but his fiery temperament and immoderate speech sometimes made him lose his sense of proportion and make statements which his enemies were quick to spread around and use against him.

Reassured by the vacancy of the imperial throne, Boniface VIII did not realize that it would be the king of France, Philip IV the Fair, son of Philip III, who had led the crusade against Aragon, who would be the principal obstacle to his ambitions. An incident early on in his reign made it possible for the Pope to declare that the French clergy need not pay any dues to the king without papal sanction. On this occasion, however, Boniface was willing to compromise and agreed to canonize Philip IV's grandfather, Louis IX. Soon afterwards the arrest of a French bishop, suspected of plotting against the king, provoked a second incident. By virtue of his precedence over the temporal powers, Boniface VIII claimed the right to investigate their administration. He summoned French prelates and university teachers to Rome to draw up a plan for the reformation of the kingdom and to censure the king, whom he criticized both for his method of government and even for his financial transactions. He talked of excommunicating Philip if he did not submit and of releasing his subjects from their bonds of

The election of the pious hermit, Celestine v, in 1294 was an attempt to end the rivalry between the Orsini and Colonna families. But his disastrous simplicity made him a tool of the King of Naples and after five months he abdicated. A detail from a fifteenth-century fresco

The French Predominance

allegiance. During the assembly of November 1302 he published the bull *Unam Sanctam* which set out in detail the papal claims. At the same time Boniface refused to accept Albert of Austria as a candidate for the imperial throne until he had sworn an oath of fealty.

Guillaume de Nogaret, a jurist as relentless as Boniface, led the counter-attack. He advised Philip IV to accuse the Pope of being illegally elected, of heresy and other crimes, and proposed that a General Council should be summoned to judge Boniface. Representatives of the French people were summoned and approved the plan. Nogaret went to Italy to make sure that the Pope was present for the opening of the Council. On 7 September 1303 the little town of Anagni was occupied. Sciarra Colonna, a mortal enemy of the Caetanis, would probably have killed Boniface if Nogaret had not intervened, but the people of Anagni, who were afraid of being accused of complicity in this scandal, soon expelled the invaders. Boniface was released, but he died a month later in Rome, aged about seventy.

The importance of the 'Anagni Incident' must not be under-estimated. It provoked a great ideological debate. The theorists, who expounded the supremacy of the monarchy, asserted the independence of the state and the laity, and were supported in their theories by the old concept of Roman law. Boniface's death did not stop Philip the Fair's action. Nogaret was determined on a posthumous trial of Boniface VIII. The conciliatory measures of Benedict XI (1303–04) did not satisfy the French Court, which insisted on a conviction. Not only Boniface VIII but the whole institution of the Papacy had been brought into discredit.

A statue of Boniface VIII on the wall of the cathedral at Anagni, his native town. In 1303 Boniface's quarrel with Philip IV of France reached a climax and he was imprisoned at Anagni and narrowly escaped assassination

The coronation of Boniface VIII from a manuscript illumination. His claim to total authority over all temporal rulers, set out in the bull *Unam Sanctam* of 1302, was principally directed at Philip IV, who retaliated by organizing fierce opposition which culminated in Boniface's humiliation at Anagni

Boniface VIII proclaiming the first Jubilee Year in 1300, which brought thousands of pilgrims flocking to Rome. A fresco by Giotto from S Giovanni in Laterano

Bonifa
tius

Right After Boniface's death Benedict XI (1303–04) adopted a conciliatory policy towards France. He is seen here with, on his left, Philip IV and Edward I of England, between whom he negotiated a truce. There are also many Dominicans in their white habits, as Benedict had been Master-General of the Order. A fresco from S Maria Novella, Florence

Left The coronation of Clement V (1305–14) inaugurated the 'Babylonian Captivity' of the Popes in Southern France. Clement was dominated by Philip IV and established the papal court at Avignon in 1309.

Left below The election of John XXII (1316–34). During his reign the papal court and administration at Avignon were strengthened and also much criticized for extravagance and corruption. Two miniatures from the *Cronaca Villani*

The French Predominance

After eleven months of hesitation marked by grave internal divisions and uncertainty about the future, the conclave elected the Archbishop of Bordeaux, Bertrand de Got, Clement V (1305–14). To the general surprise Clement, instead of coming to Rome for his coronation, had himself crowned at Lyons. The tact and geniality of the new Pope were sharply put to the test by Philip the Fair, who dropped his demand for posthumous proceedings against Boniface and instead demanded the condemnation of the Knights Templar, who held considerable property in France and who were accused of infamous practices and denial of Christ. Clement V agreed to call a General Council at Vienne on the banks of the Rhône. Although he was compelled to abandon the Templars to the mercy of judges open to pressure from the secular power and was forced to suppress the order, he himself did not condemn the Templars and transferred their assets to another order, the 'Hospitaliers' (1312).

Nevertheless, the negotiations with the King of France occupied the Pope's attention so completely that he did not once visit his See or even cross the Alps during his entire Pontificate. In 1309 he established himself in Avignon. In his absence, dissension had spread, both in Rome and in the Papal States; the Ghibelline faction had gained ascendancy over the Guelphs, who by tradition supported the Papacy in Italy. It seemed only sensible for the Pope to wait until peace had been restored before returning to Rome.

By filling the College of Cardinals with his countrymen from Gascony and with nominees of the King of France, Clement V created a majority which could choose new Popes from their own ranks. Six clerics, all born in the South of France, in the 'Langue d'Oc', were elected in succession: John XXII (1316–34), Benedict XII (1334–42), Clement VI (1342–52), Innocent VI (1352–62), Urban V (1362–70) and Gregory XI (1370–78). Regarding nepotism as a privilege of the Holy See, the Popes conferred high offices in the Church on their relations, friends and countrymen. These Frenchmen saw nothing abnormal in administering the Papacy in Provence outside a troubled Italy.

Clement v (1305–16), the first of the Avignon Popes, completed the codification of medieval canon law. In this fresco by Taddeo Gaddi he is shown with Justinian, the codifier of Roman law, and allegorical figures representing Church and State

The Avignon Papacy naturally favoured the interests of France. Moreover the temporal power of the Apostolic See which had been greatly strained under Boniface VIII continued to decline. During the disastrous Anglo-French conflict of the Hundred Years War, the most papal diplomacy could achieve was short truces and an occasional illusory peace. England repudiated the vassalage to which John Lackland had committed her at the beginning of the thirteenth century. The long-drawn-out quarrel between the Papacy and Louis of Bavaria, whom John XXII had refused to recognize as Emperor, remained unsettled. Charles IV, who was chosen by the German electors under the direction of Pope Clement VI, hastened the transformation of the Empire into a German monarchy and took little interest in Italy. It is easy to understand why the Papacy, whose political influence amongst the rapidly growing states was steadily declining, was unable to inspire a new crusade to re-conquer the Holy Land where the last Christian strongholds had been lost in 1291.

Although they were preoccupied with political struggles, the Popes never forgot their responsibility as head of the Church. Towards the middle of the thirteenth century they realized the great opportunities for promoting the Christian faith in the vast territories of Asia conquered by the Mongols. They encouraged the 'Missions' in which St Francis of Assisi had set an example. Clement V and John XXII instituted an episcopal hierarchy for China and Iran. This achievement was destroyed in the middle of the fourteenth century by a revolution in China and the wave of Moslem fanaticism. Another dream of long standing, that of union with the Greek Church, was almost realized on two occasions: at the Council of Lyons in 1274 and then during the Emperor John Paleologue's visit to Urban V in 1369. But it was not lasting. The Greeks were only interested in obtaining material aid from the West and were not willing to submit to the authority of Rome in matters of religion.

One of the most important developments in the Papacy during the late thirteenth and fourteenth centuries was the organization of the Roman Church as a pontifical monarchy. This had been taking place gradually but came to completion during the Avignon period.

Theologians and experts in canon law proclaimed the Pope as the definer of dogma, the establisher of law and the dispenser of supernatural grace; he was the fountain head of the hierarchy, the supreme judge. Papal administration was centred on him. In 1265 Clement IV declared that the

The Avignon Popes were great patrons of the arts. Clement VI bestowed a canonry on Petrarch and later sent him as papal ambassador to Naples. Nevertheless Petrarch was one of the sternest critics of the papal court and in his poems frequently pressed for the return to Rome. A manuscript illustration

Benedict XII (1334–42), who was responsible for the building of the first great papal palace at Avignon. A bust by Paolo da Siena

Pope could dispose of ecclesiastical benefices, that is to say of the offices and revenues of the Church. In fact the Popes retained the right to nominate prelates, an increasing number of canons and even parish priests, priors and chaplains and at the same time they levied taxes on the clergy they had nominated. The chancery issued decrees by the thousand. The receipts of the papal treasury were comparable with those of the larger European states. A tribunal or Rota was set up to deal with litigation.

This administration needed stability if it was to function properly and it could not adapt itself to being perpetually moved from place to place. In Avignon it was possible to achieve a permanence which had never been known before. The 'double' palace was built, an impressive building like a fortress, which can still be seen today. The part dating from Benedict XII has a monastic austerity, whereas that dating from Clement VI is gentler and more spacious, decorated with religious and secular paintings, in which the influence of Northern Europe and Italy can be recognized. Many hundreds of officials received payment in money rather than in kind, as had been the custom. The Papacy gave Avignon the status of a capital and from this period onwards it had as many as 30,000 to 40,000 inhabitants.

Were a bureaucracy and a complicated fiscal machinery appropriate to the spiritual nature of the Holy See? Voices were raised in protest. The English crown and Parliament considered it necessary to protect the English church against papal practices. Dante relegated Boniface VIII and Clement V to Hell because they had created for themselves a 'God of gold and silver'. Petrarch professed to have found neither faith nor charity at Avignon. The fanatics who preached poverty and saw themselves as the upholders of the spirit of St Francis, expected the coming of the Holy Spirit; the failure of the ascetic Celestine V did not discourage them and they were not deterred by persecution. The head of the Franciscan order, Michel de Césène and Brother William of Ockham even allied themselves with the greatest enemies of the Papacy, for whom Marsiglio of Padua acted as spokesman. Heretics, including the Waldensians and the Cathars, denounced the Church for betraying the message of the gospel in their lust for power.

This uneasy situation was aggravated by the fact that it was from Avignon and not from Rome that the orders of this rigidly organized administration proceeded. But the French Popes were well aware that the spiritual capital was still on the banks of the Tiber. In 1350 Clement VI declared that a jubilee should be celebrated in Rome. Urban V (1362–70) made an unsuccessful attempt to return. Finally Gregory XI, perhaps strengthened in his resolution by St Catherine of Siena, entered Rome on 17 January 1377. But he died in 1378 before he had had time to try and adapt the new monarchical government machine of the Papacy to the life of Rome. The French Popes had created this institution but it was weakened by temporal misfortunes, suspected of partiality and criticized for its autocratic claims, which were only accepted much later and after upheavals in which the Papacy was almost destroyed.

Detail from the Miracle of St Martial, a decoration in the Chapel of St Martial in the Palace of the Popes. According to legend St Martial restored a dead man to life by touching him with a rod given him by St Peter

Left The tomb of St Catherine of Siena in S Maria sopra Minerva, Rome. She visited Gregory XI at Avignon in 1376 and his return to Rome a year later has been attributed to her influence

Right Gregory XI returning to Rome from Avignon in 1377. A detail from a fresco by Matteo di Giovanni

9 SCHISMS AND COUNCILS

URBAN VI to EUGENIUS IV 1378-1447

JOSEPH GILL

The arrogance of Urban VI, the first Pope to be elected after the return to Rome, led the cardinals to establish a rival Pope at Avignon. For thirty years there were two Popes, one in Rome and one in Avignon. The attempt of the Council of Pisa to end the schism in 1408 only led to the establishment of a third claimant. The problem was finally solved at the Council of Constance, but only by the assertion that General Councils were superior to Popes. The Council also dealt with the Bohemian heresy and John Hus was tried and burned at the stake. Under Eugenius IV the superior authority of the Pope was reasserted and the Council which met in 1438, first in Ferrara and then in Florence, succeeded in resolving for a time the differences between the Greek and Roman churches.

THE FIRST POPE ELECTED IN ROME AFTER THE Captivity of Avignon was Urban VI (1378–89). He was however so truculent in his reforming zeal that the cardinals, his electors, fearing for their influence and privileges, pretended that his election was invalid and chose in his stead the anti-Pope Clement VII (1378–94). For the next twenty years there were two lines of 'Popes', Urban and his successors in Italy, Clement and Benedict XIII (1394–1424) in Avignon. The Church was divided and discipline languished. As a result there is no constructive development in ecclesiastical life to record, for the 'Popes' could not be prevailed on to end the Great Schism. In 1408 therefore the greater part of the cardinals of the two Curias, with the support of most Christian princes, abandoned their patrons to form the Council of Pisa, which deposed both 'Popes'. The Council of Pisa, not being summoned by a Pope, was not in the technical sense, according to tradition, a General Council. It nominated Alexander V (1409–10) as Pope, but Alexander's nomination, far from ending the schism, merely meant that there were now three claimants to the Papacy instead of two. Alexander's successor, John XXIII (1401–15) harried by political enemies and under moral pressure from Sigismund, King of the Romans, convoked a Council to meet in Constance on 1 November 1414.

The Council, whatever the validity of its terms of reference, had the support of virtually all western christendom. Sigismund arrived in person on Christmas Eve; embassies from other princes followed. The Council was divided into 'nations' for voting purposes – English, French, German, Italian and later Spanish – wherein each one of the throng of simple clerics had a deliberative vote equal to that of cardinals, bishops or abbots. The three main purposes of the gathering were unity within the Church, the extirpation of heresy, and reform. Unity was soon interpreted as the deposition of all three 'Popes' and the election of a fourth. John XXIII fled in alarm. In the absence of its head, the Council stood in danger of automatic dissolution. To give itself a juridical foundation, in its fifth session on 6 April 1415, it enunciated as a dogmatic truth what had been a tacit claim since the convocation of the Council of Pisa, that a general council 'representing the universal Church, holds its power immediately from God, and everyone, ... even if he be Pope, is bound to obey it in matters which pertain to the faith, to the eradication of this schism and to the general reform of the Church of God in head and members.' In other words, the highest authority in the Church was declared to be, not the Popes, but general councils. Thus fortified, the Fathers deposed John XXIII, who acquiesced, and Benedict XIII in his retreat in Spain, who did not; Gregory XII (1406–15), Urban's third successor, abdicated. A new Pope, recognized by virtually the whole Church, was elected on 11 November 1417 with the name of Martin V (1417–31). Unity within the Church was achieved.

Meantime the other two aims had not been forgotten. The main heresy of the day was connected with the name of John Hus, a Bohemian priest. It derived from the Bohemians' desire for ecclesiastical reform, praiseworthy in itself, but unfortunate in its developments, and the false teaching

For forty years after the return from Avignon there were two lines of 'Popes', one in Rome and one in Avignon. The Great Schism was finally ended in 1417 at the Council of Constance with the election of an entirely new Pope, Martin V. His huge statue stands in Milan Cathedral

Above The first Pope to be elected in Rome after the return from Avignon was Urban VI (1378–89). His election was marked by certain irregularities and when his autocratic methods further antagonized the French party in the College of Cardinals, they chose an anti-Pope, Clement VII, who 'ruled' from Avignon. The sarcophagus of Urban VI in the Vatican Grottoes

Below In 1408 the Council of Pisa attempted to end the schism by electing a new Pope, Alexander V. But since the others refused to resign there were then three Popes. In the third line Alexander V was succeeded by John XXIII, whose tomb by Donatello stands in the Duomo Baptistry in Florence

Schisms and Councils

Above A manuscript portrait of Gregory XII (1406–15), Urban's third successor, who abdicated to an honourable retirement in 1415 after the Council of Constance had met to put an end to the Great Schism

Left Boniface IX (1389–1404) succeeded Urban VI in the legitimate line of Popes at Rome. His statue in S Giovanni in Laterano

Schisms and Councils

The Council of Constance also discussed the reform of the Church and particularly the threat of heresy.
The teachings of the Bohemian reformer John Hus were condemned and, although he had been given a safe-conduct to Constance by the Emperor, he was burned at the stake.
A contemporary illustration of his execution

of the Englishman Wyclif. A list of Wyclif's errors was censured. John Hus, who had been given a safe-conduct by Sigismund for his journey to Constance, was tried, condemned on the evidence of his own writings and burnt at the stake with a prayer on his lips. Jerome of Prague suffered a like fate.

There remained ecclesiastical reform, by which was meant, primarily, reform of the papal Curia and its financial methods. Too many interests, however, were involved for this to be effected easily. Not only the Pope and the cardinals, but princes, bishops, chapters of cathedrals and other churches, monastic orders – all had their claims which could not be reconciled. In consequence, after much work by committees, five decrees were promulgated on 9 October 1417, of which the first became the most famous. The decree *Frequens* enacted that for the future general councils should be held regularly, the next after five years, the following one seven years later and thenceforward every ten years. The rest of the reforming legislation, arranged after Martin's accession, consisted of a few general principles chiefly concerning benefices and applicable to the whole Church and, because of the impossibility of agreeing on further legislation of universal application, concordats made separately with the five 'nations'. These were concerned with the College of Cardinals, the collation of benefices, taxes, and appeals to the Roman courts.

The council ended on 22 April 1418, when, apropos of a protest from some members, the Pope declared that he approved and ratified 'all that has been done here, touching on matters of faith, in a conciliar fashion, but not otherwise or after any other fashion'. Opinions vary as to what this papal approbation covered.

Martin V reached Florence on 26 February 1419 and stayed there till 28 September 1420, because Rome was in the hands of Queen Joan of Naples and in any case was in ruins. Other parts of the Papal States were either in revolt or had been seized by usurpers. By diplomacy and prudence the Pope slowly regained control. In 1423, five years after the close of the Council of Constance, he summoned the Council of Pavia-Siena, but the attendance was small and he quickly dissolved it. The Bohemians, far from being appeased by the action of the Council of Constance, had reacted violently. Their troops, with the zeal of fanaticism, spread terror in neighbouring Catholic countries, held Sigismund at bay and disastrously defeated several crusades organized against them by the Pope. The ecclesiastical schism between East and West was also a constant preoccupation of the Pope. Martin, at first optimistic, twice

appointed a legate for a council in Constantinople, but later became more cautious. He had just arranged for a common meeting in Italy and had besides convoked a new general council for the West to meet in Basel, when he died. Eugenius IV (1431–47), who succeeded him, was heir to both those tasks.

Very few attended the opening in 1431 of the Council of Basel. Consequently, Eugenius, involved in war round Rome, ill, and hoping for a council with the Greeks in Italy, prorogued it to meet eighteen months later in Bologna. The Fathers, however, refused to disperse and their numbers steadily increased. Indeed, basing themselves on the decree of conciliar superiority proclaimed at Constance, they bade Eugenius withdraw his dissolution and present himself before the council. Conciliarism had come to open war with the Papacy, and, as the council favoured reform, the Pope was presumed to oppose it. The nations, England and a few Italian states excepted, supported Basel. Nearly all the cardinals deserted the Pope. Eugenius made one concession after another but, in spite of the persuasions of Sigismund, crowned Holy Roman Emperor by the Pope in May 1433, the council would accept nothing that savoured of papal supremacy. In December 1433 Eugenius withdrew his dissolution. That, however, did not end the antagonism. The council really believed that it was the supreme authority in the Church and acted on its belief. It set up a Curia to transact all normal business, appointed legates *a latere*, granted indulgences and matrimonial dispensations, negotiated with Bohemians and Greeks without reference to the Pope, and legislated to reduce the Papacy to financial dependence.

This legislation, forbidding all taxes and dues at appointments to benefices which were to be filled by election and not by nomination, was ideally good but, as a measure that brooked no exception, impracticable, because it provided for no compensating sources of revenue. The Papacy was an essential part of the Church with a right to support from the Church. The council itself shortly found that, for its own maintenance and later for the upkeep of its anti-Pope, it had to have recourse to what it had forbidden to the Papacy. In addition to these chief reforms, the Council of Basel legislated also on the qualities of Popes and cardinals and on the behaviour of clerics. The sum total, however, achieved by its reforming activity was sadly out of proportion to the time and labour expended, which were dissipated far too much on the fight with the Papacy.

Discussions with the Bohemians were begun in Basel in January 1433 and continued by five embassies sent by the council to Prague and elsewhere between 1433 and 1436. The Bohemians wanted what was in effect an independent and all-inclusive Church and Communion under both kinds. The council, obviously, could not grant the former, but it allowed the latter for those who already had the practice. The agreement, more apparent than real, was proclaimed in the 'Compactata of Iglau' on 5 July 1436, which gave a certain peace to the Church (though the Bohemians steadily refused to join the Council of Basel) and let Sigismund occupy the throne.

Envoys were exchanged also with Constantinople and in September 1434 the decree *Sicut pia mater* settled the conditions on which the Greek Church would attend a council in the West. It was to take place in one of a number of specified towns. The Council of Basel, however, afraid of papal prestige in Italy, tried to impose acceptance of Avignon, a town not on the list. The Greeks refused; Eugenius remonstrated; the Council itself split on the question, the majority voting for Avignon, the 'healthier' minority for observance of the agreement. Eugenius, appealed to by the

Eugenius IV (1431–47) came into conflict with the Council of Basel, which opened in 1431 and affirmed the superiority of General Councils to the Pope.
The Council refused to accept the dissolution decreed by Eugenius, who was forced to make numerous concessions. The authority of the Pope was supported by the Emperor Sigismund. Two episodes from the life of Eugenius from the contemporary bronze doors of St Peter's by Filarete.
Far left the entry of the Pope and Sigismund into Rome and *left* the coronation of Sigismund by Eugenius in 1433

Schisms and Councils

The Romanesque façade of the Cathedral of Ferrara built in 1135. Here the Council of Ferrara first met in January 1438 in an attempt to end the differences between the Greek and Latin Churches. The Council was attended by the Emperor John Paleologus, the Patriarch of Constantinople and twenty metropolitans and representatives from Alexandria, Antioch, Jerusalem, Russia, and Georgia

Greek envoys and the minority undertook to fulfil *Sicut pia mater* and acted immediately. When in September 1437 two fleets, one papal and the other conciliar, appeared off Constantinople to transport the Greeks to Italy, Emperor and Patriarch chose the Pope's. Eugenius translated the Council of Basel to meet in Ferrara. One cardinal, a few bishops and some three hundred clerics refused and became a council in miniature – a threat to Eugenius and a reminder of the claim that General Councils were superior to Popes.

The council opened in Ferrara on 8 January 1438. Eugenius arrived on 24 January, the day on which, as it happened, the remnant at Basel declared him suspended and deprived of all power both spiritual and temporal, which it assumed for itself. The Greeks – Emperor and Patriarch of Constantinople, procurators of the other three oriental patriarchs, a score of metropolitans, clerics and courtiers, in all some 700 – reached Venice on 8 February and Ferrara in the beginning of March. They had come to work for ecclesiastical union and also to obtain military aid from the West for their homeland, threatened by the Turks. The council was solemnly inaugurated on 9 April, but, apart from some private conferences about Purgatory, did not begin its dogmatic discussions till October.

The first subject to be debated, chosen by the Greeks, was whether the Western Church had acted lawfully in adding to the Nicene Creed the words 'and from the Son' after 'I believe in the Holy Ghost ... who proceeds from the Father'. The Greeks declared the addition illegal because the Council of Ephesus (AD 431) had forbidden any change whatsoever in the Creed. The Latins maintained that the prohibition referred not to the formulation of the Creed but to its content. After fourteen sessions there was still no agreement. Then, because of plague and financial difficulties, Eugenius moved the council to Florence, where the doctrine that the addition implies was discussed – does the Holy Spirit proceed from the Father only, as the Greeks asserted, or, as the Latins held, from Father and Son. Eight sessions in March 1439 brought no accord. The Greeks refused to attend further public sessions with, as they said, their interminable arguments. They were already sixteen months away from home and no nearer union. There was an atmosphere of pessimism which was not lightened till the Pope addressed the council on 27 May 1439. Thereupon

After fourteen abortive sessions, and threatened by plague and financial difficulties, the Council was transferred from Ferrara to Florence. The movement of this great assembly was depicted in the form of the *Journey of the Magi*, a series of frescoes by Benozzo Gozzoli in the Palazzo Riccardi Medici, Florence. *Right* A detail showing John Paleologus, Emperor of Constantinople

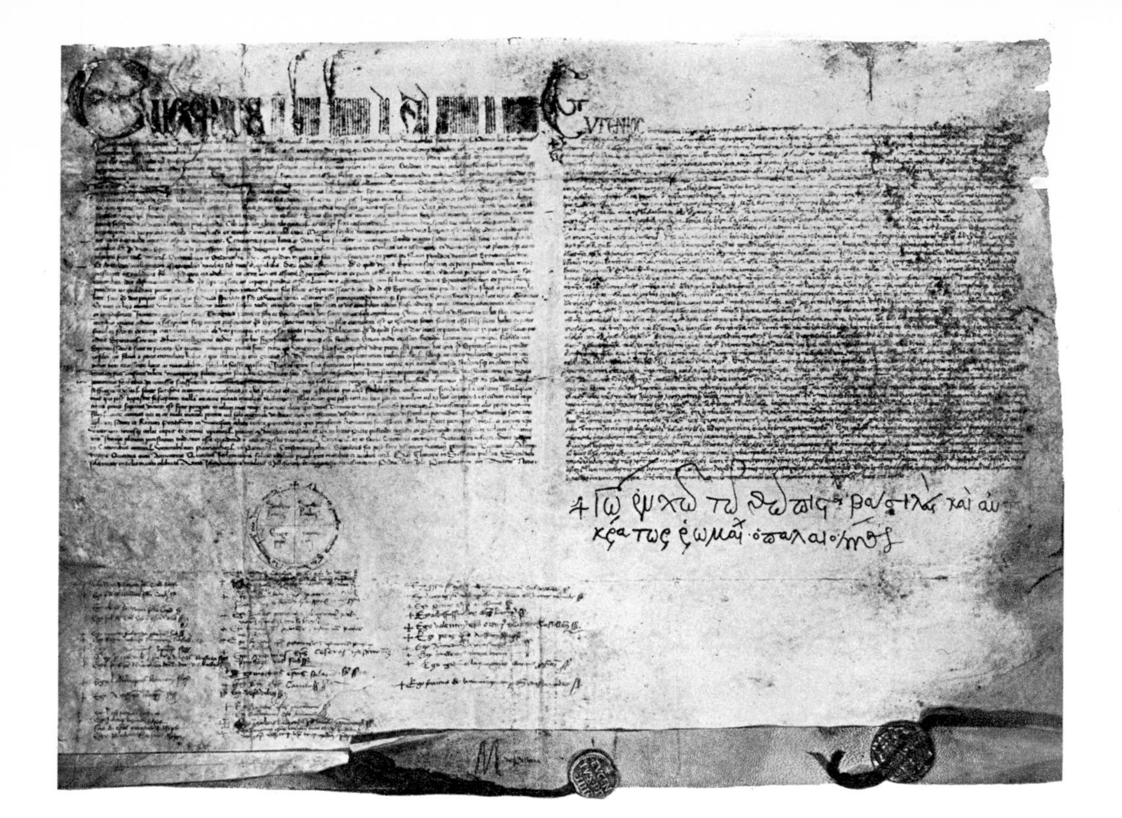

Schisms and Councils

Left In 1439 the Council at Florence pronounced a solemn decree of union between the Greek and Roman Churches. The decree, written in Latin and Greek, carries the lead seal of Eugenius IV on the bottom left and the gold seal of the Emperor John Paleologus underneath his signature on the right

Opposite Eugenius IV commissioning Rannuccio Farnese as military defender of the Papal States. The Farnese family owed their rapid rise to the patronage of Eugenius. A detail from a fresco by Francesco Salviati in the Palazzo Farnese

the unionists among the Greeks renewed their efforts. They pressed home an axiom accepted by all Greeks, that all saints must agree in faith, because as saints they are inspired by the Holy Spirit. Latin saints with their 'From the Son' and Greek saints saying 'Through the Son' had, therefore, substantially the same belief, though their expression of it differed. The two Churches, then, held the same faith and not only could, but should, unite, without either of them denying its past.

Thus, in early June, honest agreement was reached on the chief difference that divided the Churches. A few days later the Patriarch, Joseph II, died suddenly. During the next few weeks there was agreement also on the Eucharist, Purgatory and the primacy of the Pope. Union of the two Churches was solemnly promulgated in the Duomo of Florence on 6 July.

On 13 August, before the last of the Greeks had departed, Armenian delegates arrived. Union with them was proclaimed by the 'Decree for the Armenians' in December. Two years later, the Copts of Egypt and, after the translation of the council from Florence to Rome in autumn 1443, Syrians, Maronites from Cyprus and Chaldeans accepted union with Rome. The ultimate fate of all these unions is not known, but probably they lasted till the respective countries were overrun by the Turks. Certainly the union with the Greeks ended at the fall of Constantinople in 1453, but it had been seriously challenged before that. It might have had a happier issue if the crusade that Eugenius organized had been victorious. But most European countries were too engrossed in their own affairs to see further than their own immediate interests. Poles and Hungarians composed the army; the fleet was provided by the Pope, Venice and Burgundy. The crusade was vanquished at Varna in November 1444 and consequently eastern Europe was exposed for two centuries to Turkish arms.

The rump-council of Basel continued. In November 1439 it elected an anti-Pope, Felix V (1439–49), who was supported by Poland-Lithuania and a few other countries. France and Germany, while favouring conciliar superiority, declared themselves neutral as between Pope and Basel, adopted (and adapted) such Basel reforms as suited them and paid money to neither party. By ambassadors Eugenius influenced the princes and by encyclicals refuted the claims of Basel. The Council of Constance, he wrote, when it enunciated the principle of conciliar superiority, was not a general council for it represented only one of the three 'Obediences' into which the Church was split and that without a head; moreover, Basel had distorted even that principle. Frederick of Austria supported the Pope. The new schism frightened the princes. The star of Basel waned, but the *Conciliabulum* survived Eugenius who died in February 1447.

In the fifteenth century reform was greatly needed, but the measures of neither Constance nor Basel were effective, and Florence did nothing at all, though Eugenius, a reformer at heart, fostered the reforming movements within the religious orders. The extravagances of Basel illustrated the dangers inherent in the conciliarism of Constance, which would have changed the constitution of the Church from a monarchy to a kind of parliamentary régime subject to all the evils attendant on national rivalries. Florence defeated conciliarism and, even though the unions it effected did not endure, it blazed the trail for later and lasting unions by establishing the principle of all unions: unity of faith, not necessarily uniformity of rite.

10 THE RENAISSANCE POPES

NICHOLAS V to LEO X 1447-1521

GERARD CULKIN

The Popes were among the greatest patrons of art of the Renaissance and the churches and palaces of Rome are full of the finest European painting and sculpture, which they commissioned from the greatest artists of the period. Many of Rome's most beautiful churches date from this time, as does the Vatican Library with its unique collection of manuscripts. The Popes themselves were often scholars in their own right and discriminating patrons, but they became increasingly preoccupied with the splendour of their courts and the advancement of their own families. In many cases, notably the Borgia Pope, Alexander VI, their lives were openly scandalous. Despite the threat of Turkish invasion on the one hand, and on the other the growing unrest, especially in Germany, at papal financial abuses, the Popes made no attempt to set their house in order, so that the Reformation became almost inevitable.

TOMMASO PARENTUCELLI, THE CARDINAL BISHOP OF Bologna, who now succeeded as Nicholas V (1447–55), was an experienced diplomat. Within two years he brought to an end the schism which had for so long divided the Church: the anti-Pope Felix V abdicated and the Council of Basel was dissolved after formally recognizing the new Pope. It was the end of the conciliar movement, but a fresh danger now appeared in the East.

Constantinople was threatened by the Turks. In reply to the Greek Emperor's appeal, Nicholas V promised money and men but insisted that the Act of Union, which had been agreed at Florence in 1439, should first be promulgated. Against the wishes of the Greek clergy and people this was done in December 1452; less than eight months later Constantinople fell to the Turks. The renewal of the crusade was now the most urgent of all the tasks facing the Papacy.

Italy at this time was in the full tide of an astonishing outburst of creative energy in literature and the arts, and for fifty years the Popes were among the chief patrons of a movement which made of Rome the capital of the world of art. Nicholas V was the first and the best of these Renaissance Popes: undistinguished as a scholar, he was a passionate collector of manuscripts and the founder of the Vatican Library. In Rome he restored the aqueducts and more than forty churches, planned the rebuilding of St Peter's, and commissioned Fra Angelico to decorate the papal apartments. His successors were to emulate his patronage of the arts while increasingly neglecting the more important duties of their office.

Of these the first was Calixtus III (1455–58), a Spaniard, Alfonso Borgia, Bishop of Valencia and Cardinal secretary. A lawyer with little interest in the arts, from the day of his election Calixtus devoted all his energies to the urgent business of the crusade, selling the papal jewels to equip a fleet. At Belgrade in July 1456 a force under the Hungarian leader John Hunyadi, supported by crusaders from the West, inflicted a crushing defeat on the Turks. But the victory was not followed up; there was little enthusiasm for the war and a council of ambassadors summoned to Rome by the Pope in 1458 accomplished nothing. Calixtus was largely to blame for the failure of his plans; he alienated sympathy by the favours he showered on his countrymen and above all on his nephews, chief among them Rodrigo Borgia whom he made cardinal and papal chancellor.

Aeneas Silvius Piccolomini, the Cardinal of Siena, succeeded as Pius II (1458–64). A former supporter of the Council of Basel and at one time secretary of the anti-Pope Felix V, his earlier life had not been without scandal. He was a distinguished poet and scholar, the author of a remarkable history of his own times, and it was the great ambition of his life to unite all the Christian kings in a vast crusade for the recovery of Constantinople. A congress met at Mantua to discuss the plan but the crusading ideal was now dead. In Germany, rapidly falling into a state of anarchy, the Emperor Frederick had plans to conquer Hungary, which was already threatened by the Turks. The French king had his eye on Naples; Italy was hopelessly

Alexander VI (1492–1503), the Borgia Pope under whom the Renaissance Papacy reached its lowest level of corruption. A detail from Pinturicchio's fresco of the Resurrection in the Borgia Apartments of the Vatican

divided by the rivalries of the city states, and in Rome itself there were plots against the papal government. After five years of tireless effort on the part of the Pope, a fleet was finally assembled, and Pius II now announced that he would lead the crusade himself. In the summer of 1464 he left Rome for Ancona, and there he died, disillusioned, as the ships from Venice came in sight on 14 August.

Two weeks later the cardinals elected Pietro Barbo of Venice as Paul II (1464–71). A wealthy patrician, the nephew of Eugenius IV, liberal, good-natured, and with a taste for ostentation, Paul II was an indifferent scholar but a generous patron of the new art of printing and an enthusiastic collector of antiquities. In Rome he began the building of the Palazzo Venezia, one of the finest monuments of the Renaissance and the usual residence of the Popes for nearly a century.

In Rome there was much discontent with the papal government. In 1468 the papal police discovered a plot to murder the Pope and set up a republic. Among the ringleaders were two of the leading scholars of the day, Platina and the eccentric Julius Pomponius Laetus. Under torture both confessed and both were pardoned. Platina became the librarian of the Vatican and the author of a famous and scurrilous history of the Popes.

The years of Paul II's Pontificate were marked by new and alarming advances of the Turks. The fleet which Pius II had assembled was dispersed as soon as he was dead and all his successor's efforts to raise a new crusade failed before the indifference and the intrigues of the Christian kings and princes. The Pope sent money and supplies to Hungary and to Skanderbeg in Albania, but after the death of

Right Nicholas V (1447–55) was the first and one of the best of the Renaissance Popes. This fresco by Fra Angelico from the Chapel of Nicholas V shows Nicholas as Sixtus II giving alms for St Lawrence to distribute to the poor. Nicholas planned the rebuilding of St Peter's, founded the Vatican Library, and did much building in the palace, including the chapel, which he commissioned Fra Angelico to decorate

Opposite left Calixtus III (1455–58) devoted all his energies to the assembly of a crusade against the Turks, made more urgent by the fall of Constantinople in 1453. The Christian forces defeated the Turks in 1456, but the victory was not followed up. The Virgin Mary appearing to Calixtus outside the walls of Siena, by Sano di Pietro

Opposite right A miniature illuminated portrait of Paul II (1464–71) from *Antichità Romane* by Dionysius of Halicarnassus in an Italian Renaissance translation. Paul, a wealthy patrician, was an enthusiastic collector of antiquities and showed an early interest in the revolutionary art of printing

O PASTOR dESNIO ALMIO POPOL XPIANO
A TE dI SIENA ORMAI LACURA RELIdO
FA CH ALLEI VOLGA OGNI TUO SENSO HUMANO
CALISTUS III · SANUS PETRI dE SENI PIXIT

PAVLVS II VENETVS

The Renaissance Popes

Skanderbeg in 1468 the country fell to the Turks. Two years later they took the important Venetian colony of Negropont (the Peloponnese). Italy was now threatened, and some months before his death Paul II persuaded the Italian cities to form a league for the defence of the country.

His successor, Sixtus IV (1471–84), was a Franciscan friar of exemplary life, Francesco della Rovere. As Minister-General of his order he had shown outstanding talents as an administrator and reformer, but his good judgment now deserted him. Shortly after his election he made two of his numerous nephews cardinals, Giuliano, the future Pope Julius II, and the dissolute Riario, a friar like his uncle, who died within a year, worn out by his debaucheries. Five other nephews were raised to the purple, two more were married to the illegitimate daughters of the King of Naples, one to the daughter of the Duke of Milan, and another, Girolamo, to the daughter of the Duke of Urbino.

Pius II (1458–64) worked tirelessly to launch another crusade against the Turks. When a force was finally assembled he declared himself its leader, but died shortly afterwards. The arrival of Pius II in Ancona, one of a series of frescoes by Pinturicchio depicting the life of Pius in the library of the cathedral at Siena, where Pius was a cardinal

Right Sixtus IV (1471–84) appointing Platina Librarian of the Vatican, by Melozzo da Forlì. Sixtus, who had been a strict Franciscan, became as Pope a typical Renaissance monarch. He commissioned the Sistine Chapel and re-organized the Vatican Library, but his nepotism knew no bounds

Following pages Part of the ceiling of the Hall of the Liberal Arts in the Borgia Apartments, with the Borgia arms in the centre and the Borgia bull emblem on the extreme left and right. This ceiling, the work of Pinturicchio and others, is decorated with figures representing the arts and sciences. A detail showing, on the left, Rhetoric holding a sword and globe and, on the right, Geometry holding a set square and compasses, with Euclid at her feet drawing a diagram

Left A detail from Pinturicchio's fresco in the Sala dei Santi, *St Catherine of Alexandria disputing with the philosophers before the Emperor Maximian*. The figure on the right is a portrait of the Turkish prince Djem, who was a prisoner in the papal court at the time

Right The Triumph of St Thomas Aquinas by Filippo Lippi. In the right foreground are the future Medici Popes, Leo x and Clement vii, as boys. A fresco from S Maria Sopra Minerva

This excessive devotion to his family was a disaster for the Pope and for the Church. Girolamo della Rovere plotted with the Pope's bankers, the Pazzi, and the Archbishop of Florence to murder Lorenzo the Magnificent and his brother Giuliano. The attempted assassination took place in the cathedral of Florence on 26 May 1478. Giuliano was killed, but Lorenzo escaped. The plotters, including the Archbishop, were captured and executed. The Pope was in some measure privy to the plot and now excommunicated Lorenzo and declared war on Florence. The sudden shock of the capture of Otranto by the Turks in 1480 brought about a temporary truce, but later in his Pontificate Sixtus was involved in further wars with Ferrara and Milan in the interests of his ambitious nephews.

With Sixtus iv the character of the Papacy was changed. The Pope was now little more than an Italian prince, wholly absorbed by temporal interests, and, above all, by the ambitions of his family, careless of the mounting scandals in the Curia and indifferent to the needs of the Church. Sixtus did, indeed, make some attempt to stem the advance of the Turks in Europe, but with the death of Mahomet ii, the conqueror of Constantinople, in 1481, the crusade was no longer a pressing problem.

Sixtus iv, who made no serious attempt to reform the Church, was a discriminating patron of the arts: Rome was now the rival of Florence and the Pope himself was one of the greatest figures of the Renaissance. He reorganized and enlarged the Vatican Library, built roads and bridges and many new churches, among them S Maria della Pace and S Maria del Popolo. His greatest monument is the Sistine Chapel, decorated by the famous Florentine masters whom the Pope summoned to Rome: Pinturicchio, Perugino, Botticelli, Ghirlandaio.

The death of Sixtus iv in August 1484 was followed by two weeks of mob violence in Rome and a bitter contest between the rival factions in the Curia. The election of Innocent viii (1484–92) was a triumph for Cardinal Giuliano della Rovere, whose own ambitions were defeated by the intrigues of the papal chancellor, Rodrigo Borgia. The new Pope, John Baptist Cibò, was a Genoese, kindly affable, but sickly and incompetent, whose Pontificate was one of the most disastrous in the history of the Papacy.

He was the first of the Popes publicly to recognize his illegitimate children, for whom he organized splendid marriages. Within a year he drifted into a war with Ferrante of Naples who refused to pay the tribute which the Pope claimed as the King's suzerain. Innocent offered the throne of Naples to a French claimant, René of Anjou, and for a time brought Ferrante to his senses. Later he found an ally in Lorenzo the Magnificent of Florence to whose daughter he married his son, Franceschetto, and to whose son, Giovanni, a boy of thirteen, he gave the cardinal's hat.

Innocent was an improvident ruler, the papal finances were in a deplorable state, and to raise funds the Pope sold appointments in the papal court to the highest bidders who then recouped themselves by selling forged bulls. When the practice was discovered two of the chief offenders were hanged and publicly burned, but the scandal was enormous.

Only in his dealings with the Turks did Innocent achieve a modest diplomatic success. On the death of the sultan Mahomet II in 1481 his son and successor, Bajazet, quarrelled with his younger brother, Djem, who sought safety with the Knights of St John in the island of Rhodes. In 1489 Djem was handed over to the Pope as a hostage for the sultan's good behaviour.

With the accession of Rodrigo Borgia, the nephew of Calixtus III, as Alexander VI (1492–1503), the Papacy reached the depths of degradation. A cardinal and vice-chancellor of the Roman Church for thirty-five years, charming, cultured, and a notorious evil liver, Borgia bribed his way to the papal throne. He was the father of four children born of a Roman mistress, and for eleven years he sacrificed the reputation and the temporal interests of the Holy See to the ambitions of his worthless bastards. The greater scandal was the fact that the election of such a man caused scarcely a stir of protest in the Church. In Florence the Dominican friar Girolamo Savonarola, persuaded that he was inspired by God to rescue the Papacy from its shame, denounced the Pope, the Curia and the Borgia family, and appealed to the Christian kings to depose Alexander and save the Church. When, in 1494, the French king, Charles VIII, appeared in Italy to assert his claims to Milan and Naples, Savonarola greeted him as a saviour; but when Charles arrived in Rome the Pope charmed him into a humble submission of obedience, and at Florence the people, alarmed at the increasing excesses of Savonarola, burned him at the stake as a heretic.

In 1497 Alexander's favourite son, Juan, Duke of Gandia, was murdered in obscure circumstances. In his grief, as profound as it was sincere, the Pope announced that he would mend his ways and devote himself to the reform of the Church. A commission of cardinals was charged to draw up a plan of reform, but this was soon forgotten when, in the next year, the new King of France, Louis XII, who sought the nullification of his marriage, offered in return for the favour to make the Pope's son, Caesar, Duke of Valence. With Alexander VI family interest outweighed every other consideration. When he died in 1503 the Papal States had become little more than an appendage of the Borgia family.

Francesco Piccolomini, a nephew of Pius II, elected as Pius III in September 1503, died within a month after announcing that he intended to hold a general council for the reform of the Church. He was succeeded by a nephew of Sixtus IV, Girolamo della Rovere, Julius II (1503–13), who, in spite of chronic ill-health, applied himself for nearly ten years with astonishing energy and single-mindedness to the restoration of the Papal States.

Rome at this time was in a state of near anarchy: the Pope was not safe in his own city. Within three years Julius II had restored order, reformed the administration and the finances, and created a Swiss guard for his own protection. The city now underwent a remarkable transformation. New streets and roads were laid out, the bed of the Tiber was diverted to avoid the danger of flooding, the ramparts were strengthened, new churches were built and the Vatican museum was enriched with many remarkable monuments of antiquity. In 1506 the Pope laid the first

Left The Borgia crests carved in stone in the Castel Sant' Angelo and *Right* a portrait of Alexander VI, with the Borgia bulls on either side, from the Sala dei Santi in the Borgia Apartments

Above Savonarola, the fiery Dominican monk and preacher, denounced the immorality and corruption of the Renaissance Popes. But the people of Florence turned against him and he was hanged and burned as a heretic in the main square of the city. An anonymous painting

The Renaissance Popes

Right The figure of Moses by Michelangelo, from the tomb of Julius II (1503–13), which the Pope commissioned himself. Like Moses, Julius was a warrior as well as a spiritual leader and strove to maintain the papal political power in Italy

Below A silver crucifix intended for the high altar of St Peter's. Of the finest Renaissance craftsmanship, it is the work of Antonio Gentile, from a design by Michelangelo

stone of the new St Peter's. Raphael was commissioned to decorate the papal apartments and Michelangelo to prepare a fitting funeral monument for the Pope.

Much of the papal territory in Romagna was occupied by the Venetians. Julius joined the republic's enemies in the League of Cambrai and at the head of his troops recovered Faenza, Rimini and Ravenna. He then formed a Holy League in alliance with Venice, Spain and the Empire to drive the French out of Italy.

Louis XII retaliated by threatening to withdraw the Church in France from the papal obedience. Supported by nine cardinals he summoned a council which met at Pisa to hear his case against the warrior Pope. Julius II replied by calling a general council of the Church which met at the Lateran in May 1512. It was to continue until 1517; it held few sessions and it was poorly attended, but it broke the effort of the French king to divide the Church against the Pope.

Leo X (1513–21) was the last of the Renaissance Popes. Giovanni de' Medici, the eldest surviving son of Lorenzo the Magnificent of Florence and a cardinal from the age of thirteen, was cultured, kind and chaste, but completely unfitted for the task to which he was now called. But he

A portrait of Julius II as the priest in *The Miracle of the Mass at Bolsena* by Raphael. The great series of rooms in the Vatican decorated by Raphael were commissioned by Julius

Leo X (1513–21), the son of Lorenzo de Medici, the Magnificent. A weak and extravagant man, he squandered much of the achievement of Julius II. He was defeated when Francis I invaded Italy, and was forced to concede to him almost complete control of the French Church. His support of indulgences to raise money for the rebuilding of St Peter's was the immediate cause of Luther's protest. A drawing of Leo attributed to Sebastiano del Piombo

was a peace-maker. The rebel cardinals of Pisa were pardoned and restored to their offices, and in 1513 a solemn reconciliation with Louis XII took place. The new peace with France was short-lived. In 1515 Louis was succeeded by the young and energetic Francis I, and within the year a new French army shattered the Swiss and the Pope's allies at Marignano and occupied Milan. At Bologna the Pope was obliged to sign a concordat which gave Francis I almost complete control over the Church in France.

The humiliation of Bologna and the Pope's contemptuous neglect of the cardinals provoked a revolt in the Curia led by Cardinal Petrucci. A plot to poison the Pope was discovered; three at least of the cardinals were implicated and Petrucci, after trial and torture, was executed.

Leo X soon squandered the treasure accumulated by Julius II, and to raise the much-needed funds for the building of St Peter's he renewed the indulgence granted by his predecessor to those who contributed alms for the purpose. It was the scandalous preaching of this indulgence in Germany which provoked the opposition of Martin Luther; and it was Luther's passionate denunciation of the scandals of the Roman Church which prepared the way for the Protestant Reformation.

The old basilica of St Peter from a sixteenth-century fresco. Despite medieval additions and decoration, it was still basically the classical basilica built by Constantine, with the nave and double aisles. This part of the church was retained for a period when the rest was demolished for the re-building under Julius II

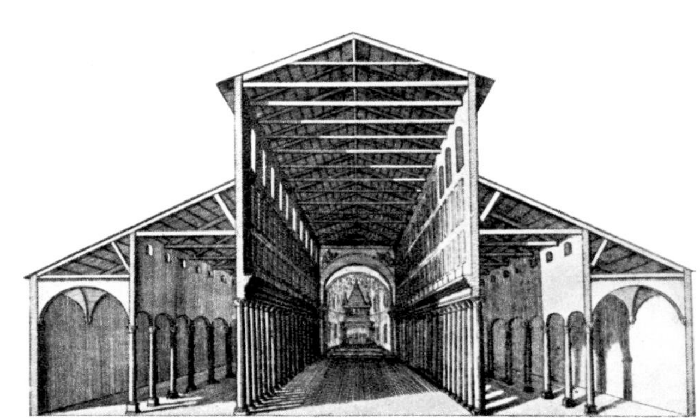

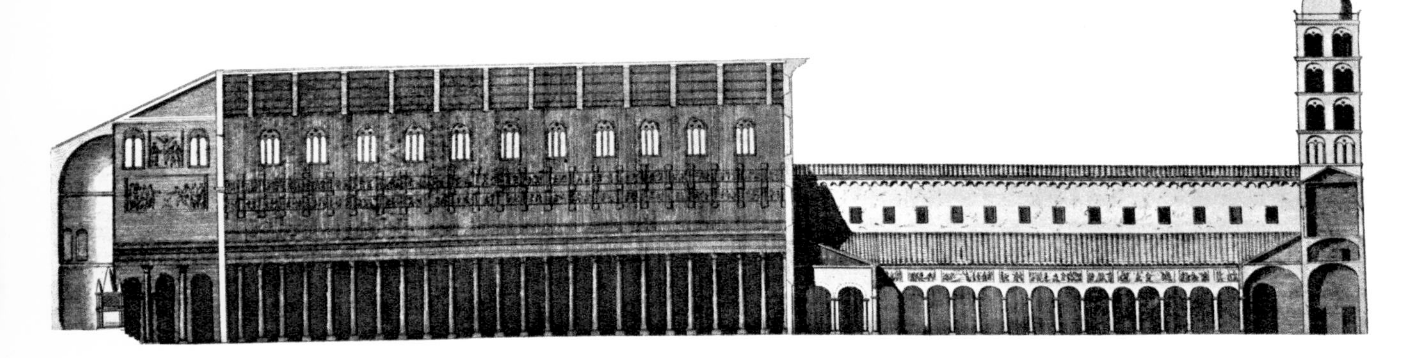

Engravings of the old basilica showing the original façade and the position of the tomb of St Peter in the apse at the end of the long nave and broad transept

11 THE BASILICA OF ST PETER AND THE VATICAN PALACES

PAOLO BREZZI

The original Vatican basilica was built by the Emperor Constantine over the traditional site of the tomb of St Peter. It was restored by Leo the Great in the middle of the fifth century. The present St Peter's is the work of the Popes of the sixteenth century, who commissioned the greatest designers, architects and artists of the time to contribute to the new basilica. Many of the most famous Vatican buildings date from the late sixteenth and seventeenth centuries, although the Sistine Chapel was begun in 1473. These buildings contain some of the finest examples of European painting and sculpture.

THE DIFFICULTIES WHICH FACED THE EMPEROR CONstantine in building the Vatican basilica were so many and so complex that nothing but the belief that he was erecting a great memorial over St Peter's tomb can explain his determination to undertake the task. The existence of a cemetery on the site, the difficult terrain and the differences in level were powerful arguments against proceeding with the enterprise.

From the beginning of the fourth century onwards the Vatican area has been the focus for impressive architectural and artistic activity, by both civil and ecclesiastical authorities. According to the *Liber Pontificalis* it was Pope Anacletus in the last quarter of the first century who built a *Memoria*, or cell, over the burial place of the apostle and initiated the custom of burying the Bishops of Rome round it. There is not sufficient information about the succeeding Popes to make any definite statement about their contribution to enlarging and beautifying the *Memoria*. Constantine endowed the basilica with a revenue of 3,710 gold *soldi* from the Imperial funds. He also gave 4,070 *soldi* to St Paul's and no less than 10,234 to the Lateran Baptistry. There is nothing to show that Bishops Miltiades and Sylvester, who held office during the reign of Constantine, were particularly concerned with the building of the Church of St Peter, nor indeed with any other enterprise. Constantine's personality dominated the whole scene.

The situation changed radically when the Emperors abandoned Rome for Byzantium and the city gradually came under ecclesiastical influence, even though from a juridical point of view the Popes did not yet enjoy really independent political power. Financially, too, the position of the Roman Church improved greatly and it had large sums available for building. One need mention only one name, that of Leo I, the Great (440–61); the *Liber Pontificalis* states that he rebuilt St Peter's, but this is probably an exaggeration. In all probability what he did was to restore the basilica – which may have been damaged during the sack of Rome by the Vandal king Genseric – and enrich it with valuable and impressive mosaics, which apparently decorated the apse and the façade at this time; on the latter were portrayed the twenty-four elders of the Apocalypse in the act of offering gifts to Christ, while above them were reproduced the symbols of the four evangelists. Half-way through the thirteenth century these mosaics could still be seen on the pediment of the basilica.

The *Itinerari*, or guide books, which have been preserved in considerable numbers, give a fairly detailed description of both the exterior and interior of the basilica as it appeared to the faithful during the High Middle Ages, while some late drawings and reproductions contain further information of great historical and artistic interest. From the spacious *piazza* – known as St Peter's *curtain* – there were thirty-five steps up to an uncovered area, paved in marble, used for the great coronation ceremonies. At the far end was the quadruple portico with slender arches along the galleries, enclosing a courtyard, in the centre of which, under a tabernacle, was the famous pine-cone ornament mentioned by Dante. The side backing on to the

St Peter's and the Vatican

Right St Peter's square decorated for the celebration of the Feast of Corpus Christi. This anonymous seventeenth-century painting shows the square after the completion of the façade of St Peter's by Maderno in 1612 and the placing of the great obelisk by Sixtus V (*d* 1590), but before Bernini started the colonnades in 1657

Left A drawing of old St Peter's and the Vatican by Marten van Heemskerck, a Dutch artist who lived in Rome from 1532 to 1536. It shows on the left the old façade with the *Loggia della Benedizione* superimposed during the reign of Pius II (1458–64). On the right is the building containing the Raphael *Logge*, or galleries, designed by Bramante to connect the Belvedere Palace and the older pontifical palaces immediately adjoining St Peter's

façade of the basilica was usually known as the *Paradise*, because it was decorated with palms, olives, cedars, and rose-trees symbolizing the earthly paradise; the celestial paradise was of course the church itself. In it were five doors with the *Regia* or Silver door in the centre, and the Roman, the *Ravegnana*, the *Guidonea* and the Door of Judgment (so called because coffins passed through it on the way to burial) on the sides, each door being placed between two columns surmounted by capitals. Marble slabs, altars and mosaics decorated the entrance, and there were many tombs of Popes, sovereigns and pilgrims set in the floor, since it was considered a great honour to be able to await the Last Judgment and the return of Christ in glory near St Peter's tomb.

The interior of the church was divided into five naves with a wide transept and a single apse; it was approximately 230 feet wide and 400 feet long. On the walls were medallions of the various Popes, as well as paintings portraying scenes from the Old and New Testaments. From the beams hung chandeliers, crosses, crowns and purple *velaria*. The upkeep of all these treasures was the responsibility of the Popes, who made any decisions about new works, restorations, modifications and extensions. A flight of eight steps led up to the High Altar, which was covered by a ciborium resting on columns of porphyry and surmounted by a gold dome, and another flight of steps led to the Confessional (or tomb), where a hundred lamps burned night and day. Amongst the priceless objects was a gold crucifix weighing two hundred pounds and a silver one of the same size. Unfortunately during the Sack of Rome by the Saracens in the middle of the ninth century the most costly and precious relics were stolen and they could not be replaced with others of the same value.

Smaller churches and oratories surrounded the Basilica of St Peter and they also received donations from the Popes – as set down in detail in the *Liber Pontificalis* under the biography of the individual Popes – and from famous people, both lay and ecclesiastical, who came on pilgrimages to Rome. There were also numerous hospices or *scholae* in the neighbourhood, which took their name from the various European peoples, for example Saxonum and Frisonum, and which owed their existence to the Popes' concern for those who undertook the long and difficult journey from their own country to the holy shrine of Peter. These *scholae* had to be maintained and the cost was met by the income from properties in various parts of Italy owned

A papal cortège crossing the bridge from the great fortress, the Castel Sant' Angelo. An anonymous early seventeenth-century painting

The architect first entrusted by Julius II with the work of rebuilding St Peter's in 1505 was Bramante. His original plan was for a huge domed church in the form of a Greek cross. He was succeeded by Raphael, who adopted the form of a Latin cross with a long nave *right* suited to great ceremonial occasions

Other designs followed. The work was continued by the seventy-year-old Michelangelo, who reverted to the form of a Greek cross *centre*, with the great dome which was his masterpiece. The engraving *far right* shows the façade as Michelangelo conceived it. His design was modified fifty years after his death by the addition of the long nave by Maderno

St Peter's and the Vatican

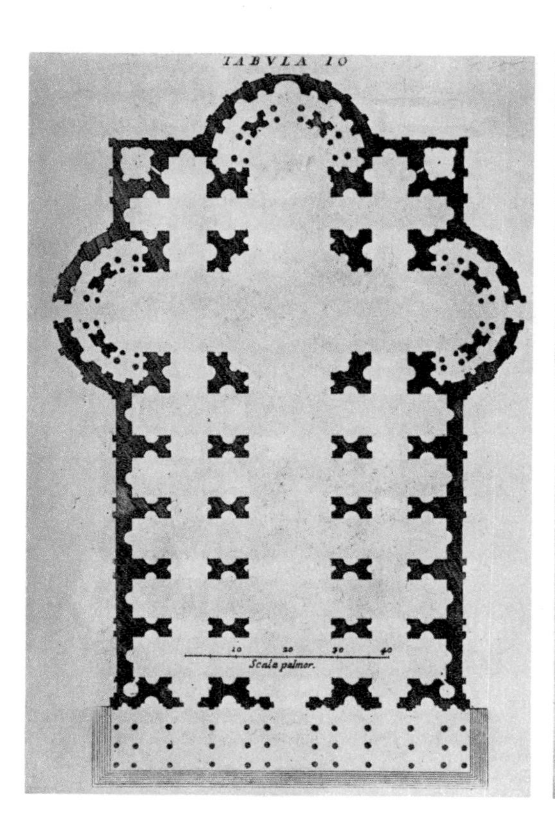

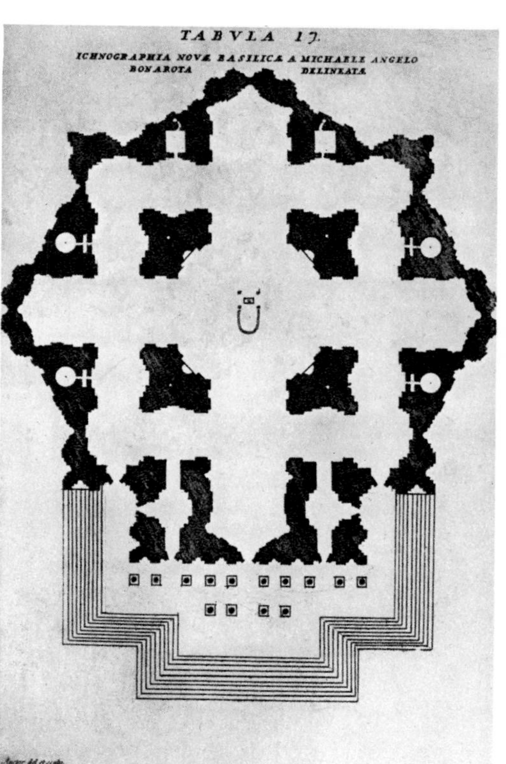

by the Popes. During the Middle Ages the Vatican area, under the spiritual and practical leadership of the Bishops of Rome, was the centre of a vigorous life, focused on the basilica. The Curia, or central government of the Church, was not located there at this time, because the Pope and his retinue lived in the Lateran *patriarchium* and only came to St Peter's in procession for certain solemn celebrations and religious functions. Of all these the most famous was undoubtedly the Jubilee of 1300 proclaimed by Boniface VIII and subsequently immortalized in the *Navicella* or *Bark of Peter* which Cardinal Stefaneschi commissioned from Giotto, whose mosaic can still be seen in the atrium of the basilica.

Though they did not live in the Vatican, the Popes did build a residence or *episcopia* there, which could be used in an emergency. It was not until the reign of Nicholas III (1277–80) that the Pope took up a permanent residence in the Vatican and traces of the building were discovered about twenty years ago. But the prolonged exile in Avignon during the fourteenth century, as well as the vicissitudes of the period of schism which followed, and the numerous risings in the city of Rome against the Holy See, put an end to any building projects. The new learning and the greater financial prosperity of the Renaissance period once again made it possible to undertake building and town-planning which were to turn the Vatican area into the heart of Christian Rome and the definitive seat of the central ecclesiastical government.

Several hundred years previously another Pope, Leo IV, who reigned in the middle of the ninth century, was responsible for the building of the city walls, known today as the Leonine walls, as a defence against the Saracens. The whole population took part in the work which was afterwards blessed by the Pope in solemn procession. The line of these walls corresponds roughly to the boundaries of the Vatican State today, with its palaces, museums, gardens and churches, which millions of visitors, both pilgrims and tourists, flock to see.

Unfortunately, as is so often the case, the new buildings grew up at the expense of the old, and Constantine's basilica was sacrificed to the pride and ambition of the Renaissance Popes, whose aim was, according to the Italian poet Foscolo, to raise 'a new Olympus to the skies'. The sacrifice was inevitable, because the fabric of the old basilica was crumbling, on account of its age and the method of its construction. Yet one cannot help feeling a certain regret, although the splendour of the new basilica more than compensated for what was destroyed.

The first Pope who thought of replacing the old St Peter's by a new building was Nicholas V (1447–55). The project was entrusted to Bernardo Rossellino who conceived a church in the shape of a Latin cross with a great dome, but work was not started until the reign of Julius II (1503–13), who laid the first stone on 18 April 1506. The building was to be based on a design by Donato Bramante who conceived a building in the form of a Greek cross with

The great reliquary by Bernini glorifying the traditional chair of St Peter. The saints at the base are the Latin Fathers, St Augustine and St Ambrose, and the Greek, St Athanasius and St John Chrysostom, symbolizing the submission of East and West to the Petrine seat

When Michelangelo died in 1564 his dome was not completed and the nave of the old basilica was still in existence. This contemporary engraving of the Pope blessing the crowds from the *Loggia della Benedizione* shows the position very clearly. The dome was completed in 1590 by Fontana

An engraving showing St Peter's Square in 1685. The façade by Maderno was completed in 1612 and Bernini's colonnades in 1663. The obelisk, which once stood in the Circus of Nero, was erected in the square in 1586

St Peter's and the Vatican

A detail from Bernini's colonnades, composed of 288 massive pillars which dwarf the passer-by. This masterpiece has been compared to 'outstretched arms gathering all men together in a gesture of charity'

The dome of St Peter's was completed to Michelangelo's plans by Domenico Fontana. Its soaring thrust to the height of the lantern is one of Michelangelo's greatest achievements

a square area in the centre surmounted by a huge cupola with four smaller cupolas at the sides. The arms of the cross ended in a semi-circular apse and had ambulatories on the outside. At the far ends were to be the *campanili*. The church's total area was to be 28,700 square yards, compared to the 17,350 square yards of the present St Peter's. The forceful personality of Julius II would have dominated the whole building, as an imposing mausoleum adorned with colossal statues was planned for the centre of the church. But the death of both the Pope and Bramante brought the work to a standstill. It was not resumed by the Popes who succeeded him – Leo X and Clement VII – due to the tragic political events of the time, in particular the Sack of Rome. Later there was a campaign to raise money to complete the building, but the dubious methods used were one of the immediate causes of the Lutheran revolt.

Without pausing to describe the contributions to the design of St Peter's made by Raphael, Peruzzi and Sangallo, we must move on to the time of Michelangelo. It was Paul III (1534–49) who entrusted the task of continuing the work on the basilica to Michelangelo, who was then over seventy. Paul III continued to support Michelangelo in spite of the bitter criticism aroused by the changes he made to the original plans. The result is there for all to admire today, but some idea of what was involved in raising a structure of this size can be gained from this contemporary account: 'Wondrous great were the mountains of stone and *pozzolana* which a single part of the foundations absorbed, so that all marvelled how so much matter could be consumed in so little time; in truth there are more works underground, because of the size of the foundations, than above.' To give a few examples: the huge pillars supporting the arches of the dome measure 233 feet in circumference; the base of the dome is 138 feet in diameter; the length of the interior is 610 feet, and the height of the dome is 390 feet on the inside and 435 feet on the outside; the statues in the niches are over sixteen feet high.

When Michelangelo died the construction of the dome had only reached the drum. Sixtus V (1585–90) put the work of constructing the vault of the dome in the hands of Giacomo della Porta and Domenico Fontana. The work was completed in twenty-two months and then the lantern was added and surmounted by the ball and cross. The front part of the church, that is to say the longer arm of the cross, had still to be built, as well as the façade. A competition for the design of the façade was won by Carlo Maderno, who decided to transform Bramante's design of a Greek cross into a Latin cross. The name of Paul V, one of the Roman Borghese family, was inscribed boldly on the completed façade. The work continued from 1607 to

1612 and vast quantities of travertine stone were used – the façade is 160 feet high and 375 feet wide. Many people, both at the time and since, have considered the final result unsatisfactory and both the designer of the façade and his patron, the Pope, came in for serious criticism, although the design has undeniable merits.

The work of completing the interior went on continuously and tombs of the various Popes gradually filled St Peter's with monuments of great beauty. The task of providing a worthy approach to the basilica took up much time and effort. It was Sixtus v who ordered the obelisk, 82 feet high and weighing about 4,500 tons, to be erected in St Peter's square. It had formerly been a *meta* or finishing post at Nero's circus. Later Lorenzo Bernini became the church's chief architect. He was responsible for the bronze baldaquin over the altar of the confessional, the great machine for the papal throne, the ciborium in the chapel of the Sacrament and the facings on the walls, all fine examples of the work of one of the greatest of the baroque architects. But his most famous achievement was the design and construction of the famous colonnade in St Peter's square, built in two arcs leading up to the basilica, and composed of 288 columns and 88 pillars and decorated with 140 statues. The two wings of the colonnade are like outstretched arms gathering all men together in a gesture of charity.

The huge task of building the colonnades was carried out by Bernini between 1657 and 1663, the central period of the pontificate of Alexander vii. It brought to a close a period of over a hundred years which had witnessed the complete renewal of the great church. It has been said with some justice that St Peter's has no unity of style, that it is theatrical, that it consists of a series of disconnected parts. Yet the total effect of St Peter's square and the basilica itself is to convey a sense of certainty, to inspire an overflowing of thanksgiving. This was the aim of the Popes who spent huge sums and overcame tremendous difficulties in order to complete work on the basilica. From the Counter-Reformation onwards the importance of St Peter's steadily increased. This is emphasized by the fact that all the offices of the Holy See were gradually transferred to the vicinity of the basilica, multiplying the number of buildings connected with it.

The eighteenth and nineteenth-century Popes continued to add to the beauties of the church; they built the great sacristy nearby, erected porches and doors, improved access to the sacred tombs under the basilica and added the two beautiful fountains in the piazza. There is hardly a Pope whose name is not associated with some improvement. In more recent times the 'spine' has been demolished, making it much easier for large crowds to move into the

A holy water stoup at the entrance to St Peter's, commissioned and dedicated by Benedict xiii. A charming detail often overlooked in the immensity of St Peter's

The nave of St Peter's in the eighteenth century. A painting by Panini conveying the massive dignity of Maderno's design

Right The interior of old St Peter's by an anonymous sixteenth-century artist. The Roman bronze *pigna*, or pine cone, stood in the atrium and is mentioned by Dante. It was later moved to form the focus of the design of the Belvedere Courtyard. A fresco from S Martino ai Monti

Following pages The Sala Regia, which is the entrance hall to the Sistine Chapel and was originally intended for the reception of foreign ambassadors. It has a magnificent Renaissance ceiling and is decorated with frescoes illustrating the power of the Church. The one on the left, by Francesco Salviati, shows Frederick Barbarossa's submission to Alexander iii at Venice

LEXANDER·PAPA·III·FRIDERICI·PRIMI·IMPERATORIS·IRAM ET
OGNITVM ET A SENATV PERHONORIFICE SVSCEPTVM OTHONE IMPERATORIS FILIO
VENETIS VICTO CAPTOQVE FRIDERICVS PACE FACTA SVPPLEX ADORAT
POLLICITVS ITA PONTIFICI SVA DIGNITAS

PAVLVS·III·PONT·MAX

The Sistine Chapel, built to the order of Sixtus IV in about 1475. The walls are decorated by some of the greatest Renaissance artists, including Botticelli, Pinturicchio and Perugino. Julius II entrusted Michelangelo with the decoration of the ceiling, which was completed in 1512. The frescoes, particularly those of Prophets and Sibyls exploit the difficult shapes in a perfect blend of painting and architecture. *The Last Judgement*, behind the altar, also by Michelangelo, was completed in 1541 and is one of his most dramatic and commanding works

square, but destroying some fine perspectives. Pius XII ordered excavations in the basilica which have considerably increased knowledge of the early history of the Church.

Once again it was Nicholas V who was first responsible for the construction of new palaces in the Vatican near St Peter's. He commissioned Fra Angelico to paint the frescoes in the Chapel of San Lorenzo. Shortly afterwards Sixtus IV ordered the construction of the famous Sistine Chapel which bears his name. From the outside it looks like a fortress with battlements, but inside it is decorated with paintings by all the greatest artists of the Italian Renaissance, culminating in the famous frescoes on the ceiling commissioned from Michelangelo by Julius II, and the *Last Judgement*, painted by Michelangelo between 1536 and 1541 under the patronage of Paul III.

Sixtus IV's successor, Innocent VIII, built the Belvedere palace, which is set a little apart from the rest of the Vatican buildings, while Alexander VI (Rodrigo Borgia) added to the splendour of his court with a series of rooms decorated with frescoes by Pinturicchio.

A magnificent French eighteenth-century monstrance in silver-gilt decorated with gems, used for displaying the Blessed Sacrament in church, or when it is carried in procession. One of the many treasures of the Vatican collection

St Peter's and the Vatican

The Cortile di S Damaso showing the *logge*, or open galleries, designed by Bramante and Raphael before they were enclosed to protect the paintings. The wing on the right was added under Gregory XIII (1572–85). An engraving from a drawing by Panini

Below A view of the Vatican gardens showing the Casino, or Coffee House, of Pius IV. It was designed by Ligorio and Peruzzi, who worked under Raphael on St Peter's in the period between Bramante and Michelangelo

In the field of secular building the name of Julius II stands out above all others, both for grandeur of conception and breadth of achievement. He was able to call on the greatest architects and painters of his day. He commissioned Bramante to re-plan the area between the residential palace and the Belvedere. The layout of this area today does not correspond with Bramante's design, but the few drawings that have survived reveal an original and impressive genius. Julius II also ordered the construction of the *Logge* which is decorated with frescoes by Raphael and paintings by other artists. He also commissioned a new papal apartment, the famous *Stanze* containing paintings by Raphael rich in theological and political meaning. In this comparatively small group of rooms is concentrated numerous masterpieces of Italian art of the early *cinquecento*. The decorations on the doors and floors and the furnishings combine with the paintings to produce the effect of a harmonious whole. The most important of the Raphael rooms is certainly the *segnatura*, so called because it was intended as the meeting place of the ecclesiastical tribunal.

It took three years, from 1508 to 1511, to complete, and it contains, besides allegories of Theology, Philosophy, Poetry and Justice and other biblical and pagan subjects allied to the central theme, the two great frescoes, *The Dispute of the Holy Sacrament* and *The School of Athens*. The Heliodorus room, named after the fresco *The Chastisement of Heliodorus*, also contains three other impressive works: *The Miracle of Bolsena*, *The Liberation of St Peter* and *St Leo the Great and Attila*. The themes of these paintings, like those in the room of the *Fire in the Borgo*, are all connected with the greatness of the Papacy and many of the Popes depicted in the narrative historical frescoes are given the features of the reigning Pope.

The zeal with which the post-Reformation Popes set out to enrich the Vatican was not limited to architecture and painting, but also included providing the Holy See with books and manuscripts by re-arranging the State papers in the Archive and collecting together the most valuable discoveries found in archaeological excavations. Thus the Vatican Library came into being with its 60,000 *codices*, including a priceless Bible and manuscripts of Virgil and Petrarch's *Canonziere*, all housed in rooms decorated with fine frescoes. The various museums were opened – Pio Clementino, Chiaramonti, Gregoriano – whose names recall the seventeenth- and eighteenth-century Popes who first created them. The secret archives were instituted in 1611 by Paul V and were later enriched by further documentary material of the greatest importance. The *nunciatures* section alone contains 6,000 volumes of diplomatic papers which are fundamental to a knowledge of every aspect and period of European history.

To Paul III we owe the Pauline Chapel and the impressive *Sala Regia*; to Pius IV the Belvedere niche and the delightful Villa Pia in the Vatican gardens; to Gregory XIII and Sixtus V the construction of the palaces round the courtyard of St Damasus, with the characteristic oblique wing which overlooks St Peter's square and is today the personal residence of the Pope. The *Scala Regia* was commissioned by Urban VIII to an ambitious and original design by Bernini. Other Popes made valuable contributions by providing buildings for specific purposes, but it was only quite recently, after the reconciliation between the Papacy and the Italian state by the Lateran agreement of February 1929, that a new impetus was given to building in the tiny Vatican City. This was aimed at fitting the new state for the tasks it would have to face. Pius XI (1922–39) built the Governatorato Palace, the railway station, the Vatican Art Gallery, the entrance to the museums and the printing house for the Vatican newspaper.

Today St Peter's and the Vatican have become a unique focus for people of every race and creed. There art is not an end in itself, and grandeur does not set out to be a sign of power. Everything combines to the glory of God and in homage to the place 'where sits great Peter's successor'.

Top The Gallery of Maps, *Galleria delle Carte Geografiche*, forms half the length of the second floor of one side of the *Cortile del Belvedere*. It was completed and decorated in 1580

Centre The Gallery of Statues was created when the Belvedere Palace was refashioned at the end of the eighteenth century by Clement XIV and Pius VI. The papal collection of antiquities had been growing steadily since the Renaissance. The collection of classical statues is now the greatest in the world

Bottom The Borgia Apartments, built for Alexander VI and his family, form another part of the Vatican palaces. Much of their Renaissance decoration, like the ceiling in the Room of the Popes, is classical in style and symbolism

Above The short reign of Adrian VI (1522–23) gave promise of long overdue reform. But his open acknowledgment of the failings of the Holy See and his pledge for reform were greeted with scepticism and he died before he could accomplish much. This detail from his tomb in S Maria dell' Anima shows his entry into Rome in 1522, having been elected *in absentia*

Left Clement VII (1523–34), the second Medici Pope, whose failure to summon a General Council and to pursue a strong policy of reform gave the Protestants an opportunity to consolidate their position. A portrait by Sebastiano del Piombo

12 THE CHALLENGE OF THE REFORMATION

ADRIAN VI to JULIUS III 1522-55

HUBERT JEDIN

Adrian VI was the first Pope to admit the need for reform within the Church, but he died before he could accomplish anything. His successor Clement VII, caught in the conflict between France and the Emperor Charles V, quarrelled with the Emperor and as a result Rome was sacked by Imperial troops in 1527. Meanwhile the Protestant movement gathered strength and Clement failed to take any decisive steps towards reform. Under Paul III a General Council was summoned to meet at Trent in 1542 to try and find a basis for agreement with the German Protestants, but the sessions during his reign and subsequently under Julius III made little progress. The Society of Jesus, approved by Paul III in 1542, was to give new strength to the Catholic Church and become a powerful supporter of the Papacy.

THE GENERATION WHICH GREW UP BETWEEN THE accession of Pope Adrian VI (1522–23) and the epoch-making papal election of 1555 witnessed the transition from the era of the Renaissance to that of Catholic reform. The revolution was achieved under the pressure of the schismatic movement which had started with Luther and Zwingli in Germany and Switzerland, reaching European proportions as it spread into Scandinavia and England and later, under Calvin, into some of the Latin countries. However, this mortal threat to the Papacy at least had the effect of liberating forces of religious revival which had long been in existence but under the Renaissance Popes had been denied an outlet. With their help, a start could be made on the long overdue reform of the Church 'in head and members', and the advance of Protestantism contained. These two strands, the self-renewal of the Church through her own reform and the self-defence of the Church in the Counter-Reformation, are closely interwoven.

The election *in absentia* of Cardinal Adrian of Utrecht on 9 January 1522, a victory for the imperial party in the College of Cardinals, seemed in itself to promise a completely new régime. This pious erstwhile teacher of theology at Louvain and tutor to Charles V was thoroughly imbued with the *devotio moderna* and had nothing in common with his predecessor. The austerity of his household arrangements and the firmness of principle he observed in filling bishoprics and bestowing benefices contrasted sharply with the indifference and irresponsible prodigality displayed by Leo X. Deeply distrustful both of the humanists who had benefited so freely from Leo's generosity and of the papal bureaucrats, the new Pope chose as his closest colleagues two fellow-countrymen, Wilhelm Enckenvoirt and Dietrich Heeze, like their master men of the highest principle, but lacking in political experience. Adrian's distrust of the Italians was intensified when he discovered that Cardinal Soderini, his political adviser, had been betraying him to the French.

Adrian was convinced that the decline of the Papacy could only be arrested by a free acknowledgement of the existing moral and structural defects within the Church, followed by their removal; he therefore instructed the nuncio Chieregati to deliver a message to the Diet of Nuremberg in the following terms: 'God has permitted this persecution of the Church because of the sins of mankind, especially of priests and prelates ... We are conscious that much that is vile has befallen this Holy See over the past years ... We have all strayed from the right path and so must all honour God and humble ourselves before Him ... For our part, we pledge ourselves that the Curia, perhaps the source of all the evil, shall be wholly renovated.' Such language had not been heard from Rome since the days of Bernard of Clairvaux. Meant to be taken seriously, this promise was greeted in Germany with contemptuous disbelief. The outstretched hand was spurned. The demand put forward by the Estates for a 'free Christian Council in German lands' to be summoned within a year, was anti-papal in implication, since 'free' in this context could only mean 'independent of the Pope'. The *Grievances of the*

Clement VII was faced with the bitter rivalry between Charles V, Emperor and King of Spain, and Francis I of France. Clement pursued a vacillating policy between the two powers. Eventually, fearful of Spanish domination in Italy, he joined Francis I's anti-Hapsburg League. These portraits by Vasari show Clement with Charles V *above* and Francis I *below*

Clement's alliance with the anti-imperial powers led to the disastrous humiliation of the Sack of Rome in 1527. The city was ravaged by the mutinous imperial troops and the Pope imprisoned in the Castel Sant' Angelo. A contemporary engraving showing German soldiers in a parody of a papal procession, while in the background are scenes of fighting and looting

German nation submitted to the Pope were anti-Roman and anti-clerical. This was not the only distress in store for Adrian. While the Lutherans were on the offensive in the north, the Turks were advancing in the east. 'Poor Christendom', cried the Pope, when he heard of the fall of Rhodes.

However regarded, the Pontificate of the last non-Italian Pope was only an episode. Even the Emperor, with whom he had personal ties of such long standing, was disappointingly slow to support his policies. As the somewhat plaintive inscription on Adrian's tomb has it, 'Alas that the work of even the best of men must be at the mercy of the age in which he lives'. He died on 14 September 1523, just a year after his entry into Rome, and is buried in the Santa Maria dell'Anima. The Roman populace gave vent to their hatred for the foreigner in a pasquinade which transformed all the unhappy Pope's virtues into vices: hypocrisy, cruelty, envy, greed; he was hated by all and loved by none.

With the election of Cardinal Giulio de' Medici, who was the posthumous illegitimate son of the Guiliano assassinated in 1478 by the Pazzi in pursuit of their vendetta, it seemed as though the golden age of the Medici had returned. Clement VII (1523–34) was certainly much less vulnerable on personal grounds than his cousin Leo had been, and was more conscientious in his attitude towards his office; but he also lacked insight into the root causes of the crisis confronting the Church. He hoped by subtle diplomacy to steer the Papacy not only through the great international conflict between the Emperor Charles V and Francis I of France but also past the rock he had special reason to fear, the General Council, which was now being demanded on all sides: in this way he imagined he would master the insurrection brewing in the Church. In the event he deceived both himself and the hopes of the humanists.

Clement's election on 19 November 1523 had once again been a victory for the imperial party over the French. Yet the new Pope hesitated over entering actively into the imperial alliance originally engineered by his cousin, and in the end, faced with the threat of Spanish domination in Italy, allowed himself to be persuaded by Giberti, his Datary, into joining the anti-Hapsburg League of Cognac (22 May 1526). This change of front brought down on him the deepest humiliation experienced by a legitimate Pope since Anagni. On 6 May 1527 the mutinous imperial army sacked Rome and imprisoned the Pope, who had only escaped by the skin of his teeth from the clutches of the marauding troops. Even after the Pope had been released from his captivity in the Castle of St Angelo, Cardinal Wolsey could seriously suggest that since his freedom of political action was so curtailed canonical measures might be needed to safeguard the independence of the Church's government. The sack of Rome meant the end of the Renaissance in the city and many people regarded it as a divine judgment. After the Peace of Barcelona (29 June 1529), which restored the Medici to Florence, Clement VII never

The challenge of the Reformation

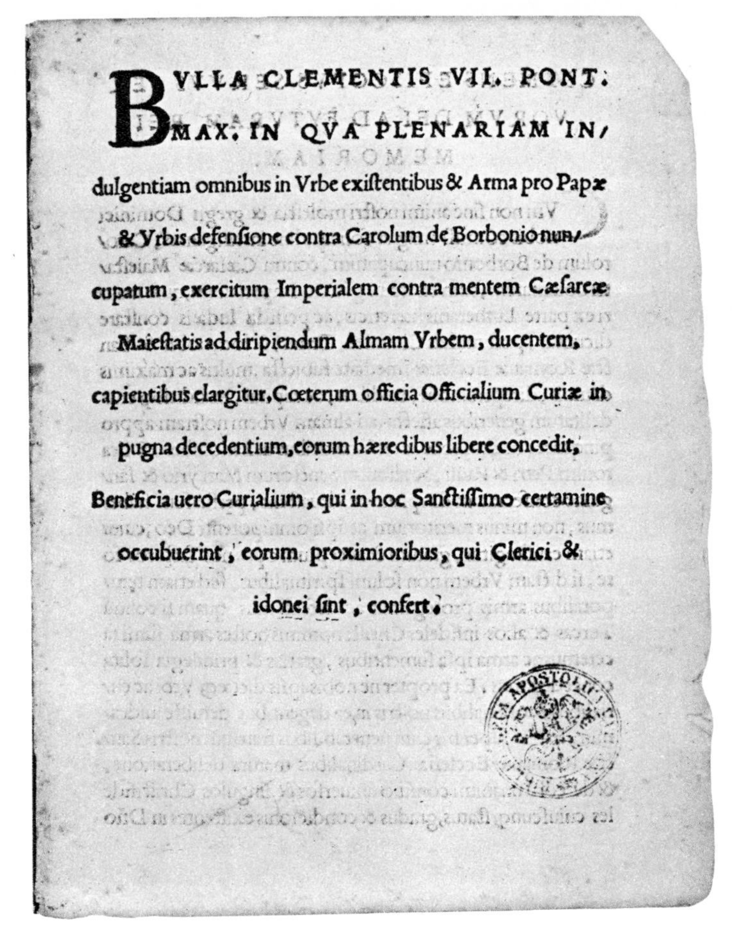

BVLLA CLEMENTIS VII. PONT. MAX. IN QVA PLENARIAM IN/dulgentiam omnibus in Vrbe existentibus & Arma pro Papæ & Vrbis defensione contra Carolum de Borbonio nun/cupatum, exercitum Imperialem contra mentem Cæsareæ Maiestatis ad diripiendum Almam Vrbem, ducentem, capientibus elargitur, Cœterum officia Officialium Curiæ in pugna decedentium, eorum hæredibus libere concedit, Beneficia uero Curialium, qui in hoc Sanctissimo certamine occubuerint, eorum proximioribus, qui Clerici & idonei sint, confert.

Right The bull issued by Clement VII during the Sack of Rome offering a plenary indulgence to anyone who would take up arms against the imperial leader Charles of Bourbon in defence of the Pope and the city

Below Martin Luther, who led Germany into religious revolt. His movement started as a protest against papal financial exactions, but soon assumed a theological form and a large proportion of the German people supported its repudiation of the papal authority

again dared to set himself openly against the Emperor.

The coronation of Charles V at Bologna (24 February 1530), the last imperial coronation to be conducted by a Pope, emphasised that a surrender had taken place; it did not imply that mutual mistrust was at an end. After long and bitter bargaining, which took place in the period before the coronation, the Pope gave a half-hearted promise to summon a General Council if the Emperor's attempt to win back the German Protestants at the forthcoming Diet of Augsburg should fail. And fail it did. The Protestant Estates adhered to the confession of faith they had prepared, the *confessio augustana*, and shortly afterwards formed themselves into the League of Schmalkalden. The Pope declared himself ready to honour his promise and call a Council, but hedged his consent with so many well-nigh impracticable conditions that the negotiations, in the hands of the nuncios Gambara and Rangoni, dragged on for a year without any definite result; since the French had not abandoned their obstructionist tactics either, this was scarcely surprising. A meeting at Marseilles between Clement VII and Francis I in October/November 1533 brought the Papacy closer to France again. A few months later, after much vacillation, the Pope at last pronounced his final verdict on the marriage of Henry VIII and Catherine of Aragon, which he upheld as valid. By the time the Act of Supremacy of 3 November 1534 had set England on the road to schism the Pope was no longer alive.

Charles v tried to stem the Lutheran tide, but without success.
In 1530 he called the German Estates to the Diet of Augsburg,
in an attempt to find a basis for agreement.
But the breach was already too wide to be easily closed
and at the Diet the Lutherans presented him with the
Augsburg Confession, a statement of their theological position.
A contemporary engraving of the scene

SANCTISSIMO. IN. CHRIS

Luther challenged the absolute authority of the Pope and the Roman Church. Others followed. In England the dispute centred on the annulment of Henry VIII's marriage to Catherine of Aragon. The petition to Clement VII supporting the annulment by the leading magnates of England in 1530. The signatures of the Archbishops of York (Wolsey) and Canterbury (Warham) are in the left-hand column

It would not be fair to say that Clement VII was actually an enemy of church reform: for example, he gave his consent to the foundation of two new orders, both of them a source of renewed strength to the Church, the Theatines, endowed by Gaetano de Tiene, and the Barnabites, founded by Antonio Maria Zaccaria. But he failed to do what was quite rightly expected of him: he took no decisive step towards reviving the Church by means of a Council. The Pope showed the same indecision in ecclesiastical matters as in politics: 'Discorre bene, ma risolve male' – 'He talks well but decides badly' – was the verdict of the Venetian ambassador, Soriano.

The new Pope, Paul III (1534–49), elected on 13 October 1554 after a rapid and virtually unanimous conclave, immediately adopted the crying necessities of Council and reform as part of his programme. Formerly the Cardinal-deacon Alessandro Farnese, Paul III was already 67 years old, but still vigorous in mind and body. The course and circumstances of his life had made him wholly a man of the Renaissance. He owed his cardinalate (conferred in 1493) to his sister Guilia's intimacy with Alexander VI; he had himself, before becoming a priest, fathered three sons and a daughter out of wedlock; the first cardinals he created, in December 1534, were his grandsons Alessandro Farnese and Guido Ascanio Sforza, aged fourteen and sixteen. The Pope loved his family dearly; its advancement was at once a constant goal of his policy and the heaviest burden on his rule. Ignoring the threatening clouds on the horizon, the papal court assumed an outward splendour almost as lavish as in the may-time of the Renaissance.

Yet this Farnese Pope, whose appearance and inner nature have been captured for us by Titian in three incomparable portraits, was also a man of sophisticated and lively intelligence. It did not escape his acute observation that his

The coronation of Charles V at Bologna in 1530, the last imperial coronation to be conducted by a Pope. A ceiling fresco by Giorgio Vasari from the Palazzo Vecchio, Florence

In 1542 Paul III summoned a Council to meet in imperial territory at Trent to combat Protestantism and institute reform. The Pope and cardinals setting out for Trent by Sebastiano Ricci

predecessor's tactic of veering from side to side, with no regard to principle, had robbed the Apostolic See of any confidence it might have inspired among the great powers, especially those loyal to the Papacy. Evasion of the Council and of reform had led only into a blind alley. Paul III based his diplomacy on the principle of strict neutrality towards the two great rival powers, France and Spain, and his ecclesiastical policy on the intention to convoke a Council and to remedy the most glaring defects in the Church. The right diagnosis had been reached, but the cure was more difficult to apply than the Pope perhaps anticipated.

In April 1536 there was a meeting in Rome between the Pope and the Emperor, who had just returned from his victorious campaign against Tunis, when it was agreed to summon a General Council to meet at Mantua. This Council never met, not so much because of the almost intolerable conditions imposed by the Duke of Mantua but because of the fresh hostilities that broke out between the Emperor and the king of France. The Protestant members of the Diet bluntly rejected the 'Pope's Council'; when the venue was changed to Vicenza, on Venetian territory, it was the bishops who remained aloof. No one now believed that a Pope could be serious in his conciliar intentions.

This failure explains why the Pope was now prepared to give at least modified support to the schemes for reunion initiated by Charles V after the armistice of Nice. The religious conferences held at Worms and Ratisbon in 1541 failed to produce agreement, despite the intervention of the Cardinal-Legate Contarini, who favoured an understanding with the Protestants; on the other hand, Protestantism was making formidable inroads in Italy itself. On 22 May 1542 the Pope summoned a Council to meet at Trent. The choice of locality met the demand for 'a Council in German lands', since Trent belonged to the Empire, and had the further advantage of being easily accessible from Italy. But this second convocation of a Council was also without effect, for Francis I once more took up arms against the Emperor. It was only after the Treaty of Crépy (18 September 1544) had been signed, with its secret clause binding France to send representatives, that the Council could at last be held, now as part of a grand design projected by the Emperor for the recovery of Christian unity: Pope and Emperor were to enter into a military alliance against the League of Schmalkalden, then, when victory had been achieved, the Council would deliver its authoritative judgment on the doctrinal controversies in the presence of the Protestants and legislate for the reform of the Church.

The first part of the plan was successfully implemented with the infliction of a total defeat on the League of Schmalkalden. Meanwhile the Council had opened on 13 December 1545 under the direction of the three papal legates, Del Monte, Cervini and Pole, and had spent the ensuing months, while the battle was raging in Germany, in debating the dogmas concerning sources of revelation (Scripture and Tradition), original sin and justification, in defining the nature of the Sacraments and in drafting decrees dealing with preaching and episcopal residence. On 11 March 1547, at the very moment when the Emperor was clinching his victory over the League of Schmalkalden, the Council transferred itself to Bologna. This move made nonsense of the master plan, for the Protestants would never consent to attend a Council sitting on papal territory. While the Spanish bishops remained at Trent, the majority continued their deliberations at Bologna, although the decrees already drafted remained unpublished. Relations between the Emperor and the Pope, already severely strained by mutual mistrust, were poisoned still further by the murder of Pierluigi

Paul III (1534–49) was a Renaissance figure in the splendour of his court and his extensive nepotism. He nevertheless agreed to summon a General Council and opened the way for the reform of the Church. One of three portraits of the Farnese Pope by Titian

Farnese, who had received the duchies of Parma and Piacenza as papal fiefs, since the imperial governor of Milan, Ferrante Gonzaga, was generally regarded as the instigator of the crime. There was no open breach, but the grand design was destroyed and the imperial plan for the Church, known as the Interim of Augsburg and introduced at the Diet held in that city in 1548, was doomed to die at birth.

Paul III has to his credit not only the convocation of the Council of Trent but also two other lasting services to the cause of Church reform. By appointing cardinals of the calibre of Contarini, Carafa, Pole and Cervini, devout men eager for reform, the Pope not only gave a fresh complexion to the College of Cardinals, which since the days of Sixtus IV had been growing more and more secular in outlook, but also made the election of a reforming Pope a genuine possibility. In approving the foundation of the Society of Jesus by St Ignatius of Loyola on 27 September 1540, Paul III enlisted an army of zealous pastors and pious masters in the service of the Papacy; the Jesuits were to build up a new élite within the Church, and undertook the systematic defence of areas where Protestantism threatened. A further reinforcement was provided by the Roman Inquisition, set up on 21 July 1542, to become the supreme (and soon the much dreaded) court in matters of doctrine.

Paul III also took the first steps towards reforming the Roman Curia. When he issued the convocation to Mantua he at the same time authorized a panel of cardinals and bishops to draw up a report on the defects in the papal bureaucracy (Chancery, Chamber, Datary and Penitentiary), which fearlessly exposed the reasons for these shortcomings. The Pope also appointed a commission to work out a detailed plan of reform, but gave way under pressure from conservative cardinals and officials; his good intentions were further weakened by the realization that any reform worth the name would entail financial sacrifices for the Pope.

So Paul III cannot really be classed with the reforming Popes; but he did prepare the way for the Tridentine reforms. His sharp ear caught the message of the times, which summoned to Council and reform, but his elderly and aristocratic hands (wonderfully rendered by Titian in the portrait of 1543) lacked the strength to cut the threads which bound him, and with him the Curia, heart and mind to the Papacy of the Renaissance. It was Paul III who commissioned Michelangelo to paint the *Last Judgement* in the Sistine Chapel and the *Conversion of St Paul* in the Capella Paolina, just as it was Paul III who appointed Michelangelo architect of the dome of St Peter's. But the tomb of this Pope (only completed in 1576 and the work of Gugliemo della Porta) is quite innocent of any religious symbol.

In the conclave that followed the death of Paul III (10 November 1549) Cardinal Reginald Pole fell short of the required two-thirds majority by only two votes. Agreement was not reached until more than three months had passed.

Paul III approves the Rule of the Society of Jesus, founded by the Spaniard Ignatius Loyola. The Jesuits were bound to complete 'military' obedience to the Pope and became one of the most important instruments of the Counter-Reformation

On 8 February 1550 Cardinal Giovanni Del Monte, the candidate favoured by the Farnese and French faction, was at last elected, to take the name of Julius III (1550–55). The new Pope, who was sixty-two, had presided over the Council of Trent, where he showed himself an able tactician; it must also be admitted that his irascible temper had made him many enemies. His uncouth exterior and somewhat rustic manners contrasted sharply with the aristocratic bearing of his predecessor, although his generosity made him a favourite with the Roman populace. He was considered a capable canon lawyer and was experienced in the ways of the Curia; but he had never been employed on diplomatic missions abroad. In spite of this drawback the

Julius III (1550–55) began his reign with enthusiastic support for reform and moved the Council back from Bologna to Trent. Little progress was made, although Julius made preparations for a grand reform bull. Later the impetus for reform slackened and the Pope spent most of his time in retreat in the Villa Giulia *below* which he built for himself outside Rome

Pope followed the advice of Dandino, his very able secretary (soon raised to the cardinalate) and reserved all important diplomatic decisions to himself. Innocenzo, his nepotic Cardinal, was quite unequal to the task.

Although Julius III was far from being a partisan of the Emperor, he at once demonstrated his willingness to conform to imperial policies and brought the Council back from Bologna to Trent. Here, while the memory of the imperial victory was still vivid, representatives of the Protestant Estates appeared before the Council for the first and last time, together with fourteen bishops from German-speaking lands; the French kept away. Negotiations with the Protestants made no progress whatever, since the parties held totally irreconcilable views on the authority of the Council and the procedure to be followed in settling doctrinal disputes. Catholic doctrine on the Sacraments of the Eucharist, Penance and Extreme Unction was defined, but no perceptible advance was made in the field of church reform. The failure of conciliar policy as initiated by Paul III finally became complete with the revolt of the German princes under the Elector Maurice of Saxony in the spring of 1552, which broke up the Council, and the conclusion of the Peace of Passau by the Emperor's brother Ferdinand, which recognized the *confessio augustana* as valid within the Empire. Moreover, the Pope was in no position to eject Ottavio Farnese, who had French support, from the Duchy of Parma, which was now lost to the Papal States.

When it became clear that Spain and Portugal were treating the still unratified reforming decrees of the Council as though they were already valid law, the Pope made exhaustive preparations for the issue of a grand reform bull, which would not only enforce the Tridentine decrees, but would also augment them by provisions dealing with papal elections and with the reform of the Curia and of the religious orders. The Pope's personal interest in this work of reform is attested by the numerous marginal notes in his own hand scattered through the documents. Yet the task remained unfinished; like his predecessors, Julius III lacked the deep sincerity and firmness of purpose needed to carry it through. He came to prefer the attractions of the villa he built for himself outside the Porta del Popolo during the last years of his Pontificate. Official business was left to languish, even the cardinals were seldom granted audience. A contemporary (the future Cardinal Seripando) remarked that the only really satisfactory event of the reign was the return of England to the Roman obedience with the accession of Mary Tudor. Cardinal Pole, the Legate appointed to England, was only admitted into the country after the marriage between Mary and Philip of Spain had been finally solemnized; the Legate completed the formalities of England's reconciliation with Rome at the palace of Whitehall on 30 November 1554. It remained an episode.

The depleted state of the funds Julius III inherited from his predecessor prevented him from acting as a patron on a generous scale; even a financier as talented as Ricci, his treasurer, was powerless to provide a remedy. A connoisseur of music, Julius appointed Pierluigi Palestrina choirmaster of St Peter's. Viewed as a whole, the Pontificate could not be described as retrogressive; but neither did it mark any significant advance. The movement towards reform, initiated by his predecessors but not consistently maintained, slackened off. Decisive steps were only taken later with the election of a series of Popes openly committed to the cause of Church reform.

Above The Council of Trent, first summoned in 1542 by Paul III, and recalled in 1560 by Pius IV, was the principal instrument of the internal reform of the Church. A representation of the Council in session by an anonymous sixteenth-century Venetian painter

Right Paul IV (1555–59) dismissed the Council of Trent and attempted to carry through reforms on his own initiative by means of bulls and decrees. Fiery and vigorous, his methods were not always popular and he became feared and hated in Rome. This head from a statue of Paul IV which stood on the Capitol, was torn down by the angry populace while he was still alive, rolled through the city and finally thrown into the Tiber. It was recovered and now stands in the Castel Sant' Angelo

13 THE TRIUMPH OF THE COUNTER-REFORMATION

MARCELLUS II to LEO XI 1555-1605

EUSEBIO REY

The period of constructive Catholic reform was inaugurated by Paul IV, whose rigorous measures were supported by the activity of the Inquisition. Under Pius IV the Council of Trent was recalled and a large number of reforming decrees were passed. These were implemented by Pius V, Gregory XIII and Sixtus V, all of whom pursued a vigorous policy of internal reform and intervened strongly in the international tensions caused by Catholic-Protestant rivalry. In Rome the city was transformed by the building projects of Sixtus V.

THE BEGINNING OF THIS PERIOD WAS MARKED BY AN event of the first importance – the Treaty of Augsburg (25 September 1555). This was not so much a religious peace as a spiritual cleavage, or rather a watershed between two epochs, one looking backwards to the past, the other facing towards the future and the results that would be produced by the formula *cujus regio ejus religio*. These results were to last until the Treaty of Westphalia, by which religious freedom was given a territorial basis. Within a few years of this same date several people holding key positions in the changing politico-religious situation in Europe had either disappeared from, or made their entrance on, the scene. Charles V, Mary Tudor, Henry II of France, Ignatius Loyola were among those who vanished. The Emperor Ferdinand I, Philip II of Spain, Elizabeth of England, Catherine de' Medici, Henry Duke of Guise (the younger leader of the Catholic League) and Henry of Navarre (the young leader of the Huguenots) took their place. There was a symbolical watershed also in the succession to the Papacy; the death of Julius III (23 March 1555) put an end to a period when the style of papal life had been tainted with worldliness, while with the election and death of the reformist Marcellus II (10 April–1 May) began a series of reforming Popes who gave a new spiritual tone to the Church.

This period can be divided into three stages, all relating to the Council of Trent: the suspension of the Council, and personal efforts at reform on the part of Paul IV (1555–59); the third and final convocation of the Council by Pius IV (1559–65); and the practical application of the Council between 1565 and 1590 by St Pius V, Gregory XIII and Sixtus V, whose death was the signal for further changes.

The governing forces behind the thoughts and actions of the leaders of the Church were, in the main, three. First the twofold conception of self-reform and counter-reform characteristic of the entire period of Catholic reform, became from 1563 onwards deliberately and openly Tridentine, in so far as it took the Council as its undisputed and indisputable standard, both in the letter and the spirit. This would not have been possible before 1563. Secondly Catholicism became contaminated by confusion of political with religious ideas. This did not show itself in controversy nor in the missions to convert the Protestants, such as that of St Peter Canisius, who was so full of understanding for members of other sects, but in political groups and in the attitude of the Catholic princes. Even the Popes contributed to this confusion. Among the Protestants there was complete identification of political with religious ends. Their interest in theological speculation was abandoned for ecclesiastical organisation, then for politics, and finally for the sword. To this was added the notion of *raison d'état* made fashionable by writers influenced by Machiavelli and Tacitus – 'the politicians'. Finally, during this period the word 'Catholicism' – the universality of the Church – gained significance. The Protestants tried to renew their claim to the word 'Catholic' (universal), but failed because of the disintegration of their dogma, and their dispersion into autonomous churches. From 1565 onwards the Catholic Church showed itself increasingly united.

The Counter-Reformation

Under the Neapolitan octogenarian, Giovanni Pietro Caraffa, Paul IV (1555–59) the recall of the Council was delayed another four years. It has often been remarked that Paul IV's virtues (asceticism, saintliness and sincere desire for reform) were in contrast with the serious failings springing from his irascible and passionate temperament and small knowledge of life and men. The latter caused him to begin his reign with two actions that were far from 'reformist' – the war with Spain for the liberation of Italy (1555–57) and his unbridled nepotism towards his undesirable Secretary of State, Cardinal Carlo Caraffa, and his brothers. He entrusted the politics and administration of his domains to them until January 1559, seven months before his death, when he expelled them from Rome, horrified by their depravity.

Paul IV made a personal effort to reform the Church rapidly by means of bulls and decrees, independently of the Council. The Reform Commission, with two hundred members presided over by himself, was succeeded by the Inquisition, to which tribunal nearly every question of reform was submitted. Everything he did showed signs of his rigorous extremism, and was based upon the Inquisition as reorganized by himself – he even prosecuted the excellent

Two of the most important instruments of the Counter-Reformation were the Society of Jesus, whose missionary efforts won back countless Protestants to the Catholic Church, and the Inquisition. The Inquisition was reconstituted and centralized for the detection and suppression of heresy by Paul IV.
Above St Ignatius Loyola, founder of the Society of Jesus, who died in 1556.
Left El Greco's portrait of Fernando Nino de Guevara, the Spanish Cardinal Inquisitor

Right Pius V (1566–72), who put in hand the implementation of the reforming decrees of the Council of Trent, particularly within the Curia itself.
A contemporary Mannerist portrait

S. IN CHRISTO PATRIS ET Dñi
N.D.Pii diuina prouidentia Papæ.iiii.

Bulla

Indictionis SACRI Oecumenici Concilii
Tridentini Celebrandi.

The most important achievements of the Council of Trent were made at the last session between 1560 and 1563 during the reign of Pius IV (1559–65). There was no longer any possibility of theological agreement with the Protestants and the Council was able to concentrate on constructive measures of reform, especially pastoral and educational. *Above* The bull issued by Pius IV in 1560, and bearing his arms, recalling the Council of Trent. *Below* The signatures on the final text of resolutions, headed by that of Cardinal Morone, the special papal legate and President of the Council

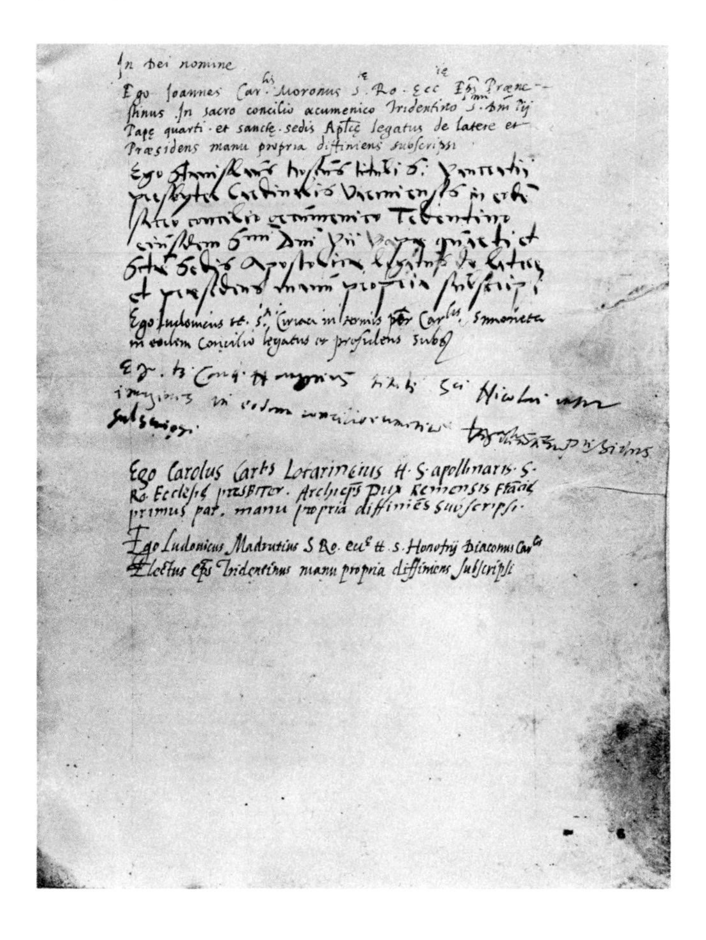

The Counter-Reformation

Cardinals Morone and Pole – and upon the Index of Prohibited Books. His reforms were hardly felt outside Rome and Italy. His principal achievement was to create a climate of reform based on the repression of customs, correction of abuses in the Curia, and restoration to health of the College of Cardinals by the creation of eighteen reformist Cardinals and the elimination of Lutheran groups.

After the collapse of the war against Philip II he became more isolationist in international relations, and when he did intervene it was because he held an anachronistic and medieval concept of his personal authority as Pope. He stubbornly continued to claim the ecclesiastical possessions which the English parliament insisted on retaining in lay hands as a condition of the *Act of Reconciliation* with Rome (1555), and would not recognize Charles V's renunciation of the Empire nor the election of his successor, Ferdinand I.

The Council was convened again for the last time by Giovanni Angelo de' Medici, Pius IV (1559–65), according to the agreement sworn in conclave. Realizing that the collaboration of the secular princes – above all of Spain, France and the Empire – was necessary, he sent his legates to them. His invitation to several Protestants was ignored. The bull of convocation was issued on 20 December 1560, but the first session did not take place until 18 January 1562, because of the resistance of Ferdinand I and Catherine de' Medici. The Council was as oecumenical as possible. In the final session 235 Fathers gave their *placet* not including the theologians and secular ambassadors. The dominating figures at the Council were Pope Pius IV and his Secretary of State Charles Borromeo, Morone (first legate since the death of Gonzaga) and the other legates Seripando, Hosio, Simoneta and Puteo; among the Fathers – the Cardinal of Lorena, the Archbishop of Braga, Bartolomeu dos Martires, and the bellicose Bishop of Granada, Pedro Guerrero; among the theologians – the Dominicans Peter de Soto, Melchior Cano, and the General of the Jesuits, Diego Lainez.

During the two years all but a few days when the Council was sitting (18 January 1562–5 December 1563) there were in this third session nine public meetings. In these the canons (dogmas) and disciplinary decrees were read, and the clergy voted *placet* or *non placet*. The Fathers and theologians had already discussed them in detail in the general congregations, and drawn up their definitive form. The theologians had in their turn held special sessions for the study and discussion of the legates' proposals.

Finally the validity of the canons and decrees issued by the two previous convocations was confirmed. In the final session approval was given to the text of all three sessions and to the petition that it should be submitted to the Pope. All the clergy and ambassadors signed before dissolving.

In 1571 Pius V organized the last crusade against the Turks, who were defeated at Lepanto. The Christian fleets before Messina, with allegorical figures representing Spain, the Papacy and Venice, a work commissioned from Giorgio Vasari by Gregory XIII

The Counter-Reformation

Bringing the Council to a conclusion was a triumph for the Church's prestige in its own eyes and those of the Protestants. The long-desired reform had been effected; it was all that could have been expected. Instead of the previous state of insecurity and anxiety there was now a feeling of confidence and liberation, which was transformed into exaltation during the Baroque era. The most far-reaching effect was to be seen in Catholic doctrine. Its fundamental dogmas were finally established in a synthesis free from all impurities or doubts. As for disciplinary matters, these were also covered by reform *in capite et in membris*. Doctrinal limits were definitely fixed and no one could overstep them without being fully aware that he was going outside

Right Gregory XIII (1572–85) continued the centralization of the Church on the Roman curia by establishing apostolic nuncios as papal representatives in favourable countries. Many German states at this time wavered between Protestantism and Catholicism. In this marble relief from S Maria dell' Anima, Rome, Gregory XIII is giving the sword and cap to Charles Frederick Duke of Cleves and Berg, one such principality

Below England, after returning to the Roman obedience under Mary Tudor, reverted to Protestantism under Elizabeth. When it was clear that diplomacy had failed, Pius V excommunicated the Queen in 1570, an act which caused grave division of loyalty amongst her Roman Catholic subjects. The bull of excommunication

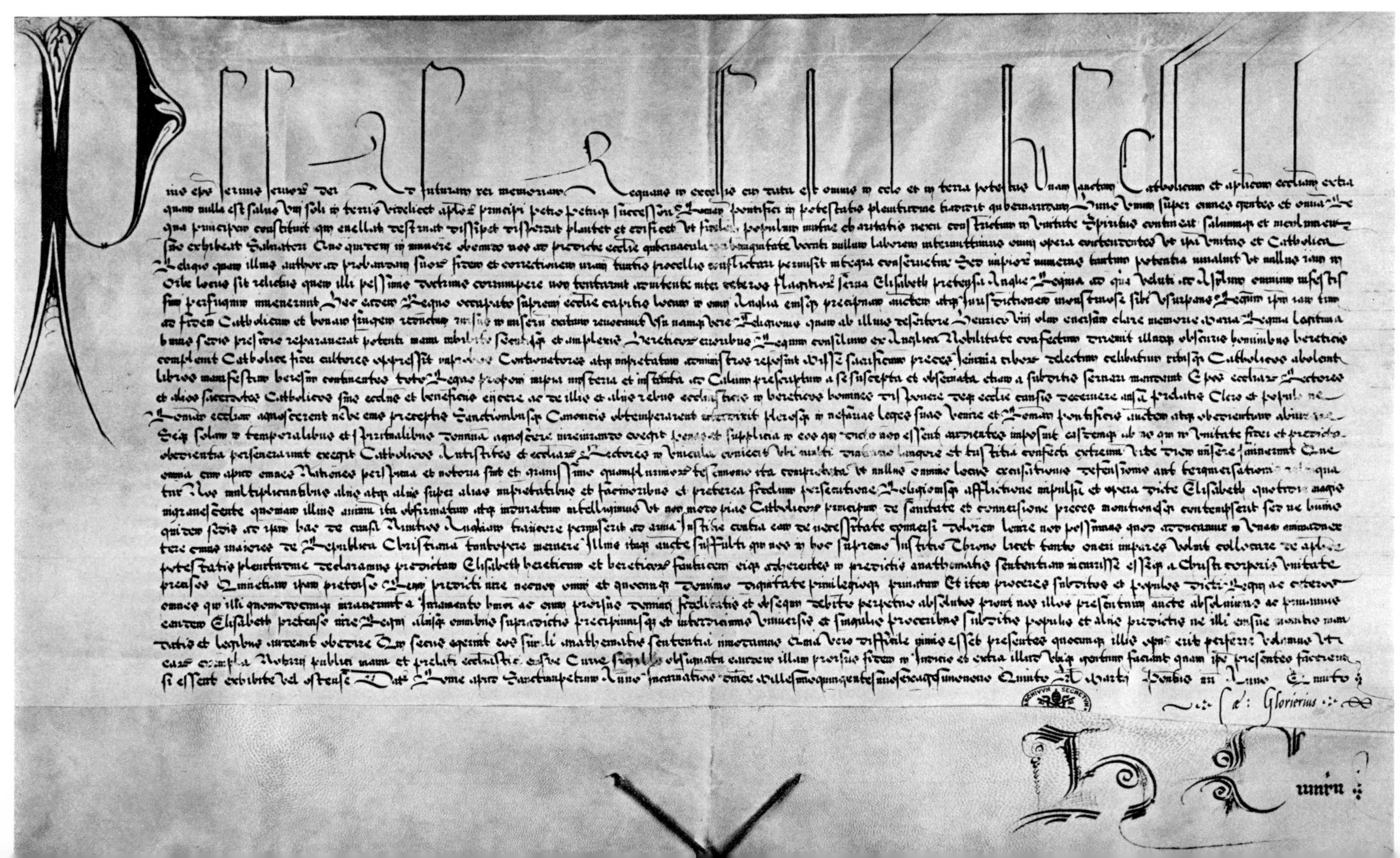

the Church. There remains the question whether the division in the Christian world, and the definite rupture with Protestantism should be attributed to the Council and the subsequent *Professio fidei tridentinae*, as some – including Catholics – would have it. Professor Hubert Jedin has recently demonstrated by historical arguments that the Council was not the cause, but only the final seal placed upon a rift which had been deliberately made by the Protestants.

Pius IV published the text of the Council in March 1564, approving and proclaiming it in the bull *Benedictus Deus*, retrospectively dated 26 January 1564. It was accepted in Portugal, Venice, the Italian States, Poland and Spain in 1564. The Catholic cantons of Switzerland and the Holy Roman Empire recognized it officially later on (1566). France was the last, and only gave official recognition to the part concerned with dogma.

The Dominican Michele Ghislieri, Pius V (1566–72) personally undertook the task of implementing the letter and the spirit of the Council. With characteristic intrepidity and enthusiasm, as well as a certain rigorousness of method, he reformed the Curia, through the agency of the uncompromising Ormaneto. He effected more moral improvements in the city of Rome even than Paul IV had done. His ecclesiastical reforms included the creation of reformist cardinals, obligatory residence of bishops and priests in their parishes, the holding of synods, the opening of seminaries and reform of religious orders. He carried out these measures throughout the Church. In the sphere of liturgical and educational reform he published the *Roman Catechism* (1566), *Breviary* (1568) and *Missal* (1570). He also edited St Thomas Aquinas' *Summa*, which was adopted as the theological text-book for the Schools. He was particularly interested in urging reform upon the secular powers, pressing the acceptance of the Council's decrees upon them, and attacking their interference in ecclesiastical affairs in the bull *In coena Domini* (1568). He took a hand in the politico-religious affairs of the day both by his writings and through his legates, administering correction or help, which was sometimes financial. Thus he excommunicated Queen Elizabeth and freed her Catholic subjects from obedience to her even at the risk of martyrdom; he rebuked the Catholic Catharine Jagellon of Sweden for using the chalice; and threatened the flighty Maximilian II with excommunication. On the other hand he supported the vacillating King Sigismund II of Poland, and gave economic and other help to the Catholic armies in Germany, the Low Countries and France. He maintained a close relationship with Venice, Florence and Philip II of Spain; and sent Cardinal Carranza of Toledo, who had been arrested for Lutheranism, to be tried in Rome. His desire to defend and spread the faith throughout the Orient led him to make contact with the Orthodox Church, and found a Holy Alliance between Spain, Venice and the Papal States against Islam. This, the last Christian crusade, was led by Don John of Austria and defeated the Turkish navy at Lepanto (9 October 1571).

St Charles Borromeo (1538–84), Cardinal Archbishop of Milan, represents the gentler side of the Counter-Reformation. He had a great influence on Gregory XIII, especially in educational reform. Here, in a painting by Orazio Borgianni, he is seen ministering to the sick in the plague which raged in Milan in 1576

During the Pontificate of the Bolognese Ugo Buoncompagni, Gregory XIII (1572–85), the efforts for reform were directed into two new and distinct channels, namely active government and educational reform. Under the spiritual influence of St Charles Borromeo, Gregory XIII succeeded in transforming the Papacy into an active centre of the Church, and maintained close contact with all other countries so as to superintend the carrying out of reform. The most significant measure along these lines was the institution of permanent *apostolic nuncios* in the place of the legates. Besides Vienna, Paris and Madrid, where he already had representatives, he established nuncios at Lucerne (1579), Gratz (1580), Cologne (1584) and other cities. To the same end he initiated relations with the Churches of the East – with those of the Slavs, the Greeks, the Maronites, the Ethiopians and even the Japanese, whose ambassadors he received.

His second campaign was inspired by the Council; its object was ecclesiastical and secular education. He founded, enlarged or assisted out of his own pocket, more than twenty-seven centres of learning. In this undertaking he

SCIPIO TVRAMINVS CRESCENTII FILVIS CV FVERIT MAGISTRATVS BICCHERNÆ
CAMERARIVS TEMPORE QVO GREGORIVS XIII PONTIFEX MAXIMVS ANNO REFORMAVERIT

Left The struggle between the Catholics and the Huguenots in France for political and religious domination came to a climax in the Massacre of St Bartholomew in 1572. This appalling act of bloodshed and treachery resulted in the slaughter of thousands of Huguenots. A painting by François Dubois, who was an eye-witness of the massacre

Left below Gregory XIII is also remembered for the reform of the calendar in 1582, known as the Gregorian Calendar. His reform was gradually accepted, first by the Catholic countries and then by the Protestants, but not by some Orthodox countries until after the First World War.
A contemporary painting showing Gregory presiding at a discussion of the calendar

Right Sixtus V (1585–90) was an energetic administrator, who organized and centralized the Curia on lines followed to this day. He restored order to the Papal States and was the greatest builder in Rome since Julius II, a fact commemorated in the borders of this contemporary engraving

made use of the Jesuits on a massive scale. Without counting the centres scattered through Protestant Europe, there were in Rome alone: the sumptuous edifice of the Collegio Romano (Gregorian University) which was then, as it is today, 'a seminary of all nations'; the German College, the soul of the Catholic revival in the Empire; the English college, a similar institution for England, imitated by Philip II in Spain at Valladolid, Seville, Salamanca, and by Cardinal Allen at Douai; the Hungarian, the Greek, the Maronite and the Armenian colleges. To complete his educational crusade he published his *Corpus Juris Canonica* (1582) and the famous *Gregorian Calendar*, which was adopted by the whole world.

In dealing with politico-religious conflicts he took the same line of repression or intervention as Pius V, but with less success. A good many of his actions are open to criticism: his rejoicings over the events of St Bartholomew's Day (1572), his negotiations with Queen Elizabeth about the treatment of the Catholics and Mary Stuart, and also his attempt to recover the wealth of the Church, so as to pay for his vast expenditure on education and politico-religious enterprises. These last measures provoked an armed rebellion and an outbreak of anarchy and banditry, which he was unable to subdue and which embittered his life.

The energetic and optimistic Franciscan, Felice Peretti of Montalto, Sixtus V (1585–90) quickly solved the two

The Counter-Reformation

Clement VIII (1592–1605) saw the victory of the Catholic party in France, when the Protestant Henry IV was converted to Catholicism from motives of political expediency and was granted absolution by the Pope. An anonymous seventeenth-century portrait of Clement

problems bequeathed him by his predecessor. In less than a year he had cleansed his domains of condottieri and bandits. Ownership of property was reorganized in two ways: a rigorous re-examination of title-deeds, as a result of which rich revenues returned to the Papacy, and the foundation of *Monti* – or bank deposits for State funds. By this means he succeeded in gathering together a treasure of four million gold scudi which he deposited in the Castle of Sant' Angelo.

His most inspired achievement was the reorganization of the Curia and the central government of the Church, by transforming the *dicasterios* into fifteen congregations, each with special functions; the reconstituted college of cardinals was divided among different congregations and contained a maximum of seventy cardinals. So as to keep in contact with all the bishops and supervise the application of the Council of Trent, he instituted *ad limina* visits (still in force today) in the bull *Romanus Pontifex*, on 20 December 1580. Out of the 'Jubilees' grew massive pilgrimages to the city of Rome, in accordance with his plan to make it the effective capital of the world.

This necessitated the transformation of the city. He dedicated all his enthusiasm for construction to this end – building gigantic aqueducts to carry the 'Acqua Felice', streets and hospitals, and beautifying the city with fountains, statues, obelisks and palaces. He was obsessed by the desire to christianize the religious buildings of Renaissance and pagan Rome. This led to a cross being substituted for Minerva's spear on the Capitol, the statues of St Peter and St Paul being placed on the restored columns of the Emperors Trajan and Marcus Aurelius, a *lignum crucis* on Nero's Egyptian obelisk. His greatest achievement in this field was the erection of the dome of St Peter's according to the designs Michelangelo had prepared twenty-five years earlier.

His intervention in politico-religious affairs revealed his view of the absolute authority of the Pope. He would never admit that 'the Pope is not Sovereign ruler of the world', and when Bellarmine published his theory of the indirect power of the Popes in temporal affairs, he tried to hand him over to the Inquisition. He excommunicated Queen Elizabeth of England for executing Mary Stuart and persecuting the Catholics, Henry of Navarre for being head of the Huguenots, Henry III for the assassination of Cardinal Guise, and Jacques Clément for the regicide of Henry III. He gave assistance to Philip II's invincible Armada, believing that it might be the means of re-Catholicizing England, and had fantastic utopian dreams of spreading the faith from Poland and Muscovy into the Orient. Yet he still had time to press on with the correction of the *Vulgate*. His Sixtine edition had later to be corrected by the Sixto-Clementine. With his death in 1590, the strictly reformist Popes came to an end.

Sixtus V was succeeded by three Popes none of whom survived for more than a few months. Clement VIII (1592–1605) was alarmed at the predominance of Spain and favoured France in order to maintain a balance of power. When Henry of Navarre, the French King, abjured the Protestant faith and became a Catholic, Clement gladly gave him absolution. Clement attempted to raise a European army for the rescue of Hungary from the Turks, but in this he was unsuccessful. Theological controversy during his reign was dominated by the controversy between the Jesuits and the Dominicans about the nature of grace, but Clement died while it was still unresolved.

In 1605 Paul V came to the throne. The growing rivalry between France and the Hapsburgs and the political and religious unrest in the German states became increasingly aggravated until the outbreak of the Thirty Years War in 1618, a watershed which marked a new phase in the history of the Papacy.

The ceiling of the Church of S Ignazio, Rome, commissioned by Gregory XV in 1622 to mark the canonization of St Ignatius Loyola. The ceiling, representing the triumph of St Ignatius, is the work of Padre Pozzo, a master of perspective painting

14 THE POPES AND THE CITY OF ROME

PAOLO BREZZI

Before Constantine there is no evidence of christian influence on the civic life of Rome, but from his death until 1870, despite the Avignon captivity and frequent invasion, Rome was essentially the papal city. Time and again the Popes defended Rome against Saracen and barbarian invasion. Later the Papacy and the government of the city became the subject of bitter rivalry between leading Roman families. Numerous attempts were made to achieve civil liberties, but there was no strong middle class to support the movement. The Popes of the sixteenth and seventeenth centuries carried out vast building projects and ruled the city and the Papal States virtually as feudal overlords. In the eighteenth and early nineteenth centuries, apart from the French Revolutionary and Napoleonic invasions, Rome remained closed within itself and the Popes allied themselves with conservative elements against the liberal and nationalist movements.
In 1870 the Risorgimento *triumphed and the Italian national state was established. The Popes remained in voluntary imprisonment in the Vatican until the establishment of the Vatican City State in 1929.*

DURING THE FIRST THREE CENTURIES OF THE CHRISTian era there is no evidence that any influence was exercised by the new religion on the public life and administration of the city of Rome. The followers of Christ were very few in number and their social importance among the one and a half million inhabitants, and in relation to the imperial political authorities, was small. The *Liber Pontificalis* speaks of the division of Rome into various ecclesiastical areas and of other measures taken by the local bishop, but we cannot be certain how reliable such information is; in any case, it seems to have been an organization quite separate from the civil administration. But the moment the Roman Empire became officially Christian, from the time of Constantine (313–37) onwards, the situation altered radically; Christian influence made itself clearly felt in the offices of state and the buildings themselves, in legislation, and in the general way of life. Rome was about to start a new historical cycle which would last many centuries and spread its glory even further afield. Nevertheless – and this is characteristic of the whole period – the territorial coexistence of two sovereignties, the papal and the secular, created problems unknown elsewhere and brought into being the *concordia discors*, which may be regarded as the symbol of Rome's history from the fourth to the nineteenth century.

It was at the time of Constantine's successors in the mid-fourth century that the question of homage to the altar of Victory was raised. Discussions took place as to whether members of the Senate should continue to pay homage to this statue, which had in the past been regarded as the divinity protecting the State. The Christian faithful could no longer accept this idolatrous gesture, but the conservative elements considered it would be an outrage to flout tradition. This controversy revealed how great were the changes required before the new religion could become a living force in an ancient civilization. The pagans defended themselves with great skill, but the cause was lost, and with the passing of time the Curia itself, where the Senate met, was transformed into a church, as if tangibly to demonstrate the change in Rome both in religious convictions and civic institutions.

Meanwhile political conditions throughout the West were deteriorating and Rome was attacked and sacked by barbarian invaders – Alaric in 410, Genseric in 455 and Ricimer in 472. This was a severe blow to the prestige of Rome, which had always been considered under the sacred and inviolable protection of the gods, and a number of famous Christian authors, such as St Augustine of Hippo, had to defend their faith against the accusation that Christianity had brought about the fall of the Empire and the end of classical civilization. This was an important phase in the transposition from temporal to spiritual jurisdiction, from the State to the Church, from imperial government to that of the Popes, and it was only by a providential interpretation of history that it became possible to justify what was happening, to discern good amidst the widespread evil, and perceive the new dispensation emerging from the ruins of the ancient Roman world.

There was a sphere in which Christian religious and

A typical scene of Roman life showing St Peter's Square at the time of the coronation of Sixtus v in 1585. Sixtus, one of the great papal builders, re-planned the city and gave fresh impetus to the rebuilding of St Peter's. This painting from the Sala Sistina shows the new dome rising behind the old church

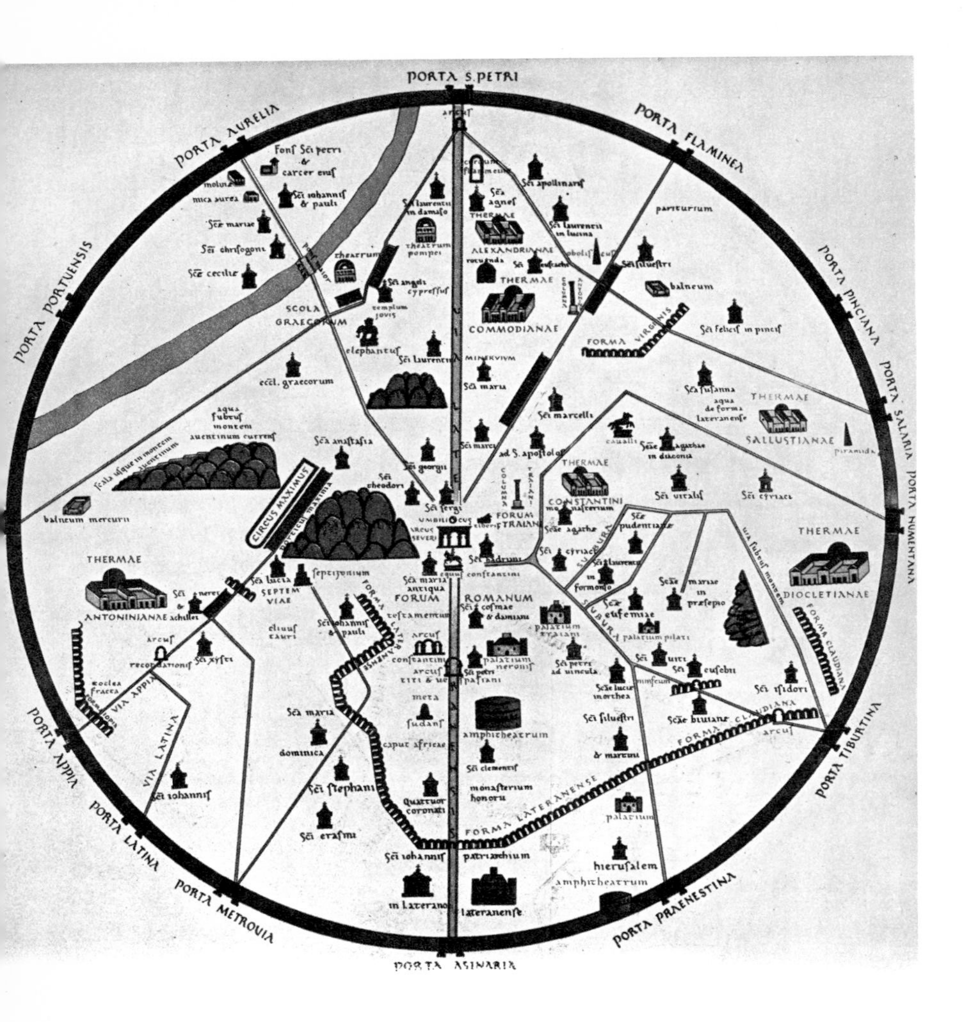

Left Rome in the eighth century from a reconstruction of a map for pilgrims in the Einsiedeln Itinerary, from the great collection of manuscripts in the Swiss Benedictine monastery. The city is half imperial, half papal. The hills of Rome are clearly marked and at the bottom is the Lateran church and palace, which until the fourteenth century were more important even than St Peter's and the Vatican, which are shown across the Tiber at the top left

ecclesiastical initiative was undoubtedly beneficial and made for progress and healthy renewal; this was in works of charity and welfare, the organization of collections (alms) and relief payments. Such measures were all the more necessary and urgent in the general administrative disorder prevalent at the time (from the middle of the fifth century onwards). They were entrusted almost exclusively to the clergy because the clergy could lay their hands on large sums of money, lived in contact with the most humble members of the community, and were inspired by a genuine spirit of brotherly love, seeing in any man in need the figure of Jesus Christ.

A great deal of information about the Pontificate of Leo I, known as the Great (441–61), can be found in his *Letters* and *Sermons*, including details of the ecclesiastical order in the city, as well as the main ceremonies and customs. It was Leo who intervened with Attila the Hun, when he was encamped near the banks of the Po at Mantua and about to attack Rome. Even if allowance is made for subsequent embellishments, the episode proves that the inhabitants trusted their bishop as *defensor civitatis* and placed themselves under his protection, that they were prepared to recognize him as their *de facto* leader in the civic and political sphere, as well as the religious.

During the following centuries Rome, while still nominally part of the Byzantine Empire and with Greek officials

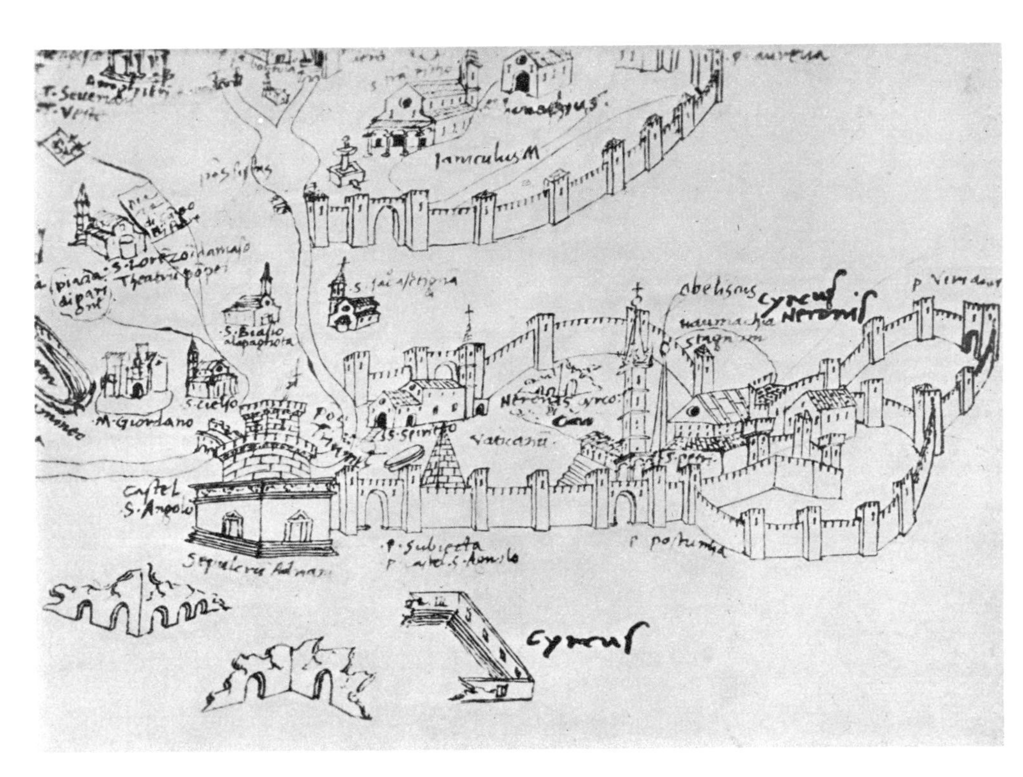

Rome in 1474, showing the Leonine walls surrounding St Peter's and the Vatican, with the Church of the Holy Spirit and the Castel Sant' Angelo to the left on the banks of the Tiber. Behind St Peter's is the hill of the Janiculum with its Roman walls. A detail from a plan of the Leonine city by Alexander Strozzi

Left Rome in 1328 shown on the reverse of a gold seal of Ludwig of Bavaria. The Tiber flows across the right-hand side, dividing at the Isola Tiberina. On the right of the river is the Castel Sant' Angelo and St Peter's; at the bottom, centre, is the Pantheon, consecrated as a church in 609, and at the top the Colosseum

The Popes and the City of Rome

Below Rome in 1549 with the Vatican and Belvedere Palaces at the top right and St John Lateran just inside the walls on the extreme left. The principal churches and antiquities are set out in the key. An engraving by Sebastian Munster

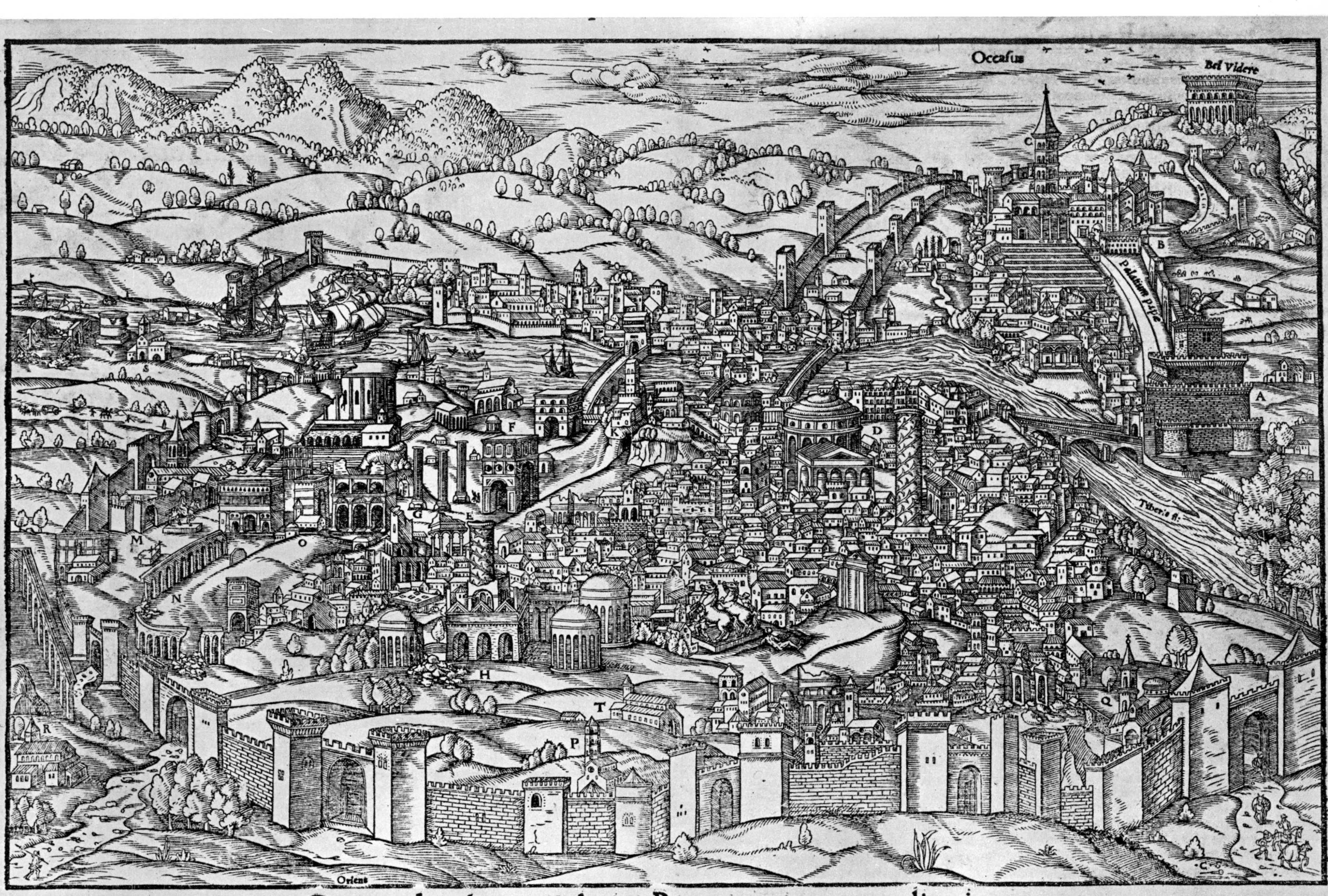

The Popes and the City of Rome

The Castel Sant' Angelo has played a dramatic part in the history of Rome. A reconstruction of the building as it was in Roman times. It was built in AD 136 as a mausoleum for Hadrian and carried on top a statue of the Emperor in a chariot drawn by four horses. In the fifth century it was fortified and incorporated into the city walls

placed over it, in practice looked to the Popes, not only for its defence and day-to-day existence, but also for artistic and cultural leadership, in so far as this was possible in those troubled times. The city's topography had also undergone considerable changes as a result of the primacy achieved by the ecclesiastical authorities. The great basilicas – lying for the most part on the outskirts – were focal points for the life of the city, and hospices and minor churches were built in their immediate vicinity. On the other hand, in certain districts, which had formerly been the site of palaces and offices of state, the population drifted away and buildings fell into decay; even the most celebrated monuments of the classical era were neglected unless they acquired Christian associations as a result of the numerous legends current in those centuries amongst the credulous and the naïve.

Among the Roman personalities of the time the outstanding figure is that of St Gregory the Great (590–604). Born of a noble family, he became a high State official and finally a monk and skilled administrator of the Church's estates. Aptly described as *consul dei*, he succeeded in applying the age-old organizational qualities of the Latins in the religious field. He kept a record of the population so as to know how many mouths had to be fed, set up appropriate centres for the distribution of food and clothing, provided for those we would today describe as refugees, and sharply upbraided those of his fellow priests who showed less zeal than himself. Later the administration of the Curia began to work even more smoothly and efficiently, with its centre in the Lateran *patriarchium* and a number of 'diaconates' attached to churches covering the various areas. These diaconates enjoyed an independent

Left The Castel Sant' Angelo in 1491, showing how the fortress dominated the right-angled bend of the Tiber and closed the entrance to the walled city of the Vatican. In the reign of Alexander VI it was joined to the Vatican by a covered passage and was used as a refuge by Clement VII during the Sack of Rome in 1527. An anonymous drawing by a Spanish artist

Right The Castel Sant' Angelo in the eighteenth century. The lower outworks were built by Urban VIII (1623–44), who took a particular interest in fortification and restored the Leonine walls. A watercolour by V. J. Nicolle

administration, made use of vacant public buildings and provided medical treatment; they were, in short, religious-social institutions whose purpose was to satisfy the elementary material and spiritual needs of the Roman people. Though the clergy inevitably played a leading role, laymen also shared in the work, not only by making generous gifts of money and property, but by individual effort by women of the aristocracy, who performed the most humble duties, and men in high places who renounced the world in order to serve God and his Church.

Unfortunately there were other sides to the picture, and it cannot be denied that with the passing of time and the constant extension of the Roman church's temporal activities, far less noble aspirations entered into the exercise of the priestly ministry. The achievement of high ecclesiastical office often became the ambition of men who were inadequately prepared for such a calling. The major Roman families set out to occupy the pontifical chair without any concern for the legitimacy of the appointment. They chose incumbents who were too young or morally unsuitable, and who interfered with good government. Between the end of the ninth and the middle of the eleventh centuries there occurred what historians have subsequently defined as the 'iron age of the Papacy' or 'the Roman pornocracy', which must be considered here not because of its repulsive or immoral aspects, but because of its influence on the life of the city. Never again did the two societies of Rome – civil and religious, lay and ecclesiastical – so intermingle that the Popes almost forgot their universal role as the head of Christendom in their concern for power in Rome.

Alberich II, *princeps omnium romanorum*, ruled the city for over twenty years, and ended by placing his own son, Octavian, on Peter's throne. This ambitious name indicated a claim that a single person embraced all power in himself and was the heir to Rome's classical and Christian traditions. He was succeeded by the Crescenzi, a bold and determined family who, after lording it over the city for fifty years and resisting the assaults made on them by the emperors of the House of Saxony, came to a tragic end when the best amongst them was hanged from the highest tower of the Castel Sant' Angelo as a warning to the people. For a short time Rome became the residence of the young Otto III, who dreamt of a spiritual and civil *renovatio* of the Roman way of life and had at his side Pope Sylvester II, the most learned man of his age. But death put an end to this noble plan and the city fell once again into the hands of the local nobility. The Tuscolani kept the Holy See and the government in their own hands through a number of Popes drawn from their family. Finally, indignation against their misdeeds, together with the revival of religious feeling expressed in the Gregorian movement for reform, led to a reaction in Rome and with the year 1059 begins a new phase in Rome's urban and ecclesiastical history.

The decisions taken by the Synod meeting in that year were to have incalculable effect on relations between the city of Rome and the Holy See, for it was agreed that the election of the Pontiff should be taken out of the hands of local elements and entrusted to the 'cardinals'. They were the title-holders (*tituli*) of the major Roman churches and were not involved in city politics and indeed were often in conflict with the secular interests. This decision had to be taken because of interference in the elections by leading lay personalities in Rome. It also marked the beginning of a division between the *curia* and the *res publica*, which soon

degenerated into deep and resentful opposition. Examples abound, as is shown by the many conflicts occurring in the twelfth century, but the climax was reached around 1144, at the time of the *renovatio senatus*, or rise of the independent commune. This development was occurring all over Italy at the time, but it is obvious that in Rome it took on a character of its own, because of the presence of the Pontiff with his high ecclesiastical authority.

For a century and a half there were a succession of revolts, expulsions of Popes, interdictions, armed clashes, truces soon broken and then patched up again, reforms of the instruments of government, the rise and fall of noble families. Needless to say, the major European developments of the time, in particular the struggle between the Papacy and the Empire influenced the situation, and so did the widespread social changes affecting the vast landed wealth of the Holy See and the Church's various other financial resources. By the end of the thirteenth century Rome was a thriving city where the arts (trade guilds) flourished, but an economically independent middle class found it difficult to assert itself because too many material interests tied the citizens to the Church's institutions. Even so attempts to assert independence did occur from time to time.

The most important Roman families between the end of the eleventh and the middle of the twelfth centuries were the Pierleoni and the Frangipane. The former, of Jewish origin, were able financiers who linked their fortunes with the victory of the Gregorian party of reform; the latter quickly threw in their lot with the old feudal order and then the Empire. Then the various Conti, Savelli, Capocci, Boveschi appeared on the Roman scene, but the whole of the thirteenth century was dominated by the enmity between the Orsini and the Colonna; the former were more 'Guelph', more favourable to the Pope, the latter, more 'Ghibelline' or supporters of the Emperor, though both families lived within the papal orbit and owed their importance to the high positions a number of their members had in the Curia. These two houses came to symbolize the frenzied vitality of the Roman aristocracy at the decline of the Middle Ages, which had been the golden age of their power. From the embattled security of their various dwellings, the Orsini and the Colonnas kept the city in a constant state of alarm; they played a decisive role in the conclaves, and sought alliances with outside powers such as the Kingdom of Naples and France. But they also encouraged the arts and surrounded themselves with a large group of supporters so as to exercise their influence on Communal administration more effectively.

Towards the end of the thirteenth century Benedetto Caetani, Pope Boniface VIII, a man of vigorous and independent mind, attempted to make his family one of the most influential in Rome by forcibly putting down the Colonnas, but he did not achieve lasting results. However, his action in proclaiming the Jubilee, or Holy Year in 1300, which drew crowds of pilgrims to Rome, demonstrated to the whole world that true papal primacy lies in the field of the spirit and can survive without political support. Nevertheless, when the reign of Boniface came to an end the Holy See was transferred for seventy years to France, and Rome declined as its main sources of wealth were exhausted. It was, however, precisely in this period that the men of the people – weary of the interminable rivalries between the nobles – made their voices heard and gave new impetus to the movement for independence. The figure of Cola di Rienzo sums up the Roman ideals of independence, nostalgia for past glory, and ambition to dominate the whole Italian peninsula, but his brief adventure in 1347 was brought to an end by his own mistakes and the united action of his enemies.

There followed a number of conspiracies aimed at restoring civic liberties to the Romans, but all of them quickly came to nothing for lack of the right economic conditions (Rome was without an industrious middle class and adequate financial resources) and because the inhabitants soon ceased to press for their rights. They preferred to hold well-paid offices in the Curia, to gravitate round the nobles, or exploit the foreigners who came to Rome in ever increasing numbers, attracted not exclusively by religious considerations as in the past, but also by the reborn passion for the classical world and a *dolce vita*, which was also widespread in circles which should have set an example of austere living. The presence of foreigners at the pontifical court is one of the most important developments in the Rome of the fifteenth and early sixteenth centuries, and one has only

Left The Castel Sant' Angelo owes its name to the legend that during the plague of 590 Gregory the Great led a pilgrimage through Rome to pray for the protection of the Virgin. An angel alighted on the mausoleum, sheathing his sword as a sign that the prayer was granted. A statue by Rafaello da Montelupo, which once stood on top of the castle

Right When the Popes succeeded to the imperial power in Rome, they also took over the defence of the city. Leo IV (847–55) was responsible for the building of the Leonine Walls round an area corresponding to the present Vatican City. They were rebuilt and restored by later Popes and by the eighteenth century had become part of the decorative landscape of Rome. A painting by Thomas Jones

The Piazza Navona in about 1630. In the foreground is the smaller of the two fountains by Bernini, which now stand in the square. This anonymous painting is earlier than the great central fountain commissioned by Innocent X (1644–55)

Above The Palazzo Borghese, the town palace of the Borghese family, bought and completed by Paul v in 1614. An eighteenth-century engraving by Giuseppe Vasi

Left The Villa Borghese, built at the beginning of the seventeenth century by Cardinal Scipio Borghese, a nephew of Paul v, who established the Borghese as one of the great patrician families of Rome. The villa is now a museum and stands in its own gardens in the North of the city just outside the old walls of Rome

to bring up the name of Borgia to evoke an atmosphere of violent passions and far from irreproachable morals. Yet there was a positive side to the picture, consisting both in the encouragement given to the arts and the reorganization of the Papal States, which abandoned their medieval structure for a more modern one, suppressing individual feudal interests and civic autonomy, so as to create unity under the Pope.

Unfortunately the Holy See was also caught up in the struggle for European supremacy waged by Spain and France throughout the first half of the sixteenth century; the worst consequence was the famous sack of Rome in 1527 by the *Landesknecht* and other German troops, who vented their anti-Roman and anti-Catholic hatred on the population, the churches and buildings of Rome. Nothing like it had happened for over a thousand years and it proved a tremendous blow, causing incalculable material damage and moral humiliation. Yet it also had a regenerating effect; it rid the city of many parasites, recalled both clergy and laymen to their duties, brought about changes in all the city's activities and made possible a revival whose effects were clearly to be seen before the century had ended. Even the city's topography altered, and whereas Rome had until then been situated within the bend of the Tiber, in an unhealthy area of narrow, tortuous streets, it now moved towards the hills (the Esquiline, the Quirinal); it was replanned on broad lines and made more beautiful, thanks to straight roads ensuring ease of communication between the most important points in the city and the venerable basilicas. The most discerning and energetic figure in the task of renewal was that of Sixtus v (Felice Peretti). Other Popes, before and after him, were mainly concerned with the reorganization of civil and ecclesiastical offices; they deprived the citizens of the last vestiges of freedom but ensured a quiet, uneventful, industrious way of life. Only a few sensational trials (the Cenci, Giordano Bruno, Galileo) created a certain unrest.

For two centuries, from the end of the sixteenth to the end of the eighteenth, Rome remained closed within itself. It was cut off to some extent from world politics, free from grave political or social unheavals, enlivened by the receptions frequently organized by foreign embassies or the wealthy aristocracy, and reminded of its lofty religious duties by the pomp and solemnity of the ceremonies held in the old and new churches, amongst which the Jubilees held regularly at intervals of twenty-five years played an important part. Behind this gay and prosperous exterior there lay much that was rotten, not only because of social injustices, which were largely ignored in the very city which was the seat of the Head of Christ's Church, but also because of an apparent insincerity which seemed to overshadow religious functions both public and private. But it would be unfair and mistaken not to mention the band of saints, men and women, Roman and Romanized, who performed their apostolate in the city, either by works of charity or by instructing the young; the name of St Philip Neri stands for a serene faith, and a ready self-sacrifice for the salvation of others. He founded the *Oratorio* near the Chiesa Nuova which had a great influence on Catholic piety and culture in Rome for several centuries. Secondary and higher education was provided by the Jesuit Roman College and the *Sapienza*.

Political and economic conditions in the city and entire Papal States were far from satisfactory. A number of new aristocratic families came to the fore and took the place of the others in the direction of church and civil affairs – Chigi, Barberini, Borghese, Odescalchi and Pamphili. Some useful measures were taken by the authorities and the building of palaces, churches, fountains and memorials went on incessantly. But the standard of living was very low and a sense of social purpose was lacking. In a Europe pervaded by revolutionary ferment and shaken at the very foundations of its traditional Christian civilization by rationalist ideologies, there was no real consciousness of the

The picture gallery of Cardinal Silvio Gonzaga, a member of one of the great Italian patrician families. This painting by Panini illustrates the opulence of the eighteenth-century princes of the Church

The Popes and the City of Rome

Right The Piazza del Quirinale in the eighteenth century by Panini, with the Quirinal Palace on the extreme left. The Quirinal, begun by Gregory XIII in 1574, was a papal palace until 1870 when it became the royal residence. The Popes frequently used it as a summer residence because of its healthy situation on the Quirinal hill. The colossal marble statue of the Horse Tamers in the centre is a classical relic

Below The Palazzo Farnese was begun in 1514 by Cardinal Alessandro Farnese, later Paul III. One of the great monuments of the High Renaissance style, the architects were Sangallo the Younger and Michelangelo. A mid-sixteenth century engraving

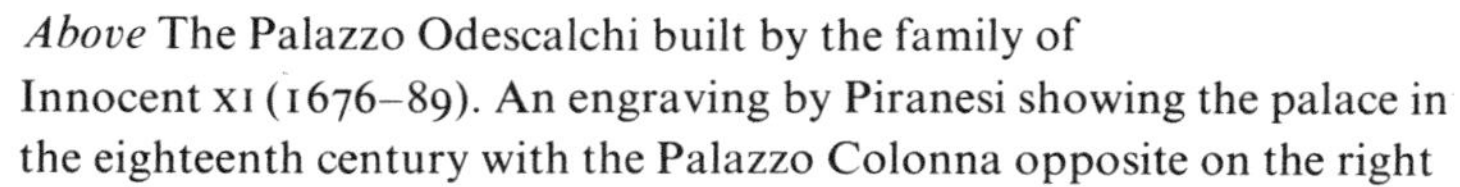

Above The Palazzo Odescalchi built by the family of Innocent XI (1676–89). An engraving by Piranesi showing the palace in the eighteenth century with the Palazzo Colonna opposite on the right

historical significance and spiritual purpose of the Papacy. Whereas in other periods corruption amongst the clergy of the Curia had been graver, what many now lacked was an awareness of the mission entrusted to Rome as the heir of a twofold temporal and spiritual empire. There were those who dreamed of its cultural supremacy, but in the eighteenth century it was only in the field of the sciences (the foundation of the Lincei Academy) and religious scholarship (the Vatican Library), that the Papacy could boast of any lasting achievement.

At the end of the eighteenth century, under the Pontificate of Pius VI (1775–99), Rome was occupied several times by the French revolutionary armies. The Papal States were declared to have lapsed, a democratic republic was set up, ecclesiastical property secularized and the social order reformed. Shortly afterwards, although Napoleon Bonaparte had made a Concordat with Pius VII (1800–23), there were new conflicts between Church and State, further violence was done to the Pontiff and the cardinals, and new administrative arrangements were made in the city of Rome. It was declared the second city of the Empire, Napoleon's long-awaited heir was named after it, ambitious plans were drawn up for modernizing the city and a marriage link was even established between Napoleon's sister and a Roman prince – Camillo Borghese married Paolina Bonaparte. But generally speaking the inhabitants remained unfriendly and suspicious, not because reform was not urgently needed, but because they were sentimentally attached to the bigoted, patriarchal system of the past and did not expect genuine improvements to descend on them from above. Popular satire – which found expression in the famous pasquinades and had never spared previous governments – lashed the new rulers unmercifully. The fall of Napoleon brought no feeling of regret; in fact the Pope was welcomed back after his long exile with unbounded and spontaneous enthusiasm.

Pius VII's wisest advisers, amongst whom Cardinal Ercole Consalvi stands out, had learned their lesson and in 1816 they promulgated with a *motu proprio* an effective and comprehensive plan for administrative reform, which went as far as was compatible with an authority such as that of the Popes, which was of its nature not democratic.

The election of Pius IX (Mastai Ferretti) in 1846, after a period of unenlightened reaction, gave rise to great hopes which were confirmed by his early actions. But soon there was a radical change in the conditions which had seemed to make possible an understanding between 'God and freedom' (to quote the current high-sounding phrase) and which might once again have given Rome a world role and a true mission. The 'Roman Question' became the most delicate and controversial issue of the Italian Risorgimento. Finally, in 1870 the city was occupied by military force, in spite of indignant protests from the Pope who shut himself up in the Vatican and branded as 'usurpers' those Italians who had taken part in the occupation. But another cycle in the history of Rome had been completed, the city once again became the political capital of a nation which had in the past looked to Rome for its laws and political institutions, while the other great Roman institution of the Papacy, relieved of the temporal power incompatible with its spiritual function, found a new energy and authority with which to speak to the world.

Left The Palazzo Corsini, rebuilt in 1729 for Cardinal Neri Corsini, nephew of Clement XII (1730–40). The famous Corsini Library founded by the two men was established there. An engraving by Giuseppe Vasi dated 1752

Right The Villa Doria Pamphili, famous for its elegant gardens above the Tiber. It was built by Algardi in about 1650 for Prince Camillo Pamphili, nephew of Innocent X. An anonymous eighteenth-century engraving

Top 'The Seven Churches of Rome', a pilgrims' guide engraved for the Jubilee Year of 1575. The pilgrims are seen visiting the churches, and kneeling before the statues of St Peter, St Mary, St John and St Paul (outside the walls). The other three traditional pilgrimage churches shown are S Lorenzo, built at the burial place of the martyr; S Croce, traditionally built by Constantine to house the relic of the True Cross brought back to Rome by his mother Helena; and S Sebastiano, built over the site of many martyrs' tombs in the catacombs below

Bottom St John Lateran and the Lateran Palace were given to the Papacy by Constantine and were the principal church of Rome and the papal residence until the time of the Avignon Papacy. St John Lateran is still the cathedral church of Rome.
A mid-seventeenth-century engraving showing the medieval palace and church just before their reconstruction

15 THE GROWTH OF THE ETERNAL CITY

PAOLO BREZZI

The unique character and appearance of Rome have been largely shaped by its importance as the seat of the Holy See and the centre of the Roman Catholic Church. Rome is dominated by its churches as is no other city. But the whole city bears witness to papal influence: the walls built by the early Popes as a defence against invasion, the great papal palaces, the many buildings erected to enhance the prestige of the Roman families, who vied with one another for ecclesiastical offices, roads, hospitals and monastic foundations. The greatest contribution to the town planning of Rome was made by Sixtus V at the end of the sixteenth century. In the seventeenth and eighteenth centuries the taste for baroque and rococo altered the appearance of the city; a new façade was added to many of the older churches and many piazzas were re-planned. The Popes were also responsible for preserving many of the great monuments of classical Rome and for important schemes of archaeological excavation.

FROM THE FIFTH CENTURY UNTIL 1870, WHEN ROME became the capital of the new united Italian state, the external appearance of the city was largely shaped by the influence of the Church. This was due not only to the vast number of churches and other ecclesiastical and monastic buildings, but also to the considerable part played by the families of the Popes and other ecclesiastics in the life of Rome and in the construction of buildings intended to enhance the prestige of a particular family or to house the branch of administration of which they were the head.

The earliest Roman churches were set up inside private houses and at the beginning of the fifth century there were twenty-five of them, at which figure they remained for some time. But side by side with them, there also came into being the great basilicas built by the Emperors and these – being for the most part situated near the place of martyrdom of some famous Christian, such as St Peter, St Paul, St Agnes, St Lawrence – were to be found outside the ancient city and this led to a shift of the population towards areas previously uninhabited. On the other hand, the old centres, such as the Forum and the Palatine, being the seat of imperial residences and official buildings, were left for a very long time without any place of worship and consequently with the passing of time were deserted by the inhabitants. In about AD 550 there were thirty-seven churches in Rome, and by the beginning of the ninth century they had increased to as many as 130, although not all owed their origin to the Popes.

From the moment Constantine made over the Palace of the Lateran (the Laterani were a noble Roman family whose houses had passed to Fausta, wife of the Emperor, who had brought them as dowry) to Pope Miltiades, this became the official seat of the Bishop of Rome and was transformed into a *patriarchium*, while nearby a basilica was built dedicated to the Saviour (afterwards to St John), which is still the Cathedral of Rome. The church, destroyed by a fire in 1308, was reconstructed by Clement V, then burned down again and rebuilt under Urban V, then finally completely renovated according to Borromini's designs under Innocent X for the Jubilee of 1650; further restoration work was carried out in 1885 by Leo XIII, who asked to be buried there (his tomb is opposite that of a great medieval Pontiff, Innocent III). The palace, as it appears today, is an austere construction built by Domenico Fontana in 1588 under Sixtus V, but when the Popes lived there it must have been situated roughly where we today find the Scala Sancta. It consisted of a collection of buildings, cloisters and small basilicas culminating in Leo III's *triclinium* (with the great mosaic, of which a more recent reconstruction still exists, portraying, amongst others, the figures of Christ, St Peter, Constantine, Charlemagne), and the *aula concilii*, erected by Urban IV and restored by Nicholas IV (a huge rectangular hall providing access to the Loggia of Blessings, added, possibly, by Boniface VIII). Two museums are at present housed in the palace, the secular one founded by Gregory XVI, the Christian by Pius IX; in the piazza stands the highest obelisk in Rome – it came from Egypt and was raised by order of Sixtus V.

The growth of the Eternal City

Innocent X ordered the reconstruction of St John Lateran for the Jubilee of 1650. The architect was Francesco Borromini, the great contemporary and rival of Bernini. The façade was designed by Alessandro Galilei in 1734 and commissioned by Clement XII. An engraving by Piranesi

It is no great distance to another famous basilica, that of S Maria Maggiore, which was also the object of unceasing papal concern and which Pope Sixtus V envisaged as the centre of a comprehensive and daring town-planning project. This church's link with the Popes is indicated by the name, Liberian, it often goes under, because according to tradition Mary appeared to Liberius, Bishop of Rome, during the night from 4th to 5th August 352 and indicated the place where the church was to be built. The present building dates from a century later at the time of Sixtus III, and was subsequently enlarged under Eugenius III in the twelfth century, and under Nicholas IV. In the seventeenth century Clement X had the rear façade built, while a hundred years later Benedict XIV restored the whole edifice, adding the main façade. Inside the most remarkable feature is the mosaics, but mention should be made of the Sistine Chapel (with the tombs of Pius V and Sixtus V) and the Pauline or Borghese Chapel, with the tombs of Paul V and Clement VIII.

Towards the end of the sixteenth century, when the Counter-Reformation had increased the prestige of the Papacy, Sixtus V conceived the idea of five wide, straight, well-paved roadways radiating from the Basilica of S Maria Maggiore, which were to have joined up the main churches of Rome. The purpose was not only to foster piety and encourage pilgrimages, but to demonstrate that the city was Christian and Catholic and not the pagan, classical city that it had appeared during the Renaissance. The plan was an ambitious one and not without its drawbacks (if death had not intervened, Sixtus V would not have hesitated

Right top The Piazza del Popolo in 1865, after it had been re-designed by Valadier in 1814 during the French occupation of Rome. The gateway was the main entrance to Rome from the North. The great obelisk was erected by Augustus in 10 BC in the Circus Maximus and was moved to its present position by Sixtus V in 1589. S Maria del Popolo, on the right, contains many masterpieces of Renaissance painting. A painting by G. Capranesi

Left A sixteenth-century engraving of S Maria Maggiore, founded in the fourth century by Pope Liberius. The engraving shows the Renaissance front, still incomplete, on the left, with the famous medieval mosaic over the entrance.
Right The Piazza dell' Esquilino and S Maria Maggiore before the addition of the baroque façade by Fuga. An anonymous eighteenth-century painting

to pull down even the Colosseum because it blocked one of his roads), but as a result a vast new area was brought within the city boundaries, following a transfer of population from the lower part, nearer the Tiber, to the higher, on the Equiline and Quirinal hills, previously almost uninhabited. This is a striking example of the important and long term influence exercised by the Popes on the expansion of the city, something which is still obvious today when we consider the area bounded by the Termini station, the Via Nazionale and the Via Cavour.

Once the new district had, so to speak, been discovered, there was a rush among the influential to develop it. Two examples will suffice: the building of the Quirinal Palace and the Palazzo Barberini, together with the replanning of the surrounding area. The first was started in 1574 to provide a more salubrious summer residence for the Curia, but with time it was so enlarged and improved as to become a sumptuous palace, with many rooms, halls, chapels and terraces, decorated with frescoes, tapestries, stucco, paintings and porcelain. The second building, one of the most imposing in the whole city, was constructed in 1625. It was commissioned from Maderno and Bernini by the powerful Barberini family, who were Florentine in origin but were by then firmly established in Rome. One of the outstanding features of the palace is the spiral staircase. Not far away is the monastery and church (containing the famous but macabre museum of 4,000 skeletons and bones of monks) commissioned by another member of the Barberini family, a cardinal and member of the Capuchin order. The road on which it was built later became the shopwindow of worldly elegance, the rendezvous of high society, the meeting-place of the strange variety of personalities who came to Rome from all parts of the world. A curious fate for a district which had been intended for a very different purpose, but this too is typical of Rome: the ability to combine the sacred and the profane, to juxtapose the spiritual and the secular, to establish relations between the black aristocracy (in other words the families owing their fortunes to the Popes and cardinals) and the newly rich.

Life was particularly difficult for the people of Rome from the seventh to the ninth century, because the lack of vigorous political leadership placed them at the mercy of outside enemies and made their livelihood precarious. The Holy See therefore set up the diaconates and *domuscultae*. This was a swift and courageous move. These diaconates had nothing to do with the seven ancient regional deaconships, but were public institutions for religious and social welfare. They flourished because they enjoyed papal support and received large donations. They had been set up in the central part of the city, often inside public buildings which had fallen into disuse (SS Cosmas and Damian, S Maria in Cosmedin, S Giorgio al Velabro, SS Nereo and Achilleo).

When times changed and the diaconates were no longer

S Paolo fuori le Mura after the fire of 1823, by Francesco Diofebi. This was one of the finest of the ancient churches of Rome until it was almost completely destroyed. The present basilica, with its double aisles, follows the plan of the old church

Above The Romanesque campanile of the church of SS Quattro Coronati. It is one of the oldest foundations in Rome and commemorates four saints martyred during the persecution of the Church under Diocletian at the end of the third century

Below A detail from one of the twelfth-century screens in S Maria in Cosmedin, one of the early churches founded in the fourth century

suited to their purpose, they were replaced by other ecclesiastical welfare organisations, also brought into being by the Popes. These were the *domuscultae*, or self-supporting farms set up in localities near Rome (Galeria, Caprarola, Anzio): wheat and vegetables were grown and animals raised for slaughter; special ration cards were held by the farmworkers and weapons provided in case of military attack. All this was done in order to ensure the livelihood of the citizens of Rome, for which the Pope was morally if not altogether juridically responsible.

In order to provide for the material needs of the citizens, the Popes also founded hospitals and similar institutions. An example is that of Santo Spirito in Sassia, which was built by Innocent III (1198–1216) on the site of the ancient hospice of the Saxons near St Peter's and which he entrusted to Guy of Montpellier and the Hospitaller Friars founded at the time in France under the title and protection of the Holy Spirit. Following a rational plan the Pope set out to make that hospital the model and centre of a vast welfare system; in fact, on the Sunday after the octave of the Epiphany, he used himself to visit it, blessing six skins of water in remembrance of the miracle at the Marriage of Cana, as mentioned in the Gospel for that day, and to symbolize the works of temporal charity. In the centuries that followed the pontiffs continued to show special affection for the Hospital of the Holy Spirit, restoring it and enlarging the sphere of its welfare activities.

S Giacomo in Augusta, S Marta, S Giovanni Calibita (or Fate-benefratelli), S Lorenzo in Fonte and S Gallicano are other hospitals which more or less directly owe their existence and maintenance to the Popes. Then there are the numerous Hospices for Pilgrims (here S Trinità is outstanding) which were especially useful during the Holy Years, or Jubilees; they did not merely provide strangers with food and shelter but offered religious instruction and sound education. Detailed information about the organization of these bodies has survived. They were founded by various Popes, who supported them financially, visited them and safeguarded their interests by appropriate measures. In a similar category is the Monte di Pietà, a State pawnshop which granted loans against pledges to the needier inhabitants, thus preventing them being exploited by usurers and private profiteers. Under Pius II and Paul II (mid-fifteenth century) this institution had become well established in Rome and, as Monaco has rightly pointed out, 'the Popes' achievement seems all the greater when it is remembered that these measures put an end to the long dispute between the Franciscans, who were in favour of the Monte di Pietà, and their opponents – on the one hand the Jews, who insisted on the right to make loans at high rates of interest, and on the other the Dominicans and Augustinians, according to whom even the low interest levied by the State pawnshops was contrary to the canons forbidding usury'. At the end of the sixteenth century Clement VIII

The history of S Maria in Trastevere is typical of that of many Roman churches. It was founded in the fifth century and still retains a basilican plan. It was rebuilt in the Middle Ages and the great choir arch is Romanesque, while the pavement is beautiful Cosmatesque work of the same period. In the sixteenth century the church was rebuilt, incorporating ancient pillars from the baths of Caracalla and a splendid Renaissance ceiling. Much of the decoration, which gives the overall feeling, is baroque. *Above* An anonymous early nineteenth-century painting showing the Renaissance façade before it was replaced later in the century by a more grandiloquent structure. *Below* The nave of the church today

housed the Monte di Pietà in a new building in a densely populated quarter of the city, while his successors up to Gregory XVI (1831–46) continued to make generous contributions to this institution.

On the artistic plane we can consider the Roman palaces, homes and villas which owe their origin to the Popes or their families; the Cancelleria, Montecitorio and San Callisto, are, or were, the headquarters of important departments of the Curia, while the Farnese, Borghese, Odescalchi, Braschi and other palaces have generally been private residences which were subsequently occupied by high-ranking foreign embassies. The first three *palazzi* mentioned are situated in districts which were typical of Rome in the various phases of its development. The Cancelleria, dating back to the time of Sixtus IV (end of the fifteenth century), is on the Via del Pellegrino, not far from the Via Giulia, which was the most elegant street in Renaissance Rome. Montecitorio, today the seat of the Italian Parliament, was constructed at the end of the seventeenth century so as to centralize under one roof the judicial departments and the courts of law, and was situated at the foot of the hills which were the favourite residential area both of the Popes and the noble families. Finally, San Callisto is in the heart of the Trastevere quarter, the stronghold of the *papalini*, or papal supporters; in it were housed the Sacred Congregations, which in the Catholic Church's administrative structure correspond to the ministries of modern governments.

The Popes were also concerned with the defence of the city. The walls surrounding Rome went back to pagan imperial times, and the Popes were repeatedly obliged to repair them, for instance after damage by siege or deterioration due to age, or to alter the line along which they ran (examples are the Leonine wall and the structure raised round St Paul's at the end of the ninth century by John VIII to protect the basilica on the Ostia road from Saracen assaults), or again simply to make them more beautiful, as was the case in the sixteenth century when Paul III commissioned Sangallo to design the famous bastions in the Ardeatino district. They also fortified the Mole Adriana, which under Gregory the Great (590–604) had become known as the Castel Sant' Angelo; on a number of occasions it was the focal point for the resistance offered by papal troops, and it was to facilitate movement from the

The growth of the Eternal City

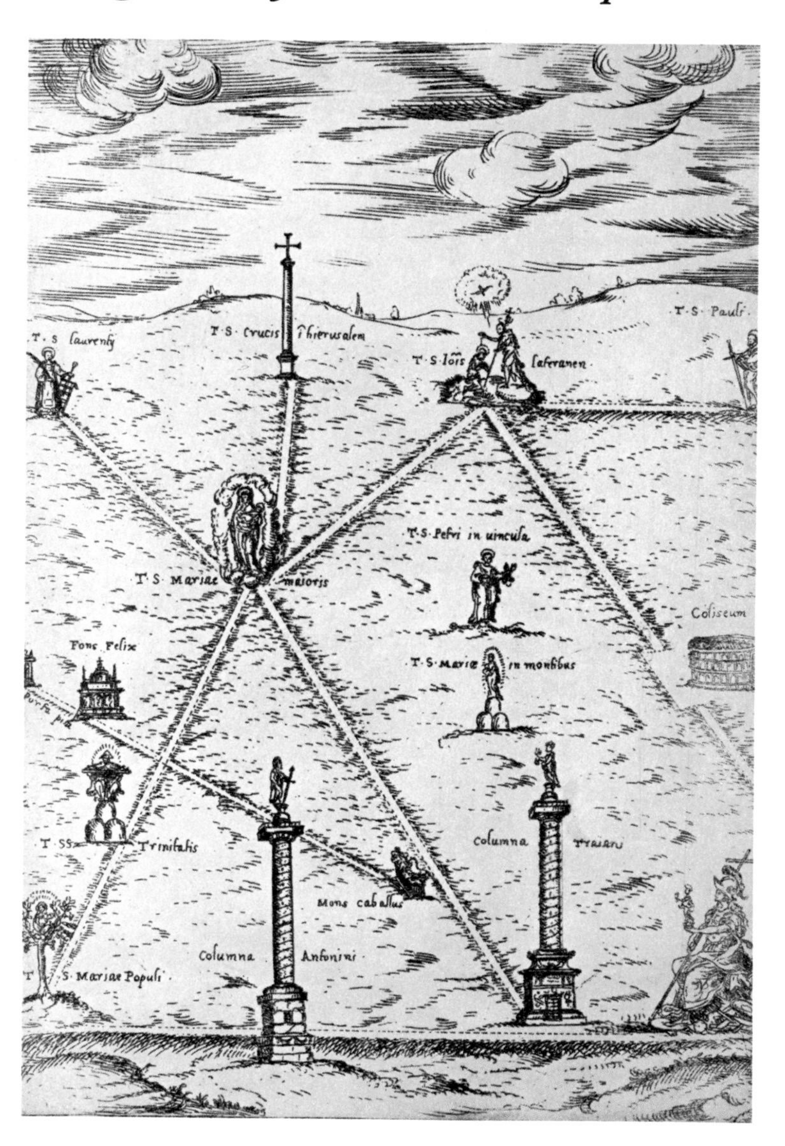

The most ambitious scheme for the re-planning of Rome was that of Sixtus V (1585–90). He set out to emphasize the Christian character of the city and conceived the idea of five great roads radiating from S Maria Maggiore and joining up the main churches of Rome. *Top right* A diagram showing Sixtus V's plan and also illustrating his scheme for placing Christian statues on the old pagan columns

Right A commemorative medal struck in 1589 in honour of Domenico Fontana, the architect commissioned by Sixtus V to erect a number of ancient obelisks in the main squares of the city

The Campidoglio, or ancient Capitoline hill, had always been the focus of civic liberty, the seat of the heads of the Commune and the meeting place of anti-ecclesiastical forces. It was not until the middle of the sixteenth century, when the people of Rome had lost all political autonomy, that the Popes made any changes to the Capitol

Paul III commissioned Michelangelo to re-design the whole square, but his project remained incomplete

Below A detail from an eighteenth-century map of Rome by Giovanni Battista Nolli showing the Capitol, with symbolic figures representing the Papacy

Vatican Palace to the castle that a covered corridor (*passetto di Borgo*) was built; it was put to good use by Clement VII during the terrible Sack of Rome carried out by the Emperor Charles V's *Landesknecht* in 1527. From Boniface IX to Nicholas V, from Alexander VI to Julius II, from Pius IV to Urban VIII, the Popes restored the castle, raised bastions, opened up the surrounding moat, erected glacis and towers, while others (particularly the Farnese Pope Paul III) adorned it with beautiful and sumptuous loggias and terraces. Often the Church's treasures were stored there, as also for some time the State Archives.

The presence of this military post was an obstacle to the development of the surrounding area (the so-called 'castle fields'), which for long remained uninhabited, while facing it, across the Tiber, rose the dwellings of the Orsini at Monte Giordano, like advance guards pointing at the Vatican.

The approach roads to the city were also kept in good repair and several Popes were responsible for erecting monumental gates along the city wall, entrusting the work to the greatest architects of the age (Michelangelo, Vignola, Bernini); by now many of these gates have been damaged or transferred elsewhere, but the one in the Piazza del Popolo still gives some idea of the old arrangement. Incidentally, the whole of the Piazza del Popolo and the slopes of the Pincio have the same appearance today as that given them in 1814 by Valadier. During their occupation of Rome the French carried out extensive reconstruction work in a dignified neo-classical style. The Popes not only carried out huge public works themselves but also preserved what had been carried out by others; this is true, for instance, of another very famous part of Rome, the Piazza di Spagna and the steps leading up to Trinità dei Monti.

The growth of the Eternal City

The Campidoglio illuminated in honour of the coronation of Clement XII in 1730. A contemporary engraving. Clement XII founded the collection of antiquities in the Capitoline Museum

Here secular buildings mingle with the ecclesiastical (the Palace of the Propaganda Fide, the Immacolata Column).

Among the works of the seventeenth and eighteenth centuries is the harbour at Ripetta, built in 1703 under Clement XI, with its elegant ramps from the river dock up to the road level; the Trevi Fountain (the joint work of Clement XII, Benedict XIV and Clement XIII); various outlets for the aqueducts; the erection of obelisks, the replanning of many squares (such as Piazza Navona and Piazza Colonna); the building of the Hospices of St Michael and others. But the main characteristic of this period is the baroque or rococo veneer added to the oldest churches, a style very popular at the time. By the use of a comparatively cheap and simple method, heavy stucco superstructures were made to cover slender columns and austere façades, so as to satisfy the taste for the opulent and the dramatic and give Rome the appearance it largely retains even today. However, as the eighteenth century proceeded, the Popes' financial difficulties increased and urban development slowed down, until the important changes in the political sphere put an end to a way of life which had altered little over the centuries.

The Campidoglio, or Capitol, had always been the focus of civic liberty, the seat of the heads of the Commune, the meeting-place for anti-ecclesiastical forces. Only from the mid-sixteenth century onwards, when all local political autonomy was lost and even the Capitol officials depended entirely on the Pontiff, is there any evidence of concern on the part of the Curia authorities for the replanning of the Campidoglio. Michelangelo's project is well known, and even though it was not completely carried out, it has nevertheless left its mark on the view which greets the visitor today (the staircase, piazza and adjacent buildings which overlook the square). The rooms inside the buildings were also improved by the addition of fine statues honouring the Popes (Urban VIII by Bernini, Innocent X by Algardi). At the time of the democratic republic in 1798 and Mazzini's republic in 1849, the Capitol at once became the symbol of revolt and of the struggle for independence.

From 1815, after their return from the exile imposed by Napoleon, until 1870, the end of the Church's temporal power, the Popes were less concerned with adding to Rome's artistic beauties than with providing for more concrete and pressing needs: roads, bridges, factories, schools and even the first railway stations, for example, at Porta Portese for the Civitavecchia line, at Porta Maggiore for Bologna, and the Termini Station for the Ceprano (Naples) and Frascati line. Public lighting was also provided, a large tobacco factory built in the Trastevere district (the present Piazza Mastai), the cemetery restored (Campo Verano near S Lorenzo without the Walls) and a start made on excavations in the Roman Forum which resulted in the first important archaeological discoveries, which were greeted with enormous interest in learned circles.

The new climate of opinion was making itself felt even in the old-established institution of the Papacy, and it was above all Pius VII (1800–23), with the help of the Secretary of State Cardinal Consalvi, and Pius IX (1846–78), advised by an able Belgian, Monsignor De Merode, who attempted to bring the administrative system up to date, to improve the standard of living, and to make life in Rome safer and more comfortable.

The Popes were responsible for most of the fountains, great and small, to be found in Rome. *Above* The Borghese heraldic beasts, the eagle and the dragon, on a drinking fountain in the Via della Conciliazone near St Peter's. *Below* The *Acqua Paola*, the grandiose fountain commissioned by the Borghese Pope Paul V from Fontana and Maderno, who incorporated some of the columns from old St Peter's into the design. An engraving by Piranesi

An early photograph of the Porta Ripetta, now demolished, looking towards Clement XI's steps

Below The Ripetta, or ancient port of Rome, as Piranesi saw it in the eighteenth century. The Customs House is on the left and the Palazzo Borghese in the centre. The fine baroque steps to the quay were built by Clement XI in 1703

16 THE POPES AND THE THIRTY YEARS WAR

PAUL V to URBAN VIII 1605-44

QUINTIN ALDEA

The Reformation left Europe deeply divided. In Italy and Spain Catholicism remained predominant and in France, after Henry IV's conversion, it was on the whole victorious. But in Germany the Catholic and Protestant states were sharply at variance and during the Thirty Years War Catholic France, for political reasons, supported the German Protestants against the Hapsburg powers of the Empire and Spain. The Papacy was mainly concerned with attempting to mediate between the Catholic powers and with a new phase of missionary activity. This period also saw important reforms in the procedure for papal elections and the selection of bishops.

THE THIRTY YEARS WAR WAS THE MOST REVEALING symptom of the constitutional malady from which Europe was suffering in the seventeenth century – political and religious disintegration. Europe suffered from an exaggeration of nationalism such as it was not to feel again until the nineteenth century.

As the number of states in any geographical area increases, instability and the danger of war increase also. The two areas of greatest instability at this time were the Holy Roman Empire and Northern Italy. If the German Empire had been as solidly united as France or Spain it might have constituted the political centre of gravity of Europe, but it was in a state of political atomization: there were seven electorates, ten *Kreise* governed by the Emperor's representatives, a string of principalities shared out among eighteen noble houses, and nearly seventy free cities. Something of the same sort was happening in the north of the Italian peninsula. Italy was made up of eleven separate domains: the Papal States, the possessions of the Catholic King of Spain (Naples, Sicily and Milan), three republics (Venice, Genoa and Lucca) and six dukedoms (Savoy, the Grand Dukedom of Tuscany, Modena, Mantua, Parma and Urbino). There were besides several noblemen exercising territorial jurisdiction, such as the Prince of Guastalla, the Marquis of Castellon and others of the Gonzaga family, the Princes of Mirandola, Massa and Monaco. All except three of these were in the north of the peninsula.

During the previous century political particularism inside the German Empire had been reinforced by religious schism, which had divided the German people into three: Catholics, Lutherans and Calvinists.

The Thirty Years War set this swarm of European states seething with unrest, and they lined up as it suited them best behind one or other of the two centres of power – the Hapsburgs or France. This warlike turmoil could not be restrained either by the marriage ties which united them with almost all the other reigning houses, or by defensive and offensive alliances against possible aggressors. Would papal mediation be more effective?

From the outbreak of the Bohemian revolution until the signing of the Treaty of Westphalia, the correspondence between the papal chancellory and the apostolic nuncios at the Catholic courts has only one theme: peace. As guardian of the peace the Pope had a twofold mission: to prevent the Catholic princes quarrelling among themselves, and to ward off aggression from heretics or the Turks. There were times when this twofold mission involved contradictory activities, as for instance in the Thirty Years War, when the House of Austria was fighting against the heretics and Turks on the one hand and against France – a Catholic country, but allied to the Protestants – on the other.

It was during the reign of Paul V (1605–21) that the Bohemian revolution occurred, an event which set the scene for the tragedy of the Thirty Years War. The conflict had from the first taken on the character of a religious war, with the spectacular episode of the defenestration of Prague (1618) and the intervention of several Protestant princes. The Calvinist Elector Palatine, Frederick V (1596–1632),

Paul V (1605–21) saw the beginning of the Thirty Years War, in which he supported the Catholic League. His monument in S Maria Maggiore includes scenes depicting the background of war

The Popes and the Thirty Years War

The political and religious unrest in Germany broke into open conflict in Bohemia when the electors refused the vacant throne to the Emperor and offered it instead to the Protestant Elector Palatine, 'the Winter King'. The outbreak of war was marked by the spectacular episode of the defenestration of Prague, when the Protestant leaders threw the Emperor's regents out of the windows of the royal palace. A contemporary engraving

was leader of the rebellion. Consequently, the Pope responded favourably to a request for help from the Emperor Matthias and the Spanish Ambassador, by giving 10,000 florins a month to the Emperor, and the Italian tithes and a subsidy of 100,000 scudi to the Catholic League.

Papal diplomacy also had an important part to play in persuading Louis XIII not to support the Elector Palatine. The fate of the usurping 'Winter King', Frederick V of the Palatinate, was decided at the celebrated battle of Weissenberg (8 November 1620). The Duke of Bavaria communicated the good news to the Pope in a slightly modified form of Caesar's famous phrase: *Veni, vidi et Deus vicit* (I came, I saw and God conquered). Two months before his death, Paul V was able to sing a Te Deum of thanksgiving for this notable victory in the national German church of Santa Maria dell' Anima in Rome. And on 28 January 1621, an apoplectic seizure put an end to his life while he was celebrating Mass.

Paul V was succeeded by Cardinal Alessandro Ludovisi, Gregory XV (1621–23), born in Bologna in 1554. He was sixty-eight years old, a man of small build, phlegmatic and placid by temperament, sparing of words and shunning human contacts. This physically feeble old man was aided in his administration by his nephew, Ludovico Ludovisi, a young man of twenty-six, possessed of noble bearing and charming manners, as well as great prudence and skill in negotiation.

Three characteristic events showed the trend of the new Pontificate: the bull relating to papal elections, the canonization of four great saints of the Counter-Reformation, and the establishment of the *de Propaganda Fide*.

Reform of the papal elections had long been considered the most radical change needed within the Church. 'It is not only a question of the health of a member but of the entire body, starting with the head', said Gregory XV in his papal bull *Aeterni Patris* (15 November 1621) speaking of the election of the Pope. The effect of the bull was that thenceforward the election would take place in closed conclave, and necessitated a majority of two-thirds of the total votes, which were registered in secret. It was also forbidden to vote for oneself. Of all the conditions imposed by the bull, the secret vote was the most important innovation, for it shut the door against many abuses.

The Pope's sympathies with the Counter-Reformation and his zeal for the propagation of the faith were symbolized in the canonization of such champions of the Counter-Reformation as the two great founders of religious orders, St Ignatius Loyola and St Philip Neri; also of the mystic and reformer of the Carmelite order, St Theresa of Jesus; and of St Francis Xavier, the apostle of the Orient (12 March 1622). 'At a time when new worlds were being discovered,' said the bull which canonized Ignatius Loyola, 'and when Luther was fighting the Catholic Church in the old world, the spirit of Ignatius Loyola was sent among us to found a Society dedicated to the conversion of pagans and heretics.' The first Pope to have been a pupil of the Jesuits wanted to express his gratitude and esteem for them by this act, just as his nephew Cardinal Ludovisi also testified to being a product of the Collegio Romano by building the church of St Ignacio at Rome.

Gregory XV's zeal for his flock was the directing force behind a great missionary movement. The distinguished Protestant historian Ranke realized more clearly than some Catholic historians have done how securely the Catholic

Gregory XV (1621–23) accomplished much in his two year Pontificate, which coincided with a lull in the Thirty Years War. One expression of his reforming zeal was the canonization of some of the chief saints of the Counter-Reformation, Ignatius Loyola, Francis Xavier, Philip Neri and Theresa of Avila, an act commemorated on the reverse of a coin of his reign

Below Bernini's famous statue of St Theresa, the mystic and founder of many Carmelite houses, who was canonized by Gregory XV in 1621

Church had been established in Central and South America under Spanish rule by the beginning of the seventeenth century; there were already five archbishoprics, twenty-seven bishoprics, four hundred religious houses and innumerable parish churches. The sacred and profane sciences were as skilfully taught in the great universities of Mexico and Lima as in the most famous European centres of learning. The conquest had become a mission, he said, and the mission a civilizing campaign.

Much the same could be said about the East Indies and all the regions under Portuguese dominion. Starting from the great Catholic headquarters at Goa, the crusade initiated by St Francis Xavier was rapidly spreading as far as the mysterious territories of China and Japan. The legendary expeditions of this great conqueror of souls had been followed, among others, by those of the famous Italian Jesuit Robert de Nobili (1577–1656), whose evangelistic methods created a regular missionary revolution, and like all new things roused fierce opposition. But Gregory XV was inspired to give them his full approval in the bull *Romanae Sedis Antistes* (31 January 1623).

The Pope cherished one great illusion throughout his Pontificate: that the marriage of the Prince of Wales with the Spanish Infanta Maria, sister of Philip IV, would be the means of the great English nation returning to their ancient faith. The Prince himself wrote to the Pope, promising to do all he could so that peace and unity should return to reign in God's Church and the Christian world, from which they had so long been absent. 'As we all acknowledge one triune God and one crucified Christ,' he wrote, 'so we may all unite in one faith and one Church.' But just when these comforting hopes seemed on the point of being realized,

The Popes and the Thirty Years War

Left Urban VIII's support of the Jesuits is commemorated in Andrea Sacchi's painting of a visit by the Pope to the Church of the Gesu. Sacchi was one of many artists to whom Urban gave papal patronage

Right Urban VIII (1623–44) ruled through the critical years of the Thirty Years War. Fearful that an imperial triumph would upset the balance of power, he withheld whole-hearted support from the imperial Catholic cause.
A bust of Urban VIII from the Castel Sant' Angelo.
During Urban's reign the papal court was dominated by members of his own family, the Barberini, four of whom he created cardinals. *Far right*
The bee, the Barberini family symbol, occurs frequently in paintings and sculpture of the period.
A motif from a mantelpiece in the Sala di Clemente VII in the Castel Sant' Angelo

the Pope died and they evaporated. Instead, God granted him the pleasure of seeing Ethiopia return to the Roman Church. On 19 December 1622, Gregory nominated as patriarch of that ancient Christian nation Doctor Alfonso Mendez, S.J. (1579–1659), who received the Emperor's oath of obedience to the Sovereign Pope.

So as to co-ordinate and direct all these missionary undertakings, he instituted the *Congregatio de Propaganda Fide* (in the bull *Inscrutabili divinae*) on the festival of Epiphany, 1622. In Urban VIII's day, the College of Propaganda was founded as a complement to this administrative missionary body; it was directed and financed by the Spanish priest Juan Bautista Vives according to the bull *Immortalis Dei* (1 August 1627). Here young men of the clergy of all nationalities were to be trained to go and propagate the gospel all over the world.

The Pontificate of Urban VIII (1623–44) was the longest of any during the six hundred years between Alexander III (*d* 1181) and Pius VI (*d* 1799). It coincided with the most decisive period of the Thirty Years War, and with the final desperate efforts of the Counter-Reformation. Hence his outstanding importance among all the seventeenth-century Popes.

Maffeo Barberini, Urban VIII, was born in 1568 into a family of Florentine merchants. The study of the classics, first in his native town and afterwards in the Collegio Romano, stimulated the brilliant literary gifts which he made use of to reform the Breviary when he was Pope.

The chief problems confronting him during his Pontificate were maintenance of peace among the Catholics, and defence against the heretics and Turks. But his desire to maintain political equilibrium led him to sympathize with France against the Hapsburgs, as was shown in particular by his negotiations with the Paris nuncio, J. Francisco Guidi di Bagno. When the dispute over the succession in Mantua suddenly developed into a European conflict, Urban VIII played a part worthy of his papal dignity, and also sent special nuncios to the courts of Vienna, Madrid and Turin, to pour oil on the troubled waters. But at the same time the Paris nuncio was secretly urging the French king and Richelieu to descend into Italy with a powerful army and 'liberate' it. This was denied by Pastor in his monumental *History of the Popes*, in which he defends Barberini's impartiality. But the truth cannot be disputed today. Even the protagonist, Bagno himself, categorically affirms the fact, and claims the glory of having 'done this great service' to his country, admitting that Cardinal Barberini offered him the means of carrying it out. So that both must have a share in the responsibility for the French invasion of Italy.

The Popes and the Thirty Years War

Another blow struck at the House of Austria by Richelieu and the nuncio Bagno was the Treaty of Fontainebleau between France and Bavaria in 1631, confirming an alliance between the Elector Duke and Louis XIII against the Hapsburgs. The ripest fruit of this alliance, for which Bagno had been working since 1628, was gathered during the Diet of Ratisbon (1630). It left the Emperor Ferdinand II politically vanquished and defenceless; the imperial General Wallenstein in disgrace; the election of the Emperor's son as King of the Romans boycotted. And a few months after the signing of the Treaty, while Wallenstein was peacefully counting geese and hunting his woods in retirement on his Bohemian farm, Gustavus Adolphus, King of Sweden, was winning one of the most important battles of modern times in the fields of Breitenfeld (17 September 1631). Thanks to two Cardinals, Richelieu and Bagno, the Catholic front had been broken.

Spanish espionage interrupted the correspondence between Bagno and Bavaria, and discovered just how much reliance could be put on Barberini's neutrality. All later attempts by the Pope to mediate between the Catholic powers were received with suspicion and mistrust. It is true that the Pope succeeded in bringing together the Congress of Cologne (1636), transferred later to Münster. But Richelieu's adroitness prolonged this indefinitely. After eight years of negotiation, Urban VIII died without seeing the hoped-for dawn of peace.

While the war was in progress, the Hapsburgs applied to him for money to carry on the struggle against the Protestants. It was decided in Vienna that the moment had arrived to make use of the treasure of the Castel Sant' Angelo (five millions in gold *scudi*), deposited there by Sixtus V in case of emergency. The Pope gave a categorical refusal. But in order not to seem to abandon the German Catholics, he gave them other help incommensurate with the magnitude of the danger. Sixtus V's millions would have decided the issue of the War.

The fact that his refusal arose from his lack of love for the House of Austria was shown some years later, by the useless war of Castro, on which he spent twelve million scudi, some of it taken from Sant' Angelo. And even more by the fabulous sum of 105 millions which he gave away in nepotism in the course of his Pontificate – a prodigality which, as we know, he regretted when he was dying.

In spite of this dark side to Pope Barberini's character, it is only fair to admit the services he rendered the Church. He repeatedly pressed for the execution of the reforms decreed by the Council of Trent, such as those concerning the residence of bishops. He prescribed new rules for the selection of candidates to bishoprics – the key to the spiritual life of the Church. To Urban VIII belongs the glory of having approved the Congregation of the Mission founded by St Vincent de Paul (12 January 1632), who also created an order of heroic women called Sisters of Mercy. We must add to these benefits, among others, his remarkable services to literature and the arts, for which Rome owes him everlasting gratitude.

One of the actions which have brought discredit on Pope Barberini's name was the condemnation of Galileo. But unjustly. Very few of his contemporaries had more admiration and esteem than he did for that great man of science. As Cardinal he was on friendly terms with him, and they used even to joke together about the view of the peripatetics that the sun and stars were made of incorruptible substance. And once when the Pope referred to the decree of 1616 against the Copernican system – and so indirectly against Galileo – he went so far as to say that if it had rested with him the decree would never have been enforced. How was it then that so well-disposed a Pope should have condemned Galileo?

One must bear in mind the two influences that were at this time deeply embedded in the Catholic schools: the peripatetic, wedded to the scholastic tradition and suspicious of everything new; and the scientific, which was more open-minded and ready to admit realities proved by

The subtle statesmanship of Cardinal Richelieu, secretly supported by Urban despite the French alliance with the Protestant states, dominated the later stages of the Thirty Years War. Richelieu laid the foundations of the absolutist policy in France, which under Louis XIV was to cause such trouble to the Papacy. A portrait by Philippe de Champaigne

Urban VIII examining plans for the rebuilding of the walls of Rome. A cartoon by Francesco Ubaldini for the Barberini tapestry factory

observation and experience. Among others the Jesuit astronomers Clavio and Grienberger, both professors of the Collegio Romano, were supporters of this second view and personal friends of Galileo. This division between the purely philosophic and the scientific attitudes would not have led to any serious conflict, if it had not been that each party interpreted Holy Writ in their own favour. Unfortunately, the theologians of the Inquisition all happened to belong to the first group, and defended their own ideas, while believing that they were defending Holy Writ. According to them the heliocentric theory was contrary to the inspiration of the Bible, and therefore 'theologically heretical and philosophically absurd and false'.

The Protestants interpreted the Bible even more literally, and Tycho Brahe himself maintained that the earth was immovable. Kepler suffered for his Copernican beliefs at the hands of his co-religionists.

All this goes to show how deep-rooted was the traditional view, and how difficult it is to change the prevailing structure of thought of any epoch. The Inquisition condemned Galileo under strong suspicion of heresy, and ordered him to abjure his errors and heresies. The astronomer preferred to remain a Christian – and submitted. 'The tragedy of Galileo's case,' as Pastor says, 'is that the outrage was committed by the representatives of the Church and in the name of religion.'

The Popes and the Thirty Years War

Left A detail of the ceiling of the hall of the Palazzo Barberini painted by Pietro da Cortona. It represents the Triumph of Divine Providence and is one of the most extravagant expressions of the baroque. *Below* The Palazzo Barberini, designed by the great baroque architects Maderno, Borromini and Bernini. An engraving by Piranesi

Above Galileo, whose theory that the sun was the centre of the universe ran counter to traditional and scholastic Catholic teaching, and led to his indictment for heresy by the Inquisition. Although a patron of literature and the arts and an admirer of Galileo's work, Urban acquiesced in his condemnation. A portrait by Sustermans

17 THE POPES AND THE ABSOLUTE MONARCHS

INNOCENT X to INNOCENT XII 1644-1700

MICHEL DIERICKX

When the Thirty Years War came to an end in 1648 the papal legate was excluded from the negotiations for the Treaty of Westphalia. The dominating personality in Europe during the next fifty years was Louis XIV. His absolutist policy and encouragement of the Gallican movement for an independent French Church inevitably led to a clash with the Papacy. The Popes were repeatedly called on to condemn the growing Jansenist movement and the quietist doctrines of Miguel Molinos spread rapidly until suppressed by Innocent XI. Louis XIV's attempts to extend the law of régale *and appoint royal nominees to all ecclesiastical benefices were firmly resisted by Innocent XI, but under Innocent XII a compromise solution was reached, although Gallicanism remained a powerful force.*

THE SECOND HALF OF THE SEVENTEENTH CENTURY was, particularly in France, a period of absolute monarchy. Political motives, and not religious convictions, determined the attitude of rulers, both in their internal policy and in their dealings with foreign powers. During this period the Popes, although they were still personally respected, lost much of their power and prestige.

Innocent X (1644–55), who had attacked his predecessor's nepotism, was soon guilty of similar practices. The influence at the papal Court acquired by Donna Olimpia Maidalchini, Innocent's brother's widow, was so great that even ambassadors and cardinals sought her favour.

The exclusion of the Pope's legate, Fabio Chigi, from the negotiations which culminated in 1648 in the Peace of Westphalia – a settlement which did the Church considerable harm – was a source of great mortification to the Pope. All he could do was to express his protest in the form of the papal bull *Zelus domus meae*, issued on 26 November 1648. He did, however, find some consolation in the Jubilee Year of 1650 when 700,000 pilgrims flocked to Rome.

Urban VIII's bull *In eminenti* of 1643 had failed to solve the problem of Jansenism, the growing heresy which opposed frequent communions. Nevertheless, Jansenism met with opposition in France not only from the Jesuits, who had attacked it from the start, but also from Saint Vincent de Paul, founder of the French Oratorians, from Monsieur Olier, founder of the Sulpicians, and soon after from the Sorbonne, from a number of bishops, and from the king himself. In 1649 Nicolas Cornet, syndic of the Faculty of Theology at the Sorbonne, extracted from Jansen's book, the *Augustinus*, five propositions which were declared heretical by the papal bull *Cum occasione* of 31 May 1653. All the French bishops, even those sympathetic to Jansenism, accepted this decree. Antoine Arnauld, 'le grand Arnauld', who succeeded Saint Cyran as leader of the Jansenists, thereupon made his historic distinction between doctrine and fact: the Pope had of course been right to condemn the five propositions, but, he maintained, they were not to be found in the *Augustinus* at all. The Sorbonne denounced Arnauld, and the Jansenist cause seemed irrevocably lost.

When Fabio Chigi, nuncio at Cologne from 1639 to 1651, and Secretary of State under Innocent X, was elected Pope Alexander VII (1655–67), hopes ran high, but few of them were realized.

On the death of his Prime Minister, Cardinal Mazarin, in 1661, Louis XIV decided to act as his own Prime Minister. Wishing to make a show of strength, he sent the Duc de Créqui to the embassy in Rome to represent him with suitable splendour. The Duke, proud and curt by nature, obeyed his orders with such offensive fidelity that the Pope's Corsican Guard, who had been sorely tried by the behaviour of the Duke's valets, broke into the embassy one day and even threatened the ambassador himself. The king took this insult very much to heart: the papal nuncio in Paris was conducted back to the frontier, the French ambassador was recalled from Rome and the Venaissin was occupied by French troops. The Pope was forced to accept the humiliating Peace of Pisa (1664), the main points

The reign of Innocent X (1644–55) was marred by nepotism and intrigue. His most important action was the condemnation of the growing Jansenist movement. Innocent was a Pamphili and this portrait by Velasquez is one of the most outstanding paintings in the great Doria Pamphili collection in Rome

The Popes and the Absolute Monarchs

Alexander VII (1655–67) came into repeated conflict with Louis XIV and had finally to accept the humiliating terms of the Peace of Pisa in 1664. A bronze medal dated 1663

A detail from the baroque fountain in the Piazza Navona which Innocent X commissioned from Bernini. The Pamphili arms can be clearly seen

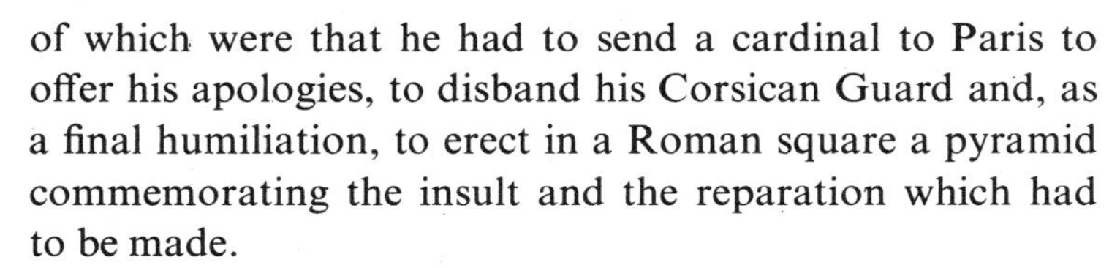

of which were that he had to send a cardinal to Paris to offer his apologies, to disband his Corsican Guard and, as a final humiliation, to erect in a Roman square a pyramid commemorating the insult and the reparation which had to be made.

In the meantime, Pascal had published his eighteen *Lettres à un Provincial*, in which he attacked the so-called 'liberal' moral teaching of the Jesuits. Written in a lively and facile style, they took the public by storm. The Jesuits were made to look ridiculous and their attempts to show that passages had been quoted out of context, or misinterpreted and so refute unjustified insinuations, met with little success. Although the Holy Office put the *Provinciales* on the index and a royal decree was issued ordering them to be burnt by the common hangman, their success could not be denied.

In an attempt to put an end to further discussion Alexander VII issued the decree *Ad sacram Beati Petri sedem* of 16 October 1656, which declared that the five propositions condemned by his predecessor were to be found in the *Augustinus* and that they had been condemned in the meaning they carried in that book. Finally, in 1665, the Pope was forced to draw up a *Formulary* of submission to be signed by all the French clergy. Four bishops refused and so did the nuns of Port-Royal, whom the Archbishop of Paris described as 'pure as angels and proud as devils'.

Although he was favourably disposed towards the Jesuits, Alexander VII also condemned forty-four 'liberal' propositions taken from Jesuit books of moral teaching.

Jesuit missionaries in China, acting on the principles of compromise advocated by the famous Matteo Ricci, allowed their Christian converts, in certain circumstances, to take part in ceremonies in honour of Confucius and of their ancestors. Certain Dominican and Franciscan missionaries, who had made converts among poor fishing communities on the Chinese coast, instructed Juan de Morales, a Dominican, to obtain a ruling from the Roman Curia on whether it was permissible to take part in these ceremonies. The congregation *de Propaganda Fide* replied in 1645 that Christians were forbidden to take part in these ceremonies in the conditions described in Morales' questionnaire. The Jesuits then drew up a counter-declaration and in 1656 a

Louis XIV receives the Cardinal Legate Chigi in audience at Fontainebleau in 1664. This magnificent Gobelin tapestry vividly portrays the splendour of the court of *Le roi soleil*

decree of the Holy Office, endorsed by Alexander VII, allowed Christians to venerate Confucius and their ancestors, provided the ceremony was purely secular and non-idolatrous. In 1669 another Dominican asked which ruling should now be applied. The reply was worthy of Solomon: 'both, according to what are the precise questions upon which a ruling is requested, the circumstances and any other relevant considerations.'

In 1654 Christina, who had ruled Sweden since the death of her father in 1632, abdicated the throne and renounced her Protestant faith. She was solemnly received into the Catholic Church in Innsbruck on 3 November 1655. On 19 December Pope Alexander VII received her in Rome with all the honours due to her rank. She was a very intelligent woman and a patron of literature and the arts, but her constant requests for money and her many eccentricities were a source of embarrassment to the Curia over a period of thirty-four years.

Alexander VII commissioned Bernini to design the famous colonnade which makes St Peter's Square the most beautiful in the world. The same artist was responsible for the decorations to the chapel of the Chigi family at Santa Maria del Popolo and added to the throne of St Peter the huge statues of St Augustine, St Ambrose, St Athanasius and St John Chrysostom.

By a rather free and somewhat ambiguous interpretation of the *Formulary* of Alexander VII, the new Pope, Clement IX (1667–69), permitted the four French Jansenist bishops and the nuns of Port-Royal to return from exile. The *Paix Clementine* remained in effect until the end of the century and enabled the Jansenists to increase their influence and to wage a secret war against the Jesuits.

Alarmed by the Turkish threat, Clement IX sought the support of the Catholic powers; he helped Venice to defend Crete against the Turks, but the island was nevertheless lost in 1669. He was succeeded by the eighty-year old Clement X (1670–76) during whose reign the question of the French *régale* first arose – a problem which was to create so many difficulties for his successor.

When Benedetto Odescalchi, Innocent XI (1676–89), was elected Pope, he was known as the 'father of the poor' and as a priest of great austerity and integrity. Undoubtedly

The Popes and the Absolute Monarchs

Alexander VII commissioned a large number of works from Bernini, pre-eminently the Scala Regia in the Vatican Palace *above* and the great colonnades enfolding St Peter's Square. The detail *left* shows the Chigi and papal arms of Alexander incorporated into the design of the colonnades

Queen Christina of Sweden renounced both her throne and her Protestantism and became a Roman Catholic in 1655. Brilliant, but unbalanced, her subsequent extravagances and eccentricities were a source of embarrassment to the Curia for thirty-four years. A portrait dated 1654 by the great French engraver Nanteuil

The Jansenist movement dominated the history of the French Church in this period and was repeatedly condemned by the Popes. It was supported by the genius of Pascal, whose *Lettres Provinciales* attacking the Jesuits, the principal opponents of the Jansenists, was put on the Index. *Below* The death mask of Pascal

he was the greatest Pope of the seventeenth century and he even had the courage to stand out against Louis XIV. He was considered a saint even during his lifetime and was venerated afterwards. He was beatified by Pius XII in 1956.

He brought order to the papal finances, which had previously shown an annual deficit of 170,000 *scudi*. He was responsible for the reform of several convents and fought against the laxity of morals in Rome.

In 1679 Innocent XI condemned sixty-five 'liberal' propositions. Without condemning 'probabilism', which the Jesuits and other teachers followed, he encouraged Thyrso Gonzalez, a Spanish Jesuit who wished to publish a book in defence of 'probabiliorism'. Probabilism taught that a really strong reason could justify a breach of a general rule of the moral law, even though stronger reasons urged the observance of the law; whereas probabiliorism laid down that one must always follow the course of action which has the strongest reasons to support it. In 1687 when a new Superior-General of the Society of Jesus was due to be elected, Thyrso Gonzalez was chosen in accordance with the Pope's request – an unaccustomed mark of obedience as far as the Jesuits were concerned.

Miguel Molinos, a Spaniard who had come to Rome in 1664, became extremely popular as a spiritual adviser and published the *Guia Espiritual*, a 'Spiritual Guide', which was quickly translated into several languages. Molinos preached 'quietism', according to which the soul should try and attain a mystical quietude, suppressing all independent desires and actions, so that the will of God was free to work unhindered. At first the Pope encouraged Molinos, but he was later forced to take action against him. Molinos was accused and later imprisoned in 1685, having admitted to improper relations with some of his penitents. In 1687 he was sentenced to life imprisonment and died nine years later. The papal decree of 20 November 1687 *Coelestis Pastor* condemned sixty-eight quietist propositions.

Innocent XI had to wage a prolonged struggle against Louis XIV. First of all there was the question of the *régale*. From time immemorial the kings of France had had the right to the income from a certain number of bishoprics during the vacancy of an episcopal see (*régale temporelle*), and also to appoint royal nominees to all ecclesiastical posts in these dioceses, except only those of parish priests

Another theological controversy in this period was roused by the 'Quietist' spiritual teaching of the Spaniard Miguel Molinos. He had many followers in Italy and France, but was condemned by Innocent XI in 1685. A contemporary portrait

The Turkish threat to Eastern Europe became increasingly grave at this time. The Turks were supported by Louis XIV and in 1683 they reached Vienna. Innocent XI succeeded in rallying the Polish and imperial forces to the relief of the city. This engraving celebrates the recapture of Budapest from the Turks in 1685, when the Turkish forces were on the retreat

(*régale spirituelle*). In 1673 a royal edict placed all the dioceses under the law of *régale*. Of the 130 French bishops, of whom fifty-nine were affected by the edict, only two protested. Innocent XI supported their action and wrote strongly worded letters to the king on three occasions; in the last of these, in 1679, he threatened him with excommunication. The king, unwilling to yield, summoned a General Assembly of the French Clergy, whose members – thirty-four bishops and thirty-eight representatives of the lower clergy – had been chosen from among the Gallican divines. After an able speech by Bossuet on the opening day, the Assembly embarked on a study of the law of *régale*. On 3 February 1682 the Assembly approved the extension of the law to all French dioceses, but the king conceded that the clergy appointed by him should be subject to a *missio canonica* from the ecclesiastical authority. On 2 April the Pope rejected this compromise proposal as being prejudicial to his authority as supreme head of the Church.

But the Assembly went very much further. On 19 March it unanimously approved the *Déclaration des quatre Articles*, drawn up by Bossuet. The first article affirmed the complete independence of the temporal power of the authority of the head of the Church; the second that the authority of the Council was superior to that of the Pope; the third that the Gallican Church enjoyed special privileges by virtue of 'special rules, customs and constitutions'; the fourth that although the Pope was the chief authority on matters of doctrine, his judgment was not final unless the consent of the Church followed. The Pope realized that the great majority of the French people supported the king and, in order to avoid a complete break, he did not condemn the *Déclaration* outright, but refused to give canonical consecration to the bishops nominated by the king. By 1688 thirty-five dioceses were without bishops.

In an attempt to set himself up as a champion of the Catholic Church Louis XIV in 1685 revoked the Edict of Nantes, which guaranteed certain rights to the Huguenots. At first the Pope approved these measures, but later withdrew

The Popes and the Absolute Monarchs

A seventeenth-century *Allegory of a Pontificate* attributed to Francesco Albani. Classical elegance allied to baroque theological extravagance typifies the period

his approbation when he saw the violence which followed.

Once again an incident provoked by Louis XIV embittered his relations with the Papacy. The foreign embassies in Rome exercised the right of asylum, but had extended this right to the whole area surrounding the residence. The Pope wished to put an end to this abuse which seriously hindered the efficiency of the Roman police. All the foreign powers agreed to comply except Louis XIV, who despatched the Marquis de Lavardin to Rome with an armed escort of 600 men. Innocent XI immediately excommunicated the French ambassador. In reply Louis XIV roused French public opinion by a well-conducted campaign; he occupied Avignon and placed the nuncio under house arrest. Innocent XI secretly informed Louis XIV that he was excommunicated. France was on the verge of schism. It was probably the king's genuine piety, his desire to remain at the head of the most important Catholic nation and the sudden changes in the European situation in 1688, which prevented him from taking the final step.

Throughout his Pontificate Innocent XI worked actively and with a certain measure of success to form a League of Catholic Nations against Islam. Only Louis XIV continued to support the Turks. In 1683 the Turks advanced right into the heart of Europe and besieged Vienna. After great difficulty the Pope succeeded in persuading the Polish king Sobieski to help the Emperor. He sent the Emperor 1,000,000 and Sobieski 500,000 florins. At the battle of Kahlenberg the Christian forces inflicted a crushing defeat on the Turks. The liberation of Vienna after a siege lasting three months is an event of the first importance. From this point onwards the Turks were on the defensive.

After the 'Bloodless Revolution' of 1688, William III, Stadholder of the United Provinces, came to the English throne and became Louis XIV's chief opponent. It has been suggested that Innocent XI was aware of the plot to depose James II in favour of William III and that he encouraged it in order to spite Louis XIV. This view is now rejected as being without foundation.

The Popes and the Absolute Monarchs

Above Innocent XI (1676–89) was the greatest Pope of this period. His whole Pontificate was overshadowed by the struggle against the absolutism and opportunism of Louis XIV, and the attempt by the French Church to maintain its national independence, classically stated in the Gallican Articles drawn up by Bossuet in 1682. A marble medallion portrait of Innocent XI

Left Innocent XII (1691–1700) inherited the struggle against Louis and the French Church. During his reign a compromise solution was reached which left the Gallican Church strongly independent until the nineteenth century. A contemporary terracotta bust

Innocent XI died on 12 August 1689, mourned and venerated by the whole of Rome. The Protestant historian Ranke is full of praise for this Pontiff who devoted his life to the renewal of the Christian spirit, to reconciling the Catholic princes and to defending the Christian West, and who did not hesitate to stand up to the most powerful monarch of his time.

He was succeeded by Alexander VIII (1689–91), whose Pontificate lasted only sixteen months. Two of his enactments must be mentioned. By the decree *Inter multiplices*, dated 4 August 1690, but promulgated on 31 January 1691, just before his death, the Pope declared both the extension of the *régale* and the *Déclaration des quatres articles* null and void. In 1690, at the instigation of the Archbishop of Malines, he condemned thirty-one Jansenist propositions taken from publications by professors of Louvain University.

In 1692, in an attempt to stamp out nepotism, Innocent XII (1691–1700), issued the bull *Romanum decet Pontificem*, which extended to the Apostolic See the sacred canons forbidding bishops to enrich their near relations at the expense of the Church.

During the War of the League of Augsburg Louis XIV found himself in need of papal support and made overtures to the Pope with a view to a reconciliation. The Pope proved willing and the following agreement was reached: the *régale* was extended to the whole of France and though the four Gallican articles were not revoked, the king ordered that they were no longer to be considered as a law of the state; finally the bishops who had been nominated by the king since 1682 received canonical consecration on condition that they expressly repudiated the *Quatre Articles*. Gallicanism still flourished, but Louis XIV had been forced to yield on some important points.

Madame Guyon, a pious, though an excitable and fanatical woman, and her spiritual director François Lacombe of the Barnabite Order were followers of Molinos and were responsible for spreading his ideas in France. The Archbishop of Paris had them arrested and Lacombe died in prison, half-mad, in 1715. Madame Guyon was released, but a commission, on which Bossuet and Fénelon served, examined her beliefs and condemned her as a quietist. Fénelon, however, was won over by Madame Guyon, who expounded to him her theories about total surrender, the call from within, silence and complete passiveness, and in 1697 he published his *Explication des maximes des saints*. He was attacked by Bossuet and the two bishops were soon engaged in a lively dispute. Under pressure from Louis XIV, Innocent XII condemned twenty-three propositions from the *Maximes* in 1699. Fénelon yielded with good grace to the Pope's ruling.

Clement IX (1667–69) was beloved by the Roman people for his simplicity and charity. During his short reign he mediated the Peace of Aix-la-Chapelle between France and Spain and sought to save Crete from the Turks. A portrait by G. B. Baciccia

CLEMENTE XI PON·M·SEDENTE
CAROLVS PRIOR PRESBYTERORVM S R E CARDINALIS BARBERINVS DE LATERE LEGATVS
AD PHILIPPVM V·HISPANIARVM REGEM CATHOLICVM, NEAPOLIM APPVLSVM, EXPLETO
FELICITER TANTO MVNERE SIBI BENIGNISSIME DE MANDATO, ANNO ÆTATIS SVÆ SEPTVAGESIMO TERTIO
IAM INCHOATO, SOSPES VRBEM INGREDITVR, AC SOLEMNI DE MORE EQVITATV CONTENDIT AD PALATIVM
APOSTOLICVM QVIRINALIS, COMMISSÆ PROVINCIÆ RATIONEM TANTO PONTIFICI EXPLICATVRVS
DIE XX IVLY MDCCII

18 THE AGE OF REASON

CLEMENT XI to CLEMENT XIV 1700-74

FERDINAND MAASS

The decline of the Popes' political influence continued and the secular powers took every opportunity to enlarge their authority at the expense of the Church. None of the Popes of this period were sufficiently strong personalities to defend either the Church's rights or her territorial possessions and the Papacy was subjected to repeated humiliations. The Jesuits were implicated in the general attack on the Church and in Portugal, France and Austria the order was suppressed. In 1773 Clement XIV was finally forced to dissolve the Society of Jesus and the Papacy lost one of its strongest bulwarks.

Left The papal legate, Cardinal Barberini, returning to the Quirinal Palace from an embassy to Philip, the disputed King of Spain, in 1702 at the beginning of the War of the Spanish Succession. The attempts of Clement XI to mediate between the rival claimants failed

EVER SINCE THE END OF THE THIRTY YEARS WAR the prestige of the Papacy had been steadily falling. At the root of this decline was the fact that men were turning away from the religious and doctrinal questions which in the past had led to so much strife and even to religious wars, and were now seeking to base human society on a natural foundation. The more abject the retreat of religion and of the Church (the community founded on religion), and the more deflated their spiritual value became, the louder grew the claims of the state, the natural human society. This new importance attached to the state was a constant incentive, particularly in non-Catholic circles, to those engaged in constructing a theoretical basis and rational superstructure for political society, using as their material subjects hitherto neglected, for example constitutional law, history, and other cognate studies. In such an atmosphere the state naturally also greatly enlarged its powers, in practice at the expense not merely of the domestic feudal nobilities, but also of the Church and Papacy, which from early in the Middle Ages had shared in secular government under a wide variety of forms, and now, even in the face of such altered conditions, still regarded this participation as their right, and a right they were not prepared to see contested. The administrators of the Church were further confirmed in this stubborn attitude when they realized that the rulers and their agents were not only insatiable in their material demands but were also using them to challenge traditional ecclesiastical and spiritual rights. The point was finally reached when the statesmen of the Enlightenment could claim that the papal Curia was lucky to have retained any influence in ecclesiastical affairs, since it was always open to the sovereign state to assume for itself any privileges not voluntarily surrendered.

For a century and more the leaders of the Church lived under the constant strain of this mortal threat to the foundations and existence of the Church and its work. It would have been little short of a miracle if they had consistently displayed the intellectual and human mastery demanded of them, if they had been able to apply at every juncture of this great trial of strength between the Church and the world just those counter-measures and tactics which at least offered, humanly speaking, some prospect of concrete results, even though they might not have produced a victory for the Church. But this was quite out of the question, for the simple reason that the secular rulers took care to use their influence in the conclave against any church dignitary whose political commitment or particular connections made it undesirable that he should become Pope. And so the Popes of the period were well-intentioned, sometimes learned and highly cultivated, pious and zealous pastors with a genuine concern for the welfare, purity and reform of the Church; but for all their good-will, they were largely deficient in just those qualities that were needed in such testing times: a surpassing knowledge of the world and of men, political acumen, initiative, energy, and not least that suppleness which could be an asset in the defence of Church privileges, especially when supported by the unyielding obstinacy that knows how and when to say '*Non*

Far left Benedict XIV (1740–58) and Cardinal Gonzaga by Panini. Writer, wit and scholar, Benedict earned the admiration of his contemporaries. He made few political concessions and effected many ecclesiastical reforms

Left Clement XIII (1758–69) was politically more rigid and less successful. He clashed with Austria and could not prevent the growing attack on the Jesuits. A portrait by P. Batoni

Clement XI supported the claims of 'James III', the Roman Catholic Stuart pretender to the English throne against the Protestant Hanoverians. After his defeat in 1715, James Stuart kept his 'court' mainly in Rome until his death in 1766. This contemporary painting by Antonio Gioninia shows him being received by a cardinal

Possumus'. Thus, as the Popes were driven step by step from the political arena, the Church's outer defences, they found they were also losing their freedom of action within their proper sphere, the ecclesiastical and spiritual. When the battle was at its fiercest during the sixties and seventies, the ordeal of the Church was so severe that Clement XIII and Clement XIV both died before their time, broken by terrible events.

Nor had the century opened auspiciously for the Papacy, since Innocent XII (1691–1700) had allowed himself to take sides in the problem of the Spanish succession, supporting the will made by the childless king of Spain, Charles II, in which the Hapsburg claim to succeed was passed over in favour of the French prince, Philip of Anjou. In the ensuing war between the Emperor and the king of Spain the neutrality of the Papal States was ignored, and the inhabitants forced to provision the imperial troops. When Clement XI (1700–21) took up arms in protest at this plundering of his subjects, at the double injustice of the taxation of the clergy and at the failure to respect his own rights as secular suzerain of certain Italian territories (Parma, Piacenza, Naples), his troops proved incapable of offering any resistance worth the name, so that the Pope was soon compelled to agree to the Emperor's chief demand, papal recognition of his brother as king of Spain. But despite this surrender (which earned the Pope some harsh reprisals from the rival Spanish claimant) the Emperor, Joseph I, still withheld his recognition of the Pope's rights over the Italian territories, and when he died suddenly the papal nuncio was unceremoniously excluded from the ensuing imperial election. Thus, even at the beginning of the period it was plain to all the world how far papal prestige had sunk.

This decline was further confirmed by the negotiations over the peace treaty, when Sicily was assigned to the Duke of Savoy, once again without any heed to papal claims to suzerainty. Without reference to Rome, the new ruler of the island was invested with the so-called *Monarchia Sicula*, which conferred sweeping ecclesiastical privileges, some of them derived from the Norman rulers of bygone centuries, the rest of very dubious origin. The fact that they continued to be claimed and exercised by the new régime even after the suspension of the *Monarchia Sicula* by the Pope in 1715 was yet another sign of the times.

The Pontificate of Clement XI was not without its battles and reverses, even in the purely spiritual sphere. Jansenism once again reared its head, and by making subtle distinctions sought to undermine the Pope's authority in matters of doctrine; amongst other things the Jansenists refused to accept the bull *Unigenitus* (1713), an important statement of dogma which condemned 101 propositions of Quesnel, and there were even some French bishops who appealed from the Pope's decision to a General Council. These 'Appellants', who defied even the Pope's excommunication, were a grave threat to the Church in France, and the danger they represented was not removed until the time of Benedict XIII (1724–30), and then only with secular assistance. So even this papal victory was not accomplished without increasing the prestige of the state. Moreover, this partial spiritual triumph, achieved by a pre-eminently pastoral Pope, was overshadowed by the malign influence of

Above Clement XI (1700–21) became embroiled in the War of the Spanish Succession and was unable to prevent the Papal States being violated by the contending armies. A contemporary engraving

Right Innocent XIII (1721–24) was a sick man, under pressure from all sides and unable to follow a consistent policy. A coin of his reign

Right Benedict XIII (1724–30), a holy pastor but a disingenuous man. His reign was overshadowed by the intrigues and ambitions of the unscrupulous Cardinal Coscia, who was imprisoned on his patron's death. A coin of his reign

Cardinal Niccolo Coscia, who had carved out a commanding position for himself under the innocent and unworldly Pope, and used it to betray the interests of the Church in his dealings with the princes, shamelessly seizing every opportunity of adding to his own fortune.

It is true that the next Pope, Clement XII (1730–40), was a man who had given many years of distinguished service to the Church; but by the time of his accession he was seventy-eight years old, and was prevented from asserting the full authority of his office by ill-health, the increasing handicaps of old age and the total blindness which descended on him soon after the start of his reign. These infirmities made him heavily dependent on his entourage, and may account for the failure of the Holy See to recover Parma and Piacenza when the line of their feudal rulers became extinct, for the unchecked encroachments of the state in the kingdom of Naples, under its fiercely anticlerical minister Tanucci, and for the continuing ill-will of Spain towards the Papacy, even after the further concessions granted by the Pope in the concordat of 1737. Nor was there much practical advantage from the condemnation of freemasonry, whose leaders certainly played a part in the international campaign against the Church, even if they were not its actual instigators. The bull of condemnation was banned in Austria, where the consort of the heiress to the throne, Maria Theresa, was himself a freemason, the first person of princely rank to be so.

In these circumstances even the scholarly Benedict XIV (1740–58), described by Macaulay as the best and wisest of Peter's 250 successors, could do little to improve or alter the position in which the Church found itself, although he was careful to yield to lay pressure only under duress, and to offer from his side every possible occasion for agreement. An Austrian envoy in Rome observed that in making political concessions the Pope was careful to surrender to temporal powers only what was already theirs. But these good intentions were soon put severely to the test. During the war of the Austrian Succession (1740–48) the neutrality of the Papal States was flagrantly ignored and the belligerents treated its territories as a kind of training ground and

Above Painting pays homage to Clement XII by L. G. Blanchet. Clement XII (1730–40), although infirm, blind for most of his reign, and politically powerless, was an enlightened patron of the arts. He started work on the new façade to the Lateran basilica seen here *right* on the reverse of a coin of his reign

Left Clement XII was responsible for the building of the beautiful Capella Corsini, dedicated to S Andreas Corsini, in the Lateran basilica. A detail of the gate to the chapel

Below The Trevi fountain, the most famous in Rome, was commissioned by Clement XII. An engraving by Piranesi

Benedict XIV opening the Porta Santa for the Jubilee of 1750. Since 1450 Jubilees have been celebrated every twenty-five years. On Christmas Eve the Pope opens the special door of St Peter's ceremonially with a silver hammer and closes it again a year later.
A drawing by Panini

transit camp. When Charles Albert of Bavaria, who had been elected Emperor despite the bitter opposition of Maria Theresa, was also recognized by the Pope, Austrian resentment was so intense that the Cardinal Secretary Valenti was deprived of the income from his ecclesiastical benefices on Austrian soil by a sequestration order which remained in force for five years. The Emperor for his part repaid the Pope for his friendly gesture by accepting a dangerous project, put forward by the Protestant princes, for the secularization of some of the south German bishoprics, which was only stopped by the anti-Bavarian policy of Austria. When this Emperor died in January 1745 he was succeeded by Francis I, husband of Maria Theresa, and despite the protests of France and Spain the Holy See again gave its consent, although the Pope could not have been overjoyed at the prospect of an Emperor known to hold 'Enlightened' views on religion and the Church. Finally, when none of the belligerent nations assembled at Aix-la-Chapelle for the peace treaty in 1748 was prepared to recognize papal suzerainty over Parma, Piacenza and Guastalla, there could be no disguising the truth, that the Church was unable to defend or maintain possessions of this nature, 'which belong to this world'.

Benedict XIV was more successful in his handling of strictly ecclesiastical affairs. He concluded formal concordats with the governments of Naples, Spain, Portugal, Sardinia and Venice; he even reached agreement with Austria about the sequestered church properties in Lombardy (*Colonica*); he set up the archbishoprics of Gorz and Udine in place of the lost patriarchate of Aquileia; he issued the so-called *Benedictina*, with its formula for the conclusion of mixed marriages, and a new edition of the Index of prohibited books; he protected the rites of the Church in the East from the effects of inadmissible methods

Benedict XIV receiving Charles III, the first Bourbon King of Naples, and later King of Spain, in the Quirinal Coffee House. A typical scene of eighteenth-century court life depicted by Panini

of attracting converts; and finally, by his moderation and good sense the Pope sought to remove some of the grounds of Jansenist protest, which was again vocal.

These were considerable achievements, and won Benedict praise even from his Enlightened contemporaries. The Pontificate of his successor, Clement XIII (1758–69), led to what in human terms must be described as disaster. Where Benedict had been flexible, the new Pope and his energetic secretary of state, Cardinal Torrigiani, were convinced that the defence of the Church must begin on its perimeter. They held therefore that it was a mistake to be liberal in making even political concessions, still less to yield ground in those areas which concerned both Church and State, where governments were seeking to obscure lines of demarcation. The Pope's arch enemy in this respect was the Austrian Chancellor, Prince Kaunitz, who for his part often remarked that the Pope might feel glad he still had any concessions to make. It was Kaunitz who first advanced the view that not only Catholic princes but all heads of state (including of course Protestant rulers) had inherited, as defenders of the Church and faith, rights of Church government once exercised by the Pope. Later he went even further and brought the Austrian church directly under the sovereign power of the state, in the system of state-church known as 'Josephism'. Similar encroachments by the state took place in other countries, and in the small duchy of Parma were so flagrant that the Pope was forced to excommunicate the Duke, whereupon the Bourbons threatened to invade the Papal States; Maria Theresa turned a deaf ear to the Pope's appeals for help and Kaunitz used the opportunity to consolidate the main outlines of his plan for a state-church, already approved by the Empress. But over and above all these formidable difficulties, there was the political persecution of the Society of Jesus. It was

In 1773 Clement XIV (1769–74) was forced to succumb to political pressures from all over Europe and dissolve the Society of Jesus. *Above* A marble bust of Clement by Christopher Hewitson and *below* the title page of the Bull suppressing the Jesuits, printed in parallel Latin and Italian for the benefit of ordinary citizens

BOLLA
DEL SOMMO PONTEFICE
CLEMENTE XIV.
Volgarizzata col Testo Latino a confronto per benefizio degli Idioti.
NELLA QUALE SI DICHIARA SOPPRESSO L' ISTITUTO
DEI GESUITI.

SI VENDE IN FIRENZE DA GIUSEPPE ALLEGRINI ALLA CROCE ROSSA.

this that really determined the fate of the Papacy during the reigns of the next two Popes.

The Jesuits were inevitably implicated in the general attack on the Church, since they were its staunchest supports. So it was that their defeat over the so-called 'affair of the rites' was noted with satisfaction by the enemies of the Order, both clerical and secular. In 1742 the Holy See, to secure uniformity of practice among missions to the peoples of the Far East, prohibited certain ceremonies such as those associated in China, Japan and India with the veneration of ancestors: the Jesuits and the local rulers regarded such rites as social rather than religious in implication. The political persecution of the order was quite unconnected with this affair. The statesmen of the Enlightenment were determined to break the Jesuits' hold over court, church and people, to expropriate the Order and to secure the interests of the state against attack from this quarter. With this programme in mind, the Portuguese minister Pombal asked in 1758 for a papal visitation of the Order. But before it had taken place the Jesuits were falsely convicted of conspiring against the king's life and were sentenced, some to prison, others to exile. In France the Order's main enemies, apart from the atheists, were the Jansenists. There the situation was brought to a head by the affair of Father LaValette, a Jesuit who had disregarded both the rules of the Church and the express command of his superiors by engaging in large-scale commercial dealings. Many merchants were ruined and the whole country roused, so that the French courts intervened and ruled that the Order as a whole was responsible for the enormous losses incurred, a decision contrary to Canon Law. When the Order contested the judgment and through its General refused to submit to the proposal for 'reform' presented soon afterwards (this was to have been achieved by the appointment of a vicar-general for France), the Society of Jesus was declared illegal in France and banned from the country. Clement XIII offered only wavering resistance to the mounting pressure applied in concert by the Bourbon courts, who now followed the French lead and demanded the complete suppression of the Order. When even Maria Theresa, anxious not to jeopardize the French marriage arranged for her daughter, Marie Antoinette, also deserted the Jesuits, Clement's successor, Pope Clement XIV (1769–1774), was forced to dissolve the Society of Jesus (1773), to avert a threat of schism.

Although the Pope had made the great sacrifice of surrendering the Jesuits, it could bring the Church no relief in the merciless struggle now being waged by the openly hostile powers. For, as Ranke long ago pointed out, the fall of the Society of Jesus deprived the Papacy of its outer defences: the inner citadel was for the first time directly exposed to attack, and sooner or later would surely – to all outward appearance at least – be taken by storm, as the next Pontificate was to show.

The Age of Reason

A contemporary engraving showing Clement XIV announcing the 'dissolution, extinction and quite abolition' of the Society of Jesus to the Spanish ambassador

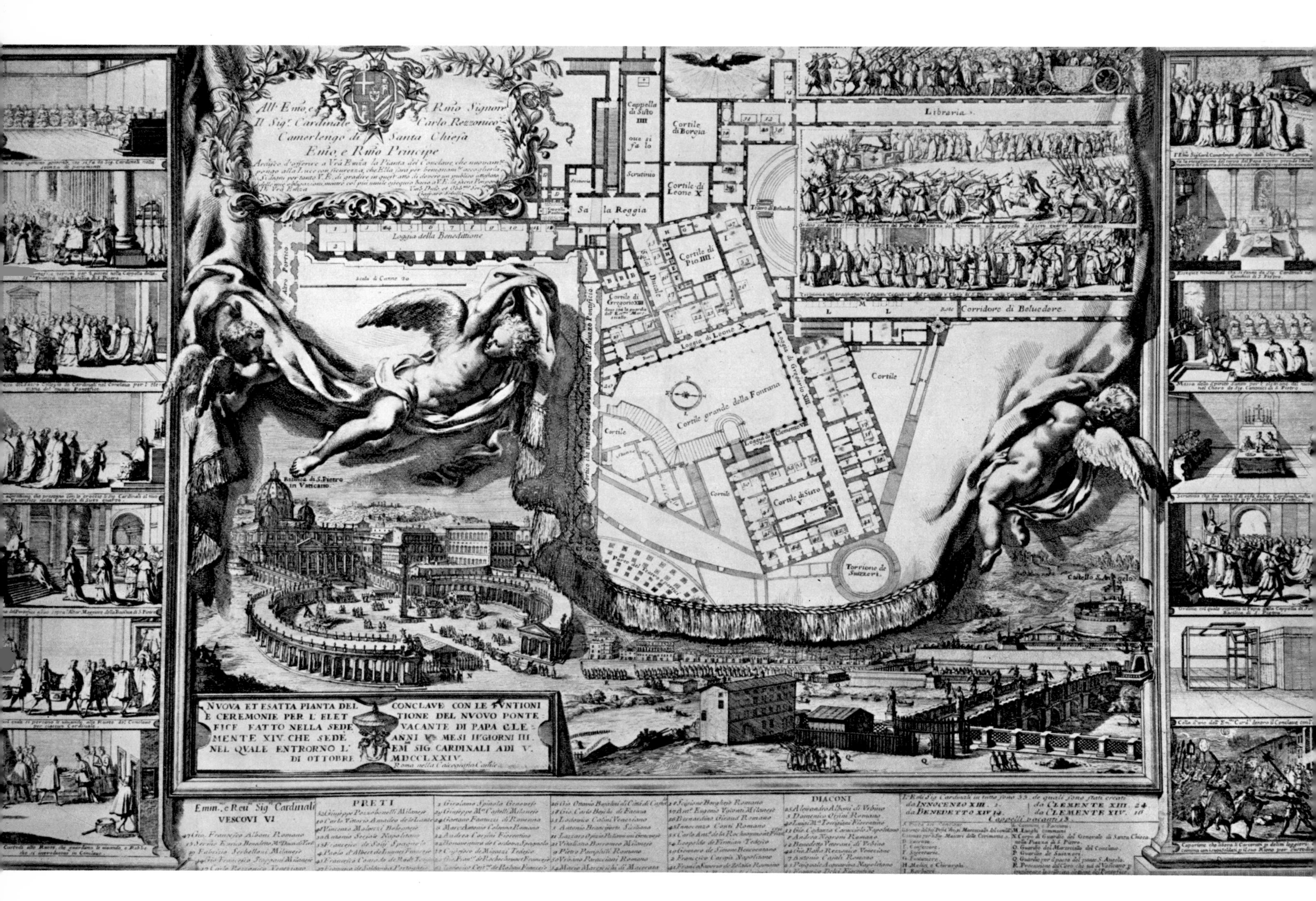

Pius VI was elected after a conclave lasting nearly five months. This contemporary engraving, dedicated to Cardinal Rezzonico, the Cardinal Camerlengo in charge of the arrangements, depicts scenes between the death of Clement XIV and the election of Pius. It shows in the centre a ground plan of the Vatican chambers in which the cardinals spent the period of the conclave

19 THE YEARS OF REVOLUTION

PIUS VI and PIUS VII 1775-1823

BURKHART SCHNEIDER

In the second half of the eighteenth century the Roman Catholic Church was subject to increasing pressure from temporal governments. Pius VI's personal visit to Joseph II in Vienna failed to stop state interference in the affairs of the Austrian Church. In France the outbreak of the Revolution brought with it the Civil Constitution of the Clergy, which deprived the Pope of any rights over the Church. In 1799 the Revolutionary armies invaded Italy and Pius VI died in captivity. The new Pope, Pius VII, bravely resisted the pressure put on him by Napoleon and then he too was imprisoned. The sufferings and personal heroism of the Pope aroused the sympathy of Europe and at the Congress of Vienna Cardinal Consalvi was able to negotiate the restoration of the Papal States. Despite the humiliations it had suffered, the institution of the Papacy survived and took on a new significance with the development of Ultramontanism, which became the predominant voice of the Church during the nineteenth century.

FOR THE FIRST TIME IN ITS WHOLE HISTORY THE Church had a Pope whose reign lasted almost as long as the twenty-five years traditionally assigned to St Peter's tenure of office in Rome; it was his fate to witness the continuation of a process already begun with the Enlightenment and the growing preference everywhere for an established national church. Papal prestige and influence steadily diminished, even in Catholic countries, to reach their nadir at the end of the century, when the Papacy seemed on the verge of extinction. The first years of the new century saw the Holy See occupied by an alien power. But it is precisely at this juncture that the characteristics of the modern Papacy begin to emerge. No longer committed to the exercise of a temporal authority, it was in this outward impotence that the Papacy now showed itself great and started to attract increased respect, even outside the Church.

Cardinal G. Angelo Braschi of Cesena, who was elected Pope in February 1775 after a protracted conclave which lasted more than four months, chose the name Pius, and thus started a modern fashion in papal nomenclature. His first aim was to restore the Eternal City to its former splendours. The magnificent sacristy he added to St Peter's was the last piece needed to complete the grand design of the whole basilica. Continuing the sixteenth-century revival of Roman traditions, the Pope had ancient obelisks re-erected in the central squares of the city, as embellishments in stone of the urban landscape. The museum of antiquities in the Vatican was enlarged, to become a worthy repository for the rich archaeological finds dug up in and around Rome. The Pope was a most generous patron of the arts, and papal Rome once again became the cultural capital of Europe, a place of pilgrimage for men of all nations. But, as might be expected, such liberality had its darker side: expenditure was far in excess of the financial resources of the Papal States, especially in view of the Pope's determination to secure a privileged position for his own family, yet another instance of the influence on him of past tradition. The Palazzo Braschi, with its magnificent staircase, is the last of a long series of papal family palaces.

The superficial glories of Rome could not disguise the fact that the Church and the Papacy were permanently on the defensive. The most immediate danger was Josephism, the system named after Joseph II of Austria (1780–90), from 1765 co-ruler with his mother, Maria Theresa. This was a mixture of Gallican ideas and the fashionable theories of the Enlightenment, with *raison d'état* as the guiding principle, and it produced a thoroughly secularized form of church. Finding that he achieved nothing through the normal diplomatic channels, in 1781 the Pope took the unusual and extreme course of seeking a personal interview with the Emperor, in the hope of altering his policy. The papal nuncio in Vienna who submitted the Pope's proposal was addressed by the Emperor in a speech prepared by the Austrian Chancellor Kaunitz, an eloquent illustration of the humiliations heaped on the Papacy: 'We shall certainly convey our heartfelt gratitude to the Pope for the honour he has condescended to propose to us. But at the same time we shall ask to be excused from accepting the proposal, in recognition of the duty laid on us to avoid any entanglement with the Holy See in the exercise of rights entrusted to the sovereign alone.' But even this barely disguised rebuff did not deter the Pope from his plan, and he actually spent the months between 22 February and 22 April 1782 in Vienna. However, the aura of splendour which surrounded the Pope during his visit was not matched by anything substantial in the way of results.

The Pope's journey to Vienna was an event of European importance, and its failure showed up the impotence of the Church. Only a little later, in 1786, Pius VI had to stand by while the Synod of Pistoia (a place very close to Rome and the Papal States) approved resolutions which endorsed not only Josephism but also Jansenist doctrines.

The French Revolution had as incisive an effect on the Church and the Papacy as on the history of the world. It was more than the reshaping of an existing order. It was,

Above Pius VI (1775–99), whose long pontificate began in splendour, with generous patronage of the arts and ended in his humiliation by the armies of the French Revolution.
A marble bust by Giuseppe Ceracchi

Below The Emperor Joseph II of Austria who gave his name to Josephism, the policy of subordination of Church to State which was bitterly opposed by the Papacy.
A contemporary engraving

Below In 1782 Pius VI took the unprecedented step of a personal visit to Vienna in an unsuccessful attempt to win Joseph II and his Chancellor Kaunitz from their anti-papal policy.
He is seen here driving through the streets of Vienna

The return visit of Joseph II to Pius VI
in Rome in 1783. A contemporary engraving

as Edmund Burke declared, 'a revolution of doctrine and theoretic dogma'. The last decade of the reign of Pius VI was in fact completely overshadowed by the French Revolution. Under the Civil Constitution of the Clergy, promulgated 12 July 1790, the Pope was deprived of any rights over the church in France, which was to be reconstructed on purely democratic lines. Louis XVI was made to confirm this constitution and also the decree issued a few months later ordering the clergy to swear acceptance of it. The Pope was well aware that Louis's position was difficult in the extreme. A month after the ecclesiastical legislation had been confirmed Pius wrote to the king: 'We have so far withheld our just repudiation of the civil constitution. Our love for you and the special affection we feel for your realm prompts us to proceed with unusual moderation.' In the event the Pope did not issue his formal condemnation until 13 April 1791, and the real persecution of the church in France began. Thousands of priests and nearly all the bishops were forced to leave the country. The Pope did everything he could for them and gave asylum to many in his own territories. And after the execution of Louis XVI on 21 January 1793 Pius openly indicted those responsible as murderers, bestowing on the king the honorary title of martyr for the holy faith.

All the hatred of the Revolution turned itself against the Church and the Papacy. Papal possessions at Avignon and in the Venaissin, previously occupied, were now annexed. A war which went badly for the Papal States was followed by the truce of Bologna (23 June 1796), which imposed conditions of great severity, for example a very heavy monetary levy and the surrender of many priceless works of art. When it came to making the peace (treaty of Tolentino, 19 February 1797) the young general Napoleon Bonaparte was able to dictate his own terms. The Papal States, although much reduced, remained for the moment in being. But within a year Rome was occupied. On 15 February 1798 it was proclaimed a republic and on 20 February the Pope was expelled. He found shelter of a kind, first in an Augustinian monastery at Siena and later, from the beginning of June, in a Carthusian house outside Florence. But when Tuscany was occupied by French troops at the end of March 1799 the Pope could no longer remain at large.

Opposite Pius VI (left) and Pius VII (right), during whose long pontificates the Papacy suffered bitter humiliation by France. But this humiliation foreshadowed the spiritual power of the Papacy when deprived of political jurisdiction. Portraits by P. Batoni and J. L. David

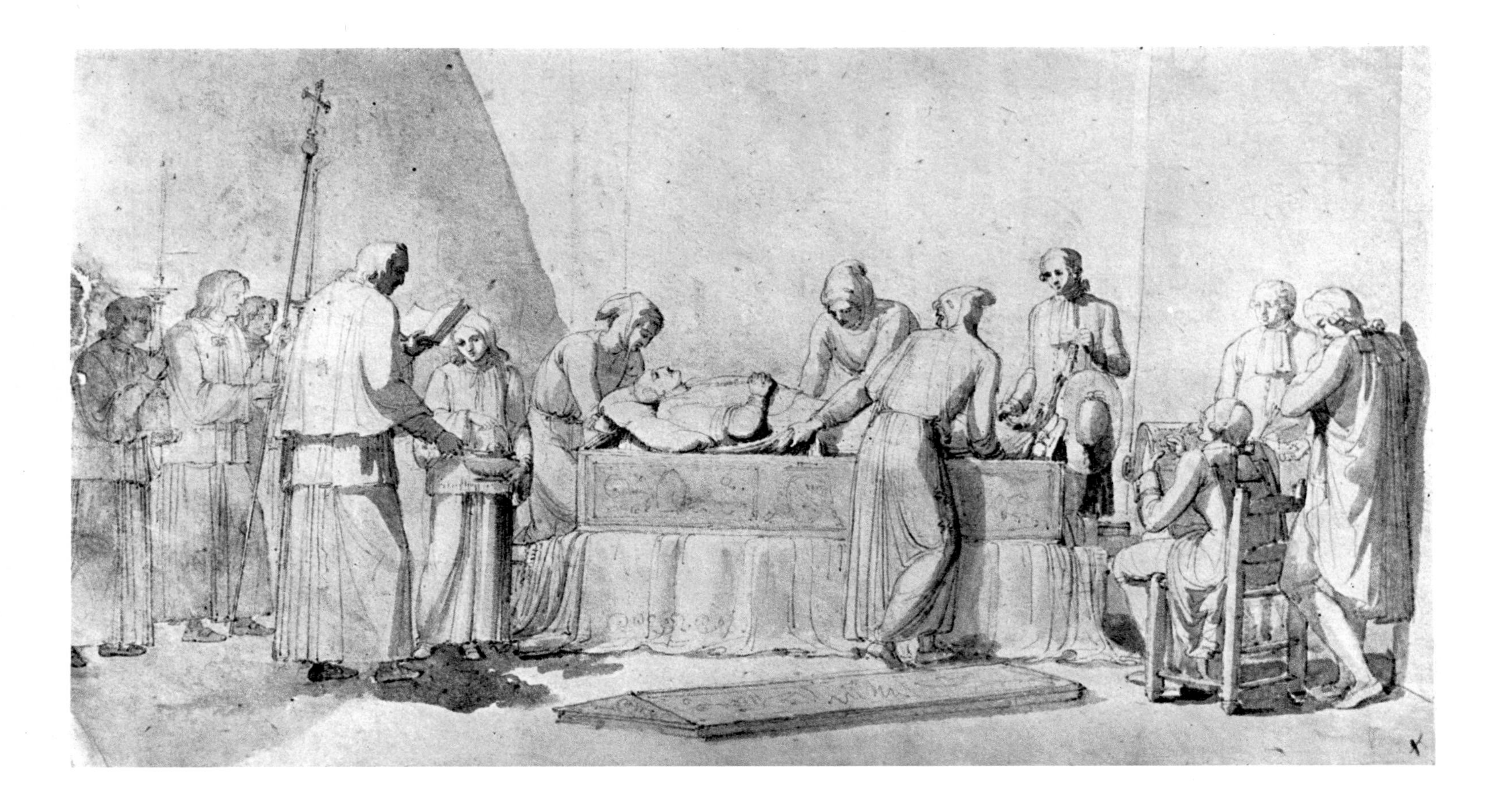

Pius VI was driven from Rome by the armies of the French Revolution and died a prisoner at Valence, after being carried, a sick man, across the Alps. An anonymous nineteenth-century drawing

Gravely ill and temporarily paralysed, he was removed from Florence on 27 March and taken first to Bologna, thence to Parma and Turin, then by way of the Mont Cenis pass to Grenoble and Briançon and finally to Valence, where he arrived on 14 July. The Directory in Paris ordered this senseless and murderous peregrination to continue, but the Pope was at the end of his strength. On 29 August 1799 he died, and his last words were 'Father forgive them'. But hatred pursued Pius VI even beyond the grave. His body was refused proper burial until January 1800, by which time Bonaparte had become First Consul; once the Concordat had been concluded he gave permission for the body to be taken to Rome. The martyred Pope made his solemn entry on 17 February 1802, to take his last resting place in the grotto of St Peter. Twenty years later Pius VII unveiled Canova's statue of his predecessor, which stands in the Confessio of St Peter, close to the tomb of the Prince of the Apostles.

With the death of Pius VI the Papacy seemed extinct. Rome was occupied, the Curia dissolved, the College of Cardinals scattered, the spirit of the Revolution had nearly the whole of Europe in its triumphant grip. However, whilst he was still in Florence Pius VI had decreed that after his death the conclave should be held wheresoever most cardinals were to be found. This turned out to be Venice, since the treaty of Campo Formio an Austrian possession. Thirty-five out of a possible total of forty-six cardinals assembled on the island of San Giorgio for the conclave, which lasted from 30 November 1799 until 14 March 1800. The election was complicated by political considerations, in particular the need to consider Austria. In the end the choice fell on the Benedictine Cardinal Barnaba Chiaramonti, Bishop of Imola. He took the name Pius VII and appointed as his closest associate Ercole Consalvi, whose diplomatic adroitness and complete reliability earned him the entire confidence of the Pope.

The articulate anti-Christianity of Revolutionary France spread to Rome when the city was invaded in 1798, the Pope expelled and a Republic proclaimed. The pagan classical celebrations in St Peter's Square at the time of the Republic, depicted by Felice Giani

LUD. DAVID
PARISIIS 1805

The Years of Revolution

In the summer of 1800 the Pope was able to return to a now liberated Rome. Two-thirds of his long reign would be passed with Napoleon in power in France. It opened with the French Concordat of 1801, engineered by the First Consul and imposed on the Church by means of very harsh sanctions; and yet with it was laid the foundation stone of the reconstructed Church. The Pope was prepared to make very large concessions, and, as he said, 'Disaster needed only a few years to do its work, though it was decades long in preparing, and so it will take centuries to rebuild the shattered house of holiness.' Napoleon for his part had a real respect for the Pope, powerless though he was, and instructed the negotiators in Rome to 'treat the Pope as though he had two hundred thousand men'. Popular feeling in Rome, however, was very bitter and found expression in doggerel such as the verse comparing the two Popes Pius:

> Pius [VI] to keep the faith gave up his power
> Pius [VII] to keep his power gave up the faith.

The little Napoleon had left to the Church was soon still further diminished. In the hope of improving the position,

Below left In the critical political situation of 1800, with Rome occupied by French troops, the cardinals had to assemble for the conclave in Venice. This election engraving shows the new Pope, Pius VII, and in the background the church of San Giorgio, where the conclave was held

Below right The last page of the account of the election of Pius VII, showing the final scrutiny on 14 March: Albani 1 vote, Chiaramonti 34

Di 14 Marzo
Mane Scrutinio
Del Sig. Albani — v. 1
Chiaramonti — v. 34

Fine

Venezia, 9. Xbre 1863.

In 1804 Pius VII was persuaded to go to Paris for Napoleon's coronation.
A detail from David's famous painting showing Pius VII a helpless onlooker, while Napoleon, having set the crown on his own head, is about to crown the kneeling Empress Josephine

The Years of Revolution

Pius accepted an invitation to attend the coronation of Napoleon in Paris at the end of 1804. The visit was as barren of practical result as his predecessor's journey to Vienna. During the next few years the Pope observed a strict neutrality and refused to be drawn into the Emperor's continental blockade; in consequence he was subjected to mounting pressure which culminated in the renewed occupation of Rome by French troops on 2 February 1808, followed in May 1809 by the annexation of the Papal States to the Empire. The Pope retaliated by issuing the Bull of Excommunication which lay in readiness, directed against 'despoilers of Peter's Patrimony and all who command, protect, advise and abet them'. Commenting on the Bull in a letter to his step-son, Eugène Beauharnais, the Emperor said, 'Does he really think his excommunication will make my soldiers' weapons drop from their hands?' There were not a few who saw the catastrophe of the Russian campaign as heaven's judgment on a scoffer. During the night of 5–6 July 1809 a surprise attack was made on the Pope in the Quirinal palace and he was carried off to the sea fortress of Savona. On the way he remarked to his companion: 'We did well to publish the Bull of Excommunication on 10 June, for what could we have done about it now?'

For more than three years Napoleon did all he could to make the Pope amenable. Cut off from the outside world, deprived of his counsellors, ignominiously treated, at the mercy of Napoleonic informers within the hierarchy, who were his only channel of communication, Pius VII was worn down and reduced to a state of exhaustion. The Emperor had him brought to Fontainebleau near Paris and forced him, weak as he was, to sign a draft concordat which deprived the Church of important rights; the Emperor then ordered the immediate publication of this document as though it were the final agreement. Those cardinals who had been under arrest or in prison because of their loyalty to the Pope were now set free and allowed to join him. Fortified by their presence and advice, Pius retracted the concessions he had made. The fall of Napoleon brought all the Pope's tribulations to an end, and on 24 May 1814 he was able to return to Rome. The Pope forgave and forgot the injuries he had suffered and during the following years repeatedly interceded for the ex-Emperor in captivity on St Helena; the Pope was even so magnanimous as to offer Napoleon's relatives a safe asylum in Rome.

The most graphic account of this unequal contest comes from the pen of Ranke, the Protestant historian: 'This was indeed a singular struggle, a struggle between one who had mastered the world more completely than any man before him and a man who was destitute and a prisoner. The one

Napoleon started his rule with the Concordat of 1801 which re-established the Church in France, but gave him substantial Gallican powers. After his coronation he embarked on the persecution of the Pope which lasted until his fall. A portrait of Napoleon by Robert Lefèvre

The last page of the Concordat of 1801 between Napoleon and Pius VII, showing the signatures of Bonaparte, First Consul, his Foreign Minister, Talleyrand, and other plenipotentiaries

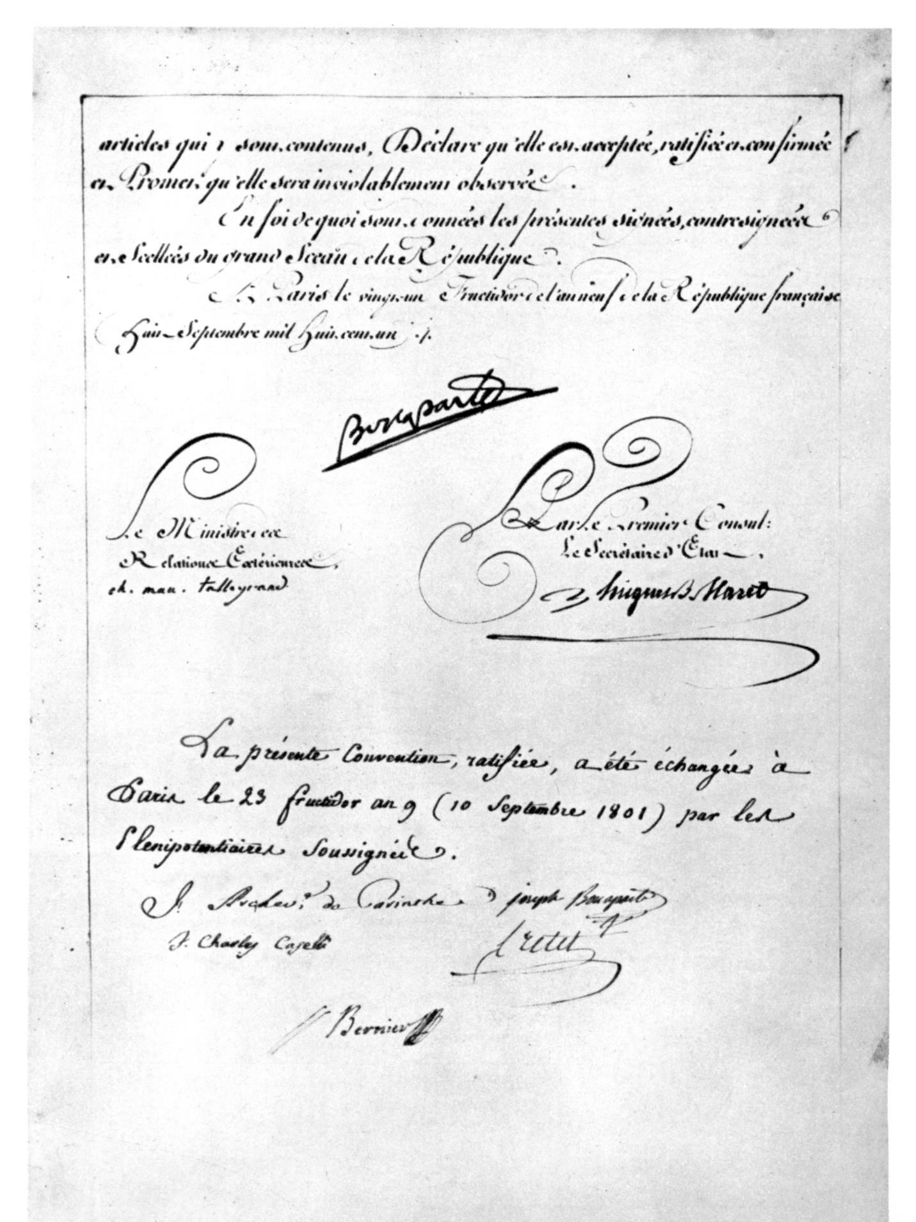

articles qui y sont contenus, Déclare qu'elle est acceptée, ratifiée et confirmée et Promet qu'elle sera inviolablement observée.

En foi de quoi sont données les présentes signées, contresignées et scellées du grand Sceau de la République.

A Paris le vingt-un Fructidor de l'an neuf de la République française (huit Septembre mil huit cent un).

Bonaparte

Le Ministre des Relations Extérieures
ch. mau. talleyrand

Par le Premier Consul:
Le Secrétaire d'Etat
Hugues B. Maret

La présente Convention, ratifiée, a été échangée à Paris le 23 fructidor an 9 (10 Septembre 1801) par les Plenipotentiaires Soussignés.

Joseph Bonaparte
J. Charles Caselli
Cretet
Bernier

In 1808 French troops again occupied Rome and the Pope became virtually a prisoner in the Quirinal palace. The Pope entering the Quirinal with his cardinals to say mass, despite the French troops and cannon. One of a series of engravings by Pinelli on the reign of Pius VII

The arrest of Pius in the Quirinal on the night of 5 July 1809, when French troops made a surprise attack on the Pope

Pius entering a carriage on the morning of 6 July before being carried off to the fortress of Savona

Left A symbolic engraving showing Pius VII, a prisoner and surrounded by enemies, but still continuing his pastoral ministry

Right At the Congress of Vienna following Napoleon's defeat at Waterloo, Cardinal Consalvi, the papal Secretary of State, succeeded in negotiating the restoration of the Papal States.
An allegorical engraving showing Consalvi presenting the figures of Romagna, Pontecorvo, Benevento and the Marches to Pius, under the auspices of a triumphant Austrian Empire (left)

basked in the enjoyment of all the splendour and power the world has to offer, was plenteously endowed with subtlety and foresight, shrewdness and energy, combined with the gifts needed to command men, and went on his way unswerving, his goal constantly before his eyes; the other, after a period of being treated with unnatural deference, was suddenly deprived of all intercourse with the world, cut off from human contacts, completely isolated. And yet his very existence was a source of power. He was allied not with open forces but with those mysterious inner powers which throughout Christendom now turned spontaneously towards him, impelled by the habit of centuries of faith and worship. All eyes were on him; his resistance to oppression, his sufferings, aroused men's sympathies all the more because they reflected an experience which was general; all this served to add immeasurably to his stature and to surround him with the glow of martyrdom.'

Consalvi, the cardinal-secretary, persuaded the Congress of Vienna to revive the Papal States. Arguments based on the historic rights of the Papacy, on the illegality of their suppression and on the importance of sovereignty as a guarantee of independent church leadership, were powerfully reinforced by the personal prestige of Pius VII. Commenting on the favourable outcome of the negotiations, Consalvi wrote: 'Had it not been for the immensely high reputation of the Holy Father and the excellent opinion men hold of his sanctity and his whole person, all would have been vain – God knows I speak the truth and do not flatter – I repeat, argument and pleading and bargaining would all have been in vain, or at best have achieved only the most meagre results.' But it was also Consalvi who had the foresight to appreciate that 'difficult though it was to recover what had been taken away – I say this quite openly – it is more difficult still to keep what has been restored. If one should make a wrong decision or an unfortunate mistake, those lands will be lost again within six months.' In fact the internal policy adopted in the Papal States was not prudent and their government became more and more of an embarrassment.

Meanwhile, the rebuilding of the ecclesiastical organization, which in many parts of Europe had been demolished by the Revolution and its aftermath, was proceeding apace. The division of the bishopric of Baltimore, hitherto the only diocese in North America, was in its way the starting point of a great upsurge in the fortunes of the Church. Although its effects were as yet imperceptible, these small beginnings were at least a partial fulfilment of the prophecy made in 1795 at the height of the Revolutionary storm by a French priest, writing to Pius VII: 'If France had to be lost to the Catholic Church, it is very likely that God is preparing his recompense in the United States.' Although at first reserved towards the struggles for independence in Latin America, during the last years of Pius VII the Papacy became somewhat less rigid in its attitude. In 1822 the first ambassador from a South American state, Cienfuegos of Chile, was received in Rome, and the first papal mission, which included the young Giovanni Mastai-Ferretti, afterwards Pope Pius IX, set out on its long journey to the remote continent.

The reassertion of the papal position achieved during the reign of Pius VII found its classical exposition in the book published by the Savoyard Joseph de Maistre in 1819 under

the title *Du Pape*. De Maistre defended the Papacy and proclaimed papal supremacy not only as an ecclesiastical institution but also as a political authority whose existence was vital to the West and to civilization generally. Experience of the disintegrating effects of the Enlightenment and of the destruction unleashed by the Revolution led to a reappraisal of traditional values. De Maistre's book became the first literary manifesto of the movement known as Ultramontanism, to become throughout the nineteenth century the most predominant voice of the Church. The Pope was now more than ever looked to as the acknowledged and actual centre of the Church, and the faithful felt themselves closely linked with him, both in his office and his person. This was not simply a matter of organization but a genuinely religious movement, bringing people and leader closer together.

Pius VII had scarcely returned to Rome before he turned his attention to the Jesuit Order, suppressed by Clement XIV in 1773; the revival of the Order in various countries had already been sanctioned, and the Pope now made the reinstatement general. Admittedly, the fresh start could only be made in a very restricted field and was a long way from redressing the losses the Church had suffered, especially in missionary activity and education. Nevertheless, the Order made itself a dominant influence in the Ultramontane movement of the new century.

It was the cardinal-secretary, Consalvi, who determined the policy adopted during this Pontificate in political dealings between the Church and the world. He stood for the view that the Church should approach secular powers, on whose good-will so much depended during the years of reconstruction, with only limited and feasible ends in view. Though there were exceptions, relations between the Holy See and national governments, particularly of non-Catholic countries such as England, Russia and Prussia, were always very friendly. The conduct of the Pope during the struggle with Napoleon had made a lasting impression. Visible evidence that this was so is to be found in the Waterloo Chamber of Windsor Castle where the Pope and Consalvi are included among the monarchs, statesmen and generals of the coalition against Napoleon whose portraits were commissioned by George IV, though in fact they have no business there, since the Holy See had been strictly neutral.

Pius VII died at the Quirinal Palace on 20 August 1823, after a long illness and six days after his eighty-first birthday. He had not been told of the disastrous fire of 16 July which had all but destroyed the very ancient basilica of St Paul outside the city walls. The faithful secretary lost office on the death of his master, and survived him by only five months. As Consalvi had remarked at the beginning of the last year of the reign, 'We shall depart together, the Pope and I.' And it is fitting that Consalvi, who probably knew Pius VII better than anyone else, should speak his epitaph: 'The outstanding features of his personality were his sweetness and moderation.'

The two Popes Pius, who both came from Cesena (they were distantly related) and whose Pontificates were among the longest in the history of the Church, were alike also in having to suffer threats, oppression and persecution. But powerless and defenceless in their own persons as they were, they made an essential contribution to establishing and strengthening the Papacy in its modern aspect.

Left Leo XII (1823–9) led the Church in the difficult years following the Napoleonic period. The bitter experiences of the immediate past led Leo and his successors to ally themselves with the reactionary, anti-liberal forces led by the Austrian Chancellor Metternich. During Leo's reign the Ultramontane movement, which exalted the authority of the Papacy above the national Churches, gathered strength. A contemporary engraving

Leo XII put in hand the rebuilding of S Paolo fuori le Mura after the disastrous fire of 1823. This was typical of his vigorous policy of rebuilding in Rome. The new church was built on the plan of the original basilica. The façade seen through the pillars of the great quadriportico

20 REACTION AND REVOLUTION

LEO XII to GREGORY XVI 1823-46

KENNETH SCOTT LATOURETTE

After the death of Pius VII the Papacy was intent on preserving the temporal power recovered at the Congress of Vienna. Relying on Austrian support, the newly restored Papal States were administered with a policy of repression that made papal rule very unpopular. After the experiences of the French Revolution the Popes looked on liberal movements of any kind with suspicion and gave their support to the conservative anti-democratic elements. On the other hand it was a period of vigorous missionary enterprise outside Europe.

THE YEARS BETWEEN THE DEATH OF PIUS VII (1823) and the accession of Pius IX (1846) were years of continued threats to the Church's faith and a rising tide of vitality in the Church. Both had begun before the quarter century and were to mount in the years which followed.

The threats were serious. Among them were the persistence of the rationalism of the eighteenth century, the de-christianization of large elements of the population, intense anti-clericalism, and the disruption of much of the inherited structure of the Church. Another was the growth of political 'liberalism', which, in spite of the efforts of Metternich and others, exploded in the revolutionary year of 1830. Very serious was the rising tide in Italy of the nationalism which under Pius IX was to erase the Papal States and render the Pope a 'prisoner in the Vatican'. Still another threat was the independence of the states which emerged from the Spanish colonial empire in the Americas. Partly because of the contest to which they gave rise between the Spanish Crown and the new governments for the control of the Church, and partly because of the penetration of the secularizing scepticism of the 'Enlightenment', the Church in that region reached a nadir. By 1827 nearly four-fifths of the episcopal sees were vacant and most of the missions to the Indians had lapsed.

At the conclusion of the Napoleonic Wars Cardinal Consalvi at the Congress of Vienna had obtained for the Papacy the restoration of the full Papal States – not only of the Patrimony of St Peter around Rome but also of the Marches around Bologna on the other side of the Apennines, where papal rule was very unpopular. It was Austrian policy at that date to dominate the Italian peninsula, and the Papacy, without serious military force of its own, could only maintain its rule over its territories by relying on Austrian support. In order to contain revolutionary outbreaks in their own territories the Popes of that period formed a sort of civic guard, known as the Centurions or *Sanfedisti*, who suppressed opposition, often with great brutality. The policy amounted to the arming of one half of the population against the other half and was vigorously criticized even in ecclesiastical circles – most notably by the then Bishop of Imola, destined to be Gregory XVI's successor as Pius IX. The experience of the Papacy at the hands of the French Revolutionaries and Napoleon caused the Papacy at this period to throw itself most strongly on to the conservative and anti-democratic side. This policy was an alliance of throne and altar, and not only caused the Papacy to condemn Lamennais' programme, as expressed in *Paroles d'un Croyant*, for a liberal and democratic Church, but even to support the Protestant King of Holland against the revolt of the Belgian Catholics and the Orthodox Czar against the revolt of the Polish Catholics.

On the other hand, in a variety of ways the Church was displaying its inherent vigour. The resurgence had begun before 1823 and was to continue long after that year. Among the many evidences were the revival of older orders and congregations and the emergence of new congregations. In the British Isles Catholic Emancipation (1829) removed the legal disabilities under which the faithful had

Two leaders of the Ultramontane movement were the Catholic writers Comte Joseph de Maistre *left* and Abbé Felicité de Lamennais *right*. They urged centralization of the Church on a strong and revived Papacy. De Maistre saw this as the political hope of a Europe shattered by the forces unleashed by the French Revolution; Lamennais saw it as the spiritual hope for the Church in the nineteenth century, but was later disillusioned by the political and intellectual conservatism of the Popes

long laboured. The geographic spread of the faith was marked. Thanks to the extensive immigration of Catholics, the United States and Canada were the scene of the rapid growth of the Church which was to continue in that and the following century. Missions were given a major impulse by several new bodies.

A feature of the revival in the life of the Church was the mounting recognition of the authority of the Pope. To this at least three trends contributed. One was the disappearance or decline of Gallicanism. In general the administrative authority of the Papacy was less challenged by the State than in the eighteenth century. A second trend was the advocacy of Catholic writers, particularly Joseph Marie Comte de Maistre and Félicité Robert de Lamennais. Their writings had their major influence in the years covered by this chapter. A third trend was represented by the *Zelanti*. In Rome a number of cardinals collectively known by that designation stood for the authority of the Pope as a defence against the 'liberal' movements of the day.

On the election of a successor to Pius VII several influences were brought to bear. From a number of quarters opposition developed to one candidate, Ercole Consalvi, Pius's great Secretary of State. To another candidate an Austrian veto was threatened. Ultimately, with the support of the *Zelanti* and in spite of French opposition, Annibale Francesco Clemente Melchior Girolamo della Genga was elected. He took the title of Leo XII (1823–29). The son

of an Italian nobleman, he had received part of his education in Rome. He had been a favourite of Pius VI and under him had served as Nuncio in several posts in Germany. During part of the Pontificate of Pius VII, when the latter was being maltreated by Napoleon, he had taken refuge in the monastery of which he was the titular head. When elected, Leo XII was physically frail – tall, pale, and emaciated. He told his fellow cardinals that they had chosen a corpse.

Although he suffered from repeated illnesses, Leo XII gave to his high office vigorous and able leadership. In a variety of ways he consistently endeavoured to improve the inner life of the Church and to extend its influence. He set an example of faithfulness in his personal devotions and of frugality in his private expenses. He spent long hours at his desk and in audiences. He officiated at masses and other public ceremonies more than had his immediate predecessors. He urged the bishops to be living exponents of sound morals and doctrine, to be faithful in their pastoral duties, and to seek to raise up and train a worthy clergy. He was adamant in forbidding nepotism by papal officials. To quicken the life of the Church and to rally it to the support of the See of Peter, he proclaimed a jubilee year. He showed initiative in putting the churches of Rome in better physical condition, in particular in the rebuilding of St Paul's Outside the Walls, and stimulating improvement in the morals of the city. He hoped thus to make Rome an inspiration to Christian life in the Church as a whole. He denounced literature which seemed to him evil and at the same time encouraged education and scholarship and enriched the Vatican Library. He opposed Gallicanism, Josephism and Febronianism. He showed favour to Lamennais, who was then vigorously championing the Papacy. He negotiated several concordats which were favourable to the Church. He risked the displeasure of the Spanish Crown by appointing bishops to the American colonies, which were in revolt against Spanish rule, without consulting Madrid, and so attempted to restore Catholic life in that vast region. He continued the policy of Pius VII in encouraging the Catholic minority in England and in showing friendship to the English College in Rome, which was preparing clergy for that country.

To many in Rome the policies of Leo XII, threatening as they did the notorious laxness of morals among the people and some of the clergy, were decidedly unwelcome. The covert opposition expressed itself more in inertia than in open dissent, but many heaved a sigh of relief when death removed the ailing Pontiff.

To the conclave which met to choose a successor to Leo XII, both France and Austria let it be known that they wished a moderate. Yet with the zealously Catholic Charles X on the throne of France and Metternich in control in Austria, this did not mean a compromise with the 'liberal' currents of the day. Presumably the two powers wished a

Two scenes of nineteenth-century life in Rome from engravings by Pinelli. *Left* A procession returning from performing the *Via Crucis* in the Colosseum and *right* a friar preaching in Lent. The hooded figures are *Sacconi*, members of a men's confraternity founded in 1729 and confined to Rome, which devoted itself to charitable works, especially the escorting of pauper funerals. Their activities were typical of nineteenth-century piety

Pope who would be more tolerant of the claims of the secular rulers and less insistent on the authority of the Holy See than Leo XII had been. The *Zelanti* could not unite on a candidate. The choice eventually fell on Francesco Saviero Castiglioni (1761–1830). Castiglioni was of a noble Italian family and had had extensive experience as a bishop and as an administrator in Rome. He was an expert in the Scriptures and canon law, with an interest in numismatics as a recreation. Pius VII had shown him favours and had created him Cardinal. Out of gratitude Castiglioni took the title of Pius VIII (1829–30). Mild in temper, he seemed to be the answer to those who wished a moderate in the Holy See.

What the record would have been had the reign lasted

Pius VIII (1829–30) was chosen as a compromise candidate, who would stand out against the growing liberal movements, but would be less insistent than his predecessor Leo XII on the claims of the Holy See, and so avoid antagonizing the secular powers. His brief reign gave promise of these hopes being fulfilled. A contemporary portrait

Above Gregory XVI (1831–46) blessing the cap and sword, which by tradition the Pope sends to Catholic Princes. Gregory set his face against all liberal movements and obtained help from Austria to suppress the growing nationalist movement in the Papal States. He sought to maintain the *status quo* and the authority of the ancient monarchies at a time when the tide against them could not be held back. An early nineteenth-century engraving

Right When the Catholic nationalist Poles rebelled against the Orthodox Czar in 1831, Gregory was in a difficult position. He publicly condemned the rising which threatened the established régime allied to Austria, although privately he remonstrated with Czar Nicholas I for the brutality with which the insurrection was suppressed. A mid-nineteenth-century painting showing the meeting between Gregory and Nicholas I, with Cardinal Acton, an English Curial cardinal, who acted as interpreter

longer can only be surmised. As it was, Pius VIII had only a little over twenty months in office. During that short time he gave some indication of following a middle course between the policy of his immediate predecessor and compromise with the forces of the age. But he warned his relatives not to come to Rome, for he wished to shun even the appearance of nepotism. Although he abolished the system of espionage created by Leo XII, Pius VIII was clearly intent on maintaining the authority of his office and the unique mission of the Catholic Church. He claimed for the See of Peter jurisdiction over the entire Church and its bishops. He condemned the opinion, then popular in some 'liberal' circles, that salvation could be obtained through any religion. He upheld the sanctity of marriage and urged the bishops to foster the religious education of the youth of their flocks. He opposed the Bible societies promoted by Protestants and condemned secret societies. In the revolutionary movements of 1830 he encouraged the bishops to remain at their posts. Unhappy as he was at these revolutions, he conferred on Louis Philippe, the nominal but lukewarm Catholic whom the Revolution of 1830 had placed on the throne of France, the traditional title associated with that crown of 'His Most Christian Majesty'.

Because of the revolutionary upheavals of 1830, both Austria and Spain, concerned for the maintenance of the *status quo*, were emphatic that they would oppose the elevation of any man to succeed Pius VIII who would be less than firm in his opposition to the 'liberal' trends of the day. The *Zelanti* were able to bring about the election of a candidate who was both fully of their mind and acceptable to Austria and Spain. The choice fell on Bartolomeo Alberto Cappellari. When in his teens, against the wishes of his family and from a deep sense of vocation, Cappellari had joined the Camaldolese, one of the strictest of the monastic orders. During the storm of the French Revolution he had boldly come out with a book, which proclaimed his confidence in the ultimate victory of the Church and the Papacy, and upheld the infallibility and temporal sovereignty of the successors of St Peter. He had been trusted by both Pius VII and Leo XII and the latter had made him Prefect of the Congregation for the Propagation of the Faith. As Pope he took the title of Gregory XVI (1831–46), in honour of Gregory XV, the founder of the Propaganda College.

As was to be expected from his background, Gregory XVI was adamant against the mounting revolutionary movements of the day. Personally kind, deeply religious, unostentatious, and active in the relief of distress, he was uncompromising in his opposition to all that smacked of 'liberalism', whether in politics or thought. Highly disciplined and abstemious in his private life, courageous, and with abounding physical energy, he was an even more tireless worker than Pius VIII. In his conservatism he was supported, and in his later years dominated, by his second Secretary of State, Lambruschini, who was insistent on the control of all society by the hierarchy and the Pope.

In Italy Gregory XVI was confronted with rising nationalism and its demand for the unification of the peninsula. Insurrection broke out in the Papal States. In the effort to obtain help from Austria to subdue it, the Pope ran foul of the rivalry between France and Austria. He promised an extensive reorganization in the papal territories, but his programme did not satisfy the radicals and he adopted repressive measures to curb the dissent.

Partly because of his former direction of the Congregation for the Propagation of the Faith, Gregory XVI gave the weight of his high office to strengthening the missionary

The advent of steam was an innovation to which Gregory XVI gave papal approval. *Opposite* A gouache celebrating an excursion on a French steamboat made by the Pope from Civitavecchia in 1835. *Left* A coin struck by Gregory to commemorate the opening of the Tiber to steam, with the Roman Port of Ripetta in the background

outposts of the Church. In Latin America he used the authority of the Holy See to promote recovery from the low ebb to which the Church had sunk earlier in the century. He created additional bishoprics in the United States and supported the bishops in that country in their struggle to maintain their prerogatives against lay trustees. He added to the number of dioceses in Canada and Australia. He reinforced the administration of the Catholic Church in England. He gave much attention to the missions in Asia and did not hesitate to oppose the claims of Portugal to the control of the Church in India.

In the internal life of the Church, Gregory XVI aided the growing devotion to the Virgin, encouraged the revival and reform of religious orders and the formation of new congregations, and promoted the cults of the saints.

In the city of Rome, Gregory furthered education and scholarly and artistic projects. He built the Etruscan and Egyptian Museums and enlarged the Lateran Museum. He carried to completion Pope Leo's rebuilding of St Paul's Outside the Walls and rebuilt the church of S Maria degli Angioli at Assisi.

During his long Pontificate Gregory appointed most of the cardinals and members of the papal Curia who survived him. Understandably, they were conservative. Many were saintly and few if any were susceptible to bribery.

In its internal life, in its geographic extent, and in its recognition of the authority of the See of Peter, Gregory's death left the Catholic Church stronger than at his accession.

Gregory XVI was a man of strict personal piety who fostered by his example the growing devotion to the Virgin Mary.
A marble monument incorporating a portrait of the Pope

The election of Pius IX was greeted with great popular enthusiasm. He opened his reign with a number of liberal reforms and schemes for the improvement of conditions in Rome, and declared an amnesty for over a thousand political prisoners. There were scenes of wild rejoicing in Rome and the Pope's carriage was pulled through the streets *above*.
Below Pius blesses the crowds demonstrating in front of the Quirinal Palace

21 PIUS IX: THE END OF TEMPORAL POWER 1846-78

E. E. Y. HALES

Pius IX opened his reign with a series of liberal reforms and the establishment of a constitutional form of government in the Papal States. But when he refused to support Piedmont against Austria in what became a crusade for national liberation, the liberals turned against him. He was forced to flee from Rome and was only restored by French intervention in 1850. Pius then abandoned all attempts at political reform and in 1861 and 1864 violently denounced the liberal movements. In 1870 the Twentieth General Council pronounced the doctrine of papal infallibility in matters of faith and morals, but before the Council was over the Papal States were finally swallowed by the Risorgimento *and Victor Emmanuel's troops occupied Rome. For the rest of his Pontificate Pius IX refused to leave the Vatican or to recognize the new Italian State. His closing years were taken up with attempts to resist Bismarck's interference in the control of the Catholic Church in Germany.*

THE ELECTION OF GIOVANNI MARIA MASTAI-FERRETTI as Pope, on 16 June 1846, when he assumed the name Pius IX (in honour of his patron Pius VII) was unexpected. Not very much was known about him, but those who did know were aware that he was rather young (he was fifty-four), and that he came from a family at Sinigaglia (on the Adriatic coast of the Papal States) which had a mild reputation for liberal leanings. For the past sixteen years he had been Bishop of Imola, in the Romagna (the north-east portion of the Papal States), where he had been outspokenly critical of the papal administration; in particular he had rebuked the voluntary papal police, known as Centurions, for their arbitrary and violent behaviour. The conclave which elected him seemed to be reacting against the authoritarian and conservative policies of his predecessor Gregory XVI; even more certainly the cardinals were reacting against the subservience to Vienna and dependence on Austrian military support which had characterized the government of his predecessor in the hands of Cardinal Lambruschini, Gregory's Secretary of State.

But neither friend, nor foe, nor the multitude to whom he was unknown, were expecting from the new Pope the cascade of liberal reforms which marked the first two years of his Pontificate and made of him the most 'enlightened' ruler of his day. First came the amnesty he gave to more than a thousand political prisoners and exiles; this sweeping act of clemency caught the imagination of Europe and America. Then there were projects for railways, for gas lighting in the streets, for reforms in education, in agriculture, in criminal jurisdiction, in the prisons. And by the end of the year 1847 the Pope had freed the press to discuss political matters and had set up a *Consulta*, with lay members, to advise the government. The way had thus been opened for the growth of a crop of newspapers and of political clubs; at Vienna the Austrian Chancellor, Prince Metternich, custodian of the *status quo* in Europe, was already foretelling disaster. But by the middle of March 1848, Metternich himself was fleeing from a revolution in Vienna and Pius, who had heard about the constitutions newly set up in Sicily and at Paris, put his own government under the control of an elective assembly and so became, in his temporal capacity, a constitutional monarch.

Whether that unique theocracy which was the papal government could have survived the control of a lay assembly, whether the Pope could successfully have ruled as a constitutional monarch in secular matters while remaining absolute in the spiritual sphere, must remain very doubtful. But this dual system was not destined to have a fair trial because King Charles Albert of Savoy went to war with the Austrians in April 1848, and liberals throughout Italy, but especially at Rome, demanded that the Pope, too, should declare war and should bless the crusade for national liberation. Faced with the prospect of participating in a war between Catholic Italians and Catholic Austrians, Pius not unnaturally declined the role he was being asked to play. He thus broke with the revolutionary liberals, who murdered his minister, Pellegrino Rossi, in October, and besieged the Pope himself in the Quirinal Palace.

In November 1848, Pius escaped in disguise to Gaeta in the Kingdom of Naples. In the following February Giuseppe Mazzini became First Triumvir of a Roman Republic.

Rome was only one of many European capitals which had fallen to the liberals in the year of revolutions. But by the summer of 1849 it was the most conspicuous, because Catholic Europe was slowly moving to restore the Pope and Mazzini, joined by Garibaldi, was bent on making a fight of it. Without support from outside, however, it was not a fight the revolutionaries could maintain and French troops entered the city in July 1849 while Austrian troops crossed the river Po into the Romagna and moved down the Adriatic coast. By April 1850, Pius IX was back in the Eternal City with his enthusiasm for sharing the government with the liberals quite quenched. Henceforward he made no more political concessions though his interest in scientific and economic improvements remained keen.

The Pope now entrusted most of the diplomatic and political business of the Papal States to his new Secretary of State, Cardinal Antonelli, a loyal, capable, obstinate man who would preserve the régime for as long as he could but who thought its days were numbered. Rome was soon in conflict not only with the liberals within the city, and at Bologna, but also with the liberal government at Turin where the new king, Victor Emmanuel, was committed to defending a democratic constitution. Since the Turin government had now embarked on a whole programme of anti-clerical legislation, closing the monasteries and convents, abolishing the feast days, secularizing marriage, and introducing divorce, the Pope's quarrel with that government became acute. And this new secularization in Italy soon became the more frightening because it was extended outside the confines of Piedmont-Savoy. Victor Emmanuel's able minister, Camillo Cavour, who had sponsored the anti-clerical legislation, succeeded in 1859 in bringing the French army of the Emperor Napoleon III into northern Italy to fight the Austrians, and as a result of this campaign the Piedmontese acquired Milan, and the Romagna made good its separation from Rome and its union with the new kingdom. Then, in the summer of 1860, Garibaldi, with his famous Thousand, landed in Sicily and drove the Bourbon government from that island and from Naples, after which he headed north. Alarmed by Garibaldi's progress Cavour sent the Piedmontese army south, through the Papal States, to meet (and to forestall) the Garibaldians and to make sure that it was his own government that annexed the Pope's territories. Faced with an enemy marching into his states, Pius, who had resolutely refused to allow his army to fight outside those states, had no inhibitions about trying to defend them against invasion; indeed, he allowed his war minister, the Belgian Monsignor de Mérode, to raise an international army for their defence which he entrusted to the veteran French general Lamoricière. But it was a raw, ill-organized force, no

The period of enlightened liberalism did not last long. In 1848 Charles Albert of Savoy declared war on Austria and called for papal support in a campaign of national liberation. Pius refused to be drawn into a conflict between Catholic Italy and Catholic Austria and the liberal elements in Rome rose against him. Two contemporary lithographs showing *top* the storming of the Quirinal, after which the Pope was forced to flee in disguise to Gaeta, and *bottom* the proclamation of a Roman Republic on the Capitoline hill

Right Giuseppe Mazzini, liberal statesman and prophet, who in February 1849 became the First Triumvir of the Roman Republic

match for the larger, better equipped, and better trained Piedmontese, and at Castelfidardo, in September, 1860, it went down to defeat. Piedmontese and Garibaldians met and embraced each other south of Rome and Pius was left with only the Patrimony of Saint Peter, a narrow strip of land along the coast in the immediate vicinity of Rome.

To Pius, who could see no virtue in handing over his territories either to the Piedmontese or to Garibaldi, what had happened was merely spoliation, made more heinous by the fact that, in all the territories taken over by Turin, in northern and southern Italy, the monasteries were closed and the anti-clerical legislation was introduced. Yet he was assured, both from Turin and from Paris, that what had been done had been in accordance with the most enlightened principles, and was in the best interests of religion. Tired of being told that he must bow before the inevitable march of 'progress, liberalism, and recent civilization' he made a violent allocution in 1861, denouncing these principles in somewhat unguarded language, a denunciation which he soon repeated and issued to an astonished world in his famous Syllabus of Errors (1864).

Left An early photograph of Pius IX, taken in about 1855. He was a warm-hearted, kindly man, but lacked the intellectual grasp and the statesmanlike qualities needed at this critical period of Italian history

Below During 1849 a European alliance was formed to restore the Pope to his temporal power. In July Mazzini was forced to abandon Rome, which was taken by French troops, and Pius was reinstated. A contemporary lithograph showing the French forces attacking Rome

Pius IX

The *volte-face* in his political attitude was now complete. The liberal innovating Pope of 1847 had become the symbol of European reaction by 1864. For in the Syllabus he denounced all the liberties fashionable in the progressive Europe of his time, such as unrestricted liberty of speech, and of the press, and equal status for all religions. He was prepared to accept these liberties as temporary expedients, which might be necessary in countries of mixed religion, but he denounced the idea that they could provide the ultimate ideal for society. 'The Church', he said, 'will never admit it as a benefit and a principle that error and heresy should be preached to Catholic peoples.' And although he never denounced democratic government as such, maintaining the Church's official indifference to forms of government, he made no secret of his preference for absolute monarchies.

The great liberals amongst the Catholics of Europe, Montalembert in France, Lord Acton in England, Döllinger in Bavaria, were deeply shocked and distressed by the Syllabus. Still more shocked, naturally enough, was liberal Protestant opinion in England, which had sympathized with Mazzini's republic at Rome, and with Turin, and believed the Papal States to be a medieval theocracy. It was an embarrassing moment for Catholics in Britain, where the Cardinal Archbishop of Westminster, Nicholas Wiseman, had only with difficulty succeeded in weathering the storm aroused by Pius IX's restoration of the Catholic hierarchy in 1850.

The Syllabus of Errors, with its accompanying encyclical, *Quanta Cura*, was issued on 8 December 1864, the Feast of the Immaculate Conception of the Blessed Virgin Mary. Ten years earlier, on that same Feast Day, the Pope had defined the dogma concerning that conception, and had thus made into an article of faith a belief which had been generally held by the Church since the early centuries of her life. Pius had a very special devotion to Our Lady and liked to use this Feast Day as the occasion for important pronouncements during his Pontificate. Two years after issuing the Syllabus he issued an invitation, on the same Feast Day, to the bishops throughout the world to come to Rome to celebrate the eighteenth centenary of the martyrdom of Saints Peter and Paul. And five years later, on the same date, he opened the Vatican Council.

But the Syllabus, though issued with some solemnity, provoked so sharp a reaction, especially in France, that 'explanations', intended to rob it of its sting, had to be put out; the most effective came from Felix Dupanloup, the Bishop of Orléans, who explained that, although the Pope had said it was an error to assert the necessity for free speech, freedom of religion, majority rule, separation of Church and State, and the rest, he had not meant that

Pius IX with King Victor Emmanuel of Savoy. Either might have headed the movement for the unification of Italy, but Pius hung back and the Piedmontese government took the lead. Although Pius remained personally friendly to the king, the government at Turin under Cavour was intensely anti-clerical and finally confiscated the Papal States. An anonymous lithograph

Cardinal Antonelli, the papal Secretary of State, a photograph taken in about 1852. From 1850 onwards he was entrusted with most of the diplomatic and political business and supported Pius in his resistance to change

Right Pius IX driving through St Peter's Square in 1855. An anonymous gouache

ONORE GLORIA
A
PIO IX.
CVI BASTO VN CIORNO
PER CONSOLARE I SVDDITI
E MARAVICLIARE IL MONDO
PACE
E
GIVSTIZIA

Left Count Camillo Cavour, Victor Emmanuel's Prime Minister, and the architect of Italian unification. Pius admired his patriotism but was shocked by his unscrupulous diplomacy and came to equate liberal democracy everywhere with Cavour's anti-clericalism
Right Garibaldi, the brilliant guerilla general and hero of Italian nationalism, whom many saw as a Messiah. In 1860 he landed in Sicily with his 'thousand', crossed to Italy and advanced towards Rome. He was met by the Piedmontese army, who had annexed the Papal States, leaving only the Patrimony of St Peter. An anonymous portrait

Opposite Pius driving through a triumphal arch erected in his honour in the Piazza del Popolo *top*. An anonymous gouache.
Bottom Pius walking in the Pincio Gardens, with St Peter's seen in the distance across the Tiber. A painting by Pio Joris

Below Pius continued to hold out in his tiny state. He is seen here in 1868 blessing papal troops at the Campo di Annibale

these ideas could not be useful at certain times and in certain places. This was the least that could be said to quieten liberal critics; just what Dupanloup meant remained, however, in dispute, and this uncertainty was one of the factors which decided the Pope in favour of summoning a General Council to Rome.

The popular expectation was that the Vatican Council, which opened at Rome on 8 December 1869, would 'explain' the Syllabus and would define with exactitude what was erroneous and what was true in the ideas of the age about the Church and her place in political society, ideas which the turbulent events in Italy had brought into the forum of public debate. But it gradually came to be seen that the most crucial question, lying behind the rest, was whether, or in what respect, the Pope was infallible when he made pronouncements such as the Syllabus. There were those, like the influential French journalist, Louis Veuillot, who were prepared not only to accept the infallibility of the Pope as a dogma, but to interpret very widely the area of the matters on which he could pronounce infallibly, while there were even some who held that his every utterance was infallible. On the other side there were some, like Bishop Dupanloup, who held that, while it might be true that the infallibility promised by Our Lord to His Church rested mainly with the Pope, it was both impracticable to define it exactly and also very unwise, in the actual state of opinion, to try to do so. So the Vatican Council divided itself into two main groups, a majority, organized by Archbishop Manning of Westminster, who wanted to secure a

definition of papal infallibility, and a minority, organized by Bishop Dupanloup, who were opposed to any definition. In the event the majority (with a good deal of backing by the Pope) won; but the minority had its influence and the definition, as it finally emerged, limited very strictly the nature of the infallibility, declaring the Pope was only infallible when he spoke '*ex cathedra*, that is when, exercising the office of pastor and teacher of all Christians, he defines with his supreme apostolic authority a doctrine concerning faith or morals to be held by the universal Church'. Such was the dogma which Pius IX read out in St Peter's on a memorable occasion, by flickering candlelight, in the midst of a thunderstorm, on 18 July 1870. Dupanloup and many of the French bishops had already left Rome; but as soon as the dogma was defined they wrote to the Pope, assuring him that they accepted the decision; indeed the dogma was accepted by the whole hierarchy of the Church, the only notable dissidents being Dr Döllinger and the small group of Old Catholics whom he led into schism in Germany.

The dogma of papal infallibility, together with one defining the papal primacy in the sphere of ecclesiastical jurisdiction, was the only important achievement of the Council. The outbreak of the Franco-Prussian War, just three days before the definition, caused the Council to be suspended, and the occupation of Rome by the troops of King Victor Emmanuel in September of the same year prevented the Pope from making any attempt to reassemble it. So the great questions raised by the Syllabus of Errors were never discussed at all. Yet, in a negative sense, some of the misgivings to which it had given rise were eased by the Council because, by limiting the papal infallibility to matters of faith and morals, the Council had made it clear that the Syllabus, and the encyclical which had accompanied it, were not infallible pronouncements.

Yet in Germany much play was made with the idea that the Council had somehow served to reinforce the Syllabus, and that the new German Empire was endangered by the excessive claims of the Church. Bismarck, Chancellor of the new Empire, launched his famous *Kulturkampf* against the German bishops, which helped to embitter the last years of the Pope's life. The Chancellor was trying to assert State control over the Church in such vital matters as the training of her priests, their public pronouncements, and the schools they ran. Pius resisted at every point and in doing so was at one with the German Church. While the Pope lived it was an *impasse*, and hundreds of the German clergy went into exile. Only in the reign of his successor, Leo XIII, was a settlement reached – with most of the concessions coming from the German Chancellor.

During the last years of his Pontificate, from the entry of the Piedmontese army into Rome in September 1870 to his death on 8 February 1878, Pius refused to emerge from his palace, calling himself the 'Prisoner in the Vatican'. By no word or act would he seem to recognize the spoliation of

The First Vatican Council opened in December 1869 under the shadow of war. The doctrinal question of papal infallibility soon came to the fore. In July 1870 the Council finally enunciated the dogma of papal infallibility in matters of faith and morals. A fresco from the Vatican showing the Council in session

his States, and especially not the seizure of the Eternal City. And he cautioned Catholics against taking any part in the politics of the new Italy, which he called the 'sub-Alpine kingdom'.

Pius IX reigned longer than any previous Pope in history and was the first to exceed the traditional twenty-five years of Saint Peter's Pontificate. His enemies were many, but they were often the keenest to acknowledge his personal fascination, his kindliness, his warmth, and especially the sense of humour which did not leave him even in his darkest days. Without much depth of intellect he had real depth of character. Despite all the disasters which he suffered – and partly because of them – he left the Papacy greatly strengthened in its hold upon the Universal Church.

Left A photograph of Pius IX taken in 1877, a year before his death, after the longest Pontificate in history. For the last eight years of his reign Pius remained a voluntary 'prisoner in the Vatican', refusing to acknowledge the new Italian state

Below Rome finally fell to the nationalist troops in September 1870, after the outbreak of the Franco-Prussian War had resulted in the withdrawal of French troops from Rome. The papal troops capitulated after the breach of the Porta Pia (Pius's own gate), portrayed in this painting by Ademollo

Inventario N°1132

SANCTISSIMI DOMINI NOSTRI

LEONIS

DIVINA PROVIDENTIA

PAPAE XIII

EPISTOLA ENCYCLICA

AD PATRIARCHAS PRIMATES
ARCHIEPISCOPOS ET EPISCOPOS UNIVERSOS CATHOLICI ORBIS
GRATIAM ET COMMUNIONEM CUM APOSTOLICA SEDE HABENTES.

ROMAE

—

MDCCCLXXIX.

Leo XIII (1878–1903) was the author and founder of modern Roman Catholic teaching on social problems, as articulated in his twelve great encyclicals, known as the 'Leonine corpus'. This new and enlightened approach gave fresh vigour to the Papacy after the reactionary policy of the last years of Pius IX's reign.

Left The title page of *Aeterni Patris* 1879, which was the first of Leo's twelve major pronouncements. It sets out the necessity for a basis of Christian philosophy to all teaching and discusses the Catholic conception of the nature of authority in the world

22 THE PAPACY AND SOCIAL REFORM: THE GREAT ENCYCLICALS

ANNE FREMANTLE

Until the second half of the nineteenth-century the Church's doctrine on social problems had never been explicitly expressed except as part of theological pronouncements. When Leo XIII came to the throne in 1878 he issued the first of eighty-six encyclicals on the social problems of the day, of which the most important was Rerum Novarum, *enunciating the Church's teaching on the rights of capital and labour. The encyclicals of St Pius X were mainly concerned with the political responsibilities of the individual Catholic, particularly with reference to the anti-clerical campaign in France. In* Quadragesimo Anno *Pius XI reaffirmed the teaching of* Rerum Novarum, *and in other encyclicals condemned Fascism, Nazism and Communism. Pius XII added encyclicals on labour relations, on international affairs, the conduct of the United Nations and the threat of scientific weapons in modern warfare. In* Mater et Magistra *John XXIII elaborated further papal teaching on social relations and in* Pacem in Terris *on international problems.*

'THE CHURCH, WHICH IS THE UNIVERSAL SOCIETY of the faithful of all languages and of all peoples, has its own social doctrine, profoundly elaborated from the first centuries on down to modern times, and studied in its progressive development under all its approaches and aspects.' So wrote the late Pope Pius XII in his allocution of 22 February 1944. Indeed, St Paul himself has much to say on social ethics, and later, St Augustine stated the tremendous principle that 'charity is no substitute for justice withheld'. But until the latter half of the nineteenth century, when materialist and atheist assumptions challenged the Church on social questions, the *expression* of this social doctrine had been an integral part of theology, neither explicitly nor separately stated. Just as the Church, on those occasions when a particular theological truth was threatened, countered by defining it, so too when issues of social existence became obscured by false solutions, the full authority of the Church was summoned to enunciate its social doctrine in clear and contemporary terms. In both instances, however, not until the menace is a distinct and present reality has the definition been made.

Yet this doctrine – spelled out in the twelve encyclicals of Pope Leo XIII that have come to be called the Leonine *corpus*, and repeated by his successors in their various encyclicals, culminating in the *Mater et Magistra* of 15 May 1961 – is not a sociology in the current sense of the term. For sociology as a science is based upon the classification of social data, from which facts are deduced to permit the adumbration of empirical laws, which laws in their turn form the subject of social philosophy. The social doctrine of the Church, on the contrary, as outlined in the so-called social encyclicals, is rather a morality of society, based upon, and rooted in, the Gospels, defined in the Epistles, expanded upon by many of the Fathers – St Basil, for example – and discussed by St Thomas Aquinas in the context of the virtue of justice.

Pope Leo XIII from the moment of his accession (7 February 1878) found himself confronted by the violence of social upheaval. He had to cope with vehemently anticlerical France, with Bismarck's German *Kulturkampf*, and with Italian revolutionaries who almost succeeded in throwing Pius IX's body into the Tiber. He had to contend, on the one hand, with an unprincipled *laissez-faire* capitalism, complacently accepting the horrors of English factories and London slums, and on the other, with a Marxist philosophy militantly atheist and materialist. His eighty-six encyclicals, produced during a papal tenure of twenty-five years, originated from his awareness that the greatest tragedy of the nineteenth century was the loss to the Church of the working classes.

'The cause of civilization lacks a solid foundation if it does not rest on the eternal principles of truth, and on the unchangeable laws of right and justice,' Pope Leo wrote in his first encyclical, *Inscrutabili* (21 April 1878). A year later, in *Arcanum* (4 August 1879), he discussed Christian marriage and insisted, among other things, on the equality of rights of husbands and wives within marriage, quoting St Jerome's statement: 'with us that which is unlawful for women is unlawful for men also, and the same restraint is imposed on equal conditions.' He also refused to concede that power over Christian marriages can ever be given to the state: the contract is inseparable from the sacrament.

In *Quod Apostolici muneris* (28 December 1878), his second encyclical, the Pope declares that the basis of authority – whether that of husband over wife, parents over children or master over servants – originates in God, and from Him derives its nature and character. And in *Aeterni Patris* (4 August 1879), the first of the round dozen of encyclicals that make up the Leonine *corpus*, the papal observation that the best way to restore the social order is by restoring the teaching of Christian philosophy in Christian schools, is followed by a reiteration of that philosophic position, and a definition of the terms in which the Church will state her argument. All authority, even in a democracy, is seen as coming from God: it is not conferred by the electors on the elected any more than it is inherited by birth in a monarchy, or inherent in some 'divine right' of kings. The electors in a democracy merely determine who will be the next president, just as in the case of royalty, the birth of a crown prince or princess establishes who will be the successor to the throne. Neither birth nor election confer power: 'they merely indicate who will administer it'.

In *Diuturnum* (29 June 1881), Leo discussed the basis of sound political government, and in *Humanum Genus* (20 April 1884), he denounced naturalism, and those who set nature and human reason above the supernatural order: the natural order and its laws are seen as part of the divine order, and subject to the supernatural order of grace. In *Immortale Dei* (1 November 1884), on the Christian constitution of states, the Pope clarified Church-State relations. The state holds its authority from God, he declared, and this divine origin of the temporal power is the most powerful guarantee the state can claim. From this it follows that states should regard the Church as the safest of their allies, and recognize their indebtedness by making public profession of religion. Then the traditional doctrine of the Two Powers is reaffirmed – 'each in its own kind supreme, each has fixed limits within which it is contained, for the powers that are, are ordained of God.' *In plurimis*, addressed to the Brazilian bishops on 5 May 1888, emphasizes that error and moral evil are the true root of social injustice. The Church never approves of the latter, but she does not believe that violence is the proper method for curing the disorders of nature. She always disapproved of slavery, which was never a natural condition, but a consequence of sin; yet she has never urged slaves to rebel. Slavery has finally disappeared as a legally recognized institution partly because the Church has so steadily disapproved of it.

In his next encyclical, the Pope defines human liberty and articulates its limits. *Libertas praestantissimum* (20 June 1888) first distinguishes clearly between natural and moral liberty. Natural liberty, the power of free choice, belongs as his birthright to every man who has the use of reason. 'As the Catholic Church declares in the strongest terms the simplicity, spirituality and immortality of the soul, so with unequalled constancy and publicity she ever also asserts its freedom.' Liberty 'belongs only to those who have the gift of reason,' wrote the Holy Father, and went on to affirm that 'freedom of choice is identical with the will'. Moral freedom is based on the assumption that that man alone is truly free who acts consistently with his reason. As St Thomas puts it: 'Everything is that which belongs to itself naturally. When it acts through a power outside itself, it does not act of itself, but through another, that is, as a slave ... But man is by nature rational ... When he sins, he acts in opposition to reason, is moved by another, and is the victim of foreign misapprehensions ... Therefore, whosoever commits sin is the slave of sin.' Or as the 'heathen philosophers' put it: 'the wise man alone is free'. This encyclical goes on to excoriate those supporters of *liberalism* who declare that the authority of the state comes from the people only, and that 'just as in every individual man, reason is his only rule of life, so the collective reason of the community should be the supreme guide in the management of all public affairs. Hence the doctrine of the supremacy of the greater number and that all right and all duty reside in the majority.' This, the Pope states abruptly, 'is simply a road leading straight to tyranny'. And he repeats St Thomas's declaration concerning tyrants: 'Whenever there exists, or there is reason to fear, an unjust oppression of the people on the one hand, or a deprivation of the liberty of the Church on the other, it is lawful to seek for such a change of government as will bring about due liberty of action.' Leo XIII goes on to declare that the 'modern liberties' of thought, speech, writing and teaching must consist in the firm resolve only to think, to say, and to write that which is true, and to will only that which is good according to natural law, human and divine law – or else such liberties simply cease to exist. For though a man is physically free to think as he pleases, to profess what religion he prefers, he is not morally free to do so, since such behaviour is not consonant with reason.

For society is not the end of man, but one of the means he uses to attain salvation. 'Nature did not fashion society with the intent that man should seek in it his last end, but that in it, and through it, he would find suitable aids whereby to attain to his own perfection,' the Pope observed. Yet even as he wrote, Leo was aware, as were all social reformers – indeed all theorists and spectators, and everyone except the most complacent meliorists – that society was far from providing suitable aids to man's perfection. For some, of whom Marx is the representative, the answer could only be to change society drastically. Others sought to alter it less radically. In England several of the early Socialists, like Charles Kingsley and Percy Widdrington, were clergymen, while in the United States Terence Powderly,

The Great Encyclicals

VENERABILIBVS FRATRIBVS
PATRIARCHIS PRIMATIBVS ARCHIEPISCOPIS EPISCOPIS
ALIISQVE LOCORVM ORDINARIIS
PACEM ET COMMVNIONEM CVM APOSTOLICA SEDE HABENTIBVS

LEO PP. XIII.

VENERABILES FRATRES

SALVTEM ET APOSTOLICAM BENEDICTIONEM

Sapientiae christianae revocari praecepta, eisque vitam, mores, instituta populorum penitus conformari, quotidie magis apparet oportere. Illis enim posthabitis, tanta vis est malorum consecuta, ut nemo sapiens nec ferre sine ancipiti cura praesentia queat, nec in posterum sine metu prospicere. — Facta quidem non mediocris est ad ea bona, quae sunt corporis et externa, progressio: sed omnis natura, quae hominis percellit sensus, opumque et virium et copiarum possessio, si commoditates gignere suavitatesque augere vivendi potest, natum ad maiora ac magnificentiora animum explere non potest. Deum spectare, atque ad ipsum contendere, suprema lex est vitae hominum: qui ad imaginem conditi similitudinemque divinam, naturà ipsà ad auctorem suum potiundum vehe-

AI VENERABILI FRATELLI
I PATRIARCHI PRIMATI ARCIVESCOVI E VESCOVI
DEL MONDO CATTOLICO
AVENTI GRAZIA E COMUNIONE COLLA SEDE APOSTOLICA

LEONE PP. XIII.

VENERABILI FRATELLI

SALUTE ED APOSTOLICA BENEDIZIONE

L'ardente brama di novità, che da gran tempo ha incominciato ad agitare i popoli, dovea naturalmente dall'ordine politico passare nell'ordine congenere dell'economia sociale. E di fatti i portentosi progressi delle arti e i nuovi metodi dell'industria: le mutate relazioni tra padroni ed operai; l'essersi in poche mani accumulata la ricchezza, e largamente estesa la povertà; il sentimento delle proprie forze divenuto nelle classi lavoratrici più vivo, e l'unione tra loro più intima: questo insieme di cose e i peggiorati costumi han fatto scoppiare il conflitto. Il quale è di tale e tanta gravità che tiene in trepida aspettazione sospesi gli animi, ed affatica l'ingegno dei dotti, i congressi dei savi, le assemblee popolari, le deliberazioni dei legislatori, i consigli dei principi: in guisa che oggi non v'ha questione che maggiormente interessi il mondo. — Ciò pertanto che a bene della Chiesa ed a comune salvezza facemmo altre volte, Venerabili Fratelli, colle Nostre Lettere Encicliche sui Poteri pubblici, la Libertà umana, la Costituzione cristiana degli Stati ed altri siffatti argomenti, che Ci parvero opportuni ad abbattere errori funesti, il medesimo crediamo per gli stessi motivi di dover fare adesso sulla *questione operaia*. Toccammo già di questa materia, come ce ne venne occasione, più di una volta: ma la coscienza dell'Aposto-

Above left Sapientiae Christianae 1890 defines the nature of Christian citizenship and states clearly that Christian duty comes before the demands of the state in case of any conflict of loyalty
Above right Rerum Novarum 1891, the greatest of Leo's encyclicals, illustrated here in its Italian edition. Cardinal Manning is said to have drafted the document, which shows a new recognition of the problems and rights of the working class and of the relations of capital and labour. It has been the basis of Roman Catholic social teaching ever since

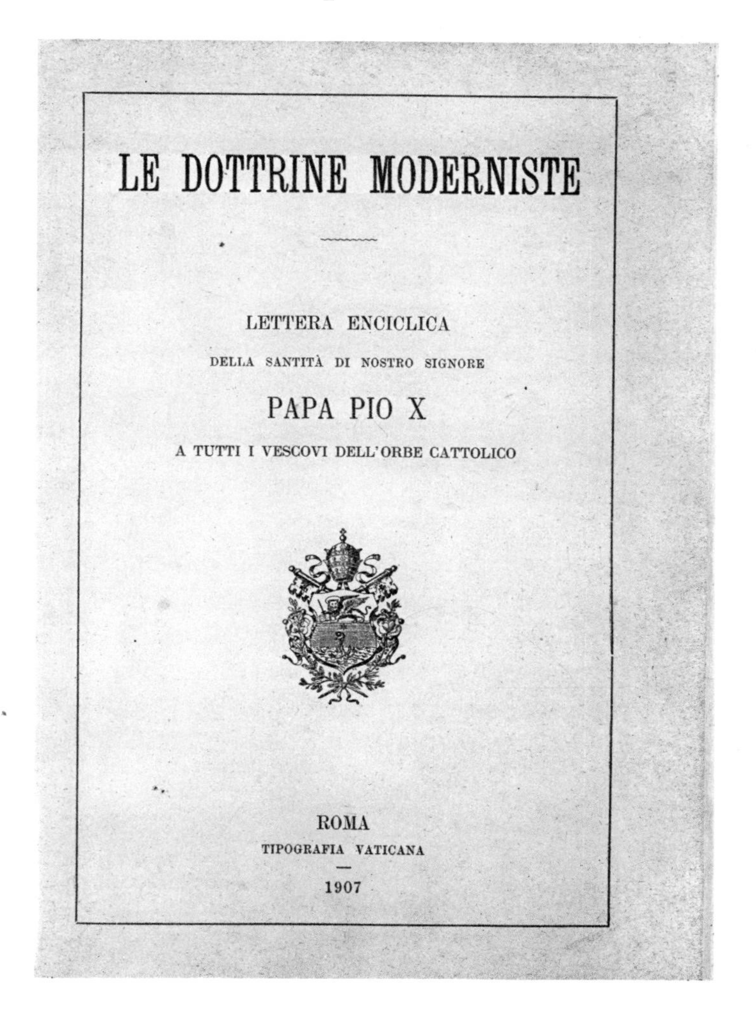

LE DOTTRINE MODERNISTE

LETTERA ENCICLICA
DELLA SANTITÀ DI NOSTRO SIGNORE
PAPA PIO X
A TUTTI I VESCOVI DELL'ORBE CATTOLICO

ROMA
TIPOGRAFIA VATICANA
1907

Right Pascendi (Le Dottrine Moderniste) was Pius X's condemnation of Catholic modernism and the attempt in philosophy or biblical studies to invoke modern fashions of thought to undermine the authority of the Church

president of the Knights of Labour (forerunner of the American Federation of Labor), was a Catholic. In Germany Archbishop Ketteler's *Christianity and the Labour Question* had given the Catholics of his nation a programme and a platform. In France a number of the Catholic reformers, such as Albert de Mun and Lacordaire, remained in the Church, while Lamennais left it.

In *Sapientiae Christianae* (10 January 1890), as in the earlier *Sancta Dei Civitas* (3 December 1880), the Pope had defined the nature of Christian citizenship: since the natural love of country and the supernatural love of God both proceed from God, who is their common author, there should be no conflict of loyalties. But if the state commands things contrary to the divine law, those commands are not lawful, and there is no sedition in refusing to obey them: it is the essential duty of Christians never to set human laws above the divine.

With this encyclical the stage was set. The preliminary encyclicals had prepared the way, and now in *Rerum Novarum*, issued on 15 May 1891, Pope Leo XIII set down the Catholic position on the condition of the working class. This great encyclical is generally supposed to have been drafted by Cardinal Manning, who had deep knowledge and practical experience of workers. It was he who had negotiated the settlement in the 1889 London dock strike: the directors of the dock companies had agreed to negotiate terms 'only if they came through Cardinal Manning'. While Temple, the Archbishop of Canterbury, had spoken harshly against the men, the Cardinal had waited hour-long, day-long, at the Mansion House in the sultry August days, in the hope of being able to bring about a settlement: 'a dying man went down to a dead city'.

Rerum Novarum 'embraced the whole social problem in its context as part of religion, politics, and the right ordering of society', and provided the basis 'for Catholic teaching on social justice ever since' (E. E. Y. Hales *The Catholic Church in the Modern World*. 'Nothing is more useful than to look upon the world as it really is – and at the same time to seek elsewhere for the solace to its troubles,' wrote the Pope in Article 18. 'The revolutionary spirit has invaded all departments of human life, and the practice of usury has reduced the masses to a condition little better than that of slavery. Socialism's remedy, to transfer all private property to the state, is against justice, since private property is a natural right, and without this right, parents cannot provide for their children.' The family precedes the state and 'has at least equal rights with the state'. The state must supply public aid to families in exceeding distress 'since each family is part of the commonwealth'. Within the state, the two classes should dwell in harmony. 'Each needs the other: capital cannot do without labour, nor labour without capital.' The employer's duty is to 'give everyone what is just'. But it is one thing to have a right to the possession of money, and quite another to have a right to use money as one wills. As St Thomas Aquinas puts it 'man should not consider his material possessions as his own, but as common to all'. Thus the regulation of working hours and conditions, the control of women's and children's labour, the right to a minimum wage, and the right – in extremity – to strike, are sanctioned and supported.

Although *Rerum Novarum* was the greatest of his encyclicals, Pope Leo XIII continued during the remainder of his long Papacy to be occupied with the condition of the working class. In *Permiti Nos* (10 July 1895) he wrote to the Belgian bishops on social problems, and in *Graves de communi* (18 January 1901) he discussed Christian democracy. For one result of *Rerum Novarum* was the formation of groups of Christian Democrats who, taking their stand on the papal directives and programmes, challenged other political parties. The Pope insisted that, if democracy is not Christian, it ceases to be a political form of government. 'For the laws of nature and of the Gospel, which ... are superior to all human contingencies ... are necessarily independent of all particular forms of civil government while, at the same time, they are in harmony with all that is not repugnant to morality and justice.'

Pope St Pius X (1903–14), in his encyclical *Il fermo proposito* (11 June 1905), laid down the norms for Catholic Action, which should 'prudently and seriously train' Catholics for political life. During his Papacy, anti-clerical legislation in France was at its most virulent, and his encyclicals *Une fois encore* of 6 January 1906 and *Vehementer nos* of 11 February 1906 refer to this, while *Pascendi* (8 September 1907) deals with the heresy of Modernism. Among the tenets condemned in the latter was the theory that 'the state must, therefore, be separated from the Church, and the Catholic from the citizen ... for the Church to trace out and prescribe for the citizen any line of action, on any pretext whatsoever, is to be guilty of an abuse of authority.'

Benedict XV spent his brief reign (1914–22) in appealing for peace. Pius XI (1922–39) roundly condemned Fascism (*Non abbiamo bisogno*: 29 June 1931), Nazism (*Mit brennender Sorge*: 14 March 1937), and Communism (*Divini Redemptoris*: 19 March 1937). In this last encyclical, after demonstrating the errors of Marxism, the Pope again sets out the mutual duties and rights of man and of society, and discusses the social and economic order. In *Ubi arcano* (23 December 1922), he wrote of the crisis in international relations: of the menace of new wars, of famine and misery, of the class struggle and the rancours between conquerors and conquered. He called to account immoderate nationalism and the materialist ethos of society, and the inclination to incite political parties to civil war. On 15 May 1931, on the occasion of the fortieth anniversary of *Rerum Novarum*, Pope Pius XI issued *Quadragesimo anno*, the second of the great 'labour' encyclicals, and essentially a re-statement of the first. Individualism and collectivism are both seen as dangers; the right to form unions is emphasized, and the Pope notes that 'just as the unity of human society cannot be founded on an opposition of classes, so also the right ordering of economic life cannot be left to a free competition of forces'.

Pope Pius XII (1939–58), in his first encyclical *Summi Pontificatus* (20 October 1939), revealed his awareness that one of the chief problems of the Church today was its relation to civil society: 'To consider the state as something ultimate to which everything else should be subordinated and directed, cannot fail to harm the true and lasting prosperity of nations.' This may occur either 'when unrestricted dominion comes to be conferred on the state as having a mandate from the nation, people or even a social order; or when the state arrogates such dominion to itself as absolute master, without any mandate whatsoever'. The Church, he notes elsewhere, 'reproves none of the different forms of government, provided they be in themselves suitable for securing the welfare of citizens.' He also made the useful distinction between 'the people' and 'the masses': 'a people lives and moves by its own vitality; the mass is inert in itself, and can only be moved from without'. Pope Pius XII was the first pope to insist on the obligation, under pain of sin, of every citizen to vote.

In his second encyclical, *Sertum laetitiae* (1 November 1939), addressed to the bishops of the United States, the Pope affirmed the absolute need for 'wealth created by God for all men to flow fairly to all according to the principles of justice and charity'. And following on the twofold nature of human labour – that it is personal and that it is necessary – he notes the corollary that the duty and the right to organize belong first to employer and employed, with the state intervening only if the two parties do not carry out their task.

During the Second World War, in his Christmas radio messages (of 1941 to 1944), Pius XII repeatedly stressed the necessity of basing peace on order, on the dignity and the duties of the human person, on social unity and the rights of labour. He advocated the internationalization of private law, and stated that the United Nations 'ought also to have the right and the power of forestalling all military intervention of one state in another, whatever the pretext under which it is effected, and also the right and power of assuming, by means of a sufficient police force, the safeguarding of order in the state which is threatened ... We desire the

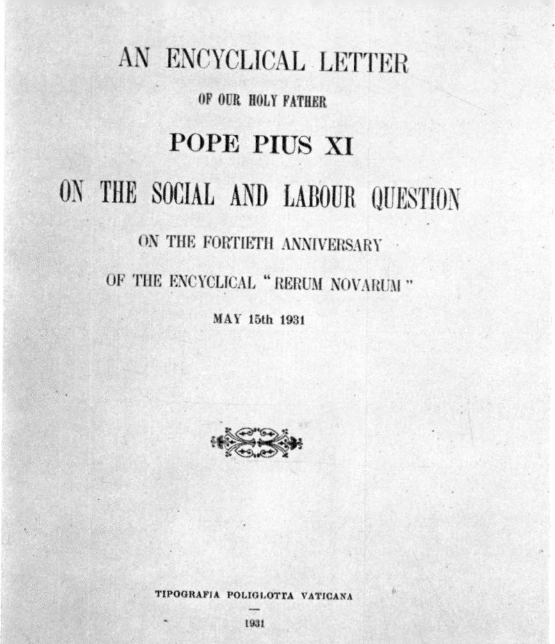

AN ENCYCLICAL LETTER

OF OUR HOLY FATHER

POPE PIUS XI

ON THE SOCIAL AND LABOUR QUESTION

ON THE FORTIETH ANNIVERSARY

OF THE ENCYCLICAL "RERUM NOVARUM"

MAY 15th 1931

TIPOGRAFIA POLIGLOTTA VATICANA

1931

Quadragesimo Anno 1931. The English edition of Pius XI's encyclical, published on the fortieth anniversary of *Rerum Novarum* and essentially a re-statement of it, with a plea for harmony in economic life

ENCYCLICAL LETTER

TO THE VENERABLE ARCHBISHOPS AND BISHOPS OF GERMANY

AND OTHER ORDINARIES

IN PEACE AND COMMUNION WITH THE APOSTOLIC SEE

ON THE CONDITION OF THE CHURCH IN GERMANY

POPE PIUS XI

VENERABLE BRETHREN

GREETING AND APOSTOLIC BENEDICTION

1. – With deep anxiety and increasing dismay We have for some time past beheld the sufferings of the Church, and the steadily growing oppression of those men and women who, loyally professing their faith in thought and deed, have remained true to her amidst the people of that land to which St. Boniface once brought the light and glad tidings of Christ and the Kingdom of God.

2. – This anxiety of Ours has not been lessened by the accurate reports dutifully brought to Us by the representatives of the most reverend episcopate, who came to visit at Our sick-bed. They related much that is consoling and edifying about the struggle for religion that is being waged by the faithful, and yet, despite their love for their people and their fatherland, with every possible attempt to reach a dispassionate judgment, they could not pass over much that is bitter and sad. After receiving their accounts, We could say in great thankfulness to God: "I have no greater grace than this, to hear that my children walk in truth."[1] But the frankness befitting Our responsible apostolic office and the desire to place before your eyes and those of the entire Christian world the actual facts in all their gravity, require Us to add: A greater anxiety, a more bitter suffering in Our pastoral care We have not, than to hear: "many leave the way of truth."[2]

[1] III John, 1, 4.
[2] II Peter, 2, 2.

Mit Brennender Sorge 1937 The English edition of Pius XI's denunciation of Hitler, three years after the concordat with the new German government. The persecution of the Church in Germany is especially condemned

DAS ERSTE RUNDSCHREIBEN UNSERES HEILIGEN VATERS PAPST PIUS XII.

SUMMI PONTIFICATUS

ÜBER DIE NOT UND DIE JRR+TÜMER UNSERER ZEIT UND DEREN ÜBERWINDUNG IN CHRISTUS

Summi Pontificatus 1939 Pius XII's first encyclical in which he emphasized the restricted authority of the state

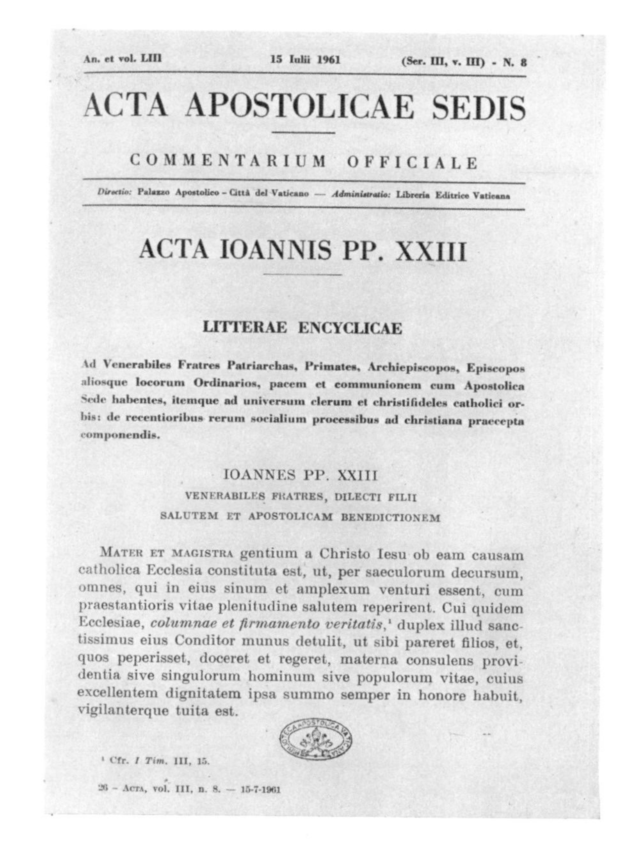

An. et vol. LIII | 15 Iulii 1961 | (Ser. III, v. III) - N. 8

ACTA APOSTOLICAE SEDIS

COMMENTARIUM OFFICIALE

Directio: Palazzo Apostolico - Città del Vaticano — *Administratio:* Libreria Editrice Vaticana

ACTA IOANNIS PP. XXIII

LITTERAE ENCYCLICAE

Ad Venerabiles Fratres Patriarchas, Primates, Archiepiscopos, Episcopos aliosque locorum Ordinarios, pacem et communionem cum Apostolica Sede habentes, itemque ad universum clerum et christifideles catholici orbis: de recentioribus rerum socialium processibus ad christiana praecepta componendis.

IOANNES PP. XXIII

VENERABILES FRATRES, DILECTI FILII

SALUTEM ET APOSTOLICAM BENEDICTIONEM

MATER ET MAGISTRA gentium a Christo Iesu ob eam causam catholica Ecclesia constituta est, ut, per saeculorum decursum, omnes, qui in eius sinum et amplexum venturi essent, cum praestantioris vitae plenitudine salutem reperirent. Cui quidem Ecclesiae, *columnae et firmamento veritatis*,[1] duplex illud sanctissimus eius Conditor munus detulit, ut sibi pareret filios, et, quos peperisset, doceret et regeret, materna consulens providentia sive singulorum hominum sive populorum vitae, cuius excellentem dignitatem ipsa summo semper in honore habuit, vigilanterque tuita est.

[1] Cfr. *I Tim.* III, 15.

26 – ACTA, vol. III, n. 8. — 15-7-1961

Mater et Magistra 1961 John XXIII's encyclical published on the seventieth anniversary of *Rerum Novarum*, which reviews the whole relationship between the Church and society and contains an outspoken condemnation of irresponsible capitalism. It recognizes that although Communism is evil, not all acts of Communists are wrong

authority of the United Nations strengthened, especially for effecting general disarmament, which we have so much at heart.' He commended the European Union, and also noted that, in the case of atomic, biological or chemical aggression, 'defending oneself against any kind of injustice is not sufficient reason to resort to war'. When the losses that such war brings are not comparable with those of the 'injustice tolerated', one may have the *obligation* of 'submitting to the injustice'.

On the seventieth anniversary of *Rerum Novarum*, 15 May 1961, Pope John XXIII (1958–63) issued *Mater et Magistra*, which reviews the whole relationship between the Church and society, between the Church and labour. While the earlier encyclicals are recalled and reaffirmed, John XXIII went much further than his predecessors in condemning *laissez-faire* capitalism, and in declaring it hardly less a menace than Communism. And though not the last word on these great themes of the Church's social doctrine, it is, at the time of writing, still the latest. In *Pacem in Terris*, issued in 1963 shortly before his death and addressed to all men of goodwill, Pope John XXIII discussed international problems, social, economic, and scientific.

Leo XIII (1878–1903) found the Papacy strong in doctrinal authority after the infallibility decree, but divested of all political power. Although he continued to refuse to recognize the Italian state, he did much to re-establish the prestige of the Papacy in the world, notably through his great social encyclicals. He is seen below with members of the Anticamera Segreta, his closest associates in the administration of the Curia

23 THE POPES IN THE MODERN WORLD

LEO XIII to PIUS XII 1878-1958

E. E. Y. HALES

Between the death of Pius IX in 1878 and the election of John XXIII in 1958 five Popes reigned. Of these three, Leo XIII, Pius X and Benedict XV spent their whole Pontificate in voluntary imprisonment within the Vatican, in protest against the Italian seizure of the Papal States. The Concordat of 1929 between Pius XI and Mussolini ended the impasse and inaugurated the present situation where the Pope is recognized as the temporal sovereign of the Vatican City. The period was one of great spiritual rebirth, of the formulation by successive Popes of the Catholic social policies and stern papal resistance to the growing threat of atheistic Communism. During the two World Wars the Popes maintained a policy of neutrality and constantly worked for international peace.

WHEN THE CONCLAVE OF FEBRUARY 1878 ELECTED Gioacchino Pecci, Leo XIII (1878–1903), to succeed Pope Pius IX it made what seemed the obvious choice. The new Pope enjoyed a reputation for moderation and diplomacy, qualities which would be sorely needed as a result of the tumultuous events of the previous pontificate, which had left the Papacy estranged from the new kingdom of Italy and – more important – from most of the governments of the modern world, and from the climate of opinion supporting them. For though, as a result of Pius IX's policies, and the work of the First Vatican Council, the authority of the Papacy was stronger within the Catholic Church than it had been for many centuries, the standing of both Papacy and Church, in Europe and the world, had not been lower since those disastrous days when Rome had been at the mercy of the French Revolution and Napoleon. At enmity with the new Italy, with Bismarck's new Germany, and with the newly established French Third Republic, the 'prisoner in the Vatican' could look for support only to defeated Austria, where the Hapsburgs were no longer in a position to help him. Scorned by progressive, enlightened, and liberal opinion – as a result of the Syllabus of Errors and similar pronouncements – the Papacy was quite commonly considered, since the loss of Rome, to be moribund.

It was Leo XIII's peculiar achievement to come to terms, of a sort, with the political Europe of his age, and even with the spirit of his age: but it is easy to exaggerate both the extent of his concessions and the extent of his achievement.

To the new Italy he yielded nothing at all, remaining a voluntary prisoner in the Vatican, refusing to recognize the new kingdom, insisting upon his rightful sovereignty over the Papal States, rejecting all compromises which did not allow him his territorial sovereignty, and maintaining the *non-expedit* of his predecessor, which forbade Catholics to vote or to take any active part in the affairs of the new government. As a result, the anti-clerical and anti-Vatican policies of the Italian government were pursued relentlessly, with suppression and spoliation of religious houses and interference with the traditional rights and liberties of the Church, especially in the field of education. This warfare, which did great harm, both to the Church and to the new kingdom, was tolerated by Leo because he believed that the new Italy was essentially unstable and would collapse, and that the rights of the Holy See would be restored. Inexorable towards Italy, he was at pains to try to achieve an understanding first with Germany and then with France. With Germany he was successful, so that Bismarck called off the persecution known as the *Kulturkampf*, though the Chancellor had little to show for his war with the Church. With France he was less successful, because his effort to persuade the French Church to accept, loyally, the Third Republic, and to give up intriguing for a return of the Bourbons, made little appeal to the French clergy. Suspected of disloyalty, these clergy consequently found themselves, in the eighteen-nineties, the victims of a political persecution comparable to that of the *Kulturkampf* in Germany.

By the end of his long reign it was becoming apparent to Leo that the new Italian kingdom was establishing itself

The Popes in the Modern World

Cardinal Rampolla, who might have been elected Pope in 1903 in succession to Leo XIII, had not Cardinal Puznya pronounced a veto in the name of the House of Hapsburg, the last example of political interference in the free election of a Pope. As Leo's Secretary of State, Rampolla had shown himself consistently friendly to France and antagonistic to the Triple Alliance and the Austrian Empire

Pius X (1903–14) was conservative in his policies, resisting the recognition of the Italian state and condemning the Modernist movement. He was a man of great simplicity and sanctity, personally loved everywhere, especially in Italy. A proposal for his canonization was made in 1923, only nine years after his death, and the ceremony finally took place in 1954. A contemporary portrait

more securely, and that no major power was any longer interested in restoring the political power of the Pope. Indeed, by achieving the Triple Alliance with Austria and Germany, the new kingdom made a restoration of the Pope's temporal power impracticable.

Leo will always be remembered for the revived study, which he inspired, of Thomist philosophy, which he made virtually the official philosophy of the Church and the basis of seminary education. But his most important achievement was to call the serious attention of Catholics to the gravity of the social question, in his famous encyclical *Rerum Novarum* (1891). Here he laid down the principle that the worker had a natural right to the 'just wage', which should be sufficient to keep himself and his family 'in decency'. It was a revolutionary pronouncement: and although in many ways the encyclical was conservative, denouncing all class war and revolution, accepting social classes as 'natural', and preferring the medieval 'vertical' guild to the 'horizontal trade union', it laid the basis for the modern social teaching of the Church.

Little improvement in the Papacy's relations either with Italy or with Europe was achieved by Leo's successor, St Pius X, who was elected in August 1903. Of humble origin, the new Pope had been greatly beloved as Patriarch of Venice, and he brought to the Vatican a simplicity of manners which contrasted with the keen ceremonial sense of his predecessor. His sincerity, indeed his sanctity, made an immediate impression on those who met him, and his canonization, on 31 May 1954, forty years after his death, gave great joy. But his Pontificate was marked, even more evidently than those of his predecessors, by conflicts, in which he showed himself intransigent. Unyielding towards the encroachments, in religious matters, of the anti-clerical French government, he saw the Church disestablished in France; indignant at the spread of Modernist ideas amongst the clergy, he denounced Modernism in an encyclical, *Pascendi dominici gregis*, of exceptional harshness, and set up an elaborate system of episcopal censorship; unwilling to see the growth of an independent, lay, political and social movement amongst Italian Catholics, he put such initiatives under clerical control.

The outbreak of the First World War, in August 1914, hastened the death of St Pius X, and that immense conflagration dominated the Pontificate of his successor, the aristocratic Benedict XV (1914–22), who was elected in September and who will always be remembered for his efforts, in the summer of 1917, to restore peace, on the basis of the *status quo*. His proposals, however, were rejected by both

The scene in St Peter's during the canonization of Pius X. His body, which now lies beneath the altar of the chapel in St Peter's dedicated to him, rests before the high altar and a vast tapestry can be seen depicting one of the two miracles which have to be proved before canonization

Left Benedict XV (1914–22), whose reign was overshadowed by the First World War. In 1917 he attempted to end the appalling bloodshed of the military stalemate by proposing peace on the basis of the territorial *status quo*, but his proposal was rejected by both sides

Opposite Pius XI (1922–39) resolutely opposed both Fascism and Communism and denounced them in outspoken terms in a number of encyclicals. He is seen *top* at the inauguration of the Vatican Wireless Station in 1931 and *bottom* at the opening of the reorganized Vatican Library in 1933

Below The most significant event of Pius XI's reign was the concordat with Italy in 1929, whereby the Papacy at last recognized the secular government of Italy and the tiny independent Vatican City State was set up. Cardinal Gasparri, the papal Secretary of State responsible for the negotiations, and Benito Mussolini with their entourages after the signing of the treaty

sides, and Italy succeeded in preventing his being represented at the peace conference at Versailles. Nevertheless it was Benedict XV who at last (1919) helped to heal the feud with Italy by removing the restrictions preventing Catholics from taking part in Italian politics, and it was in this way that Don Sturzo's *Popolari* party, forerunner of today's Christian Democrats, rapidly became politically important in the new state.

Unfortunately, however, when Italy reached her year of crisis in 1922, the new Catholic party was too young and too suspect, both at the Vatican and amongst the Italian bishops, for the new Pope, Pius XI (who succeeded Benedict XV in the same year), to give it his support. By withholding that support, and by rejecting the idea of an alliance between the Catholic *popolari* and the socialists, Pius XI undoubtedly contributed, however unwillingly, to a state of affairs which made it possible for Mussolini to take advantage of the divisions between the Italian political parties and to seize power.

But once the Fascist dictatorship was established, and its brutal and essentially pagan qualities made manifest, the Pope's voice, especially in his encyclical *Non abbiamo bisogno* (1931), provided the most effective public rebuke that Mussolini had to suffer, just as the Vatican newspaper, the *Osservatore Romano*, provided the only regular public criticism to which the dictator was subjected.

Pius XI challenged Mussolini constantly and sharply, especially in the field of education, and he denounced Hitler's régime in even stronger terms in *Mit brennender sorge* (1937). But his denunciations of atheistic Communism, especially in Russia, in Mexico, and in Spain, were more frequent and more sweeping, reaching their climax in his *Divini Redemptoris* (1937). The key *motif* of Pius XI's pontificate was his endeavour to impress upon mankind the immensity of the Communist menace. By comparison, Fascism, however pagan, was to him a power with which he was prepared to do business, and with great and lasting effect he did business with Mussolini when he achieved the Lateran treaty of 1929. By this accord the seventy-year-old quarrel between Italy and the Vatican was at last healed, the Pope giving up his claim to central Italy, and the Italian government recognizing the Pope's full independent sovereignty over the Vatican City State and providing some two billion *lire* as a partial compensation for earlier confiscations. And to the treaty was tied a concordat, by which the Italian kingdom recognized the special status of the Catholic Church in Italy. This highly realistic arrangement survived the Second World War, survived Fascism, and was accepted by all Italian parties, including the Communists, under Pius XI's successor, when the constitution of the new Italian Republic was drawn up, after the fall of the

Italian monarchy, in 1947. A determination not to allow Italy and the Vatican to be at war with each other again has taken a deep hold upon Italians of all parties as a result of their bitter experience of seventy years of conflict.

Yet, although it saw the strengthening of the settlement between Italy and the Vatican, the pontificate of Pius XI's successor, Pius XII (Eugenio Pacelli), which extended from 1939 to 1958, was a pontificate of tension. As Secretary of State during the last nine years of the reign of Pius XI, Cardinal Pacelli had helped to inspire his master's policies, negotiating his concordat with Hitler in 1933, and sharing his concern with the advances of atheistic Communism. It is therefore not surprising that, when he was elected Pope in 1939, he continued his predecessor's policies, nor that he was deeply concerned by the immensely strengthened position assumed by Moscow, in eastern Europe, after the Second World War, and by the Soviet lordship over Catholic Hungary, and over many other Catholic populations behind the Iron Curtain. In these territories the Church came under persecution and was cut off from Rome, and from the West, so that it became, in the Pope's words, 'the Church of Silence', while its leaders, notably Cardinals Mindzenty in Hungary, Beran in Czechoslovakia, and Wyszynski in Poland, suffered imprisonment or worse. And in these same years the formidable growth of Communist parties in France and Italy raised the spectre of a Soviet domination of Europe. It is against this background of desperate danger that we have to judge the action of

Above Pius XII with Cardinal Spellman, Archbishop of New York. In the struggle against Communism in the years following the Second World War it was natural for the ties between the Vatican and the Roman Catholic Church in America to become stronger

Left A jubilee brick for 1950. These bricks are used to wall up the Holy Door in St Peter's after it has been closed at the end of the Jubilee Year

Right Pius XII's pontificate (1939–58) was dominated by the Second World War and the Communist persecution of the Church in Eastern Europe. The Pope giving his blessing from the Bernini colonnade

Pius XII, in 1949, when he forbade Catholics, on pain of excommunication, to give the Communists political support.

In return, the Pope was accused from Moscow of 'warmongering' and of helping to divide the world into two camps. His own record, in his constant appeals for peace both before and during the Second World War, as well as his personal charity to war refugees, from both sides, at Rome, bore witness to his passion for peace. But it is true that in his many speeches, both during and after the war, he always linked the problem of peace with the problem of justice and that in this way he made it very clear that he did not believe that any settlement, or any international organization, could provide a true peace unless that peace were based upon freedom and justice for all peoples, and that he had particularly the peoples of eastern Europe in his mind.

Neither the exceptional gifts, as linguist, historian, theologian and diplomat, nor the intense spiritual dedication of this remarkable Pope are ever likely to be called in question, even by his opponents. But his reputation suffered somewhat, after his death, as a result of the enthusiasms engendered by his successor John XXIII's more genial and optimistic approach to the world outside the Church, and the hopes aroused by the Second Vatican Council. Certainly, in his later years, Pius XII, despite the many audiences he addressed, had become a somewhat remote and Olympian figure and one which seemed to emphasize the exclusive attributes of the Church. But the immense esteem in which he was held by Catholics, by most governments in the West, and above all by the people of Rome, was clearly demonstrated in Holy Year, 1950, the year in which he defined the dogma of the Assumption of Our Lady into Heaven. And the part which he played in the defence of western Christendom, at a time of critical challenge, as well as the element of stability he provided in an Italy torn by war and ideological conflict, may well come to be appreciated more fully in years to come.

In the years since the death of Pius XII the feeling has grown that a new era is at hand for the Church. If that proves to be so, then the Popes whom we have been discussing in this chapter are likely to be regarded, by contrast, as essentially the heirs of Pius IX's policy of resistance: resistance to the new Italy and to the inordinate claims of democracy, resistance still fiercer to the materialist teachings of Marxist Socialism and Marxist Communism. At a time of challenge they insisted on a high degree of philosophical conformity to the teachings of St Thomas as well as on a close uniformity of liturgical practice. Their greatness and their limitations the future will judge. What can be said already is that their days were stormy and that amidst the storms they stood steadfast.

Above Pius XII at the window of his apartment in the Vatican, blessing the crowds in St Peter's Square

Opposite top In 1950 Pius XII proclaimed the doctrine of the Assumption of the Blessed Virgin Mary. The Pope giving his blessing to the crowds gathered in St Peter's Square on the occasion of the proclamation. *Bottom* Pius XII talking to Monsignor Montini, now Paul VI, when he led a delegation of members of Catholic Action to the Vatican in 1956. Monsignor Montini had been in the Secretariat of State under Pius XII before becoming Archbishop of Milan

An eighteenth-century engraving showing the procedure for a conclave:
the cardinals assemble;
they hear the Mass of the Holy Spirit;
the first vote;
the scrutiny of the voting;
food arriving for the cardinals;
it is examined and passed through a hatch

24 CARDINALS AND THE CONCLAVE

CHRISTOPHER HOLLIS

For the first thousand years of the Church's history the Popes were elected by popular acclamation, a practice much open to abuse. In 1059 Nicholas II declared the formation of the College of Cardinals, which was to consist of the rectors of the leading churches in Rome, known as Cardinal-priests, the Cardinal-deacons, who presided over the Church's charitable work in different districts of Rome, and the Cardinal-bishops, who were the occupants of the seven neighbouring sees to Rome; they were to be the future papal electors. The cardinals are appointed by the Pope himself and today the College consists in part of curial officials and in part of the occupants of the most important sees in the world. To elect a Pope the cardinals meet in closed, secret conclave and a two-thirds majority is needed for election.

ACCORDING TO THE TEACHING OF THE CHURCH THE constituted orders are those of bishop, priest and the minor orders. These can only be conferred by ordination by a bishop, and every bishop has received his authority in unbroken succession from the apostles by the laying on of hands. In that sense therefore all bishops are equal. Yet, as Orwell might have put it, some bishops are more equal than others. Dioceses are grouped into provinces and over each province there is an archbishop. The archbishop presides over the meetings of his bishops, and the metropolitan, where there is a metropolitan, presides over the meetings of the bishops of the nation. Yet there is no order of archbishops. The archbishop is merely *primus inter pares*. He has no power to interfere with the bishop's exercise of his episcopal power within his own diocese. Similarly cardinals do not constitute a religious order. The cardinal, as such, is a man-created Prince of the Church.

Until late in the Middle Ages the term cardinal-priest was applied to the rectors of the leading churches in Rome. At the same time Rome was divided into regions for the purpose of charitable administration and over each of these regions a cardinal-deacon presided. As the business of the Papacy increased, the Pope called on a number of the neighbouring bishops to help him with the work, and these suburbican bishops, as they were called – the Bishops of Ostia, Porto, Santa Rufina, Albano, Sabina, Frascati and Preneste – came to be known as cardinal-bishops. The Bishop of Ostia was from the first, and still is, the Dean of the Sacred College.

During the first millennium of the Church's life the method of electing a Pope was highly irregular. Bishops at Rome, as elsewhere, were elected by popular acclamation and the popular voice often only showed itself by methods of disgraceful tumult. Local nobles and powerful monarchs did not scruple to bring pressure to bear. Meanwhile the cardinals, who had been originally only Roman officers, were becoming increasingly the main advisers of the Pope on the affairs of the Church in general. In 1059 Nicholas II in his decree *In Nomine Domini* appointed the cardinals to be the papal electors. Later in the Middle Ages, at the time of the conciliar movement, the cardinals sometimes attempted to use their position as advisers of the Pope in order to reduce the Pope to the dimensions of a constitutional monarch. 'Election-capitulations' were exacted out of Popes as conditions of their election. The Council of Basel proclaimed that it was the duty of the cardinals to rebuke any Pope who was forgetful of his duty. It was not until 1695 that Innocent XII in his constitution *Ecclesiae Catholicae* expressly condemned all such capitulations as simony. During the conciliar controversy an attempt was made to compel the Pope to obtain the consent of the cardinals before adding any new member to their company, but the attempt was not successful and the only limitation on the Pope's freedom of appointment to the College is the vague obligation imposed upon him by the Council of Trent to give a fair representation to all nations.

The appointment of cardinals rests solely with the Pope. The Pope first nominates a cardinal resident in Rome at a secret consistory. That afternoon the nominated candidates meet in the Pope's apartments, when the scarlet *zuchetta*, or skull cap, is given to them. The 'red hat' is formally conferred at the next public consistory. At the next secret consistory, the ceremony of opening and closing their mouths takes place, symbolizing the cardinals' duty to give wise counsel to the Pope and to keep his secrets. At this consistory the new cardinal receives his ring. If a cleric not resident in Rome is created cardinal, the *zuchetta* is brought to him by one of the noble guard, and, receiving it, he has to take an oath to proceed to Rome within a year for his formal initiation. A Pope sometimes makes a secret selection of someone whom he intends to create a cardinal – what is known as a cardinal *in pectore* (in his breast), but if the name of such a cardinal has not been announced before the Pope's death, the nomination is not valid. It is said that the historian Lingard was selected as a cardinal *in pectore* by Gregory XVI but, if so, Gregory died before the selection was made public and Lingard never became a cardinal. Pope John XXIII announced shortly before his death that he had selected three cardinals *in pectore*.

Above A thirteenth-century bishop's mitre embroidered with the madonna and child. In the Middle Ages the name Cardinal-bishop was given to the incumbents of the neighbouring dioceses to Rome, who gave the Pope help and advice. Today cardinals are usually bishops

Below All cardinals are chosen personally by the Pope. Their appointment is confirmed at a public consistory, at which they prostrate themselves in homage to the Pope, before receiving the traditional red hat. A photograph taken at a consistory in 1960

Pius IX conferring the red hat on Cardinal Luciano Bonaparte, great-nephew of Napoleon Bonaparte, in 1868. A contemporary engraving

The College of Cardinals consists in part of Curial officials and in part of the occupants of the most important sees throughout the world. Unless they are bishops of sees elsewhere, all cardinals are under obligation to live in Rome and indeed may not leave the city without papal permission. Only under very special circumstances, as happened for instance with Cardinal Newman, is a cardinal who has not got an episcopal see given permission to live outside Rome.

A meeting of the cardinals under the Pope's presidency is known as a consistory. Such consistories are sometimes secret and sometimes public. These meetings take place from time to time so as to give the Pope an opportunity of making a pronouncement to the world. On the death of a Pope the administration of the States of the Church passes temporarily to the College of Cardinals, which acts through the interim head of the College, known as the Cardinal Camerlengo. This responsibility in the turbulent times of the Middle Ages, when vacancies were often prolonged and when parties within the city tried to seize power by violence, was very real and very heavy.

A cardinal is a Prince of the Church and therefore ranks in the table of precedence in any country immediately after the reigning sovereign and on an equality with princes of the blood royal. In the Church he is inferior and responsible only to the Pope who alone can depose him, but the relative status of cardinals and patriarchs is a matter of controversy which is being disputed at the present General Council.

The cardinals are still divided into cardinal-bishops, cardinal-priests and cardinal-deacons, although as a general rule all of them are today in fact bishops. There is, however, no necessity for a cardinal to be even a priest. Cardinal Mazarin, Louis XIV's minister, was never a priest, nor was Cardinal Antonelli, Pius IX's Secretary of State.

The number of the cardinals was fixed by Sixtus v in 1586 at seventy-six, of whom at least six must be bishops, fifty priests and fourteen deacons, but John xxiii increased the number and after his consistory of March 1962 there were eighty-seven. At the time of his death there were eighty-five, of whom eight had been created by Pius xi, thirty-one by Pius xii and forty-six by John xxiii. Of these twenty-nine were Italian, eight French, seven from the British Commonwealth, six from Spain, five from the United States, three each from Brazil and Germany, two each from the Argentine, Ireland, Lebanon and Portugal and one each from Austria, Belgium, Chile, China, Colombia, Cuba, Ecuador, Holland, Hungary, Japan, Mexico, Peru, the Philippines, Poland, Uruguay and Venezuela. At the turn of the century there were only two cardinals – one from Australia and one from the United States – who were not resident in Europe.

By far the most important task of the College of Cardinals is that of electing a Pope in conclave at the time of a vacancy. The word 'conclave' comes from the Latin, *clavis*, a key, and is used to describe the closed room within which the cardinals are locked when they meet for a papal election. The custom of locking up the cardinals for an election originated from the election of 1271 when they delayed for two years and nine months over their deliberations until the town authorities of Viterbo where they were meeting locked them up in exasperation until they reached a decision. To prevent the recurrence of such a scandal the elected Pope, Gregory x, promulgated at the Second Council of Lyons in 1274 rules for future conclaves. On the death of a Pope the cardinals were to wait ten days so as to give their absent colleagues an opportunity to assemble. They were then all to be locked into a room, each cardinal being accompanied by one servant. During the conclave they were to hold no communication with anyone outside. If after three days they had not reached a decision they were during the next five days to receive only one dish for their midday, and one for their evening meal. After those five days, if still obstinate, they were to receive nothing but bread, water and wine until they made an election. During the period of the conclave they were to receive no payments from the papal treasury. These strict rules aroused opposition and in 1276, after they had operated at three elections, John xx revoked them. But the result was a recurrence of the scandal of absurdly protracted elections, until Boniface viii re-enacted Gregory x's provisions. Since then the

Cardinals and the Conclave

Opposite Leo x and the College of Cardinals by Giorgio Vasari, a painting in the Palazzo Vecchio, Florence

Left The most important function of the College of Cardinals is the election of a new Pope. Sebastiano Ricci (1659–1734) depicts the conclave in allegorical form, showing the dove of the Holy Spirit brooding over the vacant papal tiara

Below The period between the death of one Pope and the election of another is known as *sede vacante*. The cardinals assemble for the conclave from all over the world and the government of the Church and of the conclave during this period is in the hands of the Cardinal Camerlengo (Cardinal Chamberlain). A medal struck by Cardinal Colonna, the Governor of the conclave of 1740, which elected Benedict XIV after a *sede vacante* of seven months

Popes have always been elected in conclave, though the detailed conditions of the election have varied. Clement V, for instance, in 1351 permitted a slight amelioration of the rules of diet.

Immediately on the Pope's death the Cardinal Camerlengo verifies his death. In the presence of the papal household he strikes the Pope on the forehead with a silver mallet and calls him by his name. He then breaks his fisherman's ring and papal seals. After the nine days of the Pope's obsequies the cardinals are informed in consistory of the detailed methods of election and swear to obey them. Then they go into conclave. The door is doubly locked both from the outside and from the inside. Since 1878 there has been a kitchen within the conclave and food is provided there. Each cardinal has a cell, covered with cloth – purple if he is a creation of the last Pope, green if he is of a previous creation.

The government of the conclave is in the hands of the Camerlengo and of three cardinals-representative of the cardinal-bishops, of the cardinal-priests and of the cardinal-deacons. The morning begins with the Cardinal Dean saying mass. The other cardinals receive Communion from him and listen to a Latin allocution on their duties. They

Cardinals and the Conclave

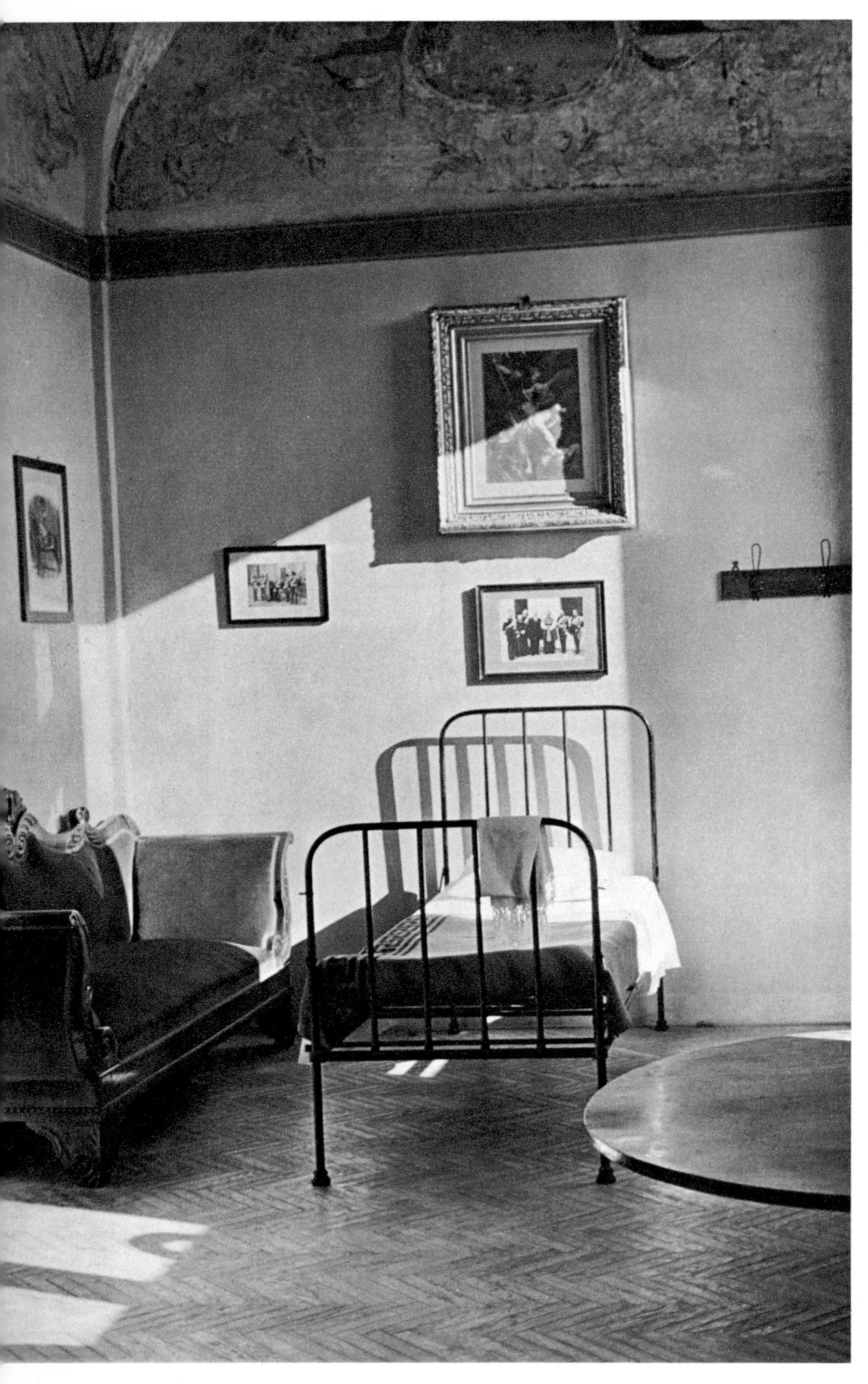

The conclave is so called because the cardinals are locked in for their deliberations and are allowed no contact with the outside world. *Above* A view of one of the bedrooms prepared for the cardinals at the 1963 conclave

Prince Chigi, Marshal of the conclave, performing the ceremony of locking the door from the outside at the conclave of 1963. The door is double locked from the inside by the Cardinal Camerlengo

Above The cardinals assembled on their thrones in the Sistine Chapel for the conclave of 1963. After a successful election all the canopies are lowered except that of the new Pope. Voting has taken place in the Sistine Chapel since the sixteenth century, except for the conclave of 1800 which took place in Venice

Signa.

Nomen.

Eligo Card.

Eligo in Summum Pontificem R.mum D. meum D. Card.

A ballot sheet for the conclave of 1800 when Pius VII was elected

Right The stove in the Sistine Chapel in which the ballot papers are burned, showing the mechanism for producing white or black smoke, according to whether the necessary two thirds majority has been obtained or not

Cardinals and the Conclave

Immediately after his election the new Pope appears on the balcony of St Peter's and is presented to the people. He then gives his first blessing, *Urbi et Orbi*, to the city and the world. Paul VI on the balcony following his election

Each Pope has his own tiara, or triple crown. The special lightweight crown presented to Paul VI on his election in 1963 by the people of Milan, where he was Archbishop

then proceed to the Sistine Chapel where, with lighted candles on the altar, prayers are said and the balloting commences. Each cardinal drops his vote into a chalice. If the vote is close, the ballot of the leading candidate is opened to make sure that he has not voted for himself. For election a two-thirds majority is necessary. At each ballot three candidates are chosen to act as *scrutatores* to preside over the voting, three as *revisores* to count the votes and three as *infirmarii* to go and fetch from their cells the votes of the sick, if any such there be. One of the *revisores* reads out the names of those voted for and, when all have been read, then the *revisores* check up to make sure that the tally is correct. The Catholic monarchs traditionally claimed a right of veto over the elections and this veto was last exercised by the Austrian Emperor through Cardinal Puzyna of Cracow against Cardinal Rampolla, Leo XIII's Secretary of State, in 1903. Pius X however formally abolished this right of veto.

After the first ballot, if the Cardinal Dean agrees, it is possible to have immediately a second ballot which is known as an *accessus* on the same form, to enable any one who wishes to change his vote. However, whether in that form or not, balloting goes on until some one obtains the requisite majority. There are two ballots every day, one in the morning and one in the afternoon. After each ballot the voting papers are put into a stove and burnt. Where there has been no election straw is mixed with the papers so as to give out black smoke. A successful ballot gives white smoke, though, as will be remembered, this device by no means worked satisfactorily at the conclave after the death of Pius XII and the crowds outside were unable to tell whether the smoke was white or black. In case of total deadlock it is possible to proceed to an election by compromise – that is to say, for all the Cardinals to delegate the task of electing a Pope to a few of their number. This method has, however, not been used since the fourteenth century. Any male Catholic can in theory be elected Pope, even though he be not as yet in holy orders, but since Urban VI (1378–89) no one has ever been elected who was not himself already a cardinal. Gregory XVI in 1831 was the last Pope who was not already a bishop.

When a decisive ballot has taken place the successful candidate is asked if he accepts election and then is asked what name he will take. The master of the ceremonies lowers the canopies over the chairs of all the cardinals other than that of the newly-elected Pope. The other cardinals then all pay him homage. The senior cardinal-deacon then announces from the balcony of St Peter's the name of the new Pope to the waiting crowds. If the Pope is not already a bishop the first ceremony is to consecrate him. The new Pope then appears on the balcony and blesses the crowd. His formal coronation follows on the next Sunday and after that he takes possession of the diocesan church of Rome, St John Lateran.

The crowds in St Peter's Square see the white smoke announcing the election of Cardinal Roncalli as John XXIII on 28 October 1958

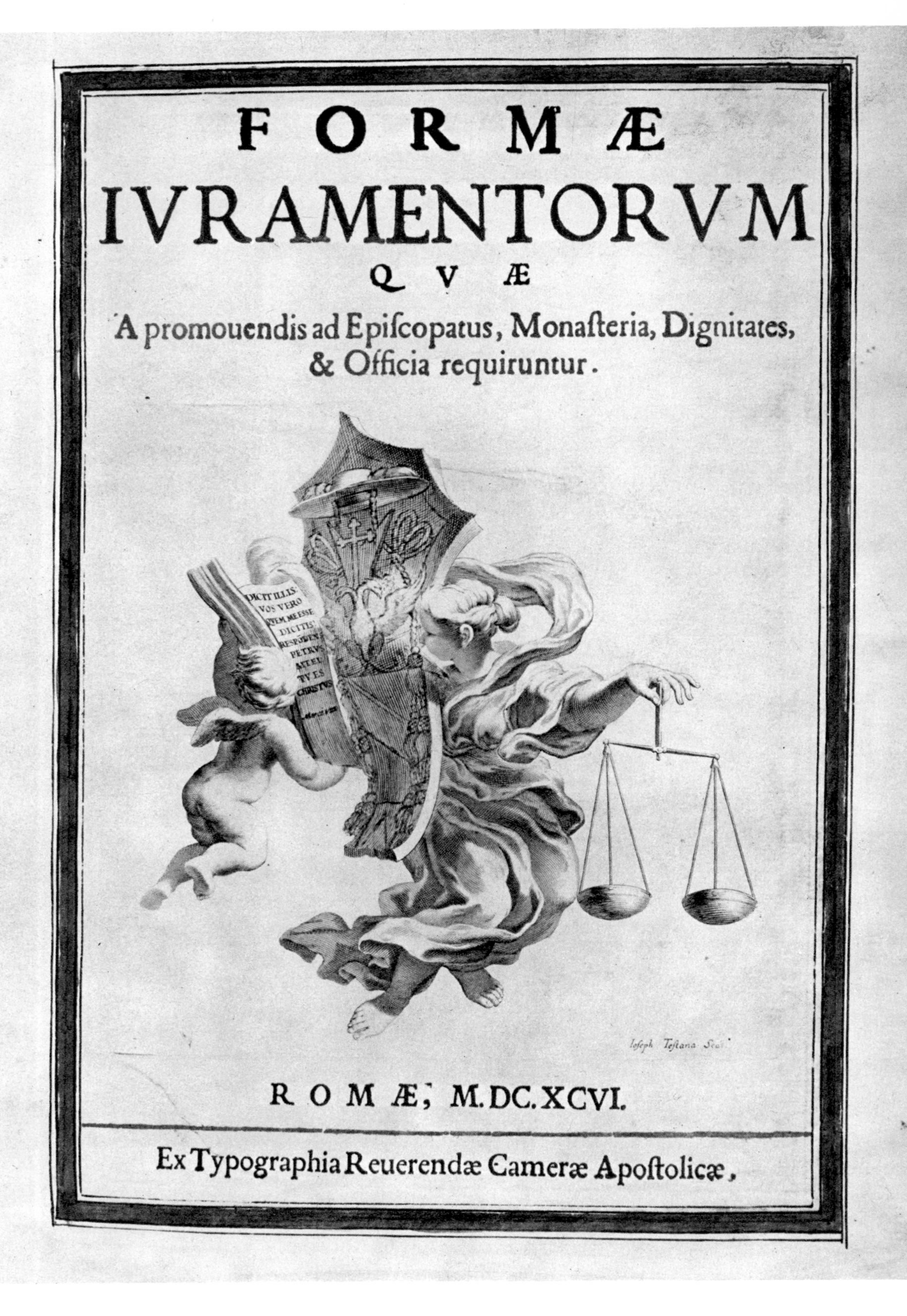
FORMÆ
IVRAMENTORVM
QVÆ
A promouendis ad Episcopatus, Monasteria, Dignitates,
& Officia requiruntur.

Ioseph Testana Sculp.

ROMÆ, M.DC.XCVI.

Ex Typographia Reuerendæ Cameræ Apostolicæ.

The major part of the administration of the central government
of the Church is dealt with by the Secretariat of State
under the Cardinal Secretary of State,
who is directly responsible to the Pope.
Top the stamp of the Secretariat of State
and *bottom* the stamp of the Cardinal Secretary of State

The title page of a book setting out the oaths required
on taking up one of the major offices of the Church.
It is dated 1696 and was issued by the Apostolic Chamber,
one of the Offices of the Curia
more recently eclipsed
by the prominence of the Secretariat

25 THE CENTRAL GOVERNMENT OF THE CHURCH

PETER CANISIUS VAN LIERDE

The government of the Church is administered by three bodies, the Congregations, the Tribunals and the Offices. The Congregations are the machinery through which the Pope exercises his legislative powers; the Tribunals exercise the Pope's judicial powers throughout the Church; and the Offices deal with the major problems of Church government, finance and the day to day administration of the Curia. The most important of the Offices is the Secretariat of State, headed by the Cardinal Secretary of State, which is directly responsible for the implementation of the policy decisions made by the Pope. It is responsible for relations with civil governments, including diplomatic negotiation of concordats ensuring freedom of worship and education for Catholics. It appoints officials of the Curia and papal legates. It controls the granting of papal subsidies and gives directives to such lay organizations as Catholic Action. The Secretariat has an ever-increasing field of activity and is the most important instrument of Church government.

CHRIST IS TEACHER, LEGISLATOR AND JUDGE. THE Pope, His Vicar on earth, must also be teacher, legislator and judge, and he exercises these powers through the organs of the central government of the Church: the Congregations, Tribunals and Offices.

The Congregations interpret the Pope's teaching and legislative powers. Through their broad activities, the Pope governs all his people. The Tribunals are responsible for the social relations of those who compose the visible society of the Church, and their activity extends the judicial power of the Pope to all territories. The Offices distribute the documents handled by the Congregations and the Tribunals and assist the Pope in the administrative work necessary for governing 500 million Catholics scattered over the face of the earth.

The Offices comprise the Apostolic Chancellery, which prepares official documents; the Apostolic Datary, which countersigns and dates official documents and manages ecclesiastical benefices; the Apostolic Chamber, which handles finance and property, and governs *sede vacante*; and lastly, the Secretariat of State. There is a great difference between the latter and the other three offices. They do not exercise powers of central government, nor do they issue decisions for dioceses, as they are primarily transmitting centres for passing on papal documents which originate from the other ministries. On the other hand, the Secretariat of State is the official secretariat of the Pope, working under his personal direction.

The world is in continuous evolution. Some institutions, indispensable in one era, lose their importance in another. The Church's manifold life, as well as the relations of the Papacy with the various states, have undergone extensive modification since the Middle Ages. This explains why the Apostolic Chancellery, the Apostolic Datary and the Apostolic Chamber, which were once so important, have been modified and reduced in their functions, while the Secretariat of State has increased in importance as the Pope's contacts with the whole Catholic Church and with secular authorities have grown. The Pope makes policy decisions, and measures based on them are communicated by the Secretariat of State.

Pius X, by the apostolic constitution *Sapienti Consilio* of 29 June 1908, divided the Secretariat into three sections, and it retains this form today. The first section handles the extraordinary affairs of the Holy See, and is presided over by the Secretary of the Congregation for Extraordinary Affairs, since the Congregation is identical with the first section. The second section is directed by the Substitute for Ordinary Affairs. The third, under the direction of the Chancellor for Apostolic Briefs, despatches documents, or briefs, relating to the business of the Secretariat of State. The whole organization of these three sections is presided over by the Cardinal Secretary of State, who is in constant touch with the Pope.

The Secretariat of State has a staff of over a hundred, most of whom are assigned to the first two sections and belonging to two categories: administrative and diplomatic. Those who do administrative work have the titles of *minutante* and *attaché*. Members of the Holy See's diplomatic

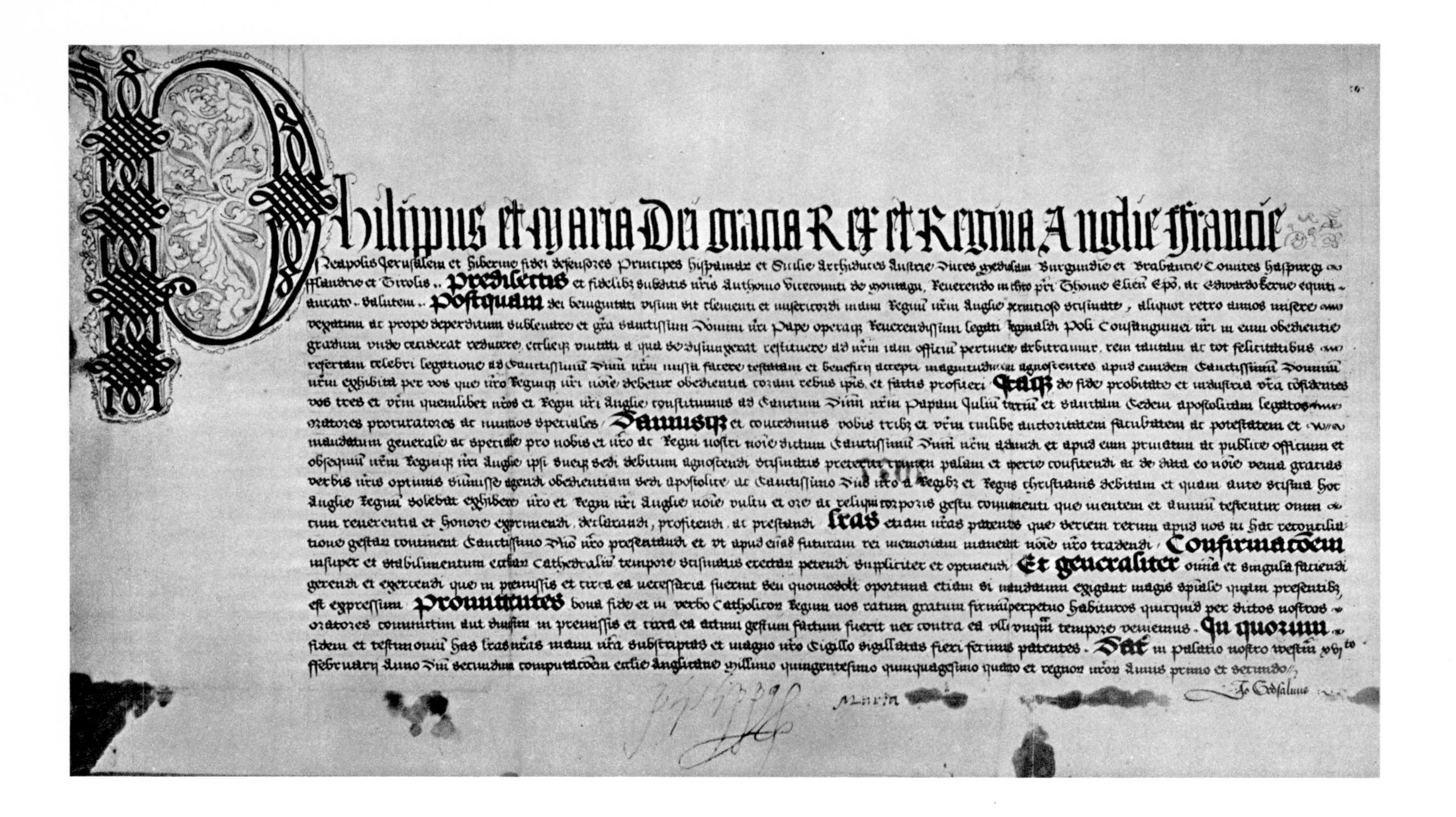

Philippus et Maria Dei gratia Rex et Regina Anglie Francie

corps hold posts in the following order: Attaché of Nunciature, Secretary of Nunciature, Auditor of Nunciature, and Counsellor of Nunciature. The Chancellor of Apostolic Briefs is assisted by a number of ecclesiastics and by several lay experts. The following chart illustrates the present organization of the Secretariat:

THE POPE

Cardinal Secretary of State

Extraordinary affairs	Ordinary affairs	Apostolic briefs
Secretary	Substitute	Chancellor of Briefs

Personnel

Administrative role	Diplomatic role
Minutante	Counsellors of Nunciature
Attachés	Auditors of Nunciature
Theologian	Secretary of Nunciature
Legal Consultant	Attachés of Nunciature

It should be added that the Cardinal Secretary of State is patron of the Pontifical Ecclesiastical Academy which prepares priests for the diplomatic service of the Holy See.

The origins of the Secretariat of State go back to the Middle Ages. The varied correspondence of the Pontiffs has been the responsibility of the Apostolic Chancellery for centuries. It is also beyond doubt that at a certain period in history the Popes made use of letters called *literae clausae*, *literae breves* and *brevia*, dealing with important matters which called for discretion. These letters bore the *bullae* of the Chancellery. The first document so stamped dates from the pontificate of Clement IV (1265–68), who wrote to Peter Grossus: *Non scribimus tibi nec familiaribus nostris sub bulla sed sub Piscatoris anulo quo Romani Pontifices in suis secretis utuntur.* ('We do not write to you nor to our own intimates under the bull-seal but by the Fisherman's ring which is used by the Pontiffs for their private correspondence.' These letters, it seems, were prepared in the Apostolic Chancellery only by a selected group of secretaries. Subsequently, around the year 1338, Benedict XII (1334–42) instituted a proper Secretariat, with personnel distinct from that of the Chancellery, to look after the secret correspondence of the Popes. This tendency for the Pope's correspondence to become more frequent, urgent and secret gave rise to new organs: the Secret Chamber, instituted by Martin V (1417–31), and the Apostolic Secretariat for official correspondence in Latin. The latter was given a definite form by Innocent VIII (1484–92) with the constitution *Non debet reprehensibile* of 31 December 1487. It was composed of twenty-four apostolic secretaries. The origin of the Chancellery of Briefs, the Secretariat of Briefs to Princes, and the

The central Government of the Church

The complexity of the machinery of central papal government goes back to medieval times. The Avignon Popes, notably Benedict XII (1334–42), created a special secretariat for the reception and filing of documents and the despatch of papal bulls and briefs, the origin of the present Secretariat of State. *Opposite* The letter of Mary Tudor and her husband Philip II of Spain, who was declared King of England in 1554, appointing three ambassadors to the court of Pope Paul III in February 1554. *Left* A few of the telegrams that came in to Cardinal Gasparri when he was Secretary of State from 1915 to 1930

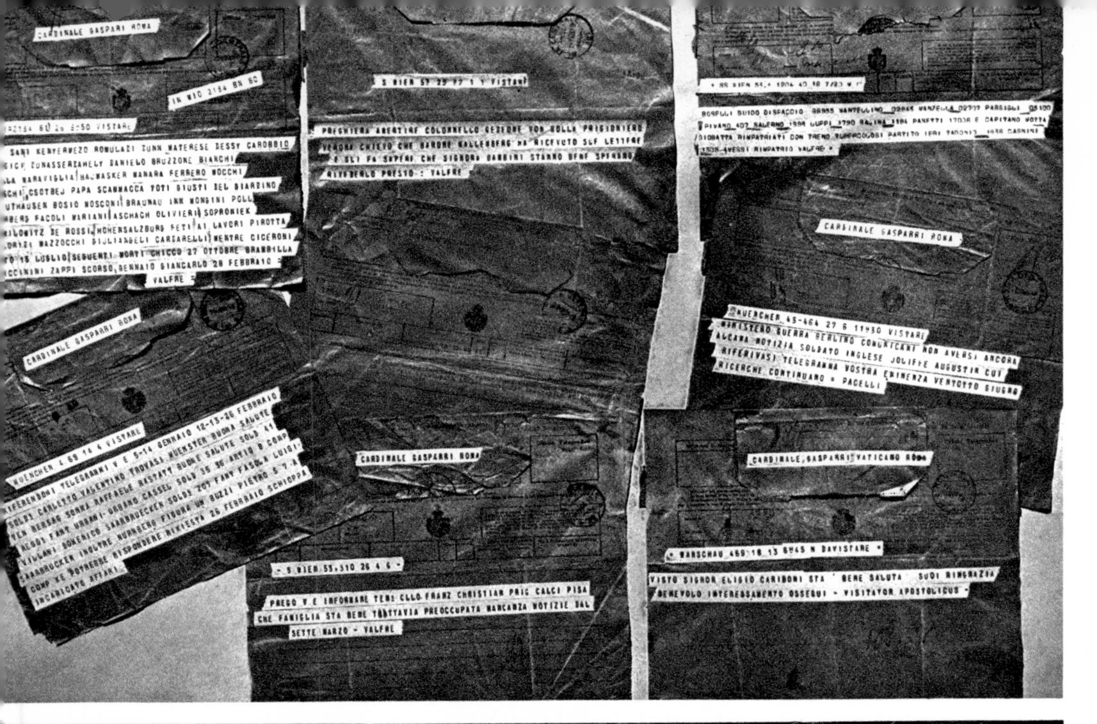

Centre One of the offices of the Secretariat of State during the First World War. An important function of the Secretariat is the appointment of the papal nuncios, who represent the Holy See in other countries, and the handling of diplomatic relations with civil governments. In the case of a great war the Papacy, through its nuncios, is one of the powers in touch with both sides

Below Cardinal Pacelli, later Pius XII, presiding as Cardinal Camerlengo over a meeting of the prelates of the Apostolic Chamber on the death in 1939 of Pius XI. On the death of a Pope all appointments in the Curia, except those of the Cardinal Camerlengo and two others, become void, and the government of the Church *sede vacante*, during the conclave, devolves on the Sacred College of Cardinals, the Cardinal Camerlengo and the Apostolic Chamber

Secretariat of Latin Letters lies in the Apostolic Secretariat.

With Leo X (1513–21) another office came into being, that of *Secretarius intimus*, also called *Secretarius Papae* or *Secretarius maior*, who was responsible for correspondence in the vernacular, in the name, but not under the signature, of the Roman Pontiff. This was used for correspondence with Apostolic nuncios having permanent diplomatic powers, an office which was then increasing in importance.

The Pope's Secretariat was later placed under the jurisdiction of the Cardinal Nephew, who almost had the rank of the Pope's Prime Minister. It underwent further development, particularly during the period of the Council of Trent. At the very beginning of his Pontificate Innocent X (1644–1655) appointed to the high office of Cardinal Nephew one who was already a cardinal and not related to the Pope. Innocent XII (1691–1700), with the bull *Romanum decet Pontificem* of 22 June 1692, finally abolished the office of Cardinal Nephew.

In 1793 Pius VI (1775–99) created a special congregation, *super negotiis extraordinariis Regni Galliarum*, to deal with the serious problems arising from the French Revolution. On 18 July 1814 Pius VII (1800–23) extended the competence of this congregation, giving it the new name of Extraordinary Congregation for the Ecclesiastical Affairs of the Catholic World, but no permanent status. Pope Leo XII (1823–29) gave it its present title: Congregation of Extraordinary Ecclesiastical Affairs, and it was Pius X (1903–14)

The Secretariat of State is responsible for all relations with civil governments and negotiates concordats regulating the powers of Church and State. *Above* The signing of the Lateran Treaty of 1929, with Cardinal Gasparri at the head of the table and Mussolini second on his right. *Below* Their signatures to the treaty

who incorporated it into the Secretariat of State as its first section with the constitution *Sapienti consilio* of 29 June 1908. Pius XI (1922–39) added the last touch when he named the Cardinal Secretary of State, who had till then been a mere member of the group of cardinals composing the congregation, prefect of the congregation. From then onwards the Cardinal Secretary of State became the effective head of all three sections, that is of the entire Secretariat of State.

The name of the first section makes it clear that it is concerned with extraordinary ecclesiastical affairs. It chiefly handles questions related to civil laws and concordats concluded between the Holy See and civil governments, apart from those matters which fall within the competence of the other Congregations and Tribunals, like the Holy Office,

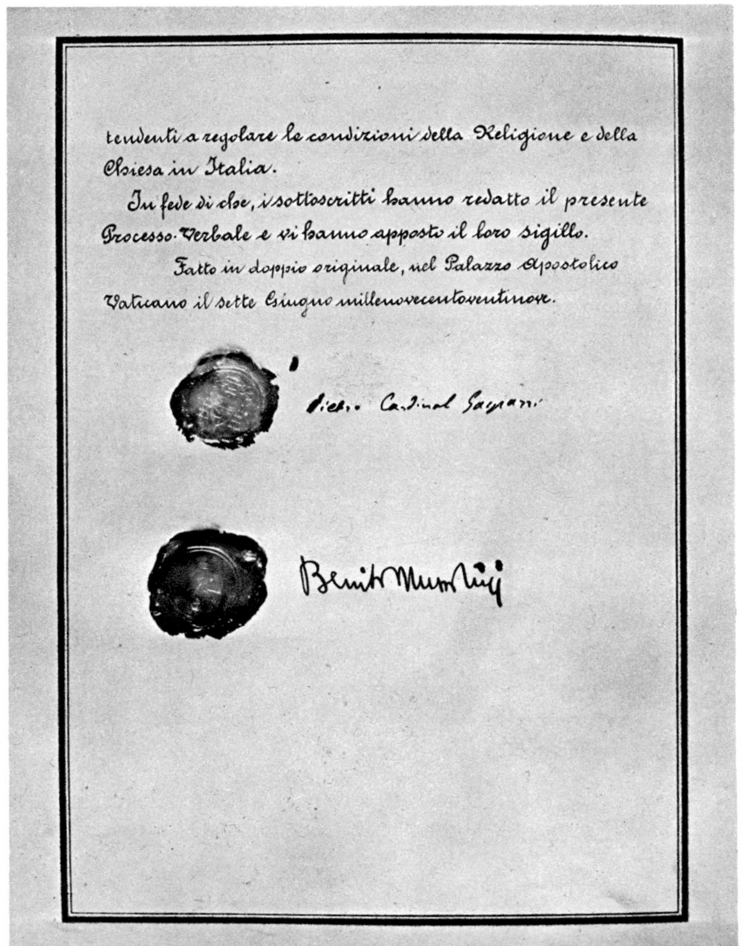

tendenti a regolare le condizioni della Religione e della Chiesa in Italia.

In fede di che, i sottoscritti hanno redatto il presente Processo-Verbale e vi hanno apposto il loro sigillo.

Fatto in doppio originale, nel Palazzo Apostolico Vaticano il sette Giugno millenovecentoventinove.

Pietro Cardinal Gasparri

Benito Mussolini

Cardinal Pietro Gasparri, one of the most outstanding Secretaries of State, who served under both Benedict XV and Pius XI. An eminent canon lawyer, he was responsible for the codification of the canon law and was the architect of the Lateran Treaty

the Consistorial Congregation and the Apostolic Penitentiary. The function of the first section is, above all, to study how the care of souls can be better provided for through mutual agreements with civil powers and with governments. They vary in form according to the nation and political events. For example, canon 255 of the Code specifies that, whenever it becomes necessary to found or dissolve dioceses or to appoint bishops in countries which require consultation on such matters, it is the Congregation for Extraordinary Affairs and not the Consistorial Congregation which undertakes the negotiations. Even in some quasi-religious matters, the Holy See concedes certain privileges to the supreme civil authority, and concordats have been drawn up with various nations, without prejudice to the prerogatives of each of the two powers and to the mutual advantage of both. Usually, on the basis of such a concordat, the Church permits governments to present the names of three candidates for the bishopric, and considers the arguments for and against a particular nomination. The first section is also concerned with concordats concluded between the Church and States to regulate religious questions protecting the interests of two conflicting parties.

When one considers the spiritual sovereignty of the Pope and the absolute independence of an authority deriving solely from God, it is easy to understand what tact, prudence and circumspection this section must exercise during its negotiations, either in writing to governments, or verbally with the ambassadors accredited to the Holy See. In these negotiations the Holy See requires that the State recognize its right to exercise its spiritual power on behalf of the faithful, and the Holy See acknowledges that the temporal power of the State should not be compromised or hindered in any manner. On these two points all discussions hinge. The Secretariat of State draws up a draft for a concordat in which are included all the articles which guarantee the free exercise of the spiritual power of the Church. Freedom of intercourse between the Holy See and all the members of the Church of the nation in question – bishops, priests, religious and laity – must be guaranteed. The Church might request certain concessions from the State which would help the clergy in the exercise of their ministry: for instance, exemption from military duty (as canon 121 of the Code specifies), and their admittance in times of war to serve as chaplains under the Military Ordinariate; the conferment of juridical personality to ecclesiastical institutions and respect for religious ceremonies. If the State recognizes the divine right of the Church over the private and public lives of citizens, it must also recognize the full validity of the Sacrament of Matrimony in its civic sense, and assure the freedom of the Catholic schools, religious instruction and spiritual assistance for men in the armed forces and the establishment of a military Ordinariate. On its part, the Church concedes to civil authorities the privilege of consultation in the creation and modification of dioceses, and so forth. These negotiations are arrived at by the give-and-take of the two contracting parties. The first section of the Secretariat of State must be courageous and sometimes bold in initiative, but at the same time prudent and judicious. It is quite understandable, therefore, that the officials responsible for such negotiations are bound to observe a secrecy similar to that of the Holy Office.

The relations between the Holy See and the civil governments do not make the Holy See a political power. Without doubt the Pope is a sovereign, but his temporal sovereignty extends only to the tiny City State of the Vatican. His spiritual sovereignty, however, surpasses all others, for it derives from the character of the Church, which prevails over every other civil society and is independent of every other sovereignty. The Pope's territorial sovereignty has no other purpose than to demonstrate and confirm his spiritual sovereignty. The Lateran treaty states that, 'to ensure the absolute and visible independence of the Holy See, to guarantee to it an indisputable sovereignty also in the international field, it has been deemed necessary to constitute, in precise detail, the status of the Vatican City, recognizing the Holy See's full ownership of it and its exclusive and absolute rights, absolute power and sovereign jurisdiction'. The purpose of the creation of the new State is: 'the fulfilment of the high mission [of the Church] in the world', that is, to ensure the Church's free, independent and visible exercise of her spiritual sovereignty.

The Holy See does not engage in any political activity as such, but aims only to create a spiritual climate within which men can attain their supernatural goal. The faithful, naturally, remain citizens of the nation to which they belong.

The second section is concerned with the ordinary affairs of the Church which are not the responsibility of the first section. It directs correspondence with the nuncios and Apostolic delegates. It refers the requests of the diplomatic representatives to the Holy See to the competent organs; it proposes the most likely candidates to the Pope for selection as nuncios and legates, and prepares the nomination of members of the Roman Curia approved by the Pope. Catholic Action and all its affiliated organizations receive directives from the second section. It also controls an office for the granting of subsidies by the Holy See, composed of a commission which examines requests and another which establishes the amount of the subsidy.

The Church grants certain decorations to priests and laymen, and for this purpose has instituted different honorary orders. These are: the Order of St Sylvester and the Order of St Gregory the Great, the Order of St Pius x, the Order of the Golden Spur and the Supreme Order of Christ. The Cross *Pro Ecclesia et Pontifice* and the *Benemerenti* Medal are honorary decorations. Recommendations for these are examined by a special office. It should be mentioned here, however, that the Secretariat of State, which is very generous in giving help where needed, is at the same time very circumspect in the granting of honours. The competent office conducts a thorough investigation of the conduct of the candidate. If the candidate for honours is a bishop, inquiries are made to the Consistorial Congregation; if a priest or layman, to the Congregation of the Council and to the bishop of the diocese. All this is done with the greatest discretion.

The work of the third section consists in compiling and transcribing the final drafts of the papal Briefs.

Top Foreign politicians and diplomats in Rome deal with the Secretariat of State. Cardinal Cicognani, the Secretary of State, receives the British Prime Minister, Mr Harold Macmillan, in February 1963.
Centre and bottom Two great Secretaries of State: Cardinal Merry del Val, an intelligent and able diplomatist who served under Pius x, and Cardinal Tardini who served under Pius XII

Finally, the offices of the Secretariat of State are divided into several sections, according to countries and languages in which officials who come from those countries work. There are sections for English, French, German, Spanish, Italian and Portuguese.

The Secretariat of State is the office of the Pope *par excellence*. It enjoys a special relation with him by reason of its constant and close contacts with him in the government of the Church. It is his chief instrument for keeping in touch with the whole world and also for transmitting his will to the other ministries of the central government. The representation of the Vatican City in other countries is exercised by the Pope through the Secretariat of State, including the permanent representatives of the Holy See in the various states, and the diplomatic representatives permanently accredited by the various states to the Holy See.

As a result of the energetic policies of recent Popes the operative field of the Secretariat of State has broadened considerably, and its work greatly increased. The twentieth century is witnessing the disappearance of a number of old customs and institutions. The Secretariat is in a position to keep abreast of these new developments and continually extends its activities. For example, the late Pope John XXIII decreed that the Pontifical Commission for Motion Pictures, Radio and Television should be annexed to it as an Office of the Holy See.

In the *Annuario Pontificio* the Secretariat of Briefs to Princes and of Latin Letters are described as forming part of the Secretariat of State, although they are at the direct disposal of the Pope. They carry out whatever orders the Supreme Pontiff may transmit to them, either personally or through the Cardinal Secretary of State. The Secretariat of Briefs to Princes is the first Latin secretariat of the Pope and of the Roman Curia. Letters to princes and to heads of state are generally in Latin and bear the signature of the Pope. The Secretariat also occupies itself with encyclicals, consistorial allocutions, *motu proprios* and some papal letters. The Secretariat of Latin Letters composes in Latin the less formal documents which are entrusted to it by the first Secretariat. Such letters are those which the Pope sends on the occasion of a centenary, to a national or international Eucharistic Congress where he is represented by a legate, and on the jubilees of bishops and priests. In some cases these letters are written in the vernacular.

A chart showing the organization of the central government of the Catholic Church. The Congregations deal with the government and policy of various specialized branches of the life of the Church, the Tribunals deal especially with judicial matters, and the Offices with the actual administration of papal rule, and relations with secular governments

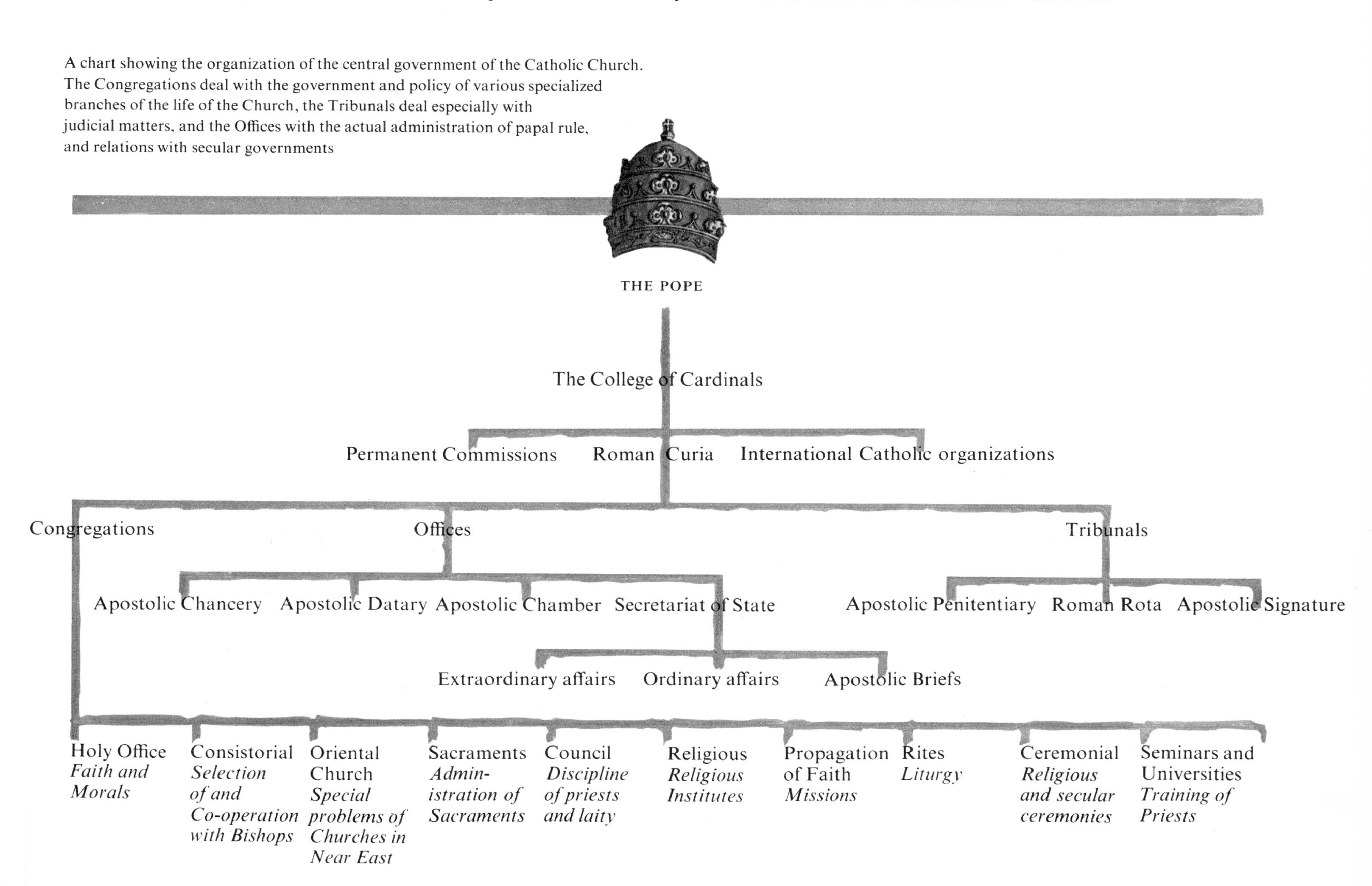

26 *JOHN XXIII AND THE SECOND VATICAN COUNCIL 1958–63*

CHRISTOPHER HOLLIS

John XXIII brought to the Holy See a warmth and humanity which endeared him to people of all nationalities and faiths. His concern for a really effective improvement in social conditions inspired his encyclical Mater et Magistra, *which called for the supplementation of a policy of national social justice with a policy of international social justice as well. In* Pacem in Terris *he made a plea for international understanding at all levels. Pope John was deeply concerned by the divisions of the Christian Church and the Second Vatican Council opened by him in October 1962, and re-summoned by Paul VI in October 1963 set out to achieve internal reform of the Catholic Church and to remove obstacles to the reunion of Christendom.*

VICTORY IN THE BATTLE OF THE REFORMATION WENT, as victories in such conflicts so often do, not to either of the protagonists but to a *tertius gaudens*. After a hundred years of interminable, if intermittent, war it was clear that neither were the Catholics strong enough wholly to suppress the Protestants, nor the Protestants strong enough wholly to suppress the Catholics. Therefore the secular national state was allowed, as the condition of peace, to assert its authority over religion. In Catholic countries the Bourbon and Hapsburg monarchies were able to obtain a power of patronage and control in the Church wholly untraditional and inordinate. The Papacy throughout the eighteenth century was in continual retreat before the Catholic monarchies and Clement XIV's suppression in 1773 of the Jesuits, the one body strong enough to make a fight against the claims of the secular state, was almost an act of papal surrender. Then in the treatment of Pius VI by the French Revolutionaries and of Pius VII by Napoleon the secular state overstepped the bounds of decency. 'C'était trop fort', as Napoleon himself confessed. As a result the nineteenth century saw a reaction towards a strong reaffirmation of papal claims in an Ultramontane form. In the first half of the century the spiritual claims of the Papacy were combined with claims to independent temporal power. A happy accident freed the Papacy from the incubus of temporal power, in 1870, and in the closing years of the century the Church came to depend less and less upon the state. With the French Republic's repudiation of the Concordat in the early years of this century, it became manifest that the Church was all the stronger for its independence of the state.

Yet each new situation creates its own problems. The nineteenth century saw not only the formal promulgation of papal infallibility but also a greatly increased centralization of ecclesiastical administration. The former was a matter of doctrine and irreformable. The latter was a matter of discipline and reformable.

In an autocracy, whether it be religious or secular, over a term of years the decisions tend no longer to be taken by the nominal autocrat. Rather does there grow up a court civil service surrounding the throne, which becomes to a large extent the repository of power. It is the power of the Roman Curia which has been one of the great problems of Catholic life for the last hundred years. It would in any event have been a serious problem. It has been made more urgent by the development of the Catholic Church in the first half of this century. The Catholic Church, formally world-wide, was at the beginning of this century in its government still in effect an entirely European body. Its cardinals were all Europeans. Hilaire Belloc in the early years of the century could write without absurdity in his *Europe and the Faith*, 'The Faith is Europe and Europe is the Faith'. Today the picture is wholly changed. In the Sacred College today there are Cardinals from Japan, China, Syria, Armenia, India, Tanganyika, and Mozambique – to name only those who are wholly without European blood. The Church is, in fact as well as in theory, world-wide to an extent that she has never been in her

John XXIII speaking at the opening of the Second Vatican Council.
The calling of the Council was an important step towards the internal reform of the Church and a significant contribution to the growing movement for Christian unity

John XXIII

John XXIII kissing the foot of the statue of St Peter on 28 June 1960, the eve of the feast day of the apostle, when the statue is robed in rich vestments

history. This extension makes a policy of decentralization more urgent even than it would otherwise have been. If the officials of the Roman Curia could hardly under modern conditions decide the problems of the Catholics of France or Spain or Germany or England or the United States, how much less is it possible that there should be taken at Rome the disciplinary decisions for Tanganyika or for Japan, for Algeria or for Uruguay? Pius XII was most keenly alive to these problems of a changing world. The years of his pontificate were years of war in which it was not possible to work out large constitutional reforms. He applied to these problems a solution characteristic, but essentially provisional. Being a man of abnormal energy, he curbed the power of bureaucracy by taking personal decisions into his own hands to a quite extraordinary degree. But he was well aware that there was no permanent solution along that road, and it is said that it had been his intention in 1954 to inaugurate a thorough reform of the Curia. But, when his health began to fail, he decided that it would be wrong and unfair to his successor to undertake a task that he would not be able to carry through.

In such a situation the question of Pius's successor was clearly of immense importance. There was much speculation who that successor would be. The name of Cardinal Roncalli was among those mentioned. Few thought of him as the favourite. Throughout the world at large he was little known, and when the news came out that an old man of seventy-eight had been elected, there was disappointment. None doubted his worthiness. But, asked the sceptics, would the cardinals have elected a man of seventy-eight had they really meant business? Is it not clear that there is a nettle to be grasped and that the Roman authorities have not had the courage to grasp it? Is it not clear that they have elected a stop-gap in the vain hope of escaping unpleasant necessity?

Angelo Joseph Roncalli was a man of humble origins from the little village of Sotto il Monte in the strongly Catholic province of Bergamo in Lombardy. His father was, and his brothers are, small peasant farmers. He himself served as a sergeant in the Italian army in the First World War. In more recent times his career had been in the papal diplomatic service where he had been *en poste* in Bulgaria, in Turkey and at Paris. Immediately before his election he was the Patriarch of Venice.

If it was the expectation that John XXIII would prove a stop-gap, that was an expectation which was very rapidly proved false. The world, which knew so little about him, within a few days began to hear tales of his kindliness and geniality – how he had stood a glass of wine to his gardener, how he had visited the inmates of a prison, how he insisted on breaking the custom that had grown up by which a Pope always eats alone, invited his peasant brothers to his table and on occasion insisted on a friend sharing his lunch, how he resumed the *de tabella* conferences with the cardinals

John XXIII being carried on the papal litter through St Peter's Square.
The Pope disliked ceremonial and made it clear that he wished it reduced to a minimum

TV SCIS QVIA DILIGO
VNA FIDES

which the more austere and less approachable Pius XII had discontinued. The irreverent nicknamed him John the Jolly. Modern means of communication – in particular the television – enable a Pope in these days to make himself, as it were, personally known to the world as was not possible for his predecessors. Pius XII had shown himself fully alive to the possibilities of these media, but, where Pius had made himself known, it is not too much to say that John made himself loved. He won the affection of men and women throughout the world, inside and outside his own communion, to an extent to which history has few parallels.

The story of religion has been marred by so much bitterness and lack of charity that the great increase of the last years of interdenominational kindness and courtesy is very much to be welcomed. To that the leaders of all denominations – the two Archbishops of Canterbury and others – have greatly contributed. The contribution both of John XXIII and his predecessor was outstanding. Yet John's contribution to Christian relations was much more than a mere contribution of courtesy, important as that would have been. Courtesy cannot of course by itself overcome deep and conscientiously held differences. The leaders of all the denominations most fully understand that these problems of the centuries cannot be merely abolished by a few words of bonhomie. Whether out of courtesy will arise a deeper understanding which may in its time lead to the healing of differences remains to be seen.

Pope John's universal popularity gave him an opportunity to speak to the world as perhaps no other man could speak. He used that opportunity in a number of ways. He pleaded with the statesmen for peace. He insisted to his own flock on the duty of gentleness and tolerance. The time has not yet come to attempt a summary of all his policies – still less of the fruits that they are likely to bear. It is perhaps better to select the three outstanding achievements of his pontificate – the achievements for which he will most certainly be remembered.

Leo XIII was the first Pope to give his mind to the problems of the new industrialism. In his *Rerum Novarum* of 1891 he laid down the Church's teaching on these matters. Forty years later, in 1931, Pius XI in *Quadragesimo Anno* repeated and brought up to date Leo's teachings. But these two encyclicals, great as they were, were both basically nationalist documents – that is to say, they laid down the principles of social justice, of the distribution of power and property and income within a single nation. But they took it almost for granted that the economic unit and the sovereign unit would be the individual nation. It was perhaps inevitable, considering the dates at which they wrote, that they should have done this, but the result is that, while they had much of the first importance to say concerning social justice within the nation, they had very little to tell us on the principles of international social justice. Yet, whereas in the nineteenth century and indeed for a large

The scene in St Peter's on 10 May 1963 when John XXIII was awarded the Balzan Peace Prize, the proceeds of which the Pope endowed as a perpetual fund to promote international peace and understanding

John XXIII

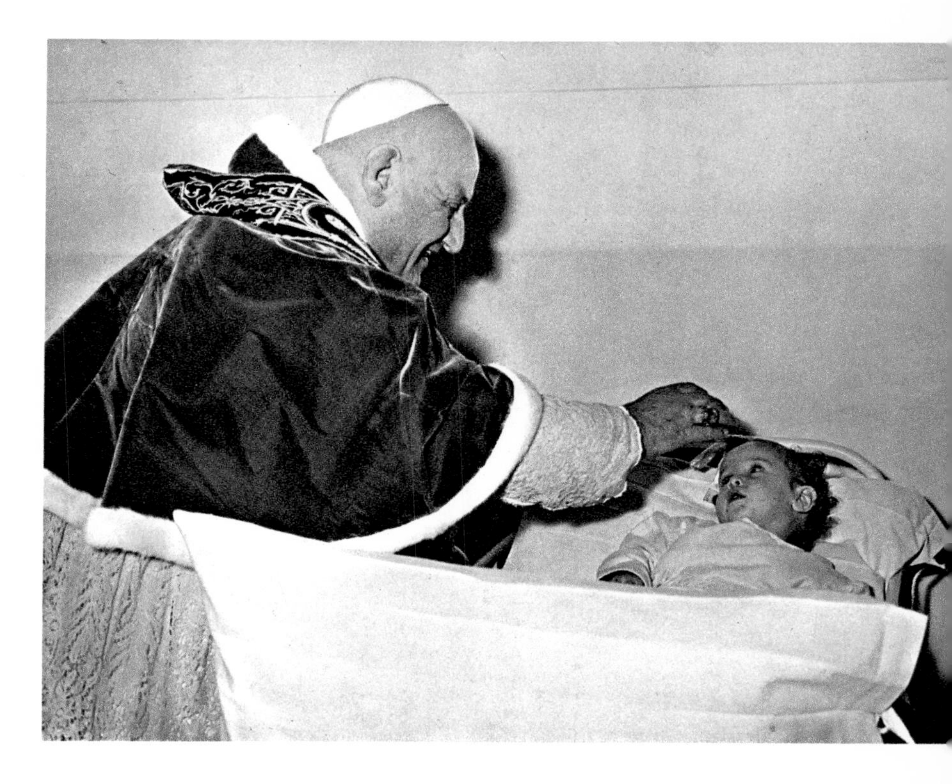

The Pope's simplicity and friendliness endeared him to all. He broke with Vatican tradition by sudden and unexpected pastoral visits in his diocese. At the first Christmas of his pontificate in 1958 he visited the Children's Hospital of the Bambino Gesù *above* and *below* the prison of the Regina Coeli

A special postal frank issued by the Vatican to mark the visit of the Archbishop of Canterbury, Dr Geoffrey Fisher, to Pope John in December 1960, a sign of the new movement for Christian unity

The procession of bishops on their way to St Peter's for the opening of the Second Vatican Council on 2 October 1962. Theological, liturgical, administrative and ecumenical questions were discussed

part of the twentieth century, wide differences of standards of living between nation and nation and between continent and continent were taken for granted as inevitable and almost a law of nature, in the post-war world it is the problem of international social justice which is the most pressing of all our economic problems. Is it just that there should be wide and, as many think, increasing differences between the standards of one country and those of another? If such differences are justifiable, by what criterion should they in justice be measured? Until Pope John's accession there was little official Catholic teaching on this subject. In his encyclical *Mater et Magistra* he bade the world turn its attention to the problem. 'It is therefore obvious,' he wrote, 'that the solidarity of the human race and Christian brotherhood demand the elimination as far as possible of these discrepancies [in living standards]. With this object in view people all over the world must co-operate actively with one another in all sorts of ways so as to facilitate the movement of goods, capital and men from one country to another. This solidarity which binds all men together as members of a common family makes it impossible for wealthy nations to look with indifference upon the hunger, misery and poverty of other nations whose citizens are unable to enjoy even elementary human rights. The nations of the world are becoming more and more dependent on one another, but even so, it will not be possible to preserve a lasting peace so long as these glaring economic and social inequalities persist.' He also commended such organizations as the FAO which are working for the alleviation of distress in the underdeveloped countries.

The Catholic Church claims to be the divinely founded Church of Christ. But Christ did not die only for Catholics. He died for all men and all men are precious in His sight. The Catholic – and the Vicar of Christ above all other Catholics – cannot deny his charity to any man. Therefore the Pope threw himself whole-heartedly, as did his predecessors, into the work of peace, pleading in his last encyclical *Pacem in Terris* for negotiation and conciliation. But there is also an international problem strictly within the Church. The problem of constitutional reform – of a certain measure of decentralization from Curial control – would in any event have called for solution. The day of the nominally Catholic, secular governments, which made excessive demands of patronage, has passed. This problem is no longer a major problem. The mid-twentieth century has other problems, which call for other remedies. The vast extension of the Church outside Europe and of its membership among non-Europeans is a challenge which calls for new policies. It was not reasonable that detailed solutions for every problem of morality or custom in such countries should have to be sought from ecclesiastical lawyers in Rome, whose whole training had been in one particular nationalist tradition. The Latin language in the liturgy could not of its nature have the meaning for a Catholic in Japan or Tanganyika, heir of a history in which the Roman Empire played no part and of a language that in no way derived from Latin, which it did for an inhabitant of one of the ancient Roman lands of Western Europe. Wisdom always lies in the middle way, and it is a curiosity, that while there are many today who think that in secular matters the hope of peace depends on our transcending national loyalties and moving forward to larger units or to a world authority, in religious matters the movement is against excessive central control and towards the concession of larger local liberties. Church and state are passing one another like two great ships that pass in the night.

Some of the 2,540 bishops who assembled for the Second Vatican Council. The Council was attended not only by bishops of the Latin rite but by bishops from the Uniate churches, ancient Eastern churches which retain their own liturgy and traditions, but acknowledge the supreme authority of the Pope

ALEXANDER
COGNITUM
VENETIS

FUGIENS·ABDIDIT·SE
TORIS·FILIO·NAVALI
ADORAT·FIDEM·ET·OBEDIENTIA
BENEFICIO·RESTITUTA

CAELORVM ✠ TV ES
FIDES
MVNDO

John XXIII

The Pope summoned the Second Vatican Council of the bishops of the world to advise him. It was still in session when he died. Its debates were carried on, before observers from other denominations with a freedom and outspokeness that have astonished the world. The details of their decisions have not yet been reached, but it has been found that the existence of an ultimate papal authority which can call a halt to any challenge to revealed truth makes possible the toleration of a very wide freedom of speech on all matters on which there is not dogmatic teaching.

The Second Vatican Council was opened by Pope John in St Peter's on 2 October 1962. To anyone who was fortunate enough to be present the occasion was unforgettable. The 744 Bishops who attended the First Vatican Council in 1869 could comfortably be accommodated in a transept. To this Second Council 2,540 bishops had come from every corner of the earth. Little more than a third of them were from European sees. They filled the whole of the main body of the Church, a forest of white mitres. The ceremony commenced at half-past eight in the morning, and shortly afterwards Pope John was carried in amid tremendous cheers. His mitre and tiara at hand, he took his seat beneath the canopy where in blazing light Bernini's dove hovers over the throne. Mass – the *Missa Papae Marcelli* – was sung and then he received the homage of the Cardinals. Finally, he pronounced his own discourse. It was a discourse deeply inspired by his own personality and by no means the collection of colourless platitudes which are sometimes considered suitable for such an occasion. Since he had summoned the bishops to give him advice it would have been absurd if he had taken the occasion to tell them in detail what advice they should give. Indeed he assured them that they would have every opportunity of debate. He rebuked with a twinkling humour those pessimists who were for ever telling him that the world was doomed to destruction. He did not believe it, nor did he believe that times of unreserved evil lay immediately before the Church. The days of the State-Church were indeed finished but he did not regret that. State patronage had often done the Church more harm than good. 'The princes of this world,' he said, 'sometimes in all sincerity intended thus to protect the Church, but more frequently this occurred not without spiritual damage and danger.' He said that this was an age in which the Church should not maintain her authority, as she sometimes had in the past, by repression but 'with the medicine of mercy rather than of severity'. He spoke of

Above The scene in St Peter's at the opening of the Council and *below* St Peter's Square illuminated on the night of the opening of the Council, when 40,000 Catholic Workers assembled with torchlights and received the papal blessing

those who were not of the Catholic fold and commended the deliberations of the bishops to the Holy Spirit. Other Councils had been summoned to define disputed doctrines. That was not the purpose of this Council. Its task was not to define new doctrines but to reform the Church – for the Church to 'bring herself up to date where required'. The doctrines of the Church were immutable. The method of imparting them must change from generation to generation.

It was a notable discourse, illuminated with Pope John's characteristic vivacity, but with the dignity which the occasion required. That evening a crowd of some forty thousand of the Catholic Workers of Rome assembled with torch lights in the Piazza of St Peter. There were cries for the Pope and he appeared smiling at a window to greet them and was received by a hurricane of cheers. Almost like a leading actor on the stage, he insisted on bringing before the crowd for their applause a few of those who had been most prominent as his collaborators in his work. Then he made to the crowd a little speech. It was not a moment for high doctrine. He told them to go home and give a kiss to their children and then to give them an extra kiss and say that it was from the Pope. He gave them his blessing and withdrew.

It is often said that within the modern evolution of the Church it is inevitable that before long there should be a non-Italian Pope. The arguments for such an experiment are powerful and it may well be that before long they will prevail. But I think that anyone who was in Rome that day cannot but feel that the problem is less simple than is sometimes thought. The Pope has to speak not only *orbi* but also *urbi*. A Pope drawn from another nation than the Italian might perhaps speak to the world with a greater authority than another Italian, and we cannot deny that his message to the world is his major message. But the Romans, who are by no means a uniformly pious or virtuous people, look on the Pope as almost a personal possession. It would be hard to imagine any non-Italian – German, American, French or English – speaking to a Roman crowd with the easy personal gaiety with which an Italian, even a Lombard Italian like Pope John, could speak. Such a manner is a gift which Italians have in general more than other people and Pope John had more than other Italians. With the wisdom of the ruler was combined the lightheartedness of the eternal child, and with them both the holiness of the saint. Whatever Popes may come, Italian or non-Italian, it is certain that there will be none again who quite fills the place in the hearts of men which John XXIII has won.

John XXIII died on 3 June 1963. On June 21 Cardinal Montini was elected to succeed him and chose for himself the name of Paul VI. Cardinal Montini had served Pius XI and Pius XII in the Secretariat of State, and then in 1954 he was appointed Archbishop of Milan. His election was not unexpected and there was little doubt that he would continue the progressive policies of his predecessor, as he has shown himself determined to do.

Paul VI, formerly Cardinal Montini, Archbishop of Milan, succeeded John XXIII in June 1963. His coronation on 30 June took place in St Peter's Square, as the basilica was prepared for the meeting of the Vatican Council. *Opposite* Paul VI being carried down the *Scala Regia* into the square, and *bottom* the coronation by Cardinal Ottaviani, the senior Cardinal-deacon. The ceremony took place against the background of the façade of St Peter's and was attended by thousands of people, representing nearly a hundred nations

Right The newly-crowned Pope being carried back through the square

Below Paul VI addressing the fourteen new bishops whom he consecrated in St Peter's on 20 October 1963, World Missionary Day

Paul VI with Patriarch Athenagoras, head of the Eastern Orthodox Church, in Jerusalem in January 1963. This was the first meeting between a Pope and an Orthodox Patriarch since the Council of Florence in 1439, and a significant expression of the movement towards greater understanding between the Churches. During his pilgrimage to the Holy Land Paul VI was greeted by scenes of great enthusiasm in both Israel and Jordan. His visit was widely regarded as a personal triumph and a sign of the growing affection and respect with which the Papacy is regarded in the twentieth century by people of all faiths and nationalities

Appendices

Maps

Europe in the reign of Innocent III 1198-1216

Italy and the Papal States in 1700

Europe and the Mediterranean in 1100 showing religious faiths

Europe in 1650 showing Roman Catholic and Protestant States

The Roman Catholic Population of the world in 1960

Chronological list of Popes

The General Councils of the Church

EUROPE IN THE REIGN OF INNOCENT III 1198–1216
NORWAY
SWEDEN
SCOTLAND
IRELAND
WALES
ENGLAND
ESTONIA
LITHUANIA
PRUSSIA
POLAND
RUSSIAN PRINCIPALITIES
FRANCE
HOLY ROMAN EMPIRE
BOHEMIA
LEON
PORTUGAL
NAVARRE
CASTILE
ARAGON
HUNGARY
CORSICA
SARDINIA
DALMATIA
BULGARIA
MOORISH DOMINIONS
KINGDOM OF SICILY
BYZANTINE EMPIRE
SELJUK DOMINIONS
ARMENIA
5
4
3
2
1
The Papal States
defined by Innocent and conceded by the Emperor in 1201
1 PATRIMONY OF ST PETER
2 DUCHY OF SPOLETO
3 MARCH OF ANCONA
4 ROMAGNA
5 LANDS OF COUNTESS MATILDA OF TUSCANY
Papal Fiefs
Other countries politically dependent on the Holy See
The Holy Roman Empire

*ITALY AND THE PAPAL STATES IN 1700**

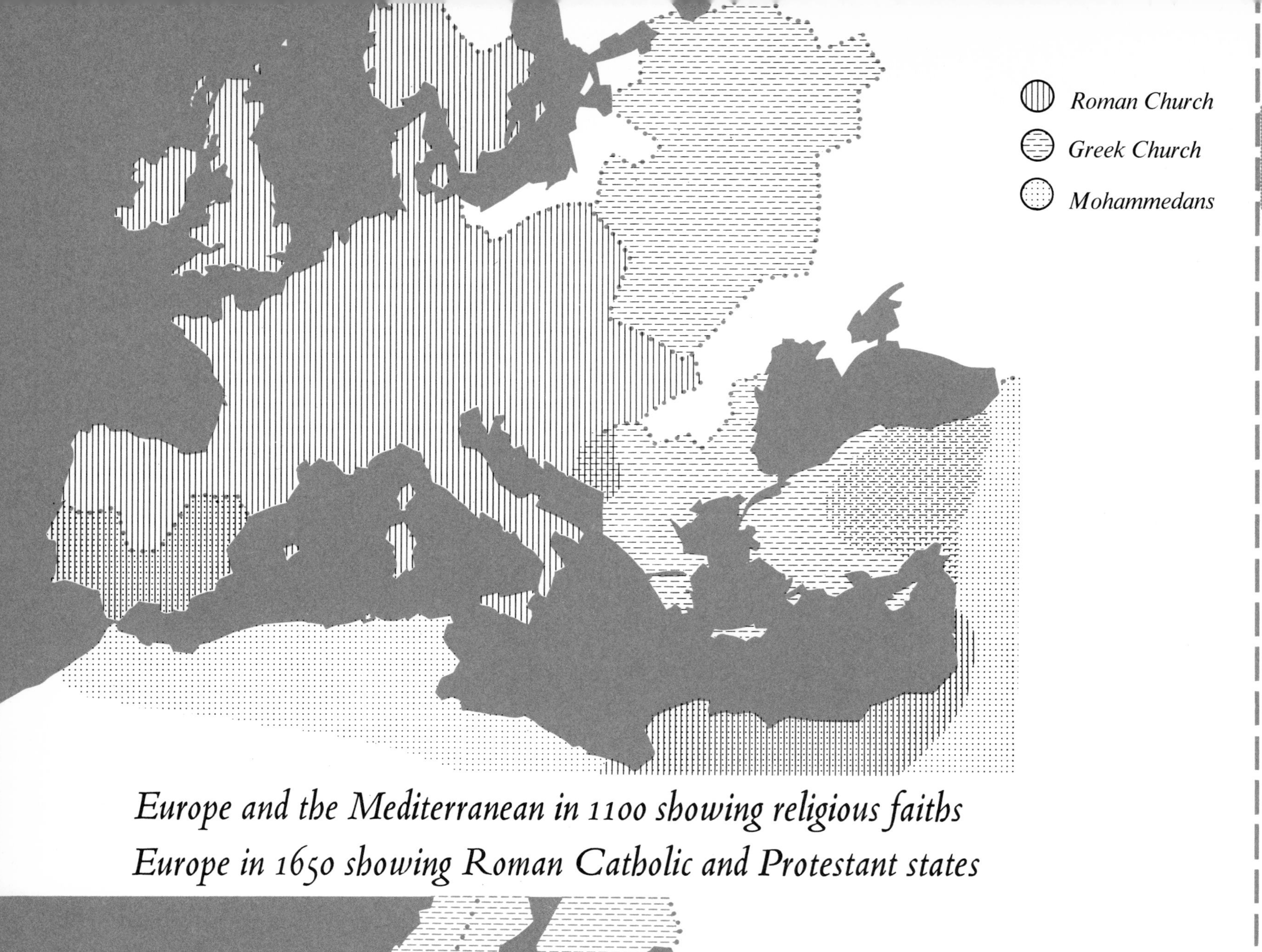

Europe and the Mediterranean in 1100 showing religious faiths

Europe in 1650 showing Roman Catholic and Protestant states

THE ROMAN CATHOLIC POPULATION OF THE WORLD IN 1960
2
1
1
1
1
1
3
1
1
1
1
1
1
1
1
1
1
1
1
1
1
1
1
2
6
1
1
7
1
4
32
over 50%
10-50%
5-10%
under 5%
of the population Roman Catholic
Figures represent the percentage of the total population of each area
Distribution of cardinals in January 1963
Cardinals attached to the Curia, who have no residential see, are shown in Rome

Chronological list of Popes

Anti-Popes in italics

Peter died *c* 67
Linus *c* 67–*c* 79
Anacletus *c* 79–*c* 90
Clement I *c* 90–*c* 99
Evaristus *c* 99–*c* 107
Alexander I *c* 107–*c* 16
Sixtus I *c* 116–*c* 25
Telesphorus *c* 125–*c* 36
Hyginus *c* 136–*c* 40
Pius I *c* 140–*c* 54
Anicetus *c* 154–65
Soter 166–74
Eleutherus 174–89
Victor I 189–98
Zephyrinus 198–217
Calixtus I 217–22
Hippolytus 217–36
Urban I 222–30
Pontianus 230–35
Anterus 235–36
Fabianus 236–50
Cornelius 251–53
Novatian 251–*c* 258
Lucius I 253–54
Stephen I 254–57
Sixtus II 257–58

Dionysius 259–68
Felix I 269–74
Eutychianus 275–83
Cajus 283–96
Marcellinus 296–304
Marcellus 307–09
Eusebius 310
Miltiades 311–14

Sylvester I 314–35
Marcus 336
Julius I 337–52
Liberius 352–65
Felix II 355–65
Damasus I 366–84
Ursinus 366–67
Siricius 384–99
Anastasius I 399–401
Innocent I 402–17
Zosimus 417–18
Boniface I 418–22
Eulalius 418–19
Celestine I 422–32
Sixtus III 432–40

Leo I 440–61
Hilarus 461–68
Simplicius 468–83
Felix II (or III) 483–92
Gelasius 492–96
Anastasius II 496–98
Symmachus 498–514
Laurentius 498–505
Hormisdas 514–23
John I 523–26
Felix III (or IV) 526–30
Boniface II 530–32
Dioscurus 530
John II 533–35
Agapetus I 535–37
Silverius 536–37
Vigilius 537–55
Pelagius I 556–61
John III 561–74
Benedict I 575–79
Pelagius II 579–90

Gregory I 590–604
Sabinianus 604–06

Boniface III 607
Boniface IV 608–15
Deusdedit 615–18
Boniface V 619–25
Honorius I 625–38
Severinus 640
John IV 640–42
Theodore I 642–49
Martin I 649–53
Eugene I 654–57
Vitalian 657–72
Adeodatus 672–76
Donus 676–78
Agatho 678–81
Leo II 682–83
Benedict II 684–85
John V 685–86
Conon 686–87
Theodore 687
Paschal 687–92
Sergius I 687–701
John VI 701–05
John VII 705–07
Sisinnius 708
Constantine 708–15
Gregory II 715–31
Gregory III 731–41
Zachary 741–52
Stephen II 752
Stephen II 752–57

Paul I 757–67
Constantine II 767–68
Philip 768
Stephen III 768–72
Adrian I 772–95
Leo III 795–816
Stephen IV 816–17
Paschal I 817–24
Eugene II 824–27
Valentine 827
Gregory IV 827–44
John 844
Sergius II 844–47
Leo IV 847–55
Benedict III 855–58
Anastasius 855

Nicholas I 858–67
Adrian II 867–72
John VIII 872–82
Marinus I 882–84
Adrian III 884–85
Stephen V 885–91
Formosus 891–96
Boniface VI 896
Stephen VI 896–97
Romanus 897
Theodore II 897
John IX 898–900
Benedict IV 900–03

Leo V 903
Christophorus 903–04
Sergius III 904–11
Anastasius III 911–13
Lando 913–14
John X 914–28
Leo VI 928
Stephen VII 929–31
John XI 931–35
Leo VII 936–39
Stephen VIII 939–42
Marinus II 942–46
Agapetus II 946–55
John XII 955–63 (deposed)
Leo VIII 963–65
Benedict V 964 (deposed)
John XIII 965–72
Benedict VI 973–74
Boniface VII 974
Benedict VII 974–83
John XIV 983–84
Boniface VII 984–85
John XV 985–96
Gregory V 996–99
John XVI 997–98
Sylvester II 999–1003
John XVII 1003
John XVIII 1003–09
Sergius IV 1009–12
Benedict VIII 1012–24
Gregory 1012
John XIX 1024–32
Benedict IX 1032–44
Sylvester III 1045
Gregory VI 1045–46
Clement II 1046–47

Damasus II 1048
Leo IX 1049–54
Victor II 1055–57
Stephen IX 1057–58
Benedict X 1058
Nicholas II 1058–61
Alexander II 1061–73
Honorius II 1061–72

Gregory VII 1073–85
Clement III 1084–1100
Victor III 1086–87
Urban II 1088–99
Paschal II 1099–1118
Theodoric 1100–02
Albert 1102
Sylvester IV 1105–11
Gelasius II 1118–19
Gregory VIII 1118–21
Calixtus II 1119–24
Honorius II 1124–30
Celestine II 1124
Innocent II 1130–43
Anacletus II 1130–38
Victor IV 1138
Celestine II 1143–44
Lucius II 1144–45
Eugene III 1145–53
Anastasius IV 1153–54
Adrian IV 1154–59

Alexander III 1159–81
Victor IV 1159–64
Paschal III 1164–68
Calixtus III 1168–79
Innocent III 1179–80
Lucius III 1181–85
Urban III 1185–87
Gregory VIII 1187
Clement III 1187–91
Celestine III 1191–98

Innocent III 1198–1216
Honorius III 1216–27
Gregory IX 1227–41
Celestine IV 1241

Innocent IV 1243–54
Alexander IV 1254–61
Urban IV 1261–64
Clement IV 1265–68
Gregory X 1271–76
Innocent V 1276
Adrian V 1276
John XXI 1276–77

Nicholas III 1277–80

Martin IV 1281–85

Honorius IV 1285–87

Nicholas IV 1288–92

Celestine V 1294

Boniface VIII 1294–1303

Benedict XI 1303–04

Clement V 1305–14

John XXII 1316–34

Nicholas V 1328–30

Benedict XII 1334–42

Clement VI 1342–52

Innocent VI 1352–62

Urban V 1362–70

Gregory XI 1370–78

Urban VI 1378–89

Clement VII 1378–94

Boniface IX 1389–1404

Benedict XIII 1394–1424

Innocent VII 1404–06

Gregory XII 1406–15

Alexander V 1409–10

John XXIII 1410–15

Martin V 1417–31

Clement VIII 1424–29

Benedict XIV 1424

Eugene IV 1431–47

Felix V 1439–49

Nicholas V 1447–55

Calixtus III 1455–58

Pius II 1458–64

Paul II 1464–71

Sixtus IV 1471–84

Innocent VIII 1484–92

Alexander VI 1492–1503

Pius III 1503

Julius II 1503–13

Leo X 1513–21

Adrian VI 1522–23

Clement VII 1523–34

Paul III 1534–49

Julius III 1550–55

Marcellus II 1555

Paul IV 1555–59

Pius IV 1559–65

Pius V 1566–72

Gregory XIII 1572–85

Sixtus V 1585–90

Urban VII 1590

Gregory XIV 1590–91

Innocent IX 1591

Clement VIII 1592–1605

Leo XI 1605

Paul V 1605–21

Gregory XV 1621–23

Urban VIII 1623–44

Innocent X 1644–55

Alexander VII 1655–67

Clement IX 1667–69

Clement X 1670–76

Innocent XI 1676–89

Alexander VIII 1689–91

Innocent XII 1691–1700

Clement XI 1700–21

Innocent XIII 1721–24

Benedict XIII 1724–30

Clement XII 1730–40

Benedict XIV 1740–58

Clement XIII 1758–69

Clement XIV 1769–74

Pius VI 1775–99

Pius VII 1800–23

Leo XII 1823–29

Pius VIII 1829–30

Gregory XVI 1831–46

Pius IX 1846–78

Leo XIII 1878–1903

Pius X 1903–14

Benedict XV 1914–22

Pius XI 1922–39

Pius XII 1939–58

John XXIII 1958–63

Paul VI 1963–

Anti-Popes in Italics

The General Councils of the Church

1 NICAEA 325 Sylvester I
Condemned the Arian heresy, which denied the full divinity of Christ, and enunciated the Nicene Creed, affirming the unity and equality of the persons of the Trinity.

2 CONSTANTINOPLE 381 Damasus I
Re-defined the nature of the Holy Ghost as the third and equal person of the Trinity, denying the heresy of Macedonius of Constantinople, who had asserted that the Holy Ghost proceeded from the Son.

3 EPHESUS 431 Celestine I
Condemned the heresy of Nestorius, Patriarch of Constantinople, which asserted that the divine nature dwelt in Christ, but that he was not fully God, nor could the Virgin Mary be called the Mother of God.

4 CHALCEDON 451 Leo I
Condemned the Monophysite heresy of Eutyches, which asserted that Christ had only a divine, and no human nature.

5 CONSTANTINOPLE 553 Vigilius
Summoned by the Emperor Justinian and overshadowed by his dispute with the Pope, who refused to join Justinian in the condemnation of three dead fifth-century heretics for Nestorianism. Vigilius was later forced to accept the Council's decision.

6 CONSTANTINOPLE 680 Agatho
Settled a long doctrinal dispute raised by the Monothelite heresy, by confirming the two wills of Christ, divine and human.

7 NICAEA 787 Adrian I
Condemned the iconoclastic movement which forbade the use of images in worship and which had many followers in the East.

8 CONSTANTINOPLE 869 Adrian II
Achieved a brief reconciliation between the Greek and Latin Churches, which had been divided by the Schism of Photius, the Patriarch of Constantinople who, supported by the Emperor Michael, had refused to accept the authority of the Pope.

9 LATERAN 1123 Calixtus II
The first General Council held in the West. Ratified the Concordat of Worms of 1122, which had settled the dispute between Papacy and Empire over the lay investiture of bishops. Condemned simony, strengthened discipline and made fiscal reforms.

10 LATERAN 1139 Innocent II
Condemned the schism of the Anti-Pope Anacletus, after a long period of disputed successions, and excommunicated his main supporter, Roger of Sicily.
The laws against simony newly defined.

11 LATERAN 1179 Alexander III
Declared that the election of Popes rested solely with the cardinals and that no lay interference, whether by the Emperor or the Roman people, was legal. A two-thirds majority was needed for a valid election. Condemned the Waldensian and Albigensian heresies. Reserved the right of canonization to the Holy See.

12 LATERAN 1215 Innocent III
Called for a new crusade. Organized measures to be taken to suppress the Albigensian heresy. Gave approval to the use of the word transubstantiation. Forbade the foundation of new religious institutions and ordered existing ones to hold a general chapter every three years.

The Council of Nicaea 787

13 LYONS 1245 Innocent IV
Summoned by the Pope in protest against the violent anti-papal policy of the Hohenstaufen Emperor Frederick II, whom the Council excommunicated and deposed. Discussed the schism between East and West and the launching of a new crusade.

14 LYONS 1274 Gregory X
Achieved temporary agreement between Eastern and Western representatives. The Greeks acknowledged the primacy of the Pope and accepted the *filioque* clause. In return they retained their creed and traditional rights. The compromise was not generally accepted in the East and had little effect.

15 VIENNE 1311 Clement V
Suppressed the order of Knights Templar for alleged heresy, immorality and financial corruption, after severe pressure from Philip IV of France.

16 CONSTANCE 1414–18 Gregory XII, Martin V
Ended the Great Schism which had divided the Church for forty years, with rival lines of Popes reigning in Rome and Avignon, by electing an entirely new Pope, Martin V. Condemned John Hus and the Bohemian reformers. Enacted some fiscal reforms, which were not for the most part enforced.

17 BASEL, FERRARA, FLORENCE 1431–39 Eugenius IV
Summoned by Martin V shortly before his death. The Council Fathers asserted the superiority of General Councils to the Pope, set up their own Curia and passed a number of reforms in finance and the method of appointment of bishops. Eugenius IV attempted to dissolve the Council, but the Fathers refused to disperse and Eugenius had to withdraw his dissolution. Re-convened at Ferrara in 1438 with representatives of the Greek Church. Moved to Florence in 1439, where on 6 July a decree of union between the Greek and Latin Churches was promulgated.

18 LATERAN 1512–17 Julius II, Leo X
Called in retaliation against a French threat to withdraw France from papal obedience, following Julius II's attempts to expel French troops from Italy. Under Leo X a Pragmatic Sanction was signed with the French King by which, in return for considerable administrative concessions, the French abandoned their plans for schism.

19 TRENT 1545–55, 1559–63 Paul III, Julius III, Pius IV
The great reforming Council which was the definitive expression of the policy of the Counter-Reformation. The early sessions were still hopeful of finding formulae by which the differences with the Protestants could be reconciled. Under Pius IV, when the impossibility of such an agreement had been recognized, a wide range of doctrinal and disciplinary reforms was passed.

20 VATICAN 1869–70 Pius IX
Proclaimed the doctrine of papal infallibility and defined its limits. Interrupted by the Franco-Prussian War and the occupation of Rome by Piedmontese armies.

21 VATICAN 1963– John XXIII, Paul VI
Summoned by John XXIII to discuss the reform and *aggiornamento* (bringing up to date) of the Church. Observers from other denominations invited to attend. Hopes expressed by both Popes that a reform of the Church might bring nearer the day of reunion of all Christendom

Top The Council of Trent 1545–63

Left The Second Vatican Council 1963

Acknowledgements

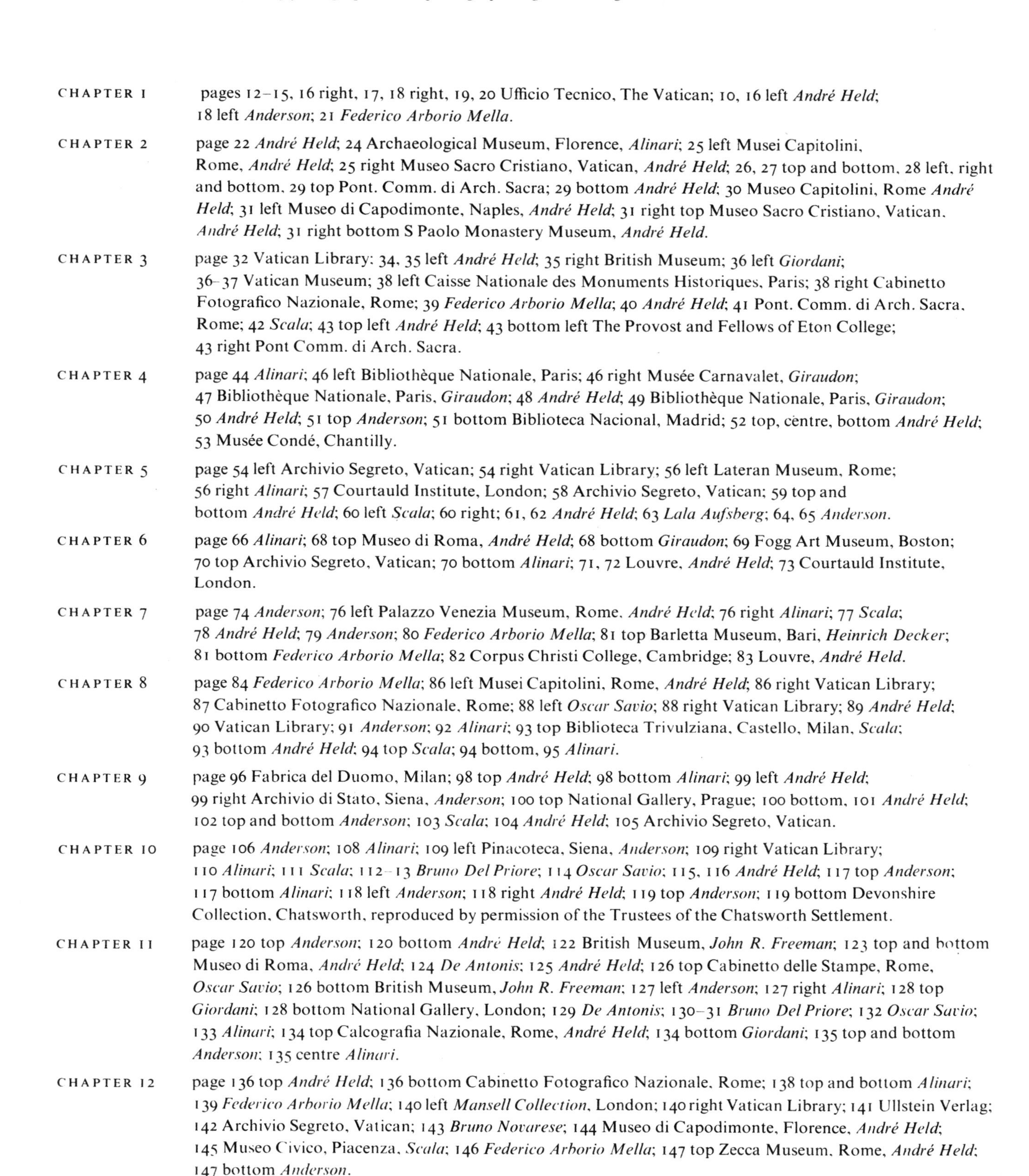

The collection of the illustrations was under the direction of Milton Gendel.
The title page ornament and the maps on pages 292–95 were drawn by Ralph Mabey.
The publishers are grateful to the following for their help in assembling the illustrative material and for permission to reproduce photographs:
The names of photographers and photographic agencies are given in italics

CHAPTER 1 pages 12–15, 16 right, 17, 18 right, 19, 20 Ufficio Tecnico, The Vatican; 10, 16 left *André Held*; 18 left *Anderson*; 21 *Federico Arborio Mella*.

CHAPTER 2 page 22 *André Held*; 24 Archaeological Museum, Florence, *Alinari*; 25 left Musei Capitolini, Rome, *André Held*; 25 right Museo Sacro Cristiano, Vatican, *André Held*; 26, 27 top and bottom, 28 left, right and bottom, 29 top Pont. Comm. di Arch. Sacra; 29 bottom *André Held*; 30 Museo Capitolini, Rome *André Held*; 31 left Museo di Capodimonte, Naples, *André Held*; 31 right top Museo Sacro Cristiano, Vatican, *André Held*; 31 right bottom S Paolo Monastery Museum, *André Held*.

CHAPTER 3 page 32 Vatican Library; 34, 35 left *André Held*; 35 right British Museum; 36 left *Giordani*; 36–37 Vatican Museum; 38 left Caisse Nationale des Monuments Historiques, Paris; 38 right Cabinetto Fotografico Nazionale, Rome; 39 *Federico Arborio Mella*; 40 *André Held*; 41 Pont. Comm. di Arch. Sacra, Rome; 42 *Scala*; 43 top left *André Held*; 43 bottom left The Provost and Fellows of Eton College; 43 right Pont Comm. di Arch. Sacra.

CHAPTER 4 page 44 *Alinari*; 46 left Bibliothèque Nationale, Paris; 46 right Musée Carnavalet, *Giraudon*; 47 Bibliothèque Nationale, Paris, *Giraudon*; 48 *André Held*; 49 Bibliothèque Nationale, Paris, *Giraudon*; 50 *André Held*; 51 top *Anderson*; 51 bottom Biblioteca Nacional, Madrid; 52 top, centre, bottom *André Held*; 53 Musée Condé, Chantilly.

CHAPTER 5 page 54 left Archivio Segreto, Vatican; 54 right Vatican Library; 56 left Lateran Museum, Rome; 56 right *Alinari*; 57 Courtauld Institute, London; 58 Archivio Segreto, Vatican; 59 top and bottom *André Held*; 60 left *Scala*; 60 right; 61, 62 *André Held*; 63 *Lala Aufsberg*; 64, 65 *Anderson*.

CHAPTER 6 page 66 *Alinari*; 68 top Museo di Roma, *André Held*; 68 bottom *Giraudon*; 69 Fogg Art Museum, Boston; 70 top Archivio Segreto, Vatican; 70 bottom *Alinari*; 71, 72 Louvre, *André Held*; 73 Courtauld Institute, London.

CHAPTER 7 page 74 *Anderson*; 76 left Palazzo Venezia Museum, Rome, *André Held*; 76 right *Alinari*; 77 *Scala*; 78 *André Held*; 79 *Anderson*; 80 *Federico Arborio Mella*; 81 top Barletta Museum, Bari, *Heinrich Decker*; 81 bottom *Federico Arborio Mella*; 82 Corpus Christi College, Cambridge; 83 Louvre, *André Held*.

CHAPTER 8 page 84 *Federico Arborio Mella*; 86 left Musei Capitolini, Rome, *André Held*; 86 right Vatican Library; 87 Cabinetto Fotografico Nazionale, Rome; 88 left *Oscar Savio*; 88 right Vatican Library; 89 *André Held*; 90 Vatican Library; 91 *Anderson*; 92 *Alinari*; 93 top Biblioteca Trivulziana, Castello, Milan, *Scala*; 93 bottom *André Held*; 94 top *Scala*; 94 bottom, 95 *Alinari*.

CHAPTER 9 page 96 Fabrica del Duomo, Milan; 98 top *André Held*; 98 bottom *Alinari*; 99 left *André Held*; 99 right Archivio di Stato, Siena, *Anderson*; 100 top National Gallery, Prague; 100 bottom, 101 *André Held*; 102 top and bottom *Anderson*; 103 *Scala*; 104 *André Held*; 105 Archivio Segreto, Vatican.

CHAPTER 10 page 106 *Anderson*; 108 *Alinari*; 109 left Pinacoteca, Siena, *Anderson*; 109 right Vatican Library; 110 *Alinari*; 111 *Scala*; 112–13 *Bruno Del Priore*; 114 *Oscar Savio*; 115, 116 *André Held*; 117 top *Anderson*; 117 bottom *Alinari*; 118 left *Anderson*; 118 right *André Held*; 119 top *Anderson*; 119 bottom Devonshire Collection, Chatsworth, reproduced by permission of the Trustees of the Chatsworth Settlement.

CHAPTER 11 page 120 top *Anderson*; 120 bottom *André Held*; 122 British Museum, *John R. Freeman*; 123 top and bottom Museo di Roma, *André Held*; 124 *De Antonis*; 125 *André Held*; 126 top Cabinetto delle Stampe, Rome, *Oscar Savio*; 126 bottom British Museum, *John R. Freeman*; 127 left *Anderson*; 127 right *Alinari*; 128 top *Giordani*; 128 bottom National Gallery, London; 129 *De Antonis*; 130–31 *Bruno Del Priore*; 132 *Oscar Savio*; 133 *Alinari*; 134 top Calcografia Nazionale, Rome, *André Held*; 134 bottom *Giordani*; 135 top and bottom *Anderson*; 135 centre *Alinari*.

CHAPTER 12 page 136 top *André Held*; 136 bottom Cabinetto Fotografico Nazionale, Rome; 138 top and bottom *Alinari*; 139 *Federico Arborio Mella*; 140 left *Mansell Collection*, London; 140 right Vatican Library; 141 Ullstein Verlag; 142 Archivio Segreto, Vatican; 143 *Bruno Novarese*; 144 Museo di Capodimonte, Florence, *André Held*; 145 Museo Civico, Piacenza, *Scala*; 146 *Federico Arborio Mella*; 147 top Zecca Museum, Rome, *André Held*; 147 bottom *Anderson*.

CHAPTER 13 page 148 top Louvre, *André Held*; 148 bottom *André Held*; 150 bottom Reinhart Collection, *André Held*; 151 *André Held*; 152 *Bruno Del Priore*; 153 top Archivio Segreto, Vatican; 153 bottom British Museum, *John R. Freeman*; 154 top *André Held*; 154 bottom Archivio Segreto, Vatican; 155 *Alinari*; 156 top Musée Cantonal des Beaux Arts, Lausanne, *Emile Gos*; 156 bottom *Federico Arborio Mella*; 157 *André Held*; 158 Museo di Roma, *André Held*; 159 *De Antonis*.

CHAPTER 14 page 160 *De Antonis*; 162 top left and right Istituto di Studi Romani; 162 bottom Cabinetto Fotografico Nazionale, Rome; 163 Istituto di Studi Romani; 164 top *André Held*; 164 bottom Cabinetto Fotografico Nazionale, Rome; 165 G. Vandolfer Collection, Cabinetto Fotografico Nazionale, Rome; 166 *André Held*; 167 top and bottom Museo di Roma, *André Held*; 168 top Borghese Gallery, Rome, *André Held*; 168 bottom *Federico Arborio Mella*; 169 Cabinetto delle Stampe, Rome; 170 top right *Anderson*; 170 top and bottom left Cabinetto delle Stampe, Rome; 170 bottom right Calcografia Nazionale, Rome, *André Held*; 171 Collection Maraini, Cabinetto Fotografico Nazionale, Rome.

CHAPTER 15 page 172 top Istituto di Studi Romani; 172 bottom, 174 top and bottom Cabinetto delle Stampe, *Oscar Savio*; 175 top and bottom, 176 Museo di Roma, *André Held*; 177 top *Anderson*; 177 bottom *André Held*; 178 top Museo di Roma, *André Held*; 178 bottom *Anderson*; 179 top Istituto di Studi Romani; 179 bottom Museo di Palazzo Venezia, Rome, *André Held*; 180 Istituto di Studi Romani; 181 Cabinetto delle Stampe, *Oscar Savio*; 182 top *André Held*; 182 bottom Cabinetto delle Stampe, *Oscar Savio*; 183 top *Oscar Savio*.

CHAPTER 16 page 184 *Alinari*; 186 Ullstein; 187 top Zecca Museum, Rome, *André Held*; 187 bottom *Alinari*; 188 Museo di Roma, *André Held*; 189 left and right *André Held*; 190 Louvre, *André Held*; 191 National Gallery, Palazzo Barberini, Rome, *André Held*; 192 *De Antonis*; 193 top Uffizi Gallery, *Anderson*; 193 bottom Calcografia Nazionale, Rome, *André Held*.

CHAPTER 17 page 194 Doria Pamphili Collection, Cabinetto Fotografico Nazionale, Rome; 196 left Museo di Palazzo Venezia, *André Held*; 196 right *Josephine Powell*; 197 *Giraudon*; 198 left and right *Giordani*; 199 top Louvre, *André Held*; 199 centre *Giraudon*; 199 bottom *Milton Gendel*; 200 Cabinetto Fotografico Nazionale, Rome; 201 Galleria Corsini, Rome, *André Held*; 202 left Museo di Roma, *André Held*; 202 right *André Held*; 203 Palazzo Corsini, Rome, *André Held*.

CHAPTER 18 page 204 top *André Held*; 204 bottom left Museo di Roma, *André Held*; 204 bottom right Galleria Corsini, Rome, *André Held*; 206 *André Held*; 207 top Calcografia Nazionale, Rome, *André Held*; 207 bottom Zecca Museum, Rome, *André Held*; 208 top Cabinetto Fotografico Nazionale, Rome; 208 bottom Zecca Mùseum, Rome, *André Held*; 209 top *André Held*; 209 bottom Calcografia Nazionale, *André Held*; 210, 211, 213 Cabinetto Fotografico Nazionale, Rome; 212 top Museo di Roma, *André Held*; 212 bottom Vatican Library.

CHAPTER 19 page 214 Calcografia Nazionale, Rome, *André Held*; 216 top left Cabinetto Fotografico Nazionale, Rome; 216 top right and bottom Osterreichisches Nationalbibliothek Bildarchiv; 217 Cabinetto Fotografico Nazionale, Rome; 218 Cabinetto delle Stampe, Rome, *Oscar Savio*; 219 top left and bottom Museo di Roma, *André Held*; 219 top right, 220 Louvre, *André Held*; 221 left and right Museo Correr, Venice; 222 top Victoria and Albert Museum, London (Apsley House Collection); 222 bottom Archivio Segreto, Vatican; 223, 224, 225 Cabinetto delle Stampe, Rome, *Oscar Savio*.

CHAPTER 20 page 226 top British Museum, *John R. Freeman*; 226 bottom *Alinari*; 228 top left *Mansell Collection*, London; 228 top right British Museum, *John R. Freeman*; 228 bottom, 229 *Milton Gendel*; 230 left *Radio Times Hulton Picture Library*; 230 right Cabinetto delle Stampe, Rome, *Oscar Savio*; 231 Mrs Douglas Woodruff, *Universal Photo Service*; 232 Museo di Roma, *André Held*; 233 top Zecca Museum, Rome, *André Held*; 233 bottom Calcografia Nazionale, Rome, *André Held*.

CHAPTER 21 page 234 top and bottom *Federico Arborio Mella*; 236 top and bottom Bertarelli Collection, *Oscar Savio*; 237 top Museo di Roma; 237 bottom left *André Held*; 237 bottom right Bertarelli Collection, *Oscar Savio*; 238 top Cabinetto delle Stampe, Rome, *Oscar Savio*; 238 bottom Museo di Roma; 239, 240 Museo di Roma, *André Held*; 241 top left Cabinetto delle Stampe, Rome, *Oscar Savio*; 241 top right *André Held*; 241 bottom Museo di Roma; 242 Vatican Museum; 243 top Museo di Roma; 243 bottom *Federico Arborio Mella*

CHAPTER 22 page 244 right *Federico Arborio Mella*; 244 left, 247–9 Vatican Library.

CHAPTER 23 page 250 top *Radio Times Hulton Picture Library*; 250 bottom Museo di Roma; 252 left Raoul Korty Collection, *Arnoldo Mondadori*; 252 right *Arnoldo Mondadori*; 253 and 254 top *Giordani*; 254, 255 *Felici*; 256, 257 *Giordani*; 258 *Federico Arborio Mella*; 259 top *Giordani*; 259 bottom *Federico Arborio Mella*.

CHAPTER 24 page 260 Vatican Library; 262 top *André Held*; 262 bottom *Giordani*; 263 *Federico Arborio Mella*; 264 *Alinari*; 265 left Museo Civico, Piacenza, *Scala*; 265 right Zecca Museum, Rome, *André Held*; 266 left *Giordani*; 266 right *Publifoto*; 267 top *Giordani*; 267 bottom left Museo Correr, Venice; 267 bottom right *Giordani*; 268 Arnoldo Mondadori, *Epoca*; 269 left *Publifoto*; 269 right *Giordani*.

CHAPTER 25 page 270 left and right, 273, 274 bottom, 275–77 *Giordani*; 272 Archivio Segreto, Vatican; 274 top *Felici*.

CHAPTER 26 page 278, 281, 283, 285–88, 289 top *Giordani*; 280 *Federico Arborio Mella*, *Associated Press*; 282 Arnoldo Mondadori, 284 left *Daily Telegraph*; 284 right *Paul Popper*; 289 bottom *Keystone Press*; 290 Catholic Universe, Associated Press.
page 296–98 Private Collection, Rome, *André Held*; 299 Royal Museum of Fine Arts, Copenhagen, *Federico Arborio Mella*; 300 top *Mansell Collection*, London; 300 bottom *Paul Popper*.

Index

Page numbers in italics refer to the illustrations

Acacius, Archbishop of Constantinople, 34, 35
Acqua Paola, the, *182*
Acton, Cardinal, *231*
Acton, Lord, 238
Adrian I, 45
Adrian II, 50
Adrian III, 53
Adrian IV, *59*, 63
Adrian VI, *136*, 137-9
Aedicula, the, *16*, *17*
Aeterni Patris, bull (1621), 186; encyclical (1879), *244*, 246
Aix-la-Chapelle, treaty of, 210
Alaric, 161
Albani, Francesco, *201*
Alberich II, 165
Albert of Austria, 88
Albigensian crusade, *68*, 69
Alexander II, 55
Alexander III, 63-4
Alexander IV, 85
Alexander V, *Anti-Pope*, 97
Alexander VI, *106*, 116, *117*, 133, 142
Alexander VII, 128, 195-7, *196*, *198*
Alexander VIII, 202
Alexander of Alexandria, 29
Alfred, King of England, 42, 50
Ambrose, St, 30, *124*
Anacletus, Pope, 18, 121
Anacletus II, *Anti-Pope*, 59
Anagni incident, 88
Anastasius I, 30
Anastasius II, Emperor, 35
Anastasius II, Pope, 35
Anastasius IV, 63
Anicetus, Pope, 18, 26
Anscar, St, 49
Anselm, St, 57
Antioch, Councils of (324), 29 (379), 30, 299
Antonelli, Cardinal, 236, *238*, 263
Arcanum, encyclical, 245
Archbishops, status of, 261
Arian controversy, 29
Arles, Council of, 29
Armenia, 105
Arnauld, Antoine, 195
Arnold of Brescia, 60, 63
Ascidas, Bishop Theodore, 35
Athenagoras, Patriarch, *290*
Attila, 33, 162
Augsburg, Diet of, 140, *141*
treaty of, 149
Augustine of Canterbury, St, 42
Augustine of Hippo, St, 245
Augustulus, Emperor, 34
Avignon, *84*, 91-4, 97, 125, 217

Baciccia, G. B., *203*
Bandinelli, Roland, *see* Alexander III
Barberini, Cardinal, *204*
Barberini, Maffeo, *see* Urban VIII
Barbo, Pietro, *see* Paul II
Barnabites, 142
Bartolo, Domenico di, *65*
Basel, Council of, 101-5, 107, 261, 300
Basilides, Bishop, 26
Batoni, P., *204*, *219*
Becket, St Thomas à, *62*
Belgrade, battle of, 107
Bellarmine, Cardinal, 158
Belloc, Hilaire, 279
Belvedere Palace, 133
Benedict I, 37
Benedict III, 50
Benedict IX, 53
Benedict XI, 88, *91*
Benedict XII, 91, 93, *93*, 272
Benedict XIII, *Anti-Pope*, 97
Benedict XIII, 207-8, *207*
Benedict XIV, 174, 181, *204*, 208-11, *210*, *211*
Benedict XV, 248, 252-5, *254*
Benedict, St, *41*, *66*
Benevento, Council of, 56
Beran, Cardinal, 256
Bernard, St, 59-60, *60*
Bernini, Gianlorenzo, 19, *124*, *127*, 128, 135, 177, 182, *187*, *196-8*
Bethlehem, 80
Bishops, status of, 261
Bismarck, 242, 245, 251
Blanchet, L. G., *208*
Boethius, 35
Bohemia, 97-101, 186-7
Bonaparte, Cardinal Luciano, *263*
Boniface III, IV and V, 42
Boniface VIII, 86-8, *88*, *89*, 94, *99*, 166, 173, 264
Boniface of Montferrat, 69
Boniface, St, 43
Borgia, Alfonso, *see* Calixtus III
Borgia, Rodrigo, 107, 115, *see* Alexander VI
Borgianni, Orazio, *155*
Borromeo, St Charles, 153, 155, *155*
Borromini, F., 173, *174*
Bossuet, J.-B., 200
Botticelli, 115
Brahe, Tycho, 193
Bramante, Donato, 125-7, *125*, 134, *134*
Braschi, Angelo, *see* Pius VI
Breakspear, Nicholas, *see* Adrian IV
Breitenfeld, battle of, 190
Budapest, *200*
Bulls, origin of, 272
Buonocompagni, Ugo, *see* Gregory XIII
Burdin, *Anti-Pope*, 58
Byzantium, *see* Constantinople

Caccianemici, Gerardo, *see* Lucius II
Caetari, Benedetto, *see* Boniface VIII
Caetennii, mausoleum of, *16*
Calixtus I, catacomb of, *27*, *28*
Calixtus II, 58-9, *58*, *59*
Calixtus III, 107, *109*
Calvin, John, 137
Cambio, Arnolfo di, 21, *21*
Camerlengo, the Cardinal, 263, 265, *273*
Campidoglio, the, *180*, 181, *181*
Canada, 228, 233
Canisius, St Peter, 149
Cappellari, Bartolomeo, *see* Gregory XVI
Capranesi, G., *175*
Carafa, Cardinal Gian Pietro, 146, *see* Paul IV
Carafa, Cardinal Carlo, 150
Cardinal Nephew, the, 273
Cardinals, choice and status of, 261-4
College of, 261-9
in conclave, 246-9
Castelfidardo, battle of, 237
Castel Sant' Angelo, 123, 139, *156*, *164-66*, 179-80
Castiglione, Francesco, *see* Pius VIII
Castiglione, Godfrey, *see* Celestine IV
Catharism, 68-9, 94
Catherine de' Medici, 149, 153
Catherine of Alexandria, St, *114*
Catherine of Aragon, 140
Catherine of Siena, St, 94, *94*
Catholic Action, *259*, 276
Cavour, Camillo, 236-7, *241*
Celestine I, 30
Celestine II, *Anti-Pope*, 59
Celestine III, 64, *65*, 67
Celestine IV, 81
Celestine V, 86, *87*, 94
Celestius, 30
Ceracchi, Giuseppe, *216*
Cerdo, 25
Cerularius, Michael, Patriarch, *51*
Cervini, Cardinal, 145, 146
Césène, Michel de, 94
Chalcedon, Council of, 34, 35, 299
Champaigne, Philippe de, *190*
Charlemagne, 20, 43, *44*, 45, 46, *46*, *47*, 49
Charles I of England, 187
Charles II, the Bald, 49
Charles II of Sicily, 86
Charles II of Spain, 206
Charles III of Naples, *211*
Charles IV, Emperor, 92
Charles V, Emperor, *138*, 139-49, *143*
Charles VIII of France, 116
Charles X of France, 229
Charles of Anjou, 84, *86*
Charles Albert, Emperor, 210
Charles Albert of Savoy, 235
Chatillon, Eudes de, *see* Urban II
Chiaramonti, Barnaba, *see* Pius VII
Chigi, Fabio, *see* Alexander VII
Chigi, Prince, *266*
Chosroes II, 42
Christina of Sweden, 197, *199*
Cibo, John Baptist, *see* Innocent VIII
Cicognani, Cardinal, *276*
Cienfuegos, Ambassador, 224
Clavio, 193
Clement I, 24
Clement III, *Anti-Pope*, 55, 56
Clement IV, 92, 272
Clement V, *90*, *91*, *92*, *92*, *94*, 173, 265
Clement VI, 91, 92, 93, 94
Clement VII, *Anti-Pope*, 97
Clement VII, *115*, 127, *136*, *138*, 139-42, 180
Clement VIII, 158, *158*, 178
Clement IX, 197, *203*
Clement X, 174, 179
Clement XI, 181, 206-8, *207*
Clement XII, 181, 208, *208*
Clement XIII, 181, *204*, 206, 211-12
Clement XIV, 206, 212, *212*, *213*, 279
Clermont, Council of, 57
Coelestis Pastor, decree, 199
Coemeterium maius, 23
College of Propaganda, 189
Colonna family, 86, 88, 166
Communism, 248, 255, 256-8
Compactata of Iglau, 101
Conclave, *260*, 264-9
Concordats with civil states, 275
Confessio Augustana, 140, 147
Congregations, functions of, 271
Extraordinary Affairs, 274-6
Ordinary Affairs, 276
Apostolic Briefs, 276, 277
Conrad III, Emperor, 63
Conrad IV, Emperor, 85
Consalvi, Cardinal Ercole, 171, 182, 218, 224, 225, *225*, 227
Consistories, 262-3, *262*
Constance, Council of, 97-100, 105, 300
Constantine the Great, 11, 18, 26, 29, 121, 161, 173
Constantinople, 45-6, 52-3, 69, 92, 101-3, 107
capture of, *70*
First Council of, 30, 299;
Second Council, 36, *37*, 299;
Third Council, Fourth Council, 299
Constantius II, 29, *30*
Constitutum (Vigilius), 36
Contarini, Cardinal, 145, 146
Conti de Segni, Lothair dei, *see* Innocent III
Coptic church, 105
Corinth, church of, 24
Cornelius, Pope, *26*
Cornet, Nicolas, 195
Corpus Juris Canonica, 157
Corsica, 85
Cortona, Pietro da, *192*
Coscia, Cardinal, 208
Cosmas, St, *35*
Cremona, Diet of, 76
Crescenzi family, 165
Crusades, first, 57;
third, 64;
fourth, 69;
Albigensian, 69
Cyprian of Carthage, 26
Cum occasione, bull, 195

Damasus, Pope, *27*, 30
Damian, St, *35*
Dandino, Cardinal, 147
Dassel, Reinhard von, 63
David, J. L., *219*, *220*, *221*
Decorations (papal awards), 276
Decretals, the, *74*, 79
della Rovere family, 110-15
della Rovere, Francesco, *see* Sixtus IV
della Rovere, Girolamo, *see* Julius II
Del Monte, Giovanni, 145, *see* Julius III
Depositio Martyrum, 16
Deusdedit, Pope, 42
Diaconates, 164-5, 177-8
Dictatus Papae, *54*, 55
Diofebi, Francesco, *176*
Dionysius of Alexandria, 26
Dionysius, Pope, 26, 29
Dioscoros, 35
Diuturnum, encyclical, 246
Divini Redemptoris, encyclical, 248, 255
Döllinger, Dr Johann, 238, 240
Dominic, St, *68*, 69, *69*
Domuscultae, 178
Domus Petri, 23
Donatello, 98
Dubois, François, *156*
Dupanloup, Felix, 238-42

Ecclesiae Catholicae, constitution, 261
Edward I of England, *91*
Election of Popes, 261, 264-9
El Greco, *83*
Elizabeth I of England, 149, *154*, 155, 157, 158
Enckenvoit, Wilhelm, 137
Ephesus, Council of, 30, 102, 299
Ethelwulf, King of England, 50
Ethiopia, 189
Eugenius III, 60-63, 174
Eugenius IV, *100*, *101*, 101-5, *104*, *105*
Eunomius, Bishop, 29
Eusebius of Caesarea, 33
Eusebius of Nicomedia, 29
Eutherius of Thiana, 30
Eutyches, Archimandrite, 34, 35

Farnese, Alessandro, 142, *see* Paul III
Farnese, Pierluigi, 145-6
Farnese, Rannucio, *104*
Fascism, 248, 255
Febronianism, 213
Felix III, 34
Felix V, *Anti-Pope*, 105, 107
Fénelon, François, 202
Ferdinand I, Emperor, 149, 153
Ferdinand II, Emperor, 190
Ferrante of Naples, 115-16
Ferrara, Council of, 102, *102*, 300
Ferretti, Mastai, *see* Pius IX
Fieschi, Sinibaldo, *see* Innocent IV
Filarete, *10*, *100*, *101*
Filioque clause, 46, 53, 102
Fisher Dr Geoffrey, *284*
Florence, Council of, *102*, 300
Fontana, Domenico, 127, *127*, 173, *179*, *182*
Fra Angelico, *68*, 107, *108*, 133
Francis I, Emperor, 210
Francis I of France, 119, *138*, 139-45
Francis, St, 69, *71*, *72*, *76*, 79, 92
Frangipani family, 57, 59, 166
Frederick Barbarossa, 63-4, *63*
Frederick II, Emperor, 73, 75-83, *76*, *80*, *81*, 85
Frederick V, Elector, 185-6
Freemasonry, 208

Gaddi, Taddeo, *92*
Galileo, 169, 190-93, *193*
Gallicanism, 228, 229
Gandia, Duke of, 116
Garibaldi, 236-7, *241*
Gasparri, Cardinal Pietro, *254*, *274*, *275*
Gelasius I, 33, 34-5
Gelasius II, *Anti-Pope*, 57-8
Genga, Francesco della, *see* Leo XII
Genseric, 121, 161
Gentile, Antonio, *118*
George IV of England, 225
Ghirlandaio, Domenico, 115
Ghislieri, Michele, *see* Pius V
Giani, Felice, *219*
Gioninia, Antonio, *206*
Giotto, *71*, *72*, *76*, *89*, 125
Giovanni, Matteo di, *95*
Gnostics, 24
Gonzaga, Ferrante, 146
Gonzaga, Cardinal Silvio, *168*
Gonzalez, Thyrso, 199
Gozzoli, Benozzo, *102*, *103*
Graves de Communi, encyclical, 248
Greek church, 34-43, 52-3, 101-5
Gregorian calendar, *156*, 157
Gregory I, 11, 20, 33, *42*, *43*, *156* 164-5, 179
Gregory III, 20, 43
Gregory IV, 46, 49, *50*
Gregory VII, *54*, 55-6, *56*, 67
Gregory VIII, 57
Gregory IX, 69, *74*, *78*, 79-80, 81
Gregory X, 85, 264
Gregory XI, 91, 94, *95*
Gregory XII, 97, *99*
Gregory XIII, 135, 149, *154*, 155-7, *156*
Gregory XV, 186, *187*
Gregory XVI, 173, 179, *230*, *231*, 232-3, *233*, 262, 269
Guevara, Fernando de, *150*
Guidi di Bagno, J. F., 189-90
Guise, Henry Duke of, 149
Gustavus Adolphus, 190
Guy of Montpellier, 178
Guyon, Mme, 202

Heeze, Dietrich, 137
Helladius of Tarsus, 30
Henoticon, 34
Henry I of England, 57, 59
Henry III, Emperor, 53
Henry IV, Emperor, 55, 56, *56*, 57
Henry IV of France, 149, 158
Henry V, Emperor, 57-9, *57*
Henry VI, Emperor, 64, 70, 73
Henry VIII of England, 140
Heraclius, Emperor, 42
Hilary, Pope, 34
Hitler, Adolf, 255, 256
Honorius I, 42
Honorius II, 59
Honorius III, 75-6, *76*, *77*
Hormisdas, Pope, 35
Hosius, 26
Hospitals and hospices of Rome, 178
Humanum genus, encyclical, 246
Hunyadi, John, 107
Hus, John, 97-100, *100*

Ignatius Loyala, St, 146, 149, *150*, 186, *187*
Ignatius of Antioch, 24
Ignatius, Patriarch, 52
Il fermo propositio, encyclical, 248
Immortale Dei, encyclical, 246
Immortalis Dei, bull, 189
In coena Domini, bull, 155
Infallibility, doctrine of, 241-2
Innocent I, 30, *31*
Innocent II, 59, *60*, *61*
Innocent III, 64, *66*, 67-73, *71*, *72*, *75*, 81, 178
Innocent IV, 81-3, 85
Innocent VI, 91
Innocent VII, 272
Innocent VIII, 115-16, 133
Innocent X, 173, *194*, 195, 273
Innocent XI, 197-202, *202*
Innocent XII, 202, *202*, 206, 261, 273
Innocent XIII, *207*
In Nomine Domini, decree, 261
In plurimis, encyclical, 246
Inquisition, the, 146, 150-53
Inscrutabili, encyclical, 245
Inscrutabili divinae, bull, 189
Iraeneus of Lyons, 24-5, 26
Irene, Empress, 45
Islam (Turkish), 45, 105, 107-15, 139, 155, 201

Jagellon, Catharine, 155
James II of England, 201
James Stuart (the Old Pretender), *206*
Jansenism, 195, *199*, 202, 207, 211, 212, 216

Jerome of Prague, 100
Jerusalem, 80
capture by Turks, 75-6
Council of, 23
Joan, Queen of Naples, 100
John I, 35
John III, 37
John IV, 42
John VIII, 179
John XII, 53
John XIII, 264
John XX, 264
John XXII, *90*, 91, 92
John XXIII, *Anti-Pope*, 97, *98*
John XXIII, 249, 262, 264, *268*, 277, *278*, 280-89, *280-83*
John of Austria, Don, 155
John Chrysostom, St, 30
John, King of England, 70, 92
John Paleologus, Emperor, 102, *103*, *105*
Jones, Thomas, *167*
Joseph I, Emperor, 206-7
Joseph II of Austria, 215, *216*, 217
Joseph II, Patriarch, 105
Josephine, Empress, *220*
Josephism, 211, 215-16, 229
Judicatum (by Pope Vigilius), 35
Julius I, 26, 29
Julius II, 116-18, *119*, 125-7, 133, 134
Julius III, 145, 146-7, *147*
Justin I, Emperor, 35
Justinian, Emperor, 36, *39*

Kahlenberg, battle of, 201
Kaunitz, Prince, 211, 215-16
Kepler, Johann, 193
Ketteler, Archbishop, 247
Kingsley, Charles, 246
Knights Hospitalers, 91
Knights Templars, 91

Lacombe, François, 202
Lacordaire, J.-B., 247
Laetus, Julius Pomponius, 108
Lambert of Ostia, *see* Honorius II
Lambruschini, Cardinal, 232, 235
Lamennais, F. R. de, 227, 228, *228*, 229, 247
Lamorcière, General, 236
Lateran Councils:
First (1123), 58, 299
Second (1139), 59, 299
Third (1178), 64, 299
Fourth (1215), 69, *73*, 299
Fifth (1512), 118, 300
Lateran Palace, *172*, 173
Lateran treaty (1929), 255, *274*
Laurentius, Deacon, 35
LaValette, Fr, 212
Lay investiture, 55-8
Leander of Seville, St, 37
Lefèvre, Robert, *222*
Legnano, battle of, 64
Leo I, *32*, 33-4, 121, 162
Leo III, Emperor, 43
Leo III, Pope, 20, *44*, 45, *47*, 173
Leo IV, 46, 50, *51*, 125
Leo IX, 53
Leo X, *115*, 118-19, *119*, 127, 137, *264*, 273
Leo XII, *226*, 228-9, 273
Leo XIII, 173, *241*, 242-8, *250*, 251-2, 283
Leonine walls, *162*, 179
Lepanto, battle of, *152*, 155
Liberal Arts, Hall of, *112-13*
Liber Censuum, 70
Liberius, Pope, *28*, 29-30, *31*, 174
Liber Pontificalis, 18, 121, 122, 161
Libertas praestantissimum, encyclical, 246
Lingard, John, 262
Lippi, Filippo, *115*
Lorenzetti, Pietro, *77*
Lothair I, 49, *49*
Lothair II, 50
Louis II, Emperor, 50
Louis VI of France, 57, 59
Louis IX of France, 81-2, *83*, 85, 86
Louis XII of France, 116, 118, 119
Louis XIII of France, 186
Louis XIV of France, 195-201, *197*
Louis XVI of France, 217
Louis of Bavaria, 92
Louis Philippe, 232
Louis the German, 49
Lucius II, 60
Ludovisi, Alessandro, *see* Gregory XV
Ludovisi, Ludovico, 186
Luther, Martin, 119, 137, *140*
Lyons, Councils of:
First (1245), 82-3, *82*, 92, 300
Lyons, Councils of: *cont.*
Second (1274), 264, 300

Macmillan, Harold, *276*
Maderno, Carlo, *126*, 127, *128*, 177, *182*
Magna Carta, 70
Mahomet II, 116
Maidalchini, Donna Olimpia, 195
Maistre, Comte Joseph de, 224-5, 228, *228*
Manfred, Regent of Sicily, 83, 85
Manning, Cardinal, 241-2, 247
Marcellus II, 149
Marcian, Emperor, 34
Marcion, Bishop, 25, 26
Maria Theresa, 208, 210, 211, 212, 215
Marie Antoinette, 212
Marsiglio of Padua, 94
Martel, Charles, 43
Martial, Bishop, 26
Martial, St, *93*
Martin I, 33, 42, *43*
Martin V, *96*, 97-101, 272
Marx, Karl, 246
Mary Stuart, 157, 158
Mary Tudor, 147, *272*
Masolino, *31*
Mastai-Ferretti, Giovanni, *see* Pius IX
Mater et Magistra, encyclical, 249, *249*, 284
Matilda of Tuscany, *56*
Matthias, Emperor, 186
Maurice, Elector of Saxony, 147
Maximian, Emperor, *114*
Maximilian II, Emperor, 155
Mazarin, Cardinal, 195, 263
Mazzini, Giuseppe, 236, *237*
Medici, Giovanni de', *see* Leo X
Medici, Giovanni Angelo de', *see* Pius IV
Medici, Giulio de', *see* Clement VII
Medici, Lorenzo de', 115, 116
Melozzo da Forlì, *60*, *111*
Mendez, Dr Alfonso, 189
Mérode, Mgr de, 236
Merry del Val, Cardinal, *276*
Metternich, Prince, 227, 229, 235
Michael, Emperor, 52
Michelangelo, 118, *118*, *125*, *126*, 127, *127*, 133, *133*, 146, *170*, 180, *180*
Midzenty, Cardinal, 256
Miltiades, Pope, 26, 121, 173
Mit brennender Sorge, encyclical, 248, 255
Molinos, Miguel, 199, *199*, 202
Monarchians, 25
Mongos, Peter, 34
Monophysitism, 34, 35, *35*, 42
Monothelitism, 42-3
Montalembert, Comte Charles de, 238
Montanists, 25
Monte di Pietà, 178
Montelupo, Rafaello de, *166*
Montfort, Simon de, 69
Montini, Mgr, *259*, *see* Paul VI
Morales, Juan de, 196
Moralia (Gregory I), 42
Morone, Cardinal, 153
Mun, Alfred de, 247
Munster, Sebastian, *163*
Murrone, Pietro di, *see* Celestine V
Mussolini, Benito, *254*, 255, *274*

Nantes, Edict of, revocation, 200
Napoleon I, 171, 217-24, *220*, *222*, 279
Napoleon III, 236
Nazareth, 80
Nazism, 248, 255
Neri, St Philip, 187, *187*
Nero, Emperor, *10*, 11
Nestorius, 30, 34, 35
Newman, Cardinal, 263
Nicaea, First Council of, 29, 299
Second Council, 299, *299*
Nicholas I, Czar, *231*
Nicholas I, Pope, *48*, 50-52
Nicholas II, 261
Nicholas III, 85, *86*, 125
Nicholas IV, 173, 174
Nicholas V, 107, *108*, 125
Nicolle, V. J., *164*
Nobili, Robert de, 187
Nogaret, Guillaume de, 88
Nolli, Giovanni Battiste, *180*
Non abbiamo bisogno, encyclical, 248, 255
Non debet reprehensibile, constitution, 272
Norbert, St, 59
Nuremberg, Diet of, 137

Ockham, William of, 94
Odescalchi, Benedetto, *see* Innocent XI
Odoacer, 34
Offices, function of, 271
Olympus, Bishop, 29
Orders, ecclesiastical, 276
Origen, 35
Orsini family, 86, 166
Otto the Great, 53, *53*
Otto III, 165
Otto IV, 73
Otranto, Capture of, 115

Pacelli, Eugenio, *273*, *see* Pius XII
Pacem in Terris, encyclical, 249, 284
Palazzo Barberini, 177, *192*, *193*
Palazzo Borghese, *169*
Palazzo Corsini, *170*
Palazzo Farnese, *170*
Palazzo Odescalchi, *170*
Palestrina, 147
Palladius of Ratiavia, 30
Panini, *128*, *134*, *168*, *204*, *210*, *211*
Parentucelli, Tomasso, *see* Nicholas V
Paris, University of, 69
Pascal, 196, *199*
Pascendi, encyclical, 248, 252
Paschal II, 57, *57*
Paschal III, *Anti-Pope*, 64
Pastoral Rule for Bishops (Gregory I), 42
Paul II, 108-10, *109*
Paul III, 127, 133, 135, 142-6, *144*, *145*, *146*, 179
Paul IV, *148*, 149, 150-53
Paul V, 127, 135, 158, *184*, 185-6
Paul VI, *269*, 288, *288*, *289*, *290*
Paul, St, 16, 23, *24*
Paul, St Vincent de, 190
Pauline Chapel, 135, 146
Pavia, Council of, 63
Pavia-Siena, Council of, 100
Pecci, Gioacchino, *see* Leo XIII
Pelagian controversy, 30
Pelagius I, 36-7
Pelagius II, 37
Pepin of Héristal, 43
Pepin the Short, 43, 45, *46*
Peretti, Felice, *see* Sixtus V
Permiti Nos, encyclical, 248
Perugino, 115
Peruzzi, 127, *134*
Peter, St, *10*, 11-20, *21*, *23-4*, *24*, *44*
tomb of, 11-20, *10-20*
Peter the Fuller, 34
Petrarch, *93*, 94
Petrucci, Cardinal, 119
Philip I of France, 56
Philip II of Spain, 147, 149, 153, 155, 158, *272*
Philip III of France, 85
Philip IV of France, 86-91, *91*
Philip Augustus, 69, 73
Philip of Anjou, 206
Philip Neri, St, 169, 186
Philip of Swabia, 73
Photius, schism of, 52-3
Piacenza, Council of, 56
Piazza dell' Esquilino, *175*
Piazza Navona, *167*
Piazza del Popolo, *175*, 180
Piazza del Quirinale, *170*
Piccolomini, Aeneas Silvius, *see* Pius II
Piccolomini, Francesco, *see* Pius III
Pierleoni family, 59, 166
Pietro, Sano di, *109*
Pinelli, *223*
Pinturicchio, *106*, *110*, *111-15*, 115, 133
Piombo, Sebastiano del, *119*, *136*
Piranesi, *170*, *174*, *182*, *183*, *209*
Pisa, Council of, 97
Peace of, 195
Pius II, 107-8, *110*
Pius III, 116
Pius IV, 135, 149, 153-5
Pius V, 149, *151*, 155
Pius VI, 171, 215-18, *216-19*, 273, 279
Pius VII, 171, *182*, 218-25, *219*, *220*, *221*, *223-25*, 273, 279
Pius VIII, 230-32, *230*
Pius IX, 171, 173, 182, 227, *234*, 235-43, *237-41*, *243*, *263*
Pius X, 248, 252, *252*, *253*, 271, 273-4
Pius XI, 135, 248, *255*, 255-6, 274, 283
Pius XII, 11, 133, 245, 248-9, *256*, *257*, 256-8, *258*, *259*, 269, 280
Platina, 108, *111*
Pole, Cardinal Reginald, 145, 146, 147, 153
Polycarp, St, 24, 25, 26
Polycrates of Ephesus, 26
Porta Ripetta, 181, *183*
Porta Santa, 210
Powderly, Terence, 246-7
Pozzo, Padre, *159*
Prague, defenestration of, 185, *186*
Professio fidei tridentinae, 155
Protestantism, 119, 137-58, 185-193, 279
Puzyna, Cardinal, 269

Quadragesimo anno, encyclical, 248, *249*, 283
Quesnel, P., 207
Quietism, 199, 202
Quirinal Palace, *170*, 177, *223*, 236
Quod Apostolici muneris, encyclical, 246

Rampolla, Cardinal, *252*, 269
Raphael, *74*, 118, *119*, 127, 134-5, *134*
Raymond VI of Toulouse, 69
Reccared, King, 37
Red wall, 13-16, *13*, *14*, *15*
Régale, 197, 199-200
Reliquary of St Peter, 124
René of Anjou, 116
Rerum Novarum, encyclical, 247-8, *247*, 252, 283
Ricci, Matteo, 196
Ricci, Sebastiano, *145*, *265*
Richelieu, Cardinal, 189-90, *190*
Ricimer, 161
Rienzo, Cola di, 166
Rimini-Selencia, Council of, 29
Risorgimento, the, 171, 235-43
Roger of Sicily, 59
Romanae Sedis Antistes, bull, 187
Romanum decet Pontificem, bull, 202, 273
Romanus Pontifex, bull, 158
Rome, Councils of, (AD 340), 29; (382), 30; (731), 43; (1074), 55
influence of Papacy on social history, 161-71
Sack of (1527), 139, *139*, *140*, 169, 180
Roncaglia, Council of, 63
Roncalli, Angelo Joseph, *see* John XXIII
Rossellino, Bernado, 125
Rossi, Pellegrino, 235

Sacchi, Andrea, *188*
Sacconi, *228*, *229*
St John Lateran, *162*, *163*, *172*, 173, *174*, 269
S Maria della Anima, 136, 139
S Maria in Cosmedin, 177, *177*
S Maria Maggiore, *31*, 174, *174*, *175*, *179*
S Maria del Popolo, 115, *175*, 197
S Maria in Trastevere, *178*
S Paolo fuori le Mura, *176*, *226*
St Peter, Basilica of, 11-20, *10-20*, 121-35, *120-32*, 160, *162*, *163*, *172*, 173, *242*, 269, *269*, *283*, *286*, 287, *289*, *300*
SS Quatro Coronati, *177*
Sala Regia, the, *130-31*
Salviati, Francesco, *64*, *104*, *130*
Sancta Dei Civitas, encyclical, 247
Sanfedisti (Centurions), 227
Sangallo, 127, *170*, 179
Sapientiae Christianae, encyclical, 247, *247*
Sapienti consilio, constitution, 271
Sardica, Council of, 29
Sardinia, 80, 85
Savonarola, Girolamo, 116, *117*
Scala Regia, 135, *198*, *288*
Schmalkalden, League of, 145
Secretariat of State, composition of, 271-2
origins and development, 272-4
functions, 274-7
Secret Chamber, the, 272
Sergius of Constantinople, 42
Sertum laetitiae, encyclical, 248
Severus of Antioch, 35
Sforza, Guido Ascanio, 142
Sicily, 70, 73, 75-6, 79, 83, 85, 207
Sicut pia mater, decree, 101-2
Siena, Guido da, *69*
Siena, Paolo da, *93*
Sigismund, Emperor, 97-102, *100*, *101*
Silverian, Pope, 42
Simon Magus, 23
Simony, 55, 58
Simplicius, Pope, 34
Siricius, Pope, 30
Sistine Chapel, 115, 133, *133*, 146, *267*, 269
Sixtus I, *31*
Sixtus II, *28*
Sixtus III, 33, 174
Sixtus IV, 110-15, *111*, 133
Sixtus V, 127, 128, 135, *157*, 157-8, *160*, 169, 173, 174, 190, 264
Skandenberg, 108-10
Society of Jesus, 146, *146*, 157, 212, *212*, *213*, 225
Soderini, Cardinal, 137
Sophronius, Archbishop of Jerusalem, 42
South America, 224, 227, 229, 233
Spellman, Cardinal, *256*
Stefaneschi, Cardinal, 125
Stephen, Pope, 26
Summi Pontificatus, encyclical, 248, *249*
Sutri, Agreement of, 57
Syllabus of Errors, 237-42, 251
Sylvester I, 26, 29, 121
Sylvester II, 165
Symmachus, Pope, *34*, 35

Tardini, Cardinal, *276*
Temple, Frederick, Archbishop, 247
Thadeus of Suessa, 82-3, *82*
Theatines, 142
Theodore I, *40*, 42
Theodoric, King, 35
Theresa of Jesus, St, 186, *187*
Thomas Aquinas, St, *115*, 246, 248
Tiene, Gaetano de, 142
Timothy the Cat, 34
Titian, *144*, 146
Tome to Flavian (Leo I), 34
Torrigiani, Cardinal, 211
Tours, Battle of, 45
Trent, Council of, 145-7, *148*, 149-55, *153*, 300, *300*
Trevi fountain, 181, *209*
Tribunals, function of, 271

Ubaldini, Francesco, *191*
Ubi arcano, encyclical, 248
Ultramontanism, 225
Unam Sanctam, bull, 88
Une fois encore, encyclical, 248
Unigenitus, bull, 207
United States of America, 224, 228, 233
Urban II, 53, 56-7, 67
Urban IV, 85, 173
Urban V, 91, 92, 94, 173
Urban VI, 97, *98*
Urban VIII, 135, 189-93, *188*, *189*, *191*

Valenti, Cardinal, 210
Valentinus, 25
Valerian, 17
Vasari, Giorgio, *79*, *138*, *143*, *152*, *264*
Vatican buildings, 122-5, 133-5, *134*, *135*, 173
Vatican City, status of, 275-6
Vatican Councils,
First (1869), 241-2, *242*, 300
Second (1962), *284*, *285*, *286-7*, 287-8, 300, *300*
Vatican Library, 107, *111*, 115, 135, 255
Vehementer nos, encyclical, 247
Velasquez, *194*
Venice, peace of, 64, *64*
Veuillot, Louis, 241
Victor I, 26
Victor III, 56
Victor IV, *Anti-Pope*, 63
Victor Emmanuel II, 236, *238*, 242
Vienne, Council of, 91
Vigilius, Pope, 35-6
Vignola, Giacomo Barozzi, 180
Villa Borghese, *168*
Villa Doria Pamphili, *171*
Villa Giulia, *147*
Visconti, Teobaldo, *see* Gregory X
Vives, Juan Bautista, 189

Wallenstein, Albrecht, 190
Westphalia, peace of, 195
Weissenberg, battle of, 186
Widdington, Percy, 246
William III of England, 201
Wiseman, Cardinal Nicholas, 238
Wolsey, Cardinal, 139, *142*
Worms, Diet of, *58*, 58-9, 64
Wyclif, John, 100
Wyszynski, Cardinal, 256

Xavier, St Francis, 186-7, *187*

Zaccaria, Antonio Maria, 142
Zachary, Pope, 43
Zelanti, 228, 230, 232
Zelus domus meae, bull, 195
Zeno, Emperor, 34
Zwingli, 137